The European Court of Human Rights as a Pathway to Impunity for International Crimes

Sonja C. Grover

The European Court of Human Rights as a Pathway to Impunity for International Crimes

Springer

Dr. Sonja C. Grover
Lakehead University
Faculty of Education
955 Oliver Road
Thunder Bay, Ontario, Canada P7B 5E1
sonja.grover@lakeheadu.ca

ISBN 978-3-642-42404-5 ISBN 978-3-642-10799-3 (eBook)
DOI 10.1007/978-3-642-10799-3
Springer Heidelberg Dordrecht London New York

Cover design: WMXDesign GmbH, Heidelberg, Germany

Printed on acid-free paper

Springer is part of Springer Science+Business Media (www.springer.com)

In loving memory of and in honour of my parents Gina and David Gazan who never lost faith in humanity when it seemed like the more rational thing to do would be the converse and whose quiet dignity is still a source of great strength and comfort to me

and

In loving memory also of my brother Albert Gazan who struggled for the rights of the dispossessed as social worker, psychologist and educator

About the Author

Sonja C. Grover, Ph.D., is a Professor at Lakehead University. In the past eight years, she has authored over 60 refereed articles on the topic of human rights and international law published in leading international human rights and law journals and contributed two book chapters for a 2007 edited volume on children's rights in Canada. She has also presented papers at various international conferences on the topic of human rights and vulnerable groups. Dr. Grover is Associate Editor of the International Journal of Human Rights. In 2007 she authored the book *Children's Human Rights: Challenging Global Barriers to the Child Liberation Movement*, published by Sandstone Academic Press; in 2008 *The Child's Right to Legal Standing* published by Lexis Nexis and in 2009 a major reference book *Prosecuting International Crimes and Human Rights Abuses Committed Against Children: Leading International Court Cases* published by Springer.

Preface

Introductory Remarks on the Perspective and Intent of the Author in Writing This Monograph

The European Court of Human Rights comments in the judgment *Korbely v. Hungary* that:

> *However, clearly drafted a legal provision may be, in any system of law, including criminal law, there is an inevitable element of judicial interpretation. There will always be a need for elucidation of doubtful points and for adaptation to changing circumstances.* Indeed, in the Convention States, the progressive development of the criminal law through judicial law making is a well-entrenched and necessary part of legal tradition...The Court's role is confined to ascertaining whether the effects of such an interpretation [interpretation by the national courts and authorities of domestic law which sometimes may refer to or incorporate international law principles or agreements] are compatible with the Convention [European Convention on Human Rights and Fundamental Freedoms] (emphasis added).[1]

This book then examines to what degree this "inevitable element of judicial interpretation" has been applied by the European Court of Human Rights in a manner consistent with the guarantees of the most fundamental human rights under international criminal, human rights and humanitarian law. In many instances, as the cases discussed will illustrate it is contended, the implicit assumption has been rather that the applicable law is intransigent, as if the law had a life of its own, rather than having life breathed into it by those jurists and legal academics and other authorities who interpret it. The end result has too often been additional suffering for victims and their surviving relatives due to the European Court of Human Rights

[1]Korbely v. Hungary (application no. 9174/02), European Court of Human Rights Grand Chamber Judgment of 19 September 2008, para. 71. http://www.menschenrechte.ac.at/orig/08_5/Korbely.pdf. Accessed 22 June 2009.

denying, in those certain cases, any modicum of a remedy in terms of (i) reparations, or (ii) in terms of the making of declarations regarding European Convention of Human rights violations, or new legal characterizations of the facts which would serve to increase the likelihood of domestic or international criminal prosecution of the applicant's tormenters. Though this book focuses on what the author holds are the European Court of Human Rights' less than shining moments, this is in no way meant to detract from the accomplishments of the Court over more than 50 years in advancing regard for and protection of human rights under the European Convention. Rather, this critical monograph is offered with great respect for the Court and with full acknowledgement of the great importance of European Court of Human Rights jurisprudence to our understanding of international human rights law in general. This critical piece, furthermore, was written out of a deep desire for the Court to deliver justice for victims of atrocity in all the cases it considers, and not just in the vast majority. For many, the European Court of Human Rights is the last and best hope for justice, and it is imperative for that reason and so many others that the Court's promise to deliver in that regard not amount, in any instance, to false advertising.

Part 1 of the monograph discusses the notion that "sovereignty" is "an attribute that states are required to exercise in accordance with international law"[2] including jus cogens principles regarding the absolute prohibition on various categories of international crime as defined under customary international law, and certain treaties such as the Rome Statute and the 1984 U.N. Treaty against Torture. This author argues that sovereign jurisdiction is exceeded in regards to the legal matters pertaining to the violation of fundamental human rights when agents of the State engage in grave human rights abuses, especially those amounting to international crimes, and the State is unwilling or unable to provide a civil or criminal law remedy to victims. The position here then is that it is *not* a colonial or Western encroachment on State sovereignty for the international criminal court in The Hague or for foreign national courts to apply universal criminal and civil law jurisdiction (extra-territorial jurisdiction) in such matters in an effort to seek justice for the victims of international crime. Indeed, the offending State forfeits its sovereignty of its own accord in respect of adjudication of such matters when it sponsors, or fails to prevent international crimes and then refuses to provide a fair and equitable remedy. This approach is in fact codified in the complementarity principle of the Rome Statute. To the extent then that the European Court of Human Rights (ECHR) declares such cases inadmissible as to the human rights complaint against the State based on State immunity, the ECHR has, it is contended, served to foster impunity based on legally insupportable grounds as will be discussed in the context of specific ECHR cases.

[2]Bennoune (2002, p. 245).

Part 2 discusses the way in which the European Court of Human Rights has often: (i) declined to discuss the systemic or widespread human rights abuses targeting certain ethnic groups such as the Roma; and (ii) declined to link ethnic discrimination – a European Convention Article 14 violation – to certain other grave Convention violations (such as infringements of European Convention Article 2 [right to life] and Article 3 [protection from torture or inhuman or degrading treatment or punishment]) by relying on an inappropriate *criminal* law standard of proof (proof 'beyond reasonable doubt') in an international *human rights* judicial proceeding. Of special interest in regards to European Court of Human Rights cases involving systemic discrimination and possible international crimes are the cases in Part 2 concerning: (i) systemic forced sterilization of Roma women in the Czech Republic and Slovakia carried out by physicians in a hospital setting in the context of C-sections and (ii) internally displaced Roma in post-conflict Kosovo placed in life threatening highly lead contaminated U.N. refugee camps in Northern Kosovo. The question is raised in Part 2 whether the latter cases involve forms of genocide and/or crimes against humanity.

The ultimate result of the Court's downgrading of the nature and gravity of the European Convention violations targeting a particular ethnic group is that the European Court of Human Rights has, in effect, contributed to decreasing the likelihood that any potential international crimes which are associated with the ECHR cases discussed in Parts 2 and 3 would be prosecuted (either domestically, or by other States exercising universal jurisdiction over international crimes, or by the international criminal court in those cases where all ICC admissibility criteria were in fact met). Recall that with respect to ICC admissibility of potential cases referred to the ICC Prosecutor by an individual or group of individuals or NGO, the Prosecutor will consider the level of outrage in the international community about the human rights violations alleged (among other admissibility criteria). Having the European Court of Human Rights disassociate ethnic hatred and systemic human rights violations targeting a certain ethnic group in such cases from the other European Convention violations serves to create the illusion that the case involves but regular serious European Convention violations rather than potentially also heinous international crimes which constitute the gravest of all human rights violations. This downgrading of the violations by the European Court of Human Rights, (the voice of the European international community), thus: (i) reduces the likelihood that the Prosecutor of the International Criminal Court will contravene the European Court of Human Rights' assessment of the *alleged* lesser gravity of the fundamental human rights violations involved (compared to international crimes), and (ii) reduces the likelihood, with respect to referred situations, that an independent ICC investigation would be initiated by the ICC Prosecutor's Office which might lead to prosecution of individual perpetrators in various cases.

As the European Court of Human Rights cases discussed in this book in Parts 2 and 3 have *not* been adjudicated by the ICC and the domestic courts have, where the question of international crimes was addressed, for the most part, if not always, negated that possibility,[3] the objective in Parts 2 and 3 is somewhat modest. That objective is simply to present the cases and *raise for the reader questions* of whether: (i) the cases potentially or likely involve international crimes, and (ii) whether the European Court of Human Rights was legally and morally obligated to address this possibility as a possibility, or as a likelihood, or even certainty (depending on the fact pattern in the specific case), and have its consideration of this issue reflected in (a) its analysis of the case and its assessment of the gravity of the alleged Convention violations; (b) its declaratory judgments and (c) its orders (orders which could include a non-pecuniary remedy in the form of admonitions to the State to end systemic ethnic persecution via certain State proactive legislative and other measures; to properly criminally investigate, prosecute and punish international crimes, to establish, where necessary, a victims' assistance fund to provide State assistance to victims in filing civil and criminal complaints relating to ethnic persecution and international crimes, etc.).

Part 3 addresses the extent to which the European Court of Human Rights applied humanitarian law principles in various cases involving ethnic targeting and probable 'war crimes' or 'crimes against humanity' in times of armed conflict. Part 3 discusses also the European Court of Human Rights apparent reluctance, in certain instances, to classify European Convention violations as international crimes even when those violations likely constitute 'war crimes' or 'crimes against humanity' in times of armed conflict.

The cases discussed in Parts 2 and 3 pose important ethical challenges and it is imperative that the European Court of Human Rights judgments in these cases be scrutinized as to their implications for our understanding of the interconnectedness of various branches of international law (i.e. international humanitarian law, international criminal law concerning the international crimes of 'genocide', 'war crimes' and 'crimes against humanity' and international human rights law). The European Court of Human Rights judgments have implications that reach far beyond simply the Court's pronouncement on European Convention violations as the cases in Parts 2 and 3 in particular illustrate.

There is a famous quote from Cicero's writing on the law; the original quote being "Those who share law must also share justice."[4] Unfortunately, as the cases discussed in this book will hopefully highlight, 'shared law' (such as, for instance,

---

[3]See, for instance, (i) the Ostrava court decision regarding refusal of compensation in the Ferencikova case of forced sterilization of a 22-year old Roma woman (sterilization without informed consent) where the Ostrava court held, despite acknowledging that forced sterilization had occurred, that the case was not an instance of genocide and was, in any event, statute-barred, and (ii) the case of Iveta Cervenakova. Ms. Cervenakova was awarded 500,000 CZK damages, (half that requested), by the Regional Court in Ostrava for forced sterilization, (where there was no signed consent, and consent was obtained verbally while the 19 year old was under the influence of anaesthesia in preparation for an imminent caesarean section). That compensation award was overturned by the Olomouc High Court by its retroactively applying to her 2007 case; a new 2008 amendment to the statute of limitations law introducing a three year statute of limitations period for the filing of "medical harm" claims (Romea 2007; The Prague Post 2008).

[4]Ishay (2007, p. 15) citing Cicero's The Laws, 52 BCE.

the *European Convention on Human Rights*) *as interpreted* does *not* always deliver what our intuitive sense tells us would amount to *justice* for the direct and indirect victims of atrocity. Rather, myopic interpretations of this shared law can, and too often do, provide for impunity for perpetrators of international crimes. We must guard against impunity cloaked in a sanctimonious version of the law which is not grounded in the reality of human suffering, but rather based on the arcane analysis of that majority of the bench that happens to hold sway in a particular legal case. *Of course, it is left to the reader, in the final analysis, to decide if and when this has occurred in the European Court of Human Rights cases examined in this book.* If nothing else, this author will have accomplished something worthwhile via this monograph if the European Court of Human Rights cases and issues discussed better highlight for the reader that the more useful version of the aforementioned Cicero quote on the relationship between law and justice might be: 'Those who share a particular version, interpretation, or vision of the law must share that version of justice that flows from the former which, in fact, may, or may not, amount to genuine justice for all.' The only course is to continue to scrutinize the judgments of the European Court of Human Rights (and those of the other international courts) and to challenge those rulings which, in whole or in part, appear: (i) to have failed to advance an appropriate level of respect for the human dignity of victims, or appear (ii) to have been defective in indirectly holding perpetrators to full account via the symbolic declaratory content of the European Court of Human Rights' judgments concerning what European Convention violations have or have not been committed. Furthermore, in regards to *European Convention on Human Rights* Article 7 alleged violations where the applicant has been convicted domestically of an international crime, the Court bears the awesome responsibility of pronouncing on whether such crimes were or were not committed as part of the process of examining State compliance with Article 7 (i.e. see the cases in Part 3). Where the Court declares no international crime was committed, and in those particular cases where this finding is in actuality incorrect on the facts, the Court inadvertently contributes to impunity and to the suffering of victims and/or their surviving relatives and muddies the historical record. Part 4 presents some concluding comments regarding the importance of moral legitimacy in the rulings of the international human rights courts.

A Brief Overview of Selected Key Aspects of the Structure and Workings of the European Court of Human Rights

The European Court of Human Rights located in Strasbourg, France was established in 1959 and operates as an international court on a full time permanent basis. The European Court of Human Rights is widely referred to as "the conscience of Europe". The *European Convention on Human Rights and Fundamental Freedoms* (also referred to as the *European Convention on Human Rights*), administered by the European Court of Human Rights, first entered into force in 1953 (and as amended by Protocol 11, entry into force in 1998) and guarantees a diverse set of civil and political rights and freedoms.

The European Court of Human Rights has 47 judges in total as its full compliment and includes one judge for every State Party to the *European Convention on Human Rights and Fundamental Freedoms* (one for every member State of the Council of Europe). The judges are elected by majority vote of the Parliamentary Assembly of the Contracting Party to *the European Convention on Human Rights and Fundamental Freedoms* from a list of three candidates nominated by the Contracting Party. The judges are expected to function as an unbiased and independent judiciary and not as representatives of any particular State or advocates for any State's interests in any particular case they are assigned. A judge elected by a particular State will not necessarily have the nationality of that State. The President of the Court, Vice-President(s) of the Court, and Section Presidents are elected by the plenary court (full court) while the Section Vice-Presidents are elected by the section (division of the Court into sections is explained below). The Registrar and two Deputy Registrars are also elected by the plenary court.

Every judge of the European Court of Human Rights is assigned to one of five sections such that the section judges represent a balanced gender and geographic mix and represent a balanced mix of the various and differing domestic legal systems of the States Parties to the European Convention of Human Rights and Fundamental Freedoms. Each of the five sections is comprised of seven judges and includes a Section President and Section Vice-President (two Section Vice-Presidents also serve as Vice Presidents of the Court as a whole) and, in addition, a Section Registrar and Deputy Section Registrar. Judges are assigned to a section for three years. The European Court of Human Rights as a whole also has an elected President.

Most of the cases heard by the European Court of Human Rights are heard by 'the Chamber' (lower court) comprised of the seven judges selected from the section to which the case was assigned. One of the seven judges is the President of the section to which the case was assigned. The lower Chamber also includes among its seven judges the judge elected by the respondent State party to the case (or another person chosen by that State Party in question who sits in the capacity of a judge in instances where the person elected is unable to serve).

The upper chamber is named the 'Grand Chamber' and it is empowered to rehear cases de novo on request by one or both parties but will do so only in very selected cases. The cases will come before the Grand Chamber for re-hearing only if accepted by the five member Grand Chamber screening panel which considers the application for a re-hearing (that application being made by one or both of the parties to the case). Alternatively, the Grand Chamber may hear the case when the lower Chamber relinquishes its jurisdiction and the case concerns central questions regarding the Convention or its application or other important questions that require clarification. The Chamber may relinquish jurisdiction to the Grand Chamber at any point prior to rendering its judgment.

The Grand Chamber is comprised of 17 judges and at least three substitute judges who can serve as alternates if one of the 17 judges of the Grand Chamber is unable to serve. The Grand Chamber includes among the 17 judges the President and Vice-Presidents of the European Court of Human Rights, and the five section

Presidents (Any Vice-President of the Court or President of a Section who is unable to sit as a member of the Grand Chamber is replaced by the Vice-President of the relevant section).

In cases to be re-heard on application for re-hearing by one or both parties (that application having been screened and accepted by a five member Grand Chamber screening panel), no judge who sat on the lower Chamber panel dealing with the case and rendered judgment will also be on the Grand Chamber panel which re-hears the case de novo with the exception of (a) the Section President of the lower Chamber that rendered the judgment and (b) the judge elected by the State that is a party to the case who previously sat as an ex officio member on the case in the lower Chamber that rendered a judgment (or the substitute judge from that State that sat on the Chamber panel that rendered judgment in the case in the lower Chamber) and (c) any judge that sat in regard to the decision on admissibility of the case.

Since the Grand Chamber is re-hearing the case de novo, the Grand Chamber is empowered to consider both admissibility and merit with respect to the allegation (s) of Convention violations it examines. The cases which are accepted by a screening panel of the Grand Chamber for re-hearing and come before the Grand Chamber must first have been ruled admissible by the lower Chamber ('the Chamber') on one or more alleged Convention violations. It is important to understand that the Grand Chamber in re-hearing a case will consider only those alleged violations in the case that have been previously ruled admissible by the Chamber (lower Court). *The Grand Chamber could reverse or affirm either or both the lower Courts rulings on admissibility or merit as regards to one or more of the alleged violations.*

Where 'the Chamber' has relinquished its jurisdiction over the case and referred the case to the Grand Chamber, the Grand Chamber will issue a ruling on admissibility of each alleged Convention/Protocol violations made in the case and, for those ruled admissible, a ruling on merit in the same judgment and a determination regarding just satisfaction (financial compensation) if any is to be awarded. Rulings are by majority vote. The Grand Chamber in all cases before it will consider the legal issues de novo (afresh) thus considering everything again (that is issues regarding law or mixed law and fact) as pertains to admissibility and merit.

The European Court of Human Rights has jurisdiction to rule via binding judgments regarding: (a) State Party violations of the *European Convention on Human Rights and Fundamental Freedoms* as modified by Protocol #11; and/or (b) State infringements of the additional protocol(s) to the *European Convention on Human Rights and Fundamental Freedoms* as set out in the most recent amended version of the Convention (where the State Party to the case has also ratified or acceded to the Protocol(s) in question), and/or (c) State violations of such additional Conventions as agreed upon by the Council of Europe which are in force (where the State Party in question has also ratified or acceded to the additional Convention(s) at issue in the case).

The European Court of Human Rights is *not* an appeal court for national courts. Therefore, the Court cannot reverse or in any way change any ruling by a national court, nor alter or quash any domestic laws of the States Parties to the European

Convention on Human Rights. The European Court of Human Rights operates as a body that helps shed light on the extent of State compliance with the European Convention on Human Rights (and its Protocols) and certain other operative European Conventions adopted by the Council of Europe and ratified or acceded to by some or all of the Council of Europe member States. This by hearing admissible cases brought by individuals, organizations or State Parties concerning alleged *European Convention of Human Rights* infringements, and by making declarations regarding alleged violations, and ordering, in the proper cases, just satisfaction and/or certain other remedies. In exceptional circumstances (i.e. where there is a risk of imminent serious physical harm to the complainant by agents of the State Party or Parties in question for whatever reason), the Court may act on behalf of the complainant to intercede with the government(s) in question to ask that certain protections be afforded the complainant by the government(s) involved as the case proceeds.

The geographical jurisdiction of the European Court of Human Rights extends only to the 47 States Parties to the *European Convention on Human Rights and Fundamental Freedoms* who comprise the Council of Europe. It should be noted that both: (a) nationals of the States Parties to the *European Convention on Human Rights and Fundamental Freedoms*, as well as (b) any other persons present in the jurisdiction of one of the States Parties to the *European Convention on Human Rights and Fundamental Freedoms*, or in a territory under the control of that State Party at the time of the alleged State Convention infringement which caused them direct, personal harms, are potentially covered by the guarantees of the Convention. Thus, State violations of the Convention may be addressed to the European Court of Human Rights by the latter individuals as well. Petitions to the Court seeking a remedy for alleged infringements of *European Convention on Human Rights* provisions may be brought by: (a) individuals directly harmed, or others accepted by the Court as the official representatives of the harmed persons (i.e. parents as complainants on behalf of a minor child victim, NGOs on behalf of victims, etc.), (b) groups of individuals directly harmed, organizations such as NGOs considered as legal entities who have members victimized, or by (c) one Convention State Party against another (though the number of inter-State petitions to the Court are very few).

The Committee of Ministers of the Council of Europe, with the assistance of the Department for the Execution of Judgments of the European Court of Human Rights, is responsible for the enforcement of the judgments made by the European Court of Human Rights.

References

Bennoune K (2002) Sovereignty vs. Suffering? Re-examining sovereignty and human rights through the lens of Iraq. EJIL 13(1):243–262

Ishay MR (2007) The human rights reader: major political essays, speeches and documents from ancient times to the present, 2nd edn. Routledge, New York

Romea (2007) Historic verdict: Court awards compensation to a Romani woman for sterilization for the first time. Press release, 12 October 2007. http://www.romea.cz/english/index.php?id=detail & detail=2007_561

The Prague Post (2008) Ostrava hospital ordered to apologize to Roma woman. Article, 12 November 2008

Acknowledgements

I extend my deepest thanks to my husband Roshan Grover for his love and his infinite patience in listening to my ramblings about the book and for his constant support, and faith in my ability to complete this rather ambitious work. I also acknowledge the support of our daughter Angeline whose pride in her mom is a source of great encouragement to me and whose own human rights advocacy work is quite admirable. My sincere thanks are extended also to Dr. Brigitte Reschke, Executive Editor for law with Springer for her invaluable advice regarding the manuscript.

Contents

PART I: Selected Factors Facilitating Impunity for International Crimes Through the European Court of Human Rights

Abstract In Part 1 various key cases are discussed which concern the contentious issue of the legal legitimacy of the notion of universal civil and universal criminal jurisdiction and whether one or both such jurisdictions is established under the *United Nations Convention Against Torture and Other Cruel, Inhuman or Degrading Treatment or Punishment* and customary international law. Such absolute universal jurisdiction or, in some instances, a restricted version of universal jurisdiction allows for legal action to be brought in the national courts of a State other than that in which the offences occurred and against persons who are not the nationals of the forum State. Such legal actions include but are not limited to civil actions for damages, extradition requests regarding foreign nationals, and warrants for the arrest of foreign nationals accused of having committed international crimes outside the forum State. Some argue such jurisdiction is not barred by any sort of immunity and under the less restrictive notion of universal jurisdiction the legal action in the forum State may be initiated whether or not the accused has ever set foot in the jurisdiction of the forum State and regardless the nationality of the victim. Issues concerning the boundaries of State sovereignty, what constitutes an 'official' act by an agent of the State, the limits of personal immunity granted to sitting or former heads of State and other high officials or diplomats are addressed. The European Court of Human Rights approach to the issue of universal jurisdiction is shown to contribute to a lack of State accountability and ultimately, in many instances, to complete impunity for individual perpetrators of international crimes such as torture and war crimes.

S.C. Grover, *The European Court of Human Rights as a Pathway to Impunity for International Crimes*,
DOI 10.1007/978-3-642-10799-3_1,

I. The European Court of Human Rights' Derogation of the Jus Cogens Nature of Certain Fundamental Human Rights

A. *Immunity as a Pathway to Impunity for International Crimes*

Introduction

The argument is made here that: (a) in cases of international crimes as defined under the Rome Statute and under certain other international law such as the *United Nations Convention Against Torture and Other Cruel, Inhuman or Degrading Treatment or Punishment*,[1] neither the State nor the individual perpetrators of international crimes are legitimately shielded by State immunity in civil actions, and (b) the State, while not criminally prosecutable as a State, should, if international law is correctly applied, be vulnerable to other mechanisms of accountability by the international community for the fostering, or failure to prevent international crimes committed by its public officials or other agents of the State while those agents were acting in their capacity as representatives of the State: (i) whether or not those agents acted with or without the authorization of the State and consistent with, or in contradiction to State instruction; (ii) whether or not the agent, if a public official, committed the offences before or during the tenure of his or her public office, and regardless whether the public official would normally be protected by diplomatic immunity accorded to a head of State, foreign ambassador or other potentially protected official, and (iii) whether or not the head of State or other person normally covered by diplomatic immunity, and now *not* in office, committed the international crime as an *alleged* official act or an act outside the jurisdiction of his or her office (but where, at the time of the commission of the international crime, the public official or other agent of the State was holding him or herself out as representing the State in carrying out, or having directed to be carried out, acts of genocide, crimes against humanity and/or war crimes).

It is time that mere rhetoric on 'immunity not leading to impunity' be replaced by the actual holding to account of States and their agents for the commission of international crimes. To effectuate such a new reality, requires challenging erroneous purportedly legal rationales under international law which lead to the perpetuation of impunity for the perpetrators of international crime. That is, the objective here is to contest the grant of immunity in cases involving international crime irrespective of how prestigious or august the body which holds that the offending State and its agents are shielded from the quest for justice by the victim of an atrocity which that body, at the same time, purports to consider an affront to humanity itself and to the conscience of the international community as a whole.

[1] *United Nations Convention Against Torture and Other Cruel, Inhuman or Degrading Treatment or Punishment*. UN General Assembly Resolution 39/46, 10 December 1984, entering into force 26 June 1987. http://www.unhchr.ch/html/menu3/b/h_cat39.htm. Accessed 17 June 2009.

The grant of immunity from civil liability to the offending State and its agents and/or the grant of State or diplomatic immunity from criminal prosecution to the accused public officials or other agents of the State it will be shown in the context of specific cases affects the substantive rights of the victims of international crime rather than simply being a purely procedural bar (that procedural bar preventing the civil dispute or criminal prosecution from being adjudicated in the national courts of a jurisdiction other than that where the offence occurred). In fact, the grant of State immunity to offending States and in some instances also their agents in such civil cases undermines the jus cogens prohibition against torture which is well-established customary international law. The implication of the grant of State immunity by the national courts of the forum State to the respondent State in civil cases where torture is alleged not as a private matter (not committed by one private citizen against another), but where the government is implicated, is that torture is being implicitly and erroneously legitimized as a State function. This implication arises in that State immunity is intended to apply only to acts within the sovereign, independent authority of the State. Hence, if the State granted immunity is one which sponsors torture by its agents within its borders, or fails to prevent its agents, acting as officials of the State, from engaging in torture within that State, torture (under the international law definition stipulated in the 1984 Treaty on Torture) is incorrectly ipso facto wrongly classified as a governmental act; a manifestation of the sovereign powers of the State. This tragic misguided illusion has potential serious adverse ramifications for peace and order in the international community and for the protection of individual and collective fundamental human rights. The European Court of Human Rights, in affirming the forum State's grant of immunity to the offending State that is directly or indirectly responsible for torture within that non-forum State's borders, thus inadvertently aids and abets the respondent State in upholding the *fallacious* contention that acts of torture (those meeting the international definition of torture under the U.N. treaty on torture) are sovereign acts (i.e. when committed by State agents or officials in their official capacity).

The proposition is here advanced that *no* State sovereignty exists in regards to international crimes from which either State or diplomatic immunity could derive and transfer to the State's public officials or other agents of the State in respect of their civil or criminal liability for their commission of international crimes. The contention here is then that State sovereignty, as currently understood, does *not* encompass a bar against universal jurisdiction (civil or criminal) in cases involving international crimes where the respondent offending State is unwilling or unable to itself provide reparations to the victims and has, furthermore, shielded the individual perpetrators from civil and/or criminal liability in the jurisdiction where the offences occurred.

The contemporary understanding of State sovereignty is a departure from the notion of State sovereignty as deriving from the sovereignty of the King where the King had absolute immunity from both civil and criminal liability whether in the domestic courts of his realm or those of a foreign jurisdiction.[2] Such an absolute

[2]McGregor (2007, pp. 903–919).

shield against accountability for the King essentially places the sovereign above the law; his authority allegedly superseding all other bodies' jurisdictional powers, such as that of the judiciary; their jurisdictional authority being considered to have been granted at the King's discretion. Such a notion rests on the faulty presumption that the King is embodied with a right and authority granted by some higher spiritual divine source. The notion of State sovereignty as unbounded (i.e. also in cases of international crime) such that the State and its agents are shielded from liability is, as McGregor[3] explains, fundamentally flawed and related to the historic notions of State sovereignty as resting in the divine right of the King. The latter notion was later re-packaged in the form of the concept of *sovereign equality* which holds that all States big and small, powerful and weak are, in theory at least (if not practice), equal and hence entitled to govern their own internal affairs without meddling by other States. The grant of State immunity thus tied into the notion of sovereign equality in that each State would grant the other protection from interference in its internal affairs without regard to any particular State characteristics or the issues at hand.

The notion of sovereign equality leads to the erroneous view that it is undemocratic under any circumstance for a *forum State* to exercise extra-territorial jurisdiction over another State in terms of assuming the role of adjudicator (via its national courts) on matters relating to international crimes committed by the agents of the offending State. Proponents of this latter view argue that only an international court may properly adjudicate on such matters since such a court is not an organ of any particular State and hence exercise of its jurisdiction does not infringe the principle of sovereign equality (though arguably hybrid courts such as the Special Court of Sierra Leone qualify as both an international court and a court importantly enmeshed in certain respects with a certain State; in this case the Court is linked to Sierra Leone and charged with applying certain pieces of Sierra Leonean criminal law regarding grave human rights abuses as well as applying certain international criminal law as embodied in its enabling statute). Sovereign equality hence is a concept that is often relied upon just as surely is the notion of State immunity to rationalize immunizing the State against the enforcement by other States of any mechanisms of accountability for international crimes which have been committed within its borders. There is, however, nothing democratic about silencing the voices of victims of atrocity who often as not are wholly or in part comprised of nationals of the offending State itself.

McGregor makes the critical point that immunity is derivative of sovereignty and hence the imagined scope of immunity is dependent on the au courant generally accepted conceptual construction of the notion of sovereignty:

> One of the further ways in which immunity has been used as a tool to sustain impunity for torture and other crimes under international law is by restating the traditional justifications for immunity. As such, courts routinely cite sovereign equality, par in parem non habet jurisdictionem [equal States cannot judge each other], dignity, comity, and international relations as legitimate and necessary bases on which to grant immunity... *no consideration*

[3]McGregor (2007, pp. 903–919).

> *is given to the contemporary meaning and evolution of such principles... immunity can only be derivative, not constitutive of these principles...* The depiction of immunity as static contradicts the progressively contracting coverage of immunity, precipitated by the evolution in sovereignty (emphasis added).[4]
>
> *If immunity derives from sovereignty, its meaning, extent, and impact must also be contingent on the current scope of sovereignty.* Yet, by simply restating the origins of immunity in sovereignty, *courts have failed to acknowledge the restrictions on the scope of immunity caused by the evolution of sovereignty over time* (emphasis added).[5]

McGregor then makes the legal argument that our contemporary vision of sovereignty contemplates that jus cogens principles such as the ban on torture from which there is no derogation possible under international law places a limit on the notion of State immunity:

> *In the case of the commission of crimes under international law, state sovereignty and the principle of parem non habet jurisdictionem no longer provide grounds on which to contest external scrutiny.* Such crimes are not considered the internal domain of one state, but the concern and responsibility of the international community as a whole (emphasis added).[6]

For most, if not all, human rights advocates, McGregor's perspective on the impact of international crime on the availability of State immunity seems incontrovertible. It would seem furthermore non-contestable that comity and good inter-State relationships are better founded on a mutual respect for the fundamental human rights of individuals and of collectives rather than on turning a blind eye to atrocity. The latter via the grant of State immunity in cases involving international crime. Such mutual respect for basic human rights would seem more conducive to long-term State and inter-State order, peace and stability. This, however, is not in fact the stance that the European Court of Human Rights has taken. Rather, the European Court of Human Rights has held that State immunity can be granted in various circumstances despite the case involving torture (and presumably other jus cogens international crimes) committed by agents of the State in their official capacity. The case of *Al-Adsani v. United Kingdom* is illustrative of the Court's reasoning in this regard. Let us then turn first to a summary of the facts of the case and its procedural history and then to an analysis and a challenge to the European Court of Human Rights conclusions in *Al-Adsani*.

Case 1: Al-Adsani v. United Kingdom (Application 35763/97) European Court of Human Rights Grand Chamber Judgment of 21 November 2001

In *Al-Adsani v. United Kingdom*[7] the European Court of Human Rights re-affirmed the grant by the U.K. courts of State sovereign immunity to Kuwait against a civil

---

[4]McGregor (2007, p. 912).

[5]McGregor (2007, p. 916).

[6]McGregor (2007, p. 916).

[7]*Al-Adsani v. United Kingdom* [2001] ECHR 752.

lawsuit filed in a U.K. court. The immunity was granted in *Al-Adsani* to Kuwait against a civil claim pursued in the U.K. courts though: (a) the claimant, Mr. Al-Adsani (a British national with dual citizenship also in Kuwait), had been severely tortured while in the territorial jurisdiction of Kuwait, and (b) despite the U.K. Courts' acceptance of the fact that Kuwait was responsible for the harms caused Mr. Al-Adsani due to torture carried out by its agents upon his person while Mr. Al-Adsani was in Kuwait. The grant of State immunity to the respondent State itself implied that the individual perpetrators who committed the torture *on behalf of the State of Kuwait* (hence 'official torture') would, in the view of the European Court of Human Rights, also have been entitled to State subject matter immunity although the court was not asked to address the latter issue which was not part of the application.

Procedural History of Al-Adsani v. United Kingdom Within the European Human Rights System

The European Court of Human Rights Grand Chamber case of *Al-Adsani v. United Kingdom* originated in a complaint filed 3 April 1997 with the European Commission on Human Rights against the United Kingdom and Northern Ireland by Mr Sulaiman Al-Adsani. Subsequent to the original filing in the case, the Commission was dissolved pursuant to reforms to the European Convention on Human Rights system. The application was then transferred to the European Court of Human Rights 1 November 1998 pursuant to Protocol 11 additional to the European Convention on Human Rights (here also referred to as the 'European Convention') after the Protocol came into force. On 19 October 1999, the European Court of Human Rights Chamber which had been allocated the case relinquished jurisdiction to the Grand Chamber of the European Court of Human Rights. This given that both parties were agreed that the case proceed directly to the Grand Chamber. The Grand Chamber ruled the Al-Adsani case admissible in a decision of 9 February 2000 after a hearing both on admissibility and merits. In an unusual move, the Grand Chamber granted a second hearing on the merits at the request of the U.K. government. The second hearing was held on 15 November 2000 jointly with another case.

The European Court of Human Rights Grand Chamber held unanimously in *Al-Adsani v. United Kingdom* that there had been no violation of Article 3 of the European Convention on Human Rights (hereafter referred to as 'the European Convention') concerning the right to be protected from torture; and by nine votes to eight that there had been no violation of Article 6(1) of the European Convention pertaining to the right to have a properly constituted tribunal fairly determine the nature of any European Convention violations which the applicant may have suffered. The European Court of Human Rights did not reach to the issue of the applicant's allegation of a violation of Article 13 of the European Convention on Human Rights concerning the right to a remedy. The European Court of Human Rights held there was no need for the Court to address the remedy issue it having been decided that there had been no violation of Articles 3 and 6(1) of the European Convention on Human Rights and Fundamental Freedoms.

Background and U.K. Proceedings in the Case of Al-Adsani v. United Kingdom

The applicant, Mr. Al-Adsani, as mentioned had dual citizenship in Britain and Kuwait at all relevant times. Being a trained pilot, he had gone to Kuwait in 1991 to serve with the Kuwaiti air force against Iraq during the Gulf War and, after the Iraqi incursion into Kuwait, he remained as a participant in the resistance struggle. Upon his return to the U.K., the applicant filed a civil lawsuit in a U.K. court against: (a) the individual perpetrators of the torture he alleged he had suffered at the hands of Kuwaiti State agents while in Kuwait, and (b) against the State of Kuwait itself seeking pecuniary reparations for the physical and psychological harms he had suffered as a result of the torture. It is important to note that the civil case against Kuwait was filed in the U.K. only after overtures for an alternative dispute mechanism to reach a mutually agreed upon settlement (i.e. through diplomatic channels with Kuwait) had been rebuffed.

The U.K. courts found the allegation that Al-Adsani had been tortured in Kuwait by agents of the Kuwaiti government (Sheikh Jaber Al-Sabah Al-Saud Al-Sabah who is related to the Emir of Kuwait and two others) on or about the dates specified by the petitioner to have been adequately substantiated by the claimant in the U.K. civil court proceedings (the alleged motive for the torture is irrelevant for the purposes of this discussion). The U.K. courts, furthermore, fully acknowledged the brutality of the injuries inflicted upon Mr Al-Adsani as a result of the torture he was subjected to while in Kuwait. These injuries included burns over 25% of his body that required many weeks of treatment in hospital both in Kuwait and upon his arrival back in the U.K.

The applicant alleged that on 2 May 1991 he had been tortured by the Kuwaiti State agents, and taken at gunpoint in a government jeep to Kuwaiti State Security Prison. The applicant further alleged that while at the prison he received beatings from prison guards and was only released after being forced to sign a false confession. His release from prison came a few days later on 5 May 1991. Mr. Al-Adsani also alleged that on 7 May 1991 he was again taken at gunpoint in a government car by the same Sheik. In this second abduction and false imprisonment, he alleged he was taken to the palace of the Emir of Kuwait's brother. At the palace, he reportedly had his head repeatedly held underwater in a swimming-pool containing corpses, and was then placed in a room where the Sheikh set fire to mattresses and he (Al-Adsani) was forced to remain in the room consequently suffering severe burns. He also alleged that while back in the U.K. he had been subjected to death threats from agents of the State of Kuwait. These threats, it was claimed, were intended to impress upon him (Al-Adsani) that he would be killed were he to take any action regarding a remedy for his victimization in Kuwait or publicize the fact that he had been tortured in Kuwait and/or reveal who had allegedly orchestrated his torture.

On 15 December 1992, Mr. Al-Adsani obtained a *default judgment against the Sheikh from a U.K. court and later was permitted to amend his statement of claim to include two further named individual defendants in the civil suit*. However, the U.K. lower court denied Mr. Al-Adsani the right to serve a writ on the State of Kuwait. The denial was based on the ground that: (a) Kuwait allegedly enjoyed State immunity as per the existing U.K. statute regarding State immunity (the 1978 U.K. State Immunity Act),[8] and (b) Kuwait allegedly enjoyed State immunity also according to the formal and customary international law on State immunity. On appeal to the U.K. Appeal Court (challenging Kuwait's right to State immunity in the case), the U.K. Appeal Court preliminarily held that Mr. Al-Adsani had established "an arguable case" (through his evidence) that Kuwait was responsible for: (a) the mental and physical suffering he had endured as result of torture he personally had endured while in Kuwait, and (b) that he continued to endure post-traumatic stress symptoms resulting from his torture experience suffered while in Kuwait.

The U.K. Appeal Court held that the following evidence supported the claimant's contention that the State of Kuwait itself bore some type of responsibility for his torture: (a) on 2 May 1991 Mr. Al-Adsani had been taken to a Kuwaiti State prison (a *government facility*), (b) on 2 and 7 May 1991, his abductors transported him in *government vehicles*, and (c) while Mr. Al-Adsani was in a Kuwaiti State prison he had been beaten by prison guards (*agents of the State*). The Appeals Court accepted then, provisionally at least, that the State of Kuwait was, at a minimum, vicariously liable for the torture of Mr. Al-Adsani and would thus be held to account unless State immunity applied.

When a writ was served on Kuwait, the State responded with an application to have the U.K. appeal proceedings struck. The Appeal Court held that it was Mr. Al-Adsani's burden to meet the standard of 'a balance of probabilities' in making out his case as to why Kuwait should not be afforded State immunity, i.e. why the case fell under the 1978 U.K. State Immunity Act statutory exception which would defeat State immunity. That statutory exception which defeated the grant of State immunity was the situation in which the personal injury to, or death of a British national was inflicted by agents of a foreign State through their actions or omissions while that British national was within U.K. jurisdiction, that is while he or she was still in the United Kingdom. The U.K. appeals court held that: (a) since the claimant was *not* contending that the acts of torture for which Kuwait was responsible occurred while the claimant was in the U.K., and (b) since the court did not find that the alleged death threats that the claimant received while back in the U.K. could be linked to the State of Kuwait, his claim did *not* fall under the exception to State immunity in the 1978 U.K. State Immunity Act. The post-traumatic stress symptoms the claimant continued to experience after his return to the U.K. were held by the U.K. Appeals Court not to have been caused by acts

[8] *1978 U.K. State Immunity Act*. http://www.law.berkeley.edu/faculty/ddcaron/Documents/RPID%20Documents/rp04038.html. Accessed 18 June 2009.

carried out by agents of Kuwait in the U.K. Hence, the post-traumatic symptoms suffered by Al-Adsani were also not sufficient, according to the U.K. Court of Appeals, to defeat Kuwait's claim to State immunity. Hence, the Court of Appeals found that the case, for all the aforementioned reasons, allegedly did not fall within the exception in the 1978 U.K. State immunity statute that would defeat the grant of immunity to Kuwait. More generally then the U.K. Appeals Court did not find an exclusionary exception to the grant of State immunity against civil claims brought in a U.K. court in cases concerning acts of torture committed within the *territorial* jurisdiction of the offending foreign State (in the instant case that foreign State being Kuwait). Adding insult to injury, Mr. Al-Adsani was then refused leave to appeal the Court of Appeal decision by the House of Lords. Subsequent to the decision by the House of Lords refusing to hear the claimant's appeal against the U.K. Court of Appeal, Mr. Al-Adsani sought redress instead through the European Court of Human Rights.

The Application to the European Court of Human Rights in Al-Adsani v. United Kingdom

Mr. Al-Adsani's application to the European Court of Human Rights claimed that his European Convention rights (European Convention on Human Rights and Fundamental Freedoms) under Article 3 (the prohibition against torture), Article 6(1) (the right to a fair hearing by an independent and impartial tribunal for the determination of his civil rights), and under Article 13 (his right to an effective remedy for violation of his European Convention rights) had been violated by the U.K.'s refusal to provide him access to the U.K. courts to seek a judicial remedy against Kuwait.

Commentary on the Reasoning of the European Court of Human Rights in Al-Adsani v. United Kingdom

1. ***Jus cogens principles are automatically incorporated into domestic law*: The** European Court of Human Rights, as previously mentioned, endorsed the U.K. Appeals Court holding of grant of State immunity to the respondent State itself in *Al-Adsani v. United Kingdom* against a civil claim. This, it will be recalled, despite the U.K. Appeal Court finding Kuwait at least vicariously liable for the torture of the complainant. The European Court of Human Rights describes the U.K. Appeals Court position as one premised on the assumption that:

> . . . international law could be used only to assist in interpreting lacunae or ambiguities in a statute [in this case the 1978 U.K. statute on State immunity], and *when the terms of a statute were clear, the statute had to prevail over international law.*[9]

[9]*Al-Adsani v. United Kingdom* [2001] ECHR 752, para 17.

Such an approach as advocated by the U.K. Appeals Court and endorsed by the European Court of Human Rights may be sensible where the domestic statute: (i) addresses domestic matters exclusively as opposed to those impacting on inter-State relations; (ii) does not impact upon individual and State rights and obligations in cases concerning grave human rights abuses such as torture, and where (iii) no international law principle has been incorporated (due to its jus cogens nature) into the national legislative scheme. Note, however, that the jus cogens nature of the customary law principle concerning the absolute ban against torture creates erga omnes obligations (obligations that are held by all States in the international community). *This suggests that this principle must be considered automatically incorporated into domestic law even if not formally so incorporated by national statute*:

> To the extent that an act of torture constitutes a violation of customary law, Canadian courts [and by extension any other national courts] may presume a violation of domestic law unless that presumption is refuted by a statute or treaty.[10]

The implication is then that the U.K. Court of Appeals' ruling (its decision later endorsed by the European Court of Human Rights) granting the State of Kuwait immunity in *Al-Adsani* was in effect inconsistent with domestic law. This since U.K. domestic law incorporates the jus cogens principle regarding the prohibition on torture and thus there is a requirement that interpretation of the U.K. State Immunity Act take account of that principle. Doing so would have led to a denial of the grant of State immunity to the respondent State of Kuwait in the case. Note also that The U.K. Courts in the Al-Adsani case, in any event, acknowledged that Kuwaiti domestic law contained a ban on torture during the time of the alleged torture incidents in *Al-Adsani*

2. **The impossibility of insulating domestic immunity statutes from international law considerations**: In the Al-Adsani case, the domestic statute involved; namely the 1978 U.K. State Immunity Act, did relate to matters beyond the domestic affairs of the State which instituted the statute. That is, the statute in question stipulated also the rights and obligations of other States (i.e. Kuwait) in the circumstances at hand and hence implicitly engaged international law concerning inter-State relations in this way also. Indeed, the U.K. Appeals Court in *Al-Adsani v. the United Kingdom* held that the 1978 U.K. State Immunity Act had the legitimate aim of comity and fostering good inter-State relations thus recognizing its relevance to international law. In addition, grave human rights abuses were central to the case (with the applicant alleging torture at the hands of agents of the foreign State) thus implicitly triggering international human rights and international criminal law considerations from the outset. Hence, international law was relevant in interpretation of the statute and its principles implicated in the case in the first instance regardless the alleged clarity of the U.K. statute at issue.

---

[10]Memo Concerning Proposed Amendments to Canada's State Immunity Law, para 2 of Part IV. http://www.law.utoronto.ca/documents/ihrp/SIA_Introductorymemo.doc. Accessed 18 June 2009.

3. **How forum States acquire extra-territorial jurisdiction in cases of so-called 'official torture' of their own nationals or of non-nationals and whether the victim suffered the torture while on the territory of the forum State or outside of that territory**: It can be argued that the proper interpretation of a domestic statute and any possible embedded, but not so obvious ambiguities in the statute may become much more apparent when the statute is viewed through the lens of certain international law principles. However, as mentioned, the European Court of Human Rights contended in *Al-Adsani*, as did the U.K. Court of Appeals in the case, that the 1978 U.K. State Immunity Act was crystal clear. More specifically, these courts held that the statute was clear as to the only exception to the grant of State immunity where the foreign State claimed such immunity. That exception, the European Court of Human Rights held, occurred when the personal injuries against the U.K. national or death of the U.K. national were due to acts for which another State was responsible *but which occurred in the United Kingdom*:

> The clear language of the 1978 Act bestowed immunity upon sovereign States for acts committed outside the jurisdiction [*of the victims home State; the U.K.*] and, by making express provision for exceptions [as when a foreign State waives immunity or the acts by the agents of the foreign State causing personal injury or death to the U.K. victim occurred in the U.K.], it excluded as a matter of construction implied exceptions. Moreover as a result, there was no room for an implied exception for acts of torture in section 1(1) of the 1978 Act [no implied exception to the grant of State immunity for torture where the torture occurred outside of the U.K.].[11]

The central issue in State immunity cases such as *Al-Adsani* concerns the implications, if any, of the jus cogens nature of the international law prohibition against torture upon State immunity. For instance, is the foreign State entitled to immunity against civil lawsuits brought by victims of torture where the claimants experienced the torture while on foreign soil and the victims bring the suit in their own domestic courts rather than in the courts of the offending foreign State (the victims being then those who have been tortured by agents of the foreign State which is now claiming State immunity).

The argument can properly be made that when a person is tortured while in a foreign State by agents of that foreign State, the courts of the victim's home State automatically acquire extraterritorial jurisdiction in the matter as a result. This extra-territorial jurisdiction confers on the courts of the victim's home State the competence to decide the legal issues concerning the offending State's obligations, and the victim's right to reparations. In such instances, the defendant State is considered complicit in the torture to the extent that its agents in their official capacity committed torture whether or not they were authorized to do so (the issue of State authorization will be discussed in detail a later note). *The extra-territorial jurisdiction of the courts in the victim's home State arises since torture is, according to international human rights and international humanitarian law, beyond the territorial jurisdiction of the offending State or any State*. Hence, no legitimate

[11] *Al-Adsani v. United Kingdom* [2001] ECHR 752, para 17.

grant of State immunity is possible in such instances whether the torture carried out by the foreign State's agents was committed against a U.K. national, or the national of another State, and regardless whether the torture occurred on U.K. soil or on foreign soil.

4. **State immunity in cases of 'official torture' is defeated *not* due to a hierarchy of international norms (where jus cogens principles supersede State immunity), but rather due to the State never having had sovereign authority in the first instance for 'official torture' to occur within its territory**: It is essential to note that the non-derogable right of all persons to be protected from torture (a jus cogens principle well-established both in customary international law and treaty law) does not defeat State immunity in such cases as Al-Adsani (though arguably it could). *There is then no need to argue a hierarchy of international norms*; though there is no suggestion here that jus cogens principles do not supersede State immunity principles (i.e. State immunity is a derogable right of the State; that is, exceptions to State immunity can legitimately occur, i.e. as when the State waives immunity, while the right to be protected from torture, in contrast, is a more fundamental non-derogable right and dictates a universal obligation agreed to internationally for each State to protect all persons against torture insofar as it reasonably can do so. The fact that the ban on torture is jus cogens international law in itself would arguably appear to confirm an international consensus on its preemptory status relative to State immunity principles. Hence, the denial of State immunity in cases such as Al-Adsani cannot be considered to reflect a unilateral reordering of international law principles by the forum State).

Let us consider then why there is *no* need for reliance on a presumed hierarchy of international norms in order to defeat State immunity in cases such as *Al-Adsani*. It is argued instead that *State sovereignty* is *not* engaged in respect of the acts of 'official torture' in the first instance in *Al-Adsani* and like cases:

> In modern times a state is . . .incapable of ordering or ratifying acts which are . . .contrary to that international law to which all states are perforce subject. Its agents, in performing such acts, are therefore acting outside their legitimate scope . . ..[12]

Hence, the offending State, having never had sovereign jurisdiction over the legal matters arising in the torture case, can thus not defend against the claim of extra-territorial jurisdiction by the national courts of the victim's home State. *The defendant State's claim of State immunity is thus ultimately defeated at the offending State's own hand. This since State sovereignty is the prerequisite for State immunity and the offending State could not, at any time, have acted in its sovereign capacity in respect of torture carried out by its own agents on behalf of the State (whether those agents acted with or without the State's authorization as will be explained).* That is, the offending State, having exceeded its territorial jurisdiction (sovereign authority) by virtue of it being vicariously or directly responsible for

[12]Glueck (1946, p. 427).

torture which occurred within its territory, is now *not* in a position to legitimately claim State sovereign immunity.

5. **The offending State has at its disposal a variety of vehicles for providing a remedy to the victim(s) of the international crime(s) committed by its public officials or other of its agents**: Nothing precludes the offending State from making fair reparations to the victim on its own initiative at some point, for instance, through diplomatic or other non-judicial channels; or through the domestic courts of the forum State (thus dropping its bogus claim to State immunity).

6. **'State sovereign immunity' is derivative (*not* constitutive) of State sovereignty and this has profound implications for the grant of State immunity**: To recap then, State immunity is defeated in instances such as Al-Adsani not because the international law on torture arguably supersedes the State immunity domestic statutes or the international treaty law on State immunity, but because State or international immunity law is State 'sovereign immunity' law. State 'sovereign immunity', as the name signifies, can only apply in respect of acts the offending State carried out through its agents which were in fact properly and lawfully under its sovereign authority (under its territorial jurisdiction); and torture is not one of those acts.

7. **An express exception in the domestic State immunity statute is *not* necessary to defeat the grant of State immunity in cases involving torture committed by agents of the State**: Torture exceeds the territorial jurisdiction (sovereign authority) of every sovereign State given the international customary law concerning the absolute prohibition against torture which, as discussed, is automatically incorporated into each State's domestic law. The jus cogens nature of the principle, furthermore, places a profound obligation on all States to take all feasible means to protect against torture occurring *in any State*. Thus, there is no possibility of the respondent State taking the default position of State immunity in fighting against civil suits brought in foreign courts regarding torture which occurred in the territory of the offending State. On this analysis then an expressly enumerated exception to State immunity in the 1978 U.K. State Immunity Act was *not* necessary for a defeat of State immunity in *Al-Adsani* contrary to the contention of both the U.K. Court of Appeals and the European Court of Human Rights.

8. **The State may be considered to have given an *express waiver* regarding the grant of State immunity in cases where it is directly or vicariously responsible for torture**: Given the long-standing customary international law prohibition against official torture in particular which is automatically incorporated into domestic law, it can properly be held that the offending State knew, or should have known, that torture was prohibited and beyond the State's sovereign authority. Hence, the fact that the non-forum foreign State is directly or vicariously responsible for torture committed by its agents may be regarded as a *de facto express waiver* of State immunity. That de facto express waiver renders the offending State – according to international immunity law and the forum State's domestic immunity law – subject to civil suits in the national courts of another State (regardless of whether the foreign offending State is in agreement or not with the forum State

exercising universal civil jurisdiction in the matter). There is then no need to argue for an implied waiver theory or to contest the notion that treaty waivers (i.e. regarding also international treaties concerning State immunity) must be express.

9. **No State immunity ratione materiae shield is available to agents of the State who commit acts of torture whether those acts are committed in accord with State instructions or State authorization or not, and regardless of the fact that the agents of the State may represent themselves as acting on behalf of the State in carrying out the torture**: As no State immunity existed in *Al-Adsani* in the first instance (given that torture is beyond the sovereign authority of the State), State immunity could *not* then have been transferred to the agents of the State responsible for the torture who held themselves out as acting on behalf of the State in committing this international crime (and irrespective of whether those agents of the State were acting with or without the blessing of the State).

10. **Torture can be an official act though unauthorized by the government**: It is the U.N. Torture Treaty definition of torture that figures most prominently in the European Court of Human Rights cases here discussed. Recall that torture, as defined under the 1984 U.N. Torture Treaty, refers to an *international crime* committed by a *representative of the State* rather than to torture committed by a private individual who is not representing the State as is reflected in Article 1of the aforementioned Treaty:

> **Article 1**
> For the purposes of this Convention, the term "torture" means any act by which severe pain or suffering, whether physical or mental, is intentionally inflicted on a person for such purposes as obtaining from him or a third person information or a confession, punishing him for an act he or a third person has committed or is suspected of having committed, or intimidating or coercing him or a third person, or for any reason based on discrimination of any kind, *when such pain or suffering is inflicted by or at the instigation of or with the consent or acquiescence of a public official or other person acting in an official capacity*. It does not include pain or suffering arising only from, inherent in or incidental to lawful sanctions (emphasis added).[13]

It is here maintained that under the 1984 U.N. Torture Treaty, any public official or other agent of the State who engages in torture under 'colour of public authority' is presumed to be acting as a representative of the State whether the act was authorized by the government or not.

11 (a) **Torture that is carried out by public officials or other agents of the State who hold themselves out to be acting on behalf of the State in carrying out the torture is: (i) an 'official' act and (ii) meets the definition of torture under the 1984 U.N. Torture Treaty, but (iii) such torture is *not* a 'sovereign' act given that it is extra-jurisdictional**: *Torture by public officials or other agents of the State is at the outset not a sovereign act since it is extra-jurisdictional (whether authorized or unauthorized), though it is still 'official' to the extent the torturer*

---

[13] *United Nations Convention Against Torture and Other Cruel, Inhuman or Degrading Treatment or Punishment.* UN General Assembly Resolution 39/46, 10 December 1984, entering into force 26 June 1987. http://www.unhchr.ch/html/menu3/b/h_cat39.htm. Accessed 17 June 2009.

holds him or herself out to be acting on behalf of the State in carrying out the torture. Thus, torture under these circumstances (committed by agents holding themselves out to be acting on behalf of the State in carrying out the torture) meets the 1984 Torture Treaty definition of official torture (see note 10 above for the definition).

At the same time, the persons carrying out the torture are not covered by State immunity despite the official character of the torture deriving from the agents' representations since simply portending to be carrying out a sovereign State function on behalf of the State is not sufficient to trigger State immunity. Rather *in order for State immunity to apply, the act must genuinely be a State function within the sovereign jurisdiction of the State which the State may then delegate to its agents for execution.*

An act such as torture can thus be an extra-jurisdictional '*official*' or '*governmental*' act. This insofar as the act is intended to be perceived by the victim as one committed on behalf of the State by an agent of the State as opposed to a private act committed by wayward officials. The principle of *respondeat superior* thus applies and the State is implicated and responsible for the conduct of the agents in committing torture whether the act was authorized or not. *Yet, such situations do not represent instances of a sovereign act since the prerequisite for a sovereign act is that it fall within the legitimate authority or jurisdiction of the State*. Nevertheless, the State itself is accountable and is not eligible for a grant of subject matter immunity as a respondent State since the State cannot extricate itself from its agents where its public officials or other agents have committed torture as officials rather than in the role of private citizen. There is then at the outset no basis for a claim of subject matter State immunity and no such State immunity against civil liability extends to the agents of the State in a torture case under the circumstances described.

(b) Consider then the similarities and differences of the view expressed by this author with the unanimous opinion of the U.K. House of Lords in *Jones* as expressed in the words of Lord Hoffman (in *Jones* the U.K. House of Lords held that *both* the State and its officials responsible for torture of the British national (and others) while the plaintiff was in the non-forum State were entitled to subject matter immunity thus reversing a Court of Appeals decision which had granted State immunity but only to the State itself). The U.K. House of Lords position is that acts which violate the jus cogens international law principles can still be 'official' (*as is agreed here*):

> The notion that acts contrary to jus cogens cannot be official acts has *not* been well received by eminent writers on international law (emphasis added).[14]

However, the disagreement arises in that the U.K. House of Lords in *Jones* went on to assert that the official status of the acts (i.e. of torture carried out under colour of public authority) confers subject matter State immunity regarding *civil* liability

---

[14]Opinion of Lord Hoffman in *Jones v. Ministry of the Interior Al-Mamlaka Al-Arabiya AS Suadiya (the Kingdom of Saudi Arabia) and others* [2006] UKHL 26, para 84.

upon the State itself, and hence also upon the agents (who carried out the acts that violate the jus cogens principle of international law regarding no derogation from the right to be protected from torture). The House of Lords in *Jones* rejected then the notion of an implied waiver of State immunity being contained in the 1984 U.N. Treaty Against Torture[15] (such that official acts of torture would not covered by subject matter immunity). The House of Lords in *Jones* held further that the U.K. national courts had no option but to bar adjudication of a civil claim against a foreign State and its agents brought in the U.K. courts where that foreign State was responsible for torture of the victim while the victim was in the foreign State:

> As Lord Millett said in *Holland v. Lampen-Wolfe* [2000] 1 WLR 1573, 1588, state immunity is *not* a "self-imposed restriction on the jurisdiction of its courts which the United Kingdom has chosen to adopt" and which it can, as a matter of discretion, relax or abandon. It is imposed by international law without any discrimination between one state and another (emphasis added).[16]

The position taken by this author, in contrast, is that no restriction on the jurisdiction of the U.K. courts existed in *Al-Adsani* or in *Jones* given that the offending States in each case, having been responsible for 'official torture', had not acted within their sovereign authority in this regard. Hence, no subject matter State immunity against civil liability for those acts was triggered, and the U.K. national courts were, as a consequence, entitled to exercise extra-territorial or universal civil jurisdiction in respect of the legal matters pertaining to the torture. That is, there is no question in these instances of having to exercise discretion and abandon or relax adherence to the international law principles relating to the sovereign equality of States and State sovereign immunity as these issues do not arise on the facts of these cases in the first instance.

(c) The view of the House of Lords in *Jones* mirrors the position of the European Court of Human Rights in *Al-Adsani* in regard to the latter court also considering state immunity ratione materiae in cases involving official torture to be a bar to adjudication of the victim's civil claim in the U.K. courts (where that victim suffered 'official torture' by agents of a foreign State while in the territory of that foreign State). In *Al-Adsani* then the European Court of Human Rights found no violation by the United Kingdom of the plaintiff's Article 6 right to access the U.K. courts in regard to adjudication of his civil claim regarding harms he suffered due to torture in Kuwait at the hands of agents of the State acting in an official capacity (arising due to a bar based on Kuwait's alleged entitlement to State immunity against civil liability). The European Court of Human Rights cited Lord Justice Stuart-Smith of the U.K. Court of Appeals in *Al-Adsani* in outlining the crux of the plaintiff's position:

---

[15] *United Nations Convention Against Torture and Other Cruel, Inhuman or Degrading Treatment or Punishment*. UN General Assembly Resolution 39/46, 10 December 1984, entering into force 26 June 1987. http://www.unhchr.ch/html/menu3/b/h_cat39.htm. Accessed 17 June 2009.

[16] Opinion of Lord Hoffman in *Jones v. Ministry of the Interior Al-Mamlaka Al-Arabiya AS Suadiya (the Kingdom of Saudi Arabia) and others* [2006] UKHL 26, para 101.

> ... in what [counsel] for the Plaintiff acknowledges is a bold submission, he contends that that section [section 1 of the 1978 U.K. State Immunity Act] must be read subject to the implication that the State is only granted immunity if it is acting within the Law of Nations. So that the section reads: 'A State *acting within the Law of Nations* is immune from jurisdiction except as provided... *The argument is ... that international law against torture is so fundamental that it is a jus cogens, or compelling law, which overrides all other principles of international law, including the well-established principles of sovereign immunity. No authority is cited for this proposition*'.[17]
>
> Notwithstanding the special character of the prohibition of torture in international law, the Court is unable to discern in the international instruments, judicial authorities or other materials before it any firm basis for concluding that, as a matter of international law, a State no longer enjoys immunity from civil suit in the courts of another State where acts of torture are alleged.[18]

The European Court of Human Rights in *Al-Adsani* thus rejected the notion that the jus cogens principle relating to the absolute ban on official torture negated the grant of subject matter State immunity to the offending State. As discussed at note 4 above, there is no need, however, to rely on a hierarchy of international norms (with jus cogens principles ranking higher in relation to State immunity rights) in order to defeat subject matter State immunity. This given that sovereignty (upon which subject matter State immunity must rest) is not absolute. Torture does not fall within any State's territorial jurisdiction or sovereign authority; hence such acts lead to a potential forfeiture of sovereignty with regard to the exclusive right to adjudicate the legal issues in the domestic courts of the State where the torture occurred. The denial of State immunity in cases such as Al-Adsani in no way undermines the possibility for respectful inter-State relations. *Rather, a denial of State immunity against civil liability in cases of 'official torture' and/or widespread or systemic torture simply allows mutual respect between nations to be grounded on each State meeting its international human rights law and international humanitarian law obligations rather than on a 'live and let live' attitude in the face of State atrocity.*

(d) The European Court of Human Rights in *Al-Adsani* accepted the plaintiff's contention that there was an Article 6 'European Convention on Human Rights' (hereafter referred to as the 'European Convention')[19] issue regarding the right to adjudication of the plaintiff's civil rights which was legitimately to be considered in the case. However, the Court did *not* consider that the reliance on State immunity by the national courts as a bar to adjudication of the civil claim against the State of Kuwait constituted a violation of the plaintiff's Article 6 European Convention right to a hearing.

---

[17] *Al-Adsani v. United Kingdom* [2001] ECHR 752, para 18.

[18] *Al-Adsani v. United Kingdom* [2001] ECHR 752, para 61.

[19] *European Convention on Human Rights and Fundamental Freedoms* (as amended by Protocol Number 11 and with protocols 1, 4, 6, 7, 12 and 13), entry into force 1 November 1998 (original Convention adopted by the Council of Europe 1950 and entered into force 3 September 1953). http://www.echr.coe.int/NR/rdonlyres/D5CC24A7-DC13-4318-B457-5C9014916D7A/0/English Anglais.pdf. Accessed 20 June 2009.

The European Court maintained rather that State immunity simply created a procedural bar to adjudication *through the U.K. courts* rather than restricting a substantive right. That is, the procedural bar, according to the European Court of Human Rights simply forced resolution in another venue. (The issue of whether State immunity creates but a *procedural* bar or restricts an individual or collective's *substantive rights* (i.e. fundamental human rights) is considered in note 12). The Court, furthermore, considered the bar to be: (i) in service of the legitimate objectives of comity and good inter-State relations and (ii) not a disproportionate restriction on the right to access the court given that it was based on a well-established international law principle concerning State immunity.[20]

(e) Note that the European Court of Human Rights in *Al-Adsani* acknowledged that Article 3 of the European Convention on Human Rights confers an extra-territorial jurisdiction though, according to the Court, only in certain limited respects:

> *In Soering... the Court recognised that Article 3 has some, limited, extraterritorial application*, to the extent that the decision by a Contracting State to expel an individual might engage the responsibility of that State under the Convention, where substantial grounds had been shown for believing that the person concerned, if expelled, faced a real risk of being subjected to torture or to inhuman or degrading treatment or punishment in the receiving country. In the judgment it was emphasised, however, that in so far as any liability under the Convention might be incurred in such circumstances, it would be incurred by the expelling Contracting State by reason of its having taken action which had as a direct consequence the exposure of an individual to proscribed ill-treatment (emphasis added)[21]

It appears that the ethic underlying non-refoulement (to prevent the victim being exposed to great physical and/or mental harms such as arise from torture and other atrocities) is applicable also in regards to providing the plaintiff access to the national courts of his or her home State for adjudication of civil claims arising from the official torture experienced while in a foreign State. To deny such access is to be complicit in the continued suffering of the victim arising from the torture in that: (i) there is no chance for the victim effectively advocating for him or herself through the courts thus interfering with his or her psychological healing and full restoration of his or her human dignity; and (ii) the victim may not be able to access the funds required to access such extraordinary services that will provide for necessary long-term and/or complex medical and psychological rehabilitation. That right to access the national courts of the victim's home State (for adjudication of the civil claim against the foreign State and its agents) requires then removal of any so-called procedural bar grounded in the State's alleged subject matter immunity. (Indeed, recognition of the psychologically restorative benefits of self-advocacy through the judicial process led the International Criminal Court in The Hague (ICC) to allow for independent legal standing for victims as witness participants rather than simply having them play the role of witnesses. Further, the

[20] *Al-Adsani v. United Kingdom* [2001] ECHR 752, para 54–56.

[21] *Al-Adsani v. United Kingdom* [2001] ECHR 752, para 39.

ICC system includes a victim fund that provides financial assistance for victims in order that they might receive the medical, psychological and other practical supports they require to start rebuilding their lives insofar as such rebuilding is in reality possible).

It appears then, for the reasons explained in this note and note 4 (amongst others to be discussed), that the refusal of the U.K. courts to exercise extra-territorial jurisdiction in *Al-Adsani* and *Jones* (with regard to adjudicating civil claims regarding the harms incurred due to official torture perpetrated on a British national abroad by agents of a foreign State) cannot be rationalized in terms of the foreign State's right to subject matter immunity. State subject matter immunity for the reasons discussed is a legally insupportable as an absolute prohibition on extra-territorial jurisdiction in cases involving official torture.

12 (a) **The grant of subject matter State immunity to foreign States in torture cases where the torture occurred within that foreign State is a restriction of substantive rights (fundamental human rights) rather than simply a procedural bar upon access to a certain forum for adjudication of legal matters**: The grant of State immunity in civil cases such as *Al-Adsani* and *Jones results in a misguided characterization of torture* (*as defined under the 1984 U.N. Torture Treaty*) *as being*: (i) *an act within the sovereign jurisdiction of the respondent State and not just an official act* (official in that the State is, at a minimum, vicariously responsible when its agents carry out torture under 'colour of public authority'), and, by extension, (ii) within the jurisdictional authority of the public officials or other agents of the State who carried it out. This is the result given the fact that State subject matter immunity is a derivative of State sovereignty; hence, the unjustified grant of State immunity implies a sovereign act where none in fact exists.

The grant of State immunity in such civil cases as Al-Adsani undermines the jus cogens international law ban on torture by negating the foundational principle that torture is always out of the sovereign jurisdiction or authority of the State and of its public officials or other agents. The grant of subject matter State immunity in such civil cases, therefore, amounts to much more than simply a procedural bar regarding in which national courts civil actions in such torture cases are to be settled: "In effect, the focus on procedure sanitizes immunity, thus legitimizing and denying the impact of immunity on impunity."[22]

Note that State sovereign immunity serves alleged State interests while sacrificing the interests of individuals (i.e. the right of victims of atrocity to access the courts and obtain a remedy for the harms suffered). This is unlike the situation with procedural bars such as time limits for filing civil suits which are focused also on the interests of individuals (i.e. enabling individuals involved to know during what period they are at risk of being sued and hence bringing the prospect of some finality to issues in dispute).

[22]McGregor (2007, p. 912).

(b) *The European Court of Human Right's affirmation of subject matter State immunity against civil liability in cases of official torture carried out by public officials and other agents of the foreign State thus implicitly, if perhaps inadvertently, breathes new life into what is clearly a dangerous and fallacious proposition, namely that torture can be regarded or properly perceived to be a justifiable governmental or sovereign act of State in some circumstances.* In contrast, the view here is that 'official torture' can never be a sovereign act and that victims have the right to seek both a criminal law and a civil remedy relying in both instances on universal jurisdiction where necessary. The following statement by the International Criminal Tribunal of the Former Yugoslavia seems consistent with the latter view:

> *The fact that torture is prohibited by a peremptory norm of international law has other effects at the inter-state and individual levels. At the inter-state level, it serves to internationally de-legitimise any legislative, administrative or judicial act authorising torture.* It would be senseless to argue, on the one hand, that on account of the jus cogens value of the prohibition against torture, treaties or customary rules providing for torture would be null and void ab initio, and then be unmindful of a State say, taking national measures authorising or condoning torture or absolving its perpetrators through an amnesty law. If such a situation were to arise, the national measures, violating the general principle and any relevant treaty provision, . . .would not be accorded international legal recognition. *Proceedings could be initiated by potential victims if they had locus standi before a competent international or national judicial body with a view to asking it to hold the national measure to be internationally unlawful; or the victim could bring a civil suit for damage in a foreign court, which would therefore be asked inter alia to disregard the legal value of the national authorising act.* What is even more important is that perpetrators of torture acting upon or benefiting from those national measures may nevertheless be held criminally responsible for torture, whether in a foreign State, or in their own State under a subsequent regime. *In short, in spite of possible national authorisation by legislative or judicial bodies to violate the principle banning torture, individuals remain bound to comply with that principle.*[23]

It appears to this author that the above statement of the International Criminal Tribunal of the Former Yugoslavia: (i) acknowledges that torture, even if officially authorized, (i.e. via national statute), is neither legal domestically (any national legislation authorizing torture is invalid), nor legal under international law (regardless any national statute purporting to have authorized it), and that (ii) victims (for instance of 'official torture') are entitled to a civil remedy in whichever court they can access if they have standing (including a court in a forum State other than that where the torture occurred) as well as being entitled to criminal law accountability for the individual perpetrators. The latter position then is consistent with the view expressed here that: (i) official torture is *not* a sovereign act; (ii) the State responsible is *not* protected from civil liability by subject matter immunity and (iii) the individual perpetrators, regardless of their personal status or the official nature

[23]*Prosecutor v. Furundzija*, International Tribunal for the Prosecution of Persons Responsible for Serious Violations of International Humanitarian Law Committed in the Territory of the Former Yugoslavia since 1991, Trial Chamber judgment, 10 December 1998 at para 155. http://www.unhcr.org/cgi-bin/texis/vtx/refworld/rwmain?docid=40276a8a4. Accessed 21 June 2009.

of their acts are *not* entitled to subject matter immunity, or personal immunity which would preclude their civil liability or their criminal prosecution. Note further that amnesty and pardons were rejected as a defense to charges of international crime (based on double jeopardy) by the international criminal court.[24] *In short, the contention here is that the international community faces no automatic procedural bar to holding those responsible for torture and other international crimes to account in an international court or in the national courts of the victim's home State even where the international crime occurred in the non-forum State and/or where the perpetrators have never been in the forum State.*

(c) Note, in contrast, that Lord Bingham of the U.K. House of Lords, in *Jones*, takes the view that the individual perpetrators of official torture, while vulnerable to universal criminal jurisdiction (barring absolute personal immunity), are *not* subject to civil liability as a consequence of civil litigation in a foreign court nor is the offending State itself (subject matter immunity allegedly being applicable to cover both the State and the individual perpetrators). Lord Bingham, in fact, considers that, in all probability, the International Criminal Tribunal of the Former Yugoslavia in the above citation at note 12(b) was *not* referring to civil liability and the operation of State immunity but rather to criminal liability alone (this though the quote clearly includes the words: "the victim could bring a *civil suit* for damage in a foreign court"). Thus, Lord Bingham states in reference to the above quote: "I do not understand the tribunal to have been addressing the issue of state immunity in *civil* proceedings..." (emphasis added).[25]

In *Pinochet (3),* the U.K. House of Lords considered that Pinochet (ex head of State of Chile) could be extradited from the U.K. (where he had been receiving medical treatment) to stand trial in Spain for torture and other crimes given that: (i) Pinochet had committed acts of torture after the 1984 Torture Treaty became law in the U.K. (thus creating a 'double criminality'); (ii) the Torture Treaty expressly conferred universal *criminal* jurisdiction on States to take the steps necessary to lead to the prosecution of torturers (Note that the 1984 Torture Treaty had already been signed and ratified by Chile at the time of the U.K. proceedings and that Chile was bound by its terms which included submitting to the sovereignty of another State if Chile declined to prosecute those who had committed official torture on behalf of Chile after the date of entry into force of the Torture Treaty in Chile); (iii) The Torture Treaty negated the U.K. State immunity provisions in regards to Pinochet: Part I of the 1978 U.K. State Immunity Act setting out State immunity provided *no immunity from criminal or civil liability* to *former Heads of State for private acts* but rather only for official acts which occurred before or during their tenure in office regardless in which State the acts were committed (State subject

---

[24]Report of the Preparatory Committee on the Establishment of an International Criminal Court, Vol. 1, p. 40, para 174 (Proceedings of the Preparatory Committee during March–April and August 1996) GAOR, 51st Sess. Supp. 22, UN Doc. A/51/22); UN Doc, A/CONF./283/2/Add. 1 (1998), Art. 19.

[25]Opinion of Lord Bingham in *Jones v. Ministry of the Interior Al-Mamlaka Al-Arabiya AS Suadiya (the Kingdom of Saudi Arabia) and others* [2006] UKHL 26, para 21.

matter immunity) while *serving* Heads of State were, according to the U.K. House of Lords, covered by absolute personal immunity from criminal and civil liability for official or private acts committed inside or outside the U.K. before or during their tenure in office. The majority of the U.K. House of Lords in *Pinochet (3)* held, however, that since all the Parties to the U.N. Torture Treaty had agreed to submit to the sovereignty of other States who could extradite torturers within their own territory to States where they would be prosecuted, or alternatively, prosecute the perpetrators themselves, they must have agreed that no immunity against *criminal liability* for 'official torture' was possible (presumably this would apply to both State subject matter immunity and personal immunity). The U.K. House of Lords regarded Pinochet (an ex head of State to be guilty of 'official torture') at the relevant times when the Torture Treaty was in force in Chile as a State Party to that Treaty. Thus, had Chile not been a Party to the Torture Convention it is doubtful that the U.K. House of Lords would have supported his extradition, i.e. based on customary jus cogens international law concerning torture.

It would appear that there is a great and unjustified reluctance on the part of most national courts (including the U.K. House of Lords) and on the part of the European Court of Human Rights to: (i) affirm the impossibility of subject matter immunity (for the offending State or for the individual perpetrators of 'official torture') whether serving or not and,(ii) the illegitimacy of absolute personal immunity in such cases for incumbent high officials such as the Head of State even though, as is argued here, *official torture is not a sovereign act (not within the State or the agents' sovereign jurisdiction) and therefore no immunity of any sort deriving from sovereignty is possible or operative*. There would seem to be, in actuality, no legitimate legal basis (under domestic or international law) for individual States to offer a foreign State subject matter immunity in cases involving official torture or to offer any form of immunity to individual perpetrators of official torture against civil or criminal liability whether serving or former Heads of State or other high official or diplomat. To suggest otherwise appears nothing more than a cynical attempt to create an air of civility around clearly distasteful and unjust outcomes for the victims of official torture and other atrocities who seek to find a remedy of sorts through the national courts of their homeland which may be a safe sanctuary in the circumstance.

13. **There is a potential spill over effect of the grant of subject matter immunity and/or diplomatic or other personal immunity for individual perpetrators in civil cases into the handling of cases involving official torture in the criminal law context**: The European Court of Human Right's affirmation of the U.K. national courts' barring adjudication of a civil claim against a foreign State (whose agents committed torture in their official capacity upon a victim who was a British national while the victim was within the foreign State territory) has a potential improper spill over into the international criminal law arena and may infect the court's reasoning in international criminal cases. More specifically, since the grant of State subject matter immunity erroneously creates the illusion that acts of official torture ostensibly fall not only into the category of an 'official' act, but also into the category of a 'sovereign' act, this bolsters the *alleged false* defense that

the acts were legitimate sovereign acts (i.e. if the objective of the torture was allegedly in the State's democratic interest). Just such a fallacious defense was raised in the Special Court of Sierra Leone (SCSL) case *Prosecutor v. Moinina Fofana and Allieu Kondewa*[26] where the SCSL trial level sentencing decisions for pro-government forces were reduced for crimes against humanity on the outrageous and unfounded rationale that the defendants had engaged in these acts (i.e. mutilation and other atrocities) to protect democracy and out of a sense of 'civic duty' (the sentences imposed were later substantially increased by the SCSL Appeals Chamber).

The bar to adjudication in the U.K. courts based on the grant of State subject matter immunity against civil liability to the defendant foreign State in cases such as Al-Adsani (and the European Court of Human Rights endorsement of that procedural bar) does nothing to foster recognition of the offending State's responsibility to hold the individual perpetrators to account in any way and, in addition, to pay restitution to the victim on behalf of the State itself. Indeed, the grant of subject matter immunity against civil liability to the offending State, and, hence, ultimately to the agents who committed torture as representatives of the State, embodies *in effect*, despite protestations to the contrary, a disregard for the rights of victims of such a grave crime as official torture. This in turn reinforces antiquated, anti-democratic notions of divine right residing in the body of the State and its delegates. The latter legally insupportable anti-democratic perspective can only serve to further perpetuate unchecked the occurrence of State-sponsored torture in the foreign State.

Further, the grant of subject matter immunity to the offending State against civil liability in an official torture case is not conducive to the initiation of inter-State petitions in the international criminal law arena where such an inter-State petition may in fact be justified, i.e. an inter-State petition to the Prosecutor of the International Criminal Court (ICC) (requesting an investigation of a *situation* in a particular State which situation allegedly involves the commission of international crimes such as systemic torture, and regarding which ICC investigation may give rise to *cases* before the ICC concerning *individual perpetrators*; amongst them high public officials who acted in their official capacity). This dampening effect on the likelihood of inter-State petitions in the international criminal law context as a consequence of the grant of State immunity against civil liability regarding torture and other atrocities arises in that State immunity undermines what should be a broad and concerted effort by all State members of the international community to hold every State accountable for international crimes occurring within its borders.

14. **The improper grant of *absolute immunity* (*immunity ratione personae*) to incumbent heads of State and certain serving high government officials and diplomats against *both civil and criminal liability* is premised on the *fallacious* notion that torture and other such acts, when carried out in an official capacity, are sovereign acts**: *If 'official torture' and other such atrocities were*

[26]*Prosecutor v. Moinina Fofana and Allieu Kondewa*, Civil Defense Forces (CDF) case, Special Court of Sierra Leone, (Case SCSL-04-14-A). http://www.sc-sl.org/CASES/CivilDefenceForces CDFCompleted/tabid/104/Default.aspx.

not erroneously considered as sovereign acts (here simply by virtue of the status of the persons implicated) then immunity *ratione personae* would *not* apply. This is clear in Lord Millet's description of the alleged foundation for a grant of *immunity ratione personae*:

> The immunity of a *serving* head of state is enjoyed by reason of his special status as the holder of his state's highest office. He is regarded as the personal embodiment of the state itself. *It would be an affront to the dignity and sovereignty of the state which he personifies and a denial of the equality of sovereign states to subject him to the jurisdiction of the municipal courts of another state, whether in respect of his public acts or private affairs.* His person is inviolable; he is not liable to be arrested or detained on any ground whatever. *The head of a diplomatic mission represents his head of state and thus embodies the sending state in the territory of the receiving state. While he remains in office he is entitled to the same absolute immunity as his head of state in relation to both his public and private acts* (emphasis added).[27]

However, it can rightfully be argued that an act does not assume sovereign status based on who commits it. This, for instance, since heads of State and other high government officials are *not* inherently endowed with sovereignty and no one person, such as a head of State, can, in actuality, legitimately embody the State symbolically or otherwise. *Rather, sovereignty rests with the people of the State under democratic notions of sovereignty, and their bestowing of sovereign authority on their government and its leadership (i.e. Head of State and head of the State's diplomatic mission) is a temporary loan which is automatically revocable when that government and/or its leadership engages in acts which are an affront to humanity as are international crimes such as official torture* (see U.N. 1984 Torture Treaty definition of torture which requires the torture be conducted by agents of the State in their official capacity),[28] or alternatively torture committed in a systemic or widespread fashion by perpetrators *who may or may not be agents of the State or may or may not be acting in an official or governmental capacity*, but who are amongst those most responsible for its occurrence in a particular situation (see the Rome Statute definition of crimes against humanity)[29] (torture may also occur as a war crime). The International Criminal Court enabling statute (the Rome Statute), it will be recalled, properly does *not* admit a bar against prosecution of individual perpetrators of international crimes under its jurisdiction based on *immunity ratione personae*. However, according to most States, and to the European Court of Human Rights, the universal criminal jurisdiction provided for under the U.N.

[27]Opinion of Lord Millet, *Pinochet* (3) at para 6 of Lord Millet's opinion. http://www.parliament.the-stationery-office.co.uk/pa/ld199899/ldjudgmt/jd990324/pino1.htm. Accessed 21 June 2009.

[28]*United Nations Convention Against Torture and Other Cruel, Inhuman or Degrading Treatment or Punishment*. UN General Assembly Resolution 39/46, 10 December 1984, entering into force 26 June 1987. http://www.unhchr.ch/html/menu3/b/h_cat39.htm. Accessed 17 June 2009.

[29]*Rome Statute of the International Criminal Court*. Text of the Rome Statute circulated as document A/CONF.183/9 of 17 July 1998 and corrected by procès-verbaux of 10 November 1998, 12 July 1999, 30 November 1999, 8 May 2000, 17 January 2001 and 16 January 2002. The Statute entered into force on 1 July 2002. http://www.un.org/children/conflict/keydocuments/english/romestatuteofthe7.html. Accessed 19 June 2009.

1984 Torture Treaty is defeated by personal immunity. Such an approach is clearly not tenable in that the International Criminal Court requires the cooperation of all States in bringing to justice those perpetrators who bear the greatest responsibility for international crimes, and who fall under ICC jurisdiction, without there being any bar based on immunity of any sort or on a national grant of amnesty.

15. **'Official' or in other words 'governmental' acts involving international crimes do *not* trigger State immunity as a function of the official nature of the acts or on any other basis neither for the offending State nor the agents of the State who are the individual perpetrators**: The view expressed here that international crimes committed by a public official or an agent of the State 'under colour of public authority' are 'official' (even though extra-jurisdictional and illegal under international law and hence not within the power of the State to authorize as a genuine State function) is consistent with the 2001 International Law Commission report on the *Responsibility of States for Internationally Wrongful Acts*:

> A particular problem is to determine whether a person who is a State organ acts in that capacity. *It is irrelevant for this purpose that the person concerned may have had ulterior or improper motives or may be abusing public power.* Where such a person acts in an *apparently* official capacity, or under *colour of authority*, the actions in question will be attributable to the State.[30]
>
> The conduct of an organ of a State or of a person or entity empowered to exercise elements of the governmental authority shall be considered an act of the State under international law if the organ, person or entity acts in that capacity, *even if it exceeds its authority or contravenes instructions* (emphasis added).[31]

The contention is here further that a state agent or public official acting under 'the colour of State authority' implicates the State though the State has no immunity to confer on its agents in the commission of a non-sovereign extra-jurisdictional act such as the commission of an international crime. Hence, neither the State nor its agents are protected by State immunity where its agents, at a minimum, appear to be acting on behalf of the State but are in fact acting outside the State's sovereign authority by committing an international crime such as torture.

16. **The loss of State immunity for the offending State and its agents responsible for international crimes such as torture committed under the appearance of public authority is *not* dependent upon *improperly* classifying the acts as unofficial or non-governmental**: The authors of the following quotes have on the position advanced by this author: (i) erroneously conflated 'sovereign' acts (which are within jurisdiction and properly regarded as State functions) with *extra-jurisdictional* governmental acts which are governmental or 'official' acts

---

[30]International Law Commission report on the *Responsibility of States for Internationally Wrongful Acts* (2001), Commentary on para 2 of Article 4 in the Draft report cited in *Jones v. Ministry of the Interior Al-Mamlaka Al-Arabiya AS Suadiya (the Kingdom of Saudi Arabia) and others* [2006] UKHL 26, para 12.

[31]International Law Commission report on the *Responsibility of States for Internationally Wrongful Acts* (2001), Commentary on Article 7: Excess of authority or contravention of instructions. http://untreaty.un.org/ilc/texts/instruments/english/draft%20articles/9_6_2001.pdf. Accessed 9 June 2009.

nonetheless; and have (ii) on the aforementioned faulty basis, incorrectly suggested that torture committed by agents of the State under the 'colour of public authority' are private, unofficial acts thus eliminating immunity for the individual perpetrators *but not for the State*:

> Can it be said that the commission of a crime which is an international crime against humanity and jus cogens is an act done in an official capacity on behalf of the state? *I believe there to be strong ground for saying that the implementation of torture as defined by the Torture Convention cannot be a state function. . ..*[32]
>
> *the requirement* [in the 1984 U.N. Treaty Against Torture] *that the pain or suffering be inflicted by a public official does no more in my view than identify the author and the public context in which the author must be acting* [*to meet the international law definition of torture*]. *It does not lend to the acts of torture themselves any official or governmental character or nature, or mean that it can in any way be regarded as an official function to inflict*, or that an official can be regarded as representing the state in inflicting, such pain or suffering. Still less does it suggest that the official inflicting such pain or suffering can be afforded the cloak of state immunity.[33]

The *denial* of State subject matter immunity, however, to *both* the offending State (for wrongful acts under international law) and its agents in cases of torture committed under the 'colour of public authority', as has been explained, is *not* reliant on *erroneously* classifying the acts of torture as 'private' or 'unofficial'. *Democratic* notions of *State* sovereignty and of the sovereign equality of States which establishes each State's right to independence and self-governance do *not* encompass the exercise of *extra jurisdictional authority* such as is, by definition, involved in the commission of international crimes well recognized by the international community as an affront to all humanity. Hence, an act can be 'governmental' and 'official' (and a 'State function' in the sense that it was conducted on behalf of the State with or without authorization) *without* being intra vires (without being within the proper jurisdiction or authority of the State). Thus, that an act such as torture is 'official' does *not* at all imply that it is a legitimate State function within the authority of the State as all proper State functions must be. More specifically, the fact that an act is 'official' or 'governmental' in and of itself tells us nothing about whether it was intra or ultra vires and, therefore, provides no information as to whether the perpetrators of the act and the State itself are or are not shielded by State immunity in regards to criminal or civil liability in respect of that act. For further discussion of this issue see the papers by Steffen Wirth and Marina Spinedi listed in the references.[34,35]

---

[32]Opinion of Lord Browne-Wilkinson, 24 March 1999 in *Pinochet* (3), para 18. http://www.parliament.the-stationery-office.co.uk/pa/ld199899/ldjudgmt/jd990324/pino1.htm. Accessed 21 June 2009.

[33]Opinion of Lord Justice Mance, *Jones v. Ministry of the Interior Al-Mamlaka Al-Arabiya AS Suadiya (the Kingdom of Saudi Arabia) and others*, Court of Appeal, [2004] EWCA Civ 1394 para 71. http://www.hrothgar.co.uk/YAWS/reps/04a1394.htm. Accessed 24 June 2009.

[34]Wirth (2002, pp. 877–893).

[35]Spinedi (2002, pp. 895–899).

17. **Universal civil and universal criminal jurisdiction pertaining to the adjudication of legal matters relating to international crimes is grounded in the sovereignty of the international community of States as a whole which sovereignty rests, in the final analysis, with all peoples in the global community**: The sovereignty manifest in the authority to adjudicate legal matters pertaining to a particular case involving international crime rests with the international community of States to the extent that the offending State is unwilling or unable to prosecute the perpetrators and/or hold them civilly liable (including certain of its own public officials or other agents) and/or to provide civil damages to the victims on behalf of the State itself.

When any particular State exercises universal civil or universal criminal jurisdiction in cases involving torture as defined under the U.N. Treaty Against Torture[36] *or under the Rome Statute,*[37] *it does so on behalf of the international community of States as a whole and not on its own behalf alone*. The search for justice in such cases is not just for the victims in the particular case, but rather for humanity as a whole (since international crimes are considered to cause injury to all peoples). Hence, the exercise of universal criminal or civil jurisdiction is within the sovereign authority of each State in cases involving international crimes (recall also that customary international law in regards to these crimes is incorporated automatically into domestic law). The exercise of universal civil or criminal jurisdiction by a State in these instances is not therefore extraterritorial (in the sense of being beyond the State's sovereign authority); though it may be exercised against foreign nationals who committed the atrocities in a foreign State rather than in the forum State (the latter being the State where the legal proceedings have been initiated). *In other words*: *"Since each sovereign power stands in the position of a guardian of international law..." each has the authority to adjudicate the civil and/or criminal law matters related to cases involving international crimes.*[38] Such a view, however, is not consistent with the rejection (by the U.K. House of Lords in *Jones*[39] and the European Court of Human Rights in *Al-Adsani)*[40] of a notion of universal *civil* jurisdiction under the U.N. Torture Treaty and especially its rejection of universal

[36]*United Nations Convention Against Torture and Other Cruel, Inhuman or Degrading Treatment or Punishment*. UN General Assembly Resolution 39/46, 10 December 1984, entering into force 26 June 1987. http://www.unhchr.ch/html/menu3/b/h_cat39.htm. Accessed 17 June 2009.

[37]*Rome Statute of the International Criminal Court*. Text of the Rome Statute circulated as document A/CONF.183/9 of 17 July 1998 and corrected by procès-verbaux of 10 November 1998, 12 July 1999, 30 November 1999, 8 May 2000, 17 January 2001 and 16 January 2002. The Statute entered into force on 1 July 2002. http://www.un.org/children/conflict/keydocuments/english/romestatuteofthe7.html. Accessed 19 June 2009.

[38]Compare Greenspan (1959, p. 420).

[39]*Jones v. Ministry of the Interior Al-Mamlaka Al-Arabiya AS Suadiya (the Kingdom of Saudi Arabia) and others* [2006] UKHL 26.

[40]*Al-Adsani v. United Kingdom* [2001] ECHR 752.

civil jurisdiction in cases concerning 'official torture' where State immunity is supposedly applicable:

> The essential ratio of the decision, as I understand it, was that international law could not without absurdity require criminal jurisdiction to be assumed and exercised where the Torture Convention conditions were satisfied and, at the same time, require immunity to be granted to those properly charged. The Torture Convention was the mainspring of the decision, *and certain members of the House expressly accepted that the grant of immunity in civil proceedings was unaffected* (emphasis added).[41]

The suggestion here, in contrast, is that the application of State immunity as a bar to civil liability in the national courts of a State other than the offending State is no more consistent with the jus cogens principle regarding torture (incorporated into the 1984 U.N. Torture Treaty) than would be a ban on universal criminal prosecution on the ground that official acts are protected by State immunity.

18. **It is a necessary pre-condition in order for State subject matter immunity to apply to the respondent State and its agents that the acts committed under "colour of public authority" were within the sovereign authority of the State which is not the case with respect to international crimes such as torture**: The U.K. House of Lords ruling in *Jones v. Ministry of the Interior Al-Mamlaka Al-Arabiya AS Suadiya (the Kingdom of Saudi Arabia) and others* holds, as here, that acts of torture committed under the appearance of public authority are 'governmental' or 'official' acts.[42] The House of Lords, however, in the Jones case further unanimously held, in contradistinction to the position taken by this author that: (i) State immunity still applies to the offending State in such instances involving 'official torture', *even if systemic* and that (ii) this alleged State immunity also covers the agents of the State responsible for the torture to the extent that those agents were, at all material times, acting in their 'official capacity' and whether or not they were instructed or authorized by the government to commit torture.

With respect, the U.K. House of Lords position insofar as the grant of State immunity in such cases as *Jones* is concerned is untenable. This given that not all 'official' acts, as previously discussed at notes 15 and 16 above are 'sovereign' (intra-jurisdictional) acts. *It is here contended that a governmental act must be within the State's sovereign authority or territorial jurisdiction for State immunity protection against civil liability to apply* (see note 4 above). After all, as Lord Millett of the U.K. House of Lords acknowledges, "*State immunity. . .is an attribute of the sovereignty of the State*" (emphasis added).[43] That sovereignty (giving rise to

---

[41]Opinion of Lord Bingham in *Jones v. Ministry of the Interior Al-Mamlaka Al-Arabiya AS Suadiya (the Kingdom of Saudi Arabia) and others* [2006] UKHL 26 at para 19 commenting on the decision by the House of Lords in the extradition case of Senator Pinochet.

[42]*Jones v. Ministry of the Interior Al-Mamlaka Al-Arabiya AS Suadiya (the Kingdom of Saudi Arabia) and others* [2006] UKHL 26.

[43]Opinion of Lord Millet, 24 March 1999 in *Pinochet* (3), para 155. http://www.parliament.the-stationery-office.co.uk/pa/ld199899/ldjudgmt/jd990324/pino1.htm. Accessed 21 June 2009.

State immunity), however, can be ruptured to a degree by internal factors as when, for instance, a State, through its agents, engages in atrocity resulting in a *very restricted* variant of 'forfeited sovereignty'[44] for that particular State: (i) limited to the loss of the exclusive right to adjudicate the legal matters pertaining to international crimes committed by agents of that State within its borders against a foreign national and (ii) with the forfeited sovereignty arising in this respect only where there is an unwillingness or inability of the offending State to assume accountability as a State itself and for the State agents involved for the official torture and to provide a civil and criminal law remedy for the victim in its own national courts.

19. **The *denial* of State subject matter immunity to those States and their agents responsible for official torture (and of personal immunity to serving Heads of States and certain other incumbent high officials) does *not* undermine the principle of the sovereign equality of States**: In no way does denying State immunity to a foreign State against civil claims in the national courts of the torture victim's home State undermine the international law principles of State 'sovereign immunity' or the 'sovereign equality' of States (the same holds true for the denial of subject matter immunity or of personal immunity to individual perpetrators irrespective of their official status). This since the State has 'sovereign immunity', as discussed, only with respect to matters that are properly within the exercise of the jurisdictional authority of the sovereign State. It is uncontested that torture of foreign nationals or anyone else for that matter, is *not* a *legitimate* State function and is not therefore within the offending State's territorial jurisdiction (though it may have occurred as an official or governmental extra-jurisdictional act). There is no insult consequently to the dignity of the foreign State (or to its high officials) for the failure to shield that State from accountability for extra-jurisdictional (non-sovereign) acts such as international crimes. One might argue in fact that the denial of State immunity in such an instance is a sign of respect for the State in that it sends the message that: (i) the international community expects more of the State and (ii) the international community has faith that the State is potentially competent and willing to ensure that in future it will not be responsible for acts (i.e. international crimes) that are an affront to humanity.

Authorities point out that contemporary international law does not regard the dignity of the State to be compromised to any extent by its accepting culpability and liability (as a State and on behalf of its agents) for fundamental human rights violations constituting international crimes (indeed the suggestion by these authorities, as has been argued here, is just the opposite):

> The relationship between State immunity and human rights should be reconsidered. Torturers and perpetrators of other serious human rights violations such as illegal detentions and enforced disappearances must not be able to hide behind the veil of immunity.

[44]See de Oliveira Moll (2003, p. 581).

> *International law should not regard it as being contrary to the dignity or sovereign equality of nations to respond to claims against them or their agents* (emphasis added).[45]
>
> the concept of the dignity of the sovereign has altered. *International law no longer regards it as being contrary to the dignity of nations to respond to claims against them* (emphasis added).[46]
>
> *It is more in keeping with the dignity of a foreign sovereign to submit himself to the rule of law than to claim to be above* it, and his independence is better ensured by accepting the decisions of courts of acknowledged impartiality, than by arbitrarily rejecting their jurisdiction (emphasis added).[47]

Holding States and individual perpetrators who are their nationals accountable for international crimes committed as 'official' acts shifts the burden regarding restoring smooth, friendly and productive inter-State relations to the offending State as it should. Such good inter-State relations *cannot*, pursuant to jus cogens principles of international law, be built on a foundation which ignores the suffering of the victims of atrocity. The denial of a grant of subject matter immunity to the offending State (as well as a denial of State immunity or personal immunity to perpetrators) conveys the message *from the international community* (through the national courts of the forum State or via an international court) that the offending State must: (a) in future demonstrate a commitment to well-established internationally codified and customary human rights norms, and (b) in the interim, provide reparations to the victim of torture or other international crimes and criminally prosecute those individual perpetrators responsible.

20. **There is a readiness of States to accept universal *criminal* jurisdiction with regard to international crimes but to resist universal *civil* jurisdiction in regards to the same matters**: Consider the comments of Justice Breyer of the Supreme Court of the United States reflecting his contention that universal civil jurisdiction in cases in which the offending foreign State is responsible directly or indirectly for international crimes ought not to be considered as an interference in sovereign equality or comity:

> Today international law will sometimes similarly reflect not only substantive agreement as to certain universally condemned behavior but also procedural agreement that universal jurisdiction exists to prosecute a subset of that behavior... That subset includes torture, genocide, crimes against humanity, and war crimes.
>
> *The fact that this procedural consensus exists suggests that recognition of universal jurisdiction in respect to a limited set of norms is consistent with principles of international*

[45]Report by the Secretary General (of the European Council on Human Rights) (SG/Inf (2006) 5, 28 February 2006) on the use of his powers under Article 52 of the European Convention on Human Rights, in the light of reports suggesting that individuals, notably persons suspected of involvement in acts of terrorism, may have been arrested and detained, or transported while deprived of their liberty, by or at the instigation of foreign agencies, with the active or passive co-operation of States Parties to the Convention or by States Parties themselves at their own initiative, without such deprivation of liberty having been acknowledged. https://wcd.coe.int/ViewDoc.jsp?Ref=SG/Inf(2006)5&Language=lanEnglish&Ver=original&Site=COE&BackColorInternet=DBDCF2&BackColorIntranet=FDC864&BackColorLogged=FDC864, at para 101(iii). Accessed 22 June 2009.

[46]Higgins (1982, p. 271).

[47]Opinion of Lord Denning in *Rahimtoola v. Nizam of Hyderabad* [1958] AC 379 at 609.

> *comity*. That is, allowing every nation's courts to adjudicate foreign conduct involving foreign parties in such cases will not significantly threaten the practical harmony that comity principles seek to protect. *That consensus concerns criminal jurisdiction, but consensus as to universal criminal jurisdiction itself suggests that universal tort jurisdiction would be no more threatening* (emphasis added).[48]

We know, however, that the reality is not in accord with Justice Breyer's expectations regarding the level of threat States generally perceive in regard to any potential universal *civil* jurisdiction (that jurisdiction being one which would provide victims of atrocity the opportunity to bring a civil suit also against *the State* in the national courts of the victim's homeland in cases involving torture committed against the victim while in a foreign land). States most often strenuously resist the application of universal civil jurisdiction and the courts, both domestic and international (including the European Court of Human Rights), have steadfastly supported the States' position on this matter.

Why then the readiness to accept universal criminal jurisdiction with respect to international crimes but not universal civil jurisdiction? The answer appears to be that resisting universal civil jurisdiction serves selfish short-term State pecuniary and other interests. While the State is *not* impleaded in the case of universal *criminal* jurisdiction, it is impleaded in the case of universal civil jurisdiction. That is, the agents of the State are liable civilly for torture as representatives of the State and hence the State, too, is civilly liable:

> States are artificial legal persons: they can only act through the institutions and agencies of the state, which means, ultimately through its officials and other individuals acting on behalf of the state.[49]
>
> ...The cases and other materials on state liability make it clear *that the state is liable for acts done under colour of public authority, whether or not they are actually authorised or lawful under domestic or international law* (emphasis added).[50]

Yet, it is to be emphasized that the State is accountable also for the criminal conduct of its agents even though the State cannot be joined as a defendant in a criminal case. The doctrine of *respondeat superior* applies making the State responsible for the actions of its agents, for instance, in regards to the commission of grave human rights abuses it would potentially have been within the State's authority and power *to prevent*. Accountability in this instance may come, for example, as the result of inter-State complaints to the International Court of Justice concerning the criminal conduct of agents of the respondent State in committing atrocities rising to the level of international crime, or State referrals of situations to the International Criminal Court (ICC) which situations include the commission of international crimes within a particular State's territory by its agents which crimes are ripe for criminal prosecution by the ICC. In both instances, the issue of whether

---

[48]Opinion of Justice Breyer in *Solsa v. Alvarez – Machain* (2004) 542 U.S. 692, p. 3.

[49]Watts, Sir Arthur (1994, p. 82).

[50]Opinion of Lord Hoffman in *Jones v. Ministry of the Interior Al-Mamlaka Al-Arabiya AS Suadiya (the Kingdom of Saudi Arabia) and others* [2006] UKHL 26, para 74.

the State's highest officials sponsored or failed to prevent or otherwise contributed to such international crimes will arise.

21. **The consequences of not affording torture victims a 'blanket right' (i.e. without requirements that the torture must have occurred in the forum State) to bring civil suits against the responsible foreign State and its agents in the national courts of the victim's home State is often the denial of a remedy**: That the courts would uphold State immunity rather than universal *civil* jurisdiction on the ground that torture can be a State act (though an extra-jurisdictional one) is disheartening. This is furthermore an ironic state of affairs in that those justices granting State immunity (in cases involving international crimes committed by agents of the foreign State in their official capacity) are presumably as much in favor of eliminating torture and other atrocities and holding States to account as are those who issue dissenting views endorsing the denial of State immunity.

At the same time, there seems to be an unwillingness amongst those in the judiciary favoring State immunity – even in cases involving torture and other atrocities – to acknowledge that often a civil remedy is the only one available to the victims. In this regard, recall that in *Al-Adsani* the institutions of the State and the operational tools of the State were utilized in the course of the Kuwaiti agents committing the grave human rights abuses against the victim claimant (i.e. the transfer of the victim to Kuwaiti State Security Prison where he was tortured and the use of government vehicles in effecting the abductions and unlawful detentions of the victim in furtherance of the torture). Hence, the illegal acts in *Al-Adsani* were done under "colour of public authority" (where 'colour of public authority' is taken to mean acting with the perceived status of 'public official' or other agent of the State on behalf of the State and *not* necessarily that the State authorized the agent to act in this fashion or instructed him or her to do so). Yet, the U.K. Court of Appeals upheld State immunity for the respondent State in the case as did the European Court of Human Rights. This despite the fact that Mr. Al-Adsani had no recourse other than to sue the agents and the State of Kuwait in a British court (i.e. he could not safely return to Kuwait and file a civil case there and all attempts to open diplomatic channels through which a settlement might have been reached with the State of Kuwait had failed). Further, note that the fact that Mr. Al-Adsani was permitted to sue the individual perpetrators and was ultimately granted a default judgment against them is inconsistent with the grant of immunity to the State of Kuwait for the reasons previously explained (i.e. the State acts through its agents and is responsible for their conduct. At the same time, State immunity *where it properly exists* transfers to the agents of the State who act in an official capacity). It would seem that the bar pertaining to civil suits against the offending State proceeding in the national courts of another State (where the case concerns official torture against a national or non-national of the forum State which torture occurred in the territory of the foreign non-forum State) has more to do with politics than with international law, i.e. the mutual interests of the States to protect against State civil liability.

In *Al-Adsani*, the victim could identify the individual perpetrators of the torture he suffered. However, where the victim cannot identify the individual perpetrators of the torture (the public officials or other agents of the State acting under 'colour of public authority') since the victim was blindfolded during the incident (as is often the case),[51] suing the State may be the only option available to the victim in his or her effort to obtain a judicial remedy. In the latter instances, the upholding of a grant of State immunity by the national courts of the forum State, even if to the respondent State alone, unjustifiably and without a supportable legal basis effectively closes the door to a remedy for the victim. Note also that in cases such as Al-Adsani, criminal prosecution may be impossible as, for instance, the circumstances in which the torture occurred may not fit the necessary criteria under the Statute of the International Criminal Court and/or the respondent State may be unwilling to extradite the defendants to stand trial in the forum State under the provisions of the 1984 Torture Treaty while, at the same time, declining to itself prosecute its officials or State agents for torture.

22. **Article 14 of the U.N. 1984 Treaty Against Torture provides for both universal civil and criminal jurisdiction in cases of 'official torture'**: Article 14 of the U.N. 1984 Treaty Against Torture reads as follows:

> 1. *Each State Party shall ensure in its legal system that the victim of an act of torture obtains redress and has an enforceable right to fair and adequate compensation, including the means for as full rehabilitation as possible.*
>
> In the event of the death of the victim as a result of an act of torture, his dependants shall be entitled to *compensation*.
>
> 2. Nothing in this article shall affect any right of the victim or other persons to compensation which may exist under national law (emphasis added).[52]

With respect, the wording of the Torture Treaty has been erroneously interpreted by various national courts such as the U.K. House of Lords and the European Court of Human Rights to exclude universal civil jurisdiction as a means to redress for the victims of official torture. In Pinochet (3), for instance, Lord Bingham and the rest of the judicial panel of the House of Lords rejected the notion of universal *civil* jurisdiction being provided for under the 1984 Torture Convention. This though Article 14 of the U.N. Torture Convention refers to the torture victim's right to obtain "redress" and his or her "enforceable right to fair and adequate compensation" and does not appear to restrict itself to universal criminal jurisdiction to the exclusion of universal civil jurisdiction. Indeed, there is no mention of State subject matter immunity against civil liability for individual perpetrators or for the State itself in the 1984 Torture Convention. However, the U.K. House of Lords in *Jones* has held that the 1984 Torture Convention, in making reference to the torture victim's "enforceable right to fair and adequate compensation", is referring to the

---

[51]Memo Concerning Proposed Amendments to Canada's State Immunity Law, Section X: Why the State rather than individuals? http://www.law.utoronto.ca/documents/ihrp/SIA_Introductory memo.doc. Accessed 18 June 2009.

[52]*United Nations Convention Against Torture and Other Cruel, Inhuman or Degrading Treatment or Punishment*. UN General Assembly Resolution 39/46, 10 December 1984, entering into force 26 June 1987. Article 14. http://www.unhchr.ch/html/menu3/b/h_cat39.htm. Accessed 17 June 2009.

victim's right to have his or her civil claims decided in the national courts of the forum State *if and only if the official torture occurred in the forum State* (i.e. at the hands of the agents of the foreign State) and *not* referring to a universal civil jurisdiction (which exists regardless of the nationality of the perpetrator or the victim and regardless in which State the torture took place).[53] *Note, however, that no qualifying language referring to the alleged necessity of the official torture having occurred in the forum State (in order for access to that State's national courts regarding a civil claim against the perpetrators and the foreign State) appears in Article 14 of the U.N. Torture Treaty thus lending no support to the House of Lords interpretation of Article 14 in this regard.* Hall in this regard states:

> In contrast to certain other provisions of the Convention [1984 U.N. Torture Convention], it contains *no* geographic limitation, such as a limitation to torture committed in the territory of a state party or subject to its jurisdiction (emphasis added).[54]

Indeed, the Committee Against Torture which monitors the 1984 Torture Treaty holds that Article 14 of the Treaty requires States to provide a civil remedy to victims regardless where the torture occurred.[55] The proviso stipulated by the U.K. House of Lords and the European Court of Human Rights in *Al-Adsani* appears then *not* to be grounded in international law but upon customary practice reflecting the political and other interests of States.

Note also that the approach of the U.K. House of Lords in *Al-Adsani* subtly transforms the civil claim in such cases to one concerning a private claim for a significant personal injury tort commonly available in Commonwealth courts, but now a civil claim surgically dissected from the international human rights law context (the U.N. Torture Convention). The Torture Treaty (incorporated into U.K. law 29 September 1988), in contrast, provides an additional international law context for a civil remedy in the national courts of the forum State under the principle of universal civil jurisdiction in response to the atrocity of official torture. It should be noted, however, that some States have taken a different approach to the issue in recent years. For instance, Canada is being urged to revise its State immunity legislation to allow for civil suits in Canada's courts by Canadian nationals against the foreign State even where the official torture did not occur in Canada.

23. **The reasoning of the U.K. House of Lords in *Jones* creates certain logical inconsistencies on the issue of extra-territorial jurisdiction**: With respect, the reasoning of the U.K. House of Lords in cases such as *Jones* results in an intolerable illogical and legally insupportable asymmetry between the application of universal criminal versus universal civil jurisdiction over the agents of the State responsible for torture and other international crimes (these courts holding that the agents of the State, having committed torture in an 'official capacity', whether authorized to do

---

[53]Chatham House: State immunity: An update in light of the Jones case. http://www.chatham house.org.uk/files/3378_il211106.pdf.

[54]Hall (2008, pp. 921–937).

[55]Committee Against Torture, Conclusions and recommendations, 34th Sess., 2–20 May 2005, UN Doc. CAT/C/CR/34/CAN, 7 July 2005, paras 4(g), 5(f).

so or not, are subject to universal *criminal* jurisdiction, unless protected by personal immunity, but not subject to universal *civil* jurisdiction).

B. *Another Landmark Case on the Issue of State Subject Matter (Functional) Immunity and Absolute Personal Immunity of Individual Perpetrators Against Civil and Criminal Liability*

Case 2: Democratic Republic of Congo v. Belgium, International Court of Justice Judgment of 14 February 2002

The International Court of Justice (ICJ) case "Case Concerning Arrest Warrant of 11 April 2000 (*Democratic Republic of Congo (DRC) v. Belgium*)":[56] The latter ICJ case concerned the issue of an international arrest warrant in absentia by a Belgian investigating magistrate against the then sitting Minister of Foreign Affairs of the DRC (M. Abdulaye Yerodia Ndombasi) alleging grave breaches of the Geneva Convention of 1949 and of the Additional protocols to the Convention[57,58,59] as well as crimes against humanity. The arrest warrant was circulated internationally through 'INTERPOL' (the International Criminal Police Organization). The DRC alleged that the arrest warrant constituted a violation "of the rule of customary international law concerning the absolute inviolability and immunity from criminal process of incumbent foreign ministers."[60] At the time of the ICJ hearing of the DRC application, Yerodia was no longer the Democratic Republic of Congo's Minister of Foreign Affairs. However, the DRC maintained that its objective

---

[56]*Democratic Republic of Congo v. Belgium*, International Court of Justice judgment of 14 February 2002 (I.C.J. Reports 2002, p. 3). http://www.icj-cij.org/docket/index.php?p1=3&p2=3&k=36&case=121&code=cobe&p3=4. Accessed 23 June 2009.

[57]Geneva Conventions (Numbers I–IV), 12 August 1949. http://www.icrc.org/Web/Eng/siteeng0.nsf/htmlall/genevaconventions. Accessed 23 June 2009.

[58]Protocol Additional to the Geneva Conventions of 12 August 1949, and relating to the Protection of Victims of *International* Armed Conflicts (Protocol 1), Adopted on 8 June 1977 by the Diplomatic Conference on the Reaffirmation and Development of International Humanitarian Law applicable in Armed Conflicts, entry into force 7 December 1979. http://www.unhchr.ch/html/menu3/b/93.htm. Accessed 23 June 2009.

[59]Protocol Additional to the Geneva Conventions of 12 August 1949, and Relating to the Protection of Victims of Non-International Armed Conflicts (Protocol II), Adopted on 8 June 1977 by the Diplomatic Conference on the Reaffirmation and Development of International Humanitarian Law applicable in Armed Conflicts entry into force 7 December 1978. http://www.unhchr.ch/html/menu3/b/94.htm. Accessed 23 June 2009.

[60]*Democratic Republic of Congo v. Belgium*, International Court of Justice judgment of 14 February 2002 (I.C.J. Reports 2002, p. 8, para 11, item 1). http://www.icj-cij.org/docket/index.php?p1=3&p2=3&k=36&case=121&code=cobe&p3=4. Accessed 23 June 2009.

remained unchanged in regards the ICJ case namely, "to have the disputed arrest warrant annulled and *to obtain redress for the moral injury suffered*."[61] It is apparent then that the DRC was relying on classical notions of sovereignty in making out its position in the Congo v. Belgium case. That is, the notion that the Minister of Foreign Affairs as a representative of the Head of State embodied the sovereignty and dignity of the Head of State and that also of the State itself. The complaints that initiated the proceeding leading to the arrest warrant were brought by twelve complainants (five of whom were Belgium nationals) and all of whom resided in Belgium. The ICJ noted that it was uncontested that the twelve complainants were *not* victims of Mr. Yerodia's criminal actions, that the alleged international crimes occurred outside of Belgium territory, that Mr. Yerodia was not a Belgium national at the time the alleged offences were committed and that he was not in Belgium at the time that the arrest warrant was issued or circulated. The international crimes for which Mr. Yerodia was charged (also crimes under Belgian law at the time), and which formed the basis for the arrest warrant issued by Belgium, concerned violations of the Geneva Conventions and its additional protocols I and II.

The ICJ held that Mr. Yerodia, as at the relevant time *incumbent* Minister of Foreign Affairs was entitled to absolute personal immunity from the criminal jurisdiction of Belgium for any international crimes (i.e. crimes against humanity or war crimes) committed before or during his tenure in office whether these acts are claimed to have been 'official' or 'private'. (In a statement obiter dictum, the ICJ in the same case seemed to imply that that even former Ministers of Foreign Affairs are entitled to absolute personal immunity for such acts (whether considered private or official) committed before or during their tenure in office). The court reasoned that any exercise of extra-jurisdictional authority by a foreign State in this regard would interfere with the ability of the official to carry out his or her functions on behalf of the State. The ICJ therefore found that both the issuance and circulation of the arrest warrant for Mr. Yerodia was unlawful under international law regarding the absolute personal immunity he enjoyed as incumbent Minister of Foreign Affairs. The ICJ ordered Belgium to cancel the arrest warrant and to notify those to whom it had been circulated not to execute it. Belgium did in fact comply with all aspects of the ICJ order.

Commentary on the International Court of Justice Judgment in Democratic Republic of Congo v. Belgium

1. **It is an affront to the dignity of the State *not* to hold Heads of State and other high ranking officials accountable for international crimes committed before, or during their tenure in office**: The International Court of Justice in the Yerodia

---

[61] *Democratic Republic of Congo v. Belgium*, International Court of Justice judgment of 14 February 2002 (I.C.J. Reports 2002, p. 14, para 31). http://www.icj-cij.org/docket/index.php?p1=3&p2=3&k=36&case=121&code=cobe&p3=4. Accessed 23 June 2009.

case noted that it is well-established international law that "as also diplomatic and consular agents, certain holders of high-ranking office in a State, such as the Head of State, Head of Government and Minister for Foreign Affairs, enjoy immunities from jurisdiction in other States, both civil and criminal".[62] The ICJ also observed that:

> In customary international law, the immunities accorded to Ministers for Foreign Affairs are not granted for their personal benefit, but to ensure the effective performance of their functions on behalf of their respective States.[63]

This author has, in contrast to the International Court of Justice (ICJ) position in the *Democratic Republic of Congo v. Belgium*, argued that there is no affront to the dignity of the State when Ministers of Foreign Affairs or others who would normally be entitled to claim absolute personal immunity are held criminally and civilly liable for international crimes committed before, or during their tenure in office whether or not they continue to hold that or another high government office. Indeed, it is instead an affront to the dignity of the State to suggest (by the implication deriving from the grant of personal immunity to high government officials responsible for international crimes namely, official torture, genocide, crimes against humanity and/or war crimes) that the State's sovereign authority extends to the commission of international crimes by its high officials. The denial of absolute personal immunity in cases such as that of Mr. Yerodia would have the salutary effect of emphasizing, on behalf of the international community, that: (i) "the effective performance of . . .functions on behalf of their respective States" by high government officials and diplomats does *not* include the commission of international crimes, and that (ii) direct or indirect responsibility of these officials for the commission of international crimes will trigger a loss of personal immunity regardless whether in all other respects the official did carry out the legitimate functions of government which are covered by sovereign immunity.

2. **There is, in fact, no legally supportable basis for the ICJ contention that a high governmental official who has committed international crimes, whether before or during office, is entitled to absolute personal immunity** (i.e. on the grounds that to do otherwise would interfere with that official carrying out the duties of his or her office and with his or her ability to travel internationally as is required by the office). After all, that official has insulted the dignity of all peoples (and the international community of independent States) through his or her acts given that such international crimes as mentioned have been long recognized as an affront to humanity under international customary and particular treaty law. Further, it is unclear why the international community (through a recognition of

[62] *Democratic Republic of Congo v. Belgium*, International Court of Justice judgment of 14 February 2002 (I.C.J. Reports 2002, p. 21, para 51). http://www.icj-cij.org/docket/index.php?p1=3&p2=3&k=36&case=121&code=cobe&p3=4. Accessed 23 June 2009.

[63] *Democratic Republic of Congo v. Belgium*, International Court of Justice judgment of 14 February 2002 (I.C.J. Reports 2002, p. 21, para 53). http://www.icj-cij.org/docket/index.php?p1=3&p2=3&k=36&case=121&code=cobe&p3=4. Accessed 23 June 2009.

absolute personal immunity for perpetrators of international crimes who happen to hold high government or diplomatic office) should essentially provide certain perpetrators a 'free pass' such that they may potentially continue to perpetrate such international crimes with impunity while in office.

3. **Personal Immunity is, in fact, *not* a pre-emptory principle where international crimes have been committed before or during tenure in office**: The International Court of Justice ruling that Mr. Yerodia was entitled to absolute personal immunity went on to make the following holding:

> It should further be noted that the rules governing the jurisdiction of national courts must be carefully distinguished from those governing jurisdictional immunities: jurisdiction does not imply absence of immunity, while absence of immunity does not imply jurisdiction. *Thus although various international conventions or the prevention and punishment of certain serious crimes impose on States obligations of prosecution or extradition, thereby requiring them to extend their criminal jurisdiction, such extension of jurisdiction in no way affects immunities under customary international law, including those of Ministers for Foreign Affairs.* These remain opposable before the courts of a foreign State, even where those courts exercise such a jurisdiction under these conventions (emphasis added).[64]

It is no doubt the case that the Democratic Republic of Congo and Mr. Yerodia were entitled to their day in court in *Democratic Republic of Congo v. Belgium* before the International Court of Justice (ICJ) and before the national courts of Belgium. It does *not* at all follow, contrary to the contention of the ICJ in the case, that universal criminal (or civil) jurisdiction *when applicable* does not negate absolute personal immunity. Indeed, were absolute personal immunity a peremptory principle, as in effect it was improperly regarded by the ICJ in *Democratic Republic of Congo v. Belgium*, extra-jurisdictional authority in the form of universal criminal or civil jurisdiction would effectively have no substance or import.

4. **Universal criminal jurisdiction is international customary law and there is no sovereignty rationale for absolute personal immunity when international crimes have been committed before, during or after the tenure as Head of State or the high official has held government office**: The attempt of the ICJ to assuage the wounds of Mr. Yerodia's victims and of all those in the international community who respect fundamental human rights (despite its holding that Mr. Yerodia was entitled to absolute personal immunity) is reflected in the following:

> *The Court emphasizes, however, that the immunity from jurisdiction enjoyed by incumbent Ministers for Foreign Affairs does not mean that they enjoy impunity in respect of any crimes they might have committed, irrespective of their gravity.* Immunity from criminal jurisdiction and individual criminal responsibility are quite separate concepts. While jurisdictional immunity is procedural in nature, criminal responsibility is a question of substantive law. Jurisdictional immunity may well bar prosecution for a certain period or for certain offences; it cannot exonerate the person to whom it applies from all criminal responsibility.

---

[64]*Democratic Republic of Congo v. Belgium*, International Court of Justice judgment of 14 February 2002 (I.C.J. Reports 2002, p. 25, para 59). http://www.icj-cij.org/docket/index.php?p1=3&p2=3&k=36&case=121&code=cobe&p3=4. Accessed 23 June 2009.

> Accordingly, the immunities enjoyed under international law by an incumbent or former Minister for Foreign Affairs do not represent a bar to criminal prosecution in certain circumstances.
>
> First, such persons enjoy no criminal immunity under international law in their own countries, and may thus be tried by those countries' courts in accordance with the relevant rules of domestic law.
>
> Secondly, they will cease to enjoy immunity from foreign jurisdiction if the State which they represent or have represented decides to waive that immunity.
>
> Thirdly, *after a person ceases to hold the office of Minister for Foreign*
>
> *Affairs*, he or she will no longer enjoy all of the immunities accorded by international law in other States. Provided that it has jurisdiction under international law, a court of one State may try a *former* Minister for Foreign Affairs of another State in respect of acts committed prior or subsequent to his or her period of office, as well as in respect of acts committed during that period of office *in a private capacity.*
>
> Fourthly, an *incumbent or former* Minister for Foreign Affairs may be subject to criminal proceedings before certain international criminal courts, where they have jurisdiction. . ..
>
> Accordingly, the immunities enjoyed under international law by an incumbent or former Minister for Foreign Affairs do not represent a bar to criminal prosecution in certain circumstances (emphasis added).[65]

Note that the International Court of Justice in the above citation appears to be suggesting that even after such high officials leave office they are shielded by absolute personal immunity in respect of *official* functions carried out before or during their tenure in office (see paragraph five of the citation above from the ICJ judgement in *Democratic Republic of Congo v. Belgium).* In this regard, the ICJ opinion in this case appears to contradict the U.K. House of Lords judgment in Pinochet (3) (and general practice), at least insofar as the outcome, though somehow the ICJ does not find a contradiction in terms of the reasoning in the two cases. Generally, the international law on immunity provides for (i) absolute personal immunity (ratione personae) with respect to *serving* heads of State and certain incumbent high officials or diplomats, covering *both* official and private acts, and for (ii) the immunity of ordinary officials or agents of the State including former heads of State with respect to subject matter immunity (ratione materiae); that is with respect only to *official acts* carried out before or during office.

We have already addressed the fact that the grant of such absolute personal immunity, or alternatively of State subject matter immunity, implicates substantive law and does not just represent a procedural bar to adjudication in a particular forum (see note 12 above). Indeed, the ICJ concedes that an incumbent or former official with a status akin to that of Mr. Yerodia (even absent any waiver of immunity) is subject to the jurisdiction of an international criminal court (such as the International Criminal Court in The Hague). That jurisdiction in regards to the International Criminal Court in The Hague includes jurisdiction over so-called private or non-official acts and official acts constituting international crimes

---

[65] *Democratic Republic of Congo v. Belgium*, International Court of Justice judgment of 14 February 2002 (I.C.J. Reports 2002, p. 25, para 60–61). http://www.icj-cij.org/docket/index.php?p1=3&p2=3&k=36&case=121&code=cobe&p3=4. Accessed 23 June 2009.

committed by the high official before assuming office, during or after assuming office. Hence, there is, in reality, no legitimate rationale for absolute personal immunity in respect of criminal liability for international crimes for which an incumbent high government official or diplomat or other high official is in some manner responsible (despite the reference by the ICJ to such a right perhaps even extending to former heads of State). In both situations (exercise of universal criminal jurisdiction by a foreign State, or by an international criminal court), according to the claims of the offending State and its defendant high official, the sovereignty of the State, allegedly shielded by immunity (whether via State subject matter and/or personal immunity of high officials) has been unlawfully encroached. *Note also that, according to the International Law Commission, universal criminal jurisdiction is*: (i) *part of international customary law* (universal criminal jurisdiction here referring to the ability of a State to try persons for certain types of crimes committed outside that State's territory regardless of the nationality of the perpetrator or the victim and even though there is no direct link to the forum State in terms of the impact of the crimes on that forum State or in any other way) as well as being (ii) incorporated into certain treaty law (i.e. the 1984 U.N. Treaty on torture and the 1949 Geneva Convention as well as Protocol I to that Convention).[66] There is then no legally supportable rationale for the grant of absolute personal immunity to such high officials as a shield to the exercise of universal criminal jurisdiction by a State in such a case.

Further, amnesty granted by the offending State to its nationals who are perpetrators of official torture is also *not* a shield to the exercise of universal *criminal* jurisdiction by a foreign State when the defendant's home State is unwilling or unable to prosecute its agents for this international crime. With respect to determinations pertaining to the import of the jus cogens international legal norm regarding torture, there are significant contradictions in the various rulings of the European Court of Human Rights (ECHR). Recall that the European Court of Human Rights affirmed the State immunity accorded Kuwait by the U.K. courts in the Al-Adsani *civil* case (where State subject matter immunity would, as has been discussed, then properly apply also to the agents responsible for the torture committed under 'colour of public authority' had that issue been before the ECHR in the case which it was not). At the same time, the European Court of Human Rights in *Ould Dah v. France* has *rejected* the notion that amnesty can serve as such a shield in overriding universal criminal jurisdiction of a foreign State (i.e. France) which jurisdiction is based on the jus cogens principle regarding the absolute ban on torture as articulated in the 1984 U.N. Torture Treaty. The *Ould Dah v. France* case was hence ruled inadmissible by the ECHR. The ECHR attempted to distinguish the *Ould Dah v. France* case from *Al-Adsani* based on the fact that *Ould Dah v. France* involved universal criminal jurisdiction and issues relating to amnesty. However, it is unclear why the jus cogens principle is the operative principle in an amnesty case and not an immunity civil case such as *Al-Adsani* when issues of comity and State

[66] Galicki (2006).

sovereign equality are implicated in both. Consider also that jus cogens principles as discussed are regarded as part of customary international law that are automatically incorporated into domestic law while amnesty, of course, is based on national law in the first instance thus again creating a parallel.[67]

The following options are potentially available alone or in concert unimpeded by immunity considerations: (i) the *forum State* exercising universal criminal jurisdiction over a high official or other State agent based on the U.N. Torture Treaty, customary international law ('extradite or prosecute') or obligations under the Rome Statute (which may be incorporated into domestic law) *despite the defendant's claim of State subject matter or absolute personal immunity* and/or (ii) the exercise of universal criminal jurisdiction by an *international criminal court* in the same case. Any alleged distinction in the feasibility of either option (i.e. the contention that State-exercised universal criminal jurisdiction may be defeated by absolute personal immunity claims such as would be applicable if no international crime were involved) is grounded not on international law, but rather on inter-State politics and the application of comity in a morally offensive and legally indefensible manner. Such an approach as advocated by the ICJ does nothing to foster domestic peace or international tranquility founded on human rights and mutual self-interest but a self-interest yet conducive to the long-term well being of the international community as a whole. *It is here suggested then that the principle of the sovereign equality of States is compromised neither by: (i) any State exercising universal criminal or civil jurisdiction over perpetrators of international crimes where the offending State declines or is unable to hold these perpetrators to account nor by (ii) any international criminal court, such as the permanent court in The Hague, which exercises such jurisdiction in the same circumstances.* This in that, in both instances, there is *no* basis rooted in State sovereignty which would give rise to immunity of any sort for acts which under international customary and treaty law are clearly beyond the sovereign authority of the State. Consistent with such a view consider that the International Law Commission maintains that there are various prosecutorial options available; each equally feasible and potentially even operative in parallel where necessary:

> . . .the Commission has introduced a concept of "triple alternative", considering a possibility of parallel jurisdictional competence to be exercised not only by interested States, but also by international criminal courts. . .Alternative competencies of the International Criminal Court, established on the basis of the Rome Statute of 1998, are generally known. The Statute gives a choice between exercising jurisdiction over an offender by the State itself or having him surrendered to the jurisdiction of the International Criminal Court.[68]

[67] *Ould Dah v. France*, (Application no 13113/03), European Court of Human Rights, 17 March 2009. http://www.unhcr.org/refworld/docid/49d474a12.html. Accessed 27 June 2009 (French only).

[68] Galicki (2006, para 52 and 54, p. 16).

The International Law Commission also notes that some jurists of the International Court of Justice have found that the principle of 'extradite or prosecute' is a jus cogens principle of customary international law.[69]

C. Torture Versus Inhuman or Degrading Treatment or Punishment: Implications for Universal Criminal Jurisdiction and the Chances for Impunity

Introduction

In this section, we will consider the European Court of Human Rights excessive deference to the State at the expense of jus cogens principles regarding international crimes. More specifically, we will examine whether the Court in Ireland v. United Kingdom overextended its application of the principle of 'margin of appreciation' when it ruled that: (i) the United Kingdom had employed 'inhuman or degrading treatment' in regards to 14 IRA alleged terrorists rather than 'torture'; hence protecting the State (the U.K.) from the spectre of foreign States potentially exercising universal criminal justice in bringing the U.K. agents responsible to justice, and (ii) when it ruled that the U.K.'s systemic violations of Article 3 of the Convention did not in any way undermine the alleged legitimacy of the extra-judicial powers that the U.K. had implemented, or the manner in which the State had instructed these powers were to be executed. There was no problem, according to the European Court of Human Rights, with the fact that the impugned U.K. legislation granting the government extra-judicial powers did not at the outset also provide for a guarantee of the Convention rights secured under Article 3 (the right to be protected from torture or inhuman or degrading treatment or punishment). It was not until such cases had occurred (12 in August and 2 in October 1971 had surfaced and become public), and then only some time later, about March 1972, that explicit directives against the use of interrogation techniques that violated Article 3 of the European Convention were issued by the U.K. government. Nor was there a problem with the emergency U.K. legislation, according to the European Court of Human Rights, despite the fact that: (i) the Convention, under Article 15, provides for no derogation from the rights under Articles 3 in times of public emergency such as was present in Northern Ireland at the time and (ii) the State did know, or should have known, that violations of Convention Article 3 were occurring; especially given that certain U.K. agents were trained in an official setting to employ such techniques as constituted violations of Article 3 of the Convention. *That is, the Commission found, and it was uncontested, that the techniques had been orally taught to members of the RUC (Royal Ulster Constabulary) by the English Intelligence Centre at a seminar held in April 1971* which is shortly before their implementation against the 12 IRA members in

[69]Galicki (2006, para 55, pp. 16–17).

August 1971 (this is not to negate the fact that the U.K. legislation did *not* officially authorize torture or inhuman treatment).[70]

In *Ireland v. the United Kingdom* we consider an inter-State case in which the European Court of Human Rights essentially defined away torture through some fairly blatant semantic gymnastics thus inadvertently undermining certain fundamental human rights guarantees. Had the European Court of Human Rights affirmed that the United Kingdom had specifically employed a practice of 'torture' against 14 alleged Irish terrorists, (as had the European Commission), this would have potentially established universal criminal jurisdiction for foreign States (pursuant to international customary law; and contemporary understandings of obligations under the Article 3(a) prohibition against torture in the 1949 Geneva Conventions) to prosecute the torturers (provided that the U.K. itself had been unwilling to do so). Note that Article 3(c) of the 1949 Geneva Conventions[71] also included a prohibition against: "Outrages upon personal dignity, in particular, humiliating and degrading treatment." We will consider the *devolution* of Article 3 of the *Geneva Convention* as incorporated into the *European Convention on Human Rights and Fundamental Freedoms* in the case commentary section. The *Ireland v. the United Kingdom* case highlights the issue of: (i) whether derogation of the *European Convention on Human Rights'* prohibition against torture and/or inhuman or degrading treatment or punishment can ever be justified in times of emergency when the peace and security of a community is threatened; a topic with currency given the recent controversies regarding treatment of alleged terrorists at Abu Ghraib prison in Baghdad and at Guantanamo Bay, Cuba, and (ii) whether the *jus cogens* principle regarding torture was somehow undermined in the ruling of the European Court of Human Rights in the Ireland v. United Kingdom case despite the Court's holding to the contrary.

Case 3: *Ireland v. United Kingdom*

Procedural History and Background Relating to Ireland v. United Kingdom

The *Ireland v. United Kingdom* case pertained to the first inter-State petition before the European Court of Human Rights and, indeed, the first inter-State application before any international human rights tribunal. The case originated in an application by Ireland against the government of the 'United Kingdom of Great Britain and Northern Ireland' brought before the European Commission on Human Rights (hereafter referred to as 'the Commission') 16 December 1971. The instant case

---

[70] *Ireland v. the United Kingdom* (Application 5310/71), European Court of Human Rights, 13 December 1977. http://www.unhcr.org/refworld/docid/3ae6b7004.html. Accessed 27 June 2009, para 221–222; see also para 97.

[71] *Geneva Conventions* (Numbers I–IV), 12 August 1949. http://www.icrc.org/Web/Eng/siteeng0.nsf/htmlall/genevaconventions. Accessed 23 June 2009.

concerned alleged violations of the *European Convention on Human Rights*[72] (hereafter referred to as 'the Convention') by the respondent government. The violations related to infringements of the guarantee of protection against torture and against inhuman or degrading treatment as well as violations of a number of other Convention violations. The focus in this discussion will, however, be on the alleged torture and its implications for the matter of the potential for universal criminal jurisdiction to try the perpetrators should the United Kingdom be unwilling or unable to do so.

The case was registered with the European Court of Human Rights 10 March 1976 for consideration of, among other things; the Commission's finding that the respondent government had seriously breached Article (3) of the European Convention on Human Rights and Fundamental Freedoms. *More specifically, the Commission had made a finding that agents of the respondent government had committed 'torture' against 14 captured and detained members of the Irish Republican Army but against no other IRA detainees. This it found amounted to a practice of torture. With regard to other Convention violations, the Commission found that there had also been a pattern or practice of such infringements (such as, for instance, Article 3 violations constituting 'inhuman or degrading treatment') rather than only isolated incidents.*

The events giving rise to the complaint occurred during August 1971 – December 1975; the period when the respondent government was exercising "extra-judicial powers of arrest, detention and internment."[73] These extraordinary measures were considered by the respondent government to be necessary to quell the activity of the Irish Republican Army (the IRA) and that of the opposing Protestant extremists; both of which it considered terrorist groups. The IRA was considered an illegal organization in the U.K. a well as in Northern Ireland (the group did not accept Northern Ireland as part of the U.K., nor did it accept the governing apparatus of the independent Republic of Ireland which excluded the Northern Ireland counties)[74] The European Court of Human Rights noted that the internal hostilities in Northern Ireland had, up to March 1975, (according to the statistics provided by the respondent government), resulted in over

[72] *European Convention on Human Rights and Fundamental Freedoms* (as amended by Protocol Number 11 and with protocols 1, 4, 6, 7, 12 and 13), entry into force 1 November 1998 (original Convention adopted by the Council of Europe 1950 and entered into force 3 September 1953). http://www.echr.coe.int/NR/rdonlyres/D5CC24A7-DC13-4318-B457-5C9014916D7A/0/EnglishAnglais.pdf. Accessed 20 June 2009.

[73] *Ireland v. the United Kingdom* (Application 5310/71), European Court of Human Rights, 13 December 1977. http://www.unhcr.org/refworld/docid/3ae6b7004.html. Accessed 27 June 2009, para 11.

[74] *Ireland v. the United Kingdom* (Application 5310/71), European Court of Human Rights, 13 December 1977. http://www.unhcr.org/refworld/docid/3ae6b7004.html. Accessed 27 June 2009, para 16.

1,100 persons being killed, over 11,500 persons being injured and more than 140,000,000 pounds (in British currency) worth of property destroyed.[75]

It was uncontested that on 9 August 1971, twelve people were arrested and that in October 1971 two additional persons were arrested (suspected or confirmed IRA members); all of whom were targeted for, and whom did indeed receive treatment classified by the captors as 'interrogation in depth'. This treatment consisted of five specific techniques that the Commission held unanimously met the criteria for 'torture'. *The Commission maintained that 'torture' involved much more severe suffering than the treatment constituting the inhuman or degrading treatment referred to in Article 3 of the European Convention on Human Rights.* The Commission further established that the five techniques in question included the following (although importantly, there was still uncertainty regarding exactly how these were carried out, i.e. precisely how long each technique would be imposed on each detainee at one session, or over how many sessions in total, etc.):

> (a) wall-standing: forcing the detainees to remain for periods of some hours in a "stress position", described by those who underwent it as being "spreadeagled against the wall, with their fingers put high above the head against the wall, the legs spread apart and the feet back, causing them to stand on their toes with the weight of the body mainly on the fingers";
> (b) hooding: putting a black or navy coloured bag over the detainees' heads and, at least initially, keeping it there all the time except during interrogation;
> (c) subjection to noise: pending their interrogations, holding the detainees in a room where there was a continuous loud and hissing noise;
> (d) deprivation of sleep: pending their interrogations, depriving the detainees of sleep;
> (e) deprivation of food and drink: subjecting the detainees to a reduced diet during their stay at the centre and pending interrogations.[76]

It should be noted that the respondent government in the instant case: (i) stipulated to the European Commission on Human Rights' finding that the techniques in question had been authorized at a very high governmental level, but that, at the same time, performance of these techniques was never issued as an order in an official document, and agreed that the interrogation techniques in question were never outlined in writing; though agents were specifically trained in their use, and *(ii) did not contest the Commission finding that these five so-called 'interrogation techniques' as applied in the instant case constituted a 'practice' of 'torture'*. However, the European Court of Human Rights majority held that it was *not* bound by the findings of the Commission in this case, or any other though that view was *not* a unanimous one for the Court as we will discuss.

Further, note that the respondent government had provided financial compensation to the aforementioned 14 victims of the five contentious interrogation

[75] *Ireland v. the United Kingdom* (Application 5310/71), European Court of Human Rights, 13 December 1977. http://www.unhcr.org/refworld/docid/3ae6b7004.html. Accessed 27 June 2009, para 12.

[76] *Ireland v. the United Kingdom* (Application 5310/71), European Court of Human Rights, 13 December 1977. http://www.unhcr.org/refworld/docid/3ae6b7004.html. Accessed 27 June 2009, para 96.

techniques. In addition, the respondent government had given an undertaking to the European Court of Human Rights that these techniques would no longer be employed and had implemented a number of concrete preventive measures to that end.

Commentary on Ireland v. United Kingdom

1. **The European Court of Human Rights' basis for exercise of its jurisdiction in *Ireland v. United Kingdom***: Despite the fact that: (a) the U.K. had promised not to utilize these five interrogation techniques in future; (b) had taken what appeared to be, on their face, appropriate preventive measures in this regard; and (c) had compensated the victims, the European Court of Human Rights held that it still had jurisdiction over the case. *In particular, the Court held that it was essential for the Court to make a ruling on key matters such as whether the five interrogation techniques at the heart of the case constituted torture as the European Commission on Human Rights had ruled*:

> Nevertheless, the Court considers that the responsibilities assigned to it within the framework of the system under the Convention extend to pronouncing on the *non-contested* allegations of violation of Article 3 (art. 3). *The Court's judgments in fact serve not only to decide those cases brought before the Court but, more generally, to elucidate, safeguard and develop the rules instituted by the Convention, thereby contributing to the observance by the States of the engagements undertaken by them as Contracting Parties* (Article 19) (art. 19).[77]

Thus, as alluded to in the above quote, the Court's judgment in the case is intended to provide guidance regarding (among other things) what constitutes 'torture' as opposed to 'inhuman' or 'degrading' treatment or punishment. This latter distinction, we will discover, has profound implications for how each State Party understands its respective rights and obligations (i) as a member of the international community; (ii) as a State which has signed and ratified the *European Convention on Human Rights*, and (iii) as a States Party accepting the jurisdiction and competence of the European Court of Human Rights (e.g. to decide disputes between the contracting States Parties to the Convention). We will return to this point later and whether or not the Court's ruling in fact provides appropriate guidance on: (i) what constitutes torture and (ii) the jurisdictional mandate of the States Parties to the European Convention on Human Rights under that Convention and various other international legal instruments in regards to the prevention of torture, the prosecution of individual perpetrators, and the holding to account, in some fashion, of the offending State itself.

2. **The European Court of Human Rights consideration of individual cases of Article 3 violations in *Ireland v. United Kingdom* only as proof of a practice**:

---

[77] *Ireland v. the United Kingdom* (Application 5310/71), European Court of Human Rights, 13 December 1977. http://www.unhcr.org/refworld/docid/3ae6b7004.html. Accessed 27 June 2009, para 154.

The British government had argued that the violations of Article 3 of the European Convention (considered by the Commission to have constituted inhuman or degrading treatment, and, in respect of five interrogation techniques, torture) did *not* represent a pattern or practice, but rather isolated individual cases. The respondent government thus contended that the individual victims of such Article 3 violations could, and should have pursued domestic remedies, and that these domestic remedies needed to be exhausted before the victims could bring the case to the European Court of Human Rights (these domestic remedies had not been exhausted, if indeed they had in fact been available, given the climate of the time).

The European Court of Human Rights, in contrast, held that its role was to determine whether there had been a *pattern or practice* of violations of Article 3 of the Convention as opposed to making determinations on whether or not certain individuals had been the victims of torture or inhuman or degrading treatment per se. This mandate for the Court arose, it held, given that: (i) this had been the issue upon which the Commission had ruled, and (ii) the Commission had made a finding that a *pattern* of Article 3 violations had occurred, and not just isolated cases of torture and other lesser forms of inhuman or degrading treatment. The Court held that an accumulation of identical or like individual cases which are sufficiently interconnected could amount to a pattern or practice. Hence, the Court could consider the individual case, but only in an effort to determine if there was proof of a practice of torture and not to make rulings on individual claims under the Convention. (The case thus did *not* advance the rights of individual victims to any pecuniary and/or non-pecuniary reparations under the Convention over and above what the U.K. had provided). In considering the issue of whether there was a pattern or practice of certain Convention violations, the Court held it was *not* necessary that the individual victims involved would have exhausted all domestic remedies before the issue of a pattern or practice of violations could be considered by the Court (unlike the situation when an individual or group of similarly situated complainants brought a case before the Court). One could argue, however, that *where there is strong prima facie evidence for a pattern or practice of Convention violations*, the requirement of exhaustion of domestic remedies (in deciding admissibility of a case to the European Court of Human Rights) should be abandoned even when the complainant is an individual (or collection of individuals) as opposed to a State. This in order that the Court not rule inadmissible systemic patterns or practices of the State which constitute grave human rights abuses and which may even rise to the level of, for instance, crimes against humanity or war crimes depending on the context as defined under the Rome Statute[78]

Note also in regards to the issue of the admissibility of cases involving a pattern or practice of Convention violations, that often the respondent State is highly

---

[78]*Rome Statute of the International Criminal Court.* Text of the Rome Statute circulated as document A/CONF.183/9 of 17 July 1998 and corrected by procès-verbaux of 10 November 1998, 12 July 1999, 30 November 1999, 8 May 2000, 17 January 2001 and 16 January 2002. The Statute entered into force on 1 July 2002. http://www.un.org/children/conflict/keydocuments/english/romestatuteofthe7.html. Accessed 19 June 2009.

uncooperative in providing information on the matter as was the situation in the U.K.'s dealings with the Commission in *Ireland v. United Kingdom*. This is especially likely when the violations are very grave as in the instant case. Hence, victims may be unable to obtain from the State all of the information which would allow them, if at all, in a reasonable time, to exhaust all domestic remedies before an impartial set of domestic tribunals or courts. For this reason also it is suggested that admissibility rules on the issue of exhaustion of domestic remedies should be relaxed in cases involving a pattern or practice of violations; especially, but not limited to, cases where the violations involve serious mental or physical harms or death.

3. **Implications of a finding of a practice of Article 3 violations for State responsibility**: The finding of a pattern or practice was essential in regards to holding the high level official authorities of the State accountable for the Convention violations since: (i) the State, according to the Court, could *not* reasonably claim to be unaware of such a pattern or practice of Convention violations by its agents or officials, and (ii) such high level authorities are required, under the *European Convention on Human Rights and Fundamental Freedoms*, to accept responsibility for the conduct of their subordinates in a circumstance where they were aware or should have been aware of this pattern of conduct.[79]

4. **The five interrogations techniques induced intense suffering according to the European Court but were nevertheless *not* classed by the European Court of Human Rights as 'torture'**: Note the following European Court of Human Rights findings (articulated in the majority judgment) concerning the severity of suffering induced by the five interrogation techniques:

> *The five techniques were applied in combination*, with premeditation and *for hours at a stretch; they caused, if not actual bodily injury, at least intense physical and mental suffering to the persons subjected thereto and also led to acute psychiatric disturbances during interrogation*. . .The techniques . . .were such as to arouse in their victims feelings of fear, anguish and inferiority capable of humiliating and debasing them and possibly breaking their physical or moral resistance (emphasis added).[80]

It is entirely unclear, given the above, on what basis the European Court of Human Rights held that the five interrogation techniques, as applied in combination in the instant case, did not amount to torture *given the level of mental and physical suffering the Court itself held the techniques caused*. (Note that the subtitle for Article 3 in the European Convention on Human Rights refers only to 'torture' and reads "Prohibition of torture" also suggesting an equivalency between torture and the terms inhuman or degrading treatment also listed in Article 3).

5. **The European Commission in *Ireland v. United Kingdom* listened to approximately one hundred witnesses while the European Court of Human**

[79] *Ireland v. the United Kingdom* (Application 5310/71), European Court of Human Rights, 13 December 1977. http://www.unhcr.org/refworld/docid/3ae6b7004.html. Accessed 27 June 2009, para 159.

[80] *Ireland v. the United Kingdom* (Application 5310/71), European Court of Human Rights, 13 December 1977. http://www.unhcr.org/refworld/docid/3ae6b7004.html. Accessed 27 June 2009, para 167.

Rights did *not* have the benefit of hearing the witnesses on the stand or of directly assessing witness demeanor and credibility in delivering their testimony: While the European *Commission* on Human Rights made a finding supporting Ireland's claim that the aforementioned five interrogation techniques constituted torture – which the respondent government, the United Kingdom of Great Britain and Northern Ireland, did *not* contest – the European *Court* of Human Rights found that these techniques constituted *not* 'torture'; but rather 'inhuman or degrading treatment' (that is, treatment causing less suffering than torture).

Note that the European *Commission*, in classifying the five interrogation techniques as torture, had had the benefit of listening in vivo to one hundred witnesses, and hence could assess their demeanor and credibility on the stand in testifying regarding: (i) their *subjective experiences of suffering* through one or more of the five contentious 'interrogation techniques', and (ii) in giving their rendition of the objective facts regarding the circumstances leading up to, during and after the interrogation techniques they experienced. Hence, the Commission had *not* relied only on documentary evidence from witnesses and on medical reports, while the European Court of Human Rights was restricted to relying upon transcripts and other documentary evidence. In fact, Judge Zekia, who rendered a separate opinion, had disagreed with the Court's majority view that the Court was not bound by the findings of fact of the Commission. Judge Zekia held that findings of fact and evidence were under the Commission's purview according to the Convention rules, and should be reviewed by the Court only if there were compelling grounds for doing so. When one considers that: (i) it was only the Commission that heard witnesses, (ii) that the Commission's finding was unanimous that the contentious five interrogation techniques constituted torture and (iii) that *no new evidence* had been presented to the Court that had not been before the Commission; it would appear that no such compelling grounds for altering the Commission's finding in this regard existed, nor were any such alleged grounds advanced by the Court. Yet, the Court *in effect* made critical new findings of fact by *overturning* the Commission ruling that the five interrogation techniques constituted torture.

The standard of proof relied upon by both the Commission and the European Court of Human Rights was one of 'beyond a reasonable doubt' although the Court held that "such proof may follow from the coexistence of sufficiently strong, clear and concordant inferences or of similar unrebutted presumptions of fact."[81]

6. **The European Court of Human Rights in *Ireland v. United Kingdom* created the illusion that the notion of torture has a well-understood defined scope and that the designation is not simply dependent on the subjective assessment of the facts by the Court hearing the case**: *The European Court of Human Rights thus, as mentioned, classified the five 'interrogation techniques' (used by the RUC, with authorization of the U.K. government, against the 14 IRA*

[81]*Ireland v. the United Kingdom* (Application 5310/71), European Court of Human Rights, 13 December 1977. http://www.unhcr.org/refworld/docid/3ae6b7004.html. Accessed 27 June 2009, para 161(3).

members) as inhuman or degrading treatment per se rather than as torture. This then differed from the conclusion of the European Commission on Human Rights which had found that the techniques, as implemented, constituted torture. The Court did *not* in fact explain in what way the European Commission allegedly erred in its analysis in order to reach its purportedly incorrect conclusion that the five interrogation techniques constituted torture. The European Court instead simply held that the five interrogation techniques did not rise to the level of cruelty and suffering required for the classification of torture:

> Although the five techniques, as applied in combination, undoubtedly amounted to inhuman and degrading treatment, although their object was the extraction of confessions, the naming of others and/or information and although they were used systematically, *they did not occasion suffering of the particular intensity and cruelty implied by the word torture as so understood.*[82]

With respect, the latter citation from the Court majority judgment in *Ireland v. United Kingdom* reflects what appears to be circular reasoning as follows: The five [interrogation] techniques are not torture because "they did not occasion suffering of the particular intensity and cruelty implied by the word torture" and The five techniques "did not occasion suffering of the particular intensity and cruelty associated with torture since they are not torture." Circular reasoning in this instance is no more helpful in clarifying matters than is usually the case. Note also the use of the words "as so understood" in the quote immediately above from the majority judgment in *Ireland v. United Kingdom*. The words "as so understood" here, used as they are in connection with the word "torture", and given the entire context created by the above quote, implies *erroneously* that: (i) the Court can distinguish precisely when it should or should not classify something as 'torture' and (ii) that it can make this distinction using a reasonably accurate assessment of the intensity of suffering involved and the presence, if any, of cruelty. However, the scope of what constitutes 'torture' versus so-called 'inhuman or degrading treatment' not amounting to torture (assuming for a moment for the sake of argument that such a distinction exists) is completely unclear. As noted by Judge Gerald Fitzmaurice in his separate opinion in the instant case, the words "as so understood" in connection with the term 'torture' give a false sense that the Court knows the exact boundaries of the phenomenon of torture:

> This wording [referring to the wording of Article 3 of the European Convention on Human Rights], perhaps deliberately because of the virtual impossibility of arriving at any completely satisfactory definition of the notions involved, attempts none respecting torture, inhuman treatment, or degrading treatment. It is thus left to be determined in the light of the circumstances of each particular case whether what occurred amounted to, or constituted the specified treatment [i.e. torture]. Such a determination must necessarily be an entirely subjective one, so that differently constituted courts or commissions, functioning at different periods, might, on the basis of similar or analogous facts, reach different conclusions in

[82] *Ireland v. the United Kingdom* (Application 5310/71), European Court of Human Rights, 13 December 1977. http://www.unhcr.org/refworld/docid/3ae6b7004.html. Accessed 27 June 2009, para 167.

border-line, or even not so border-line, cases. *It results that there is little practical utility in speaking of torture or inhuman treatment, etc. "according to", or "within the meaning (or 'scope' or 'intention') of", Article 3 (art. 3) – (although the Judgment, probably by an oversight, uses such language here and there), – for that Article ascribes no meaning to the terms concerned, and gives no guidance as to their intended scope.*[83]

7. **There are implications in terms of extra-territorial jurisdiction (i.e. universal criminal jurisdiction and arguably also universal civil jurisdiction to be exercised by foreign States) when an offending State uses 'torture'**: It is important to note that the European Court of Human Rights finding in *Ireland v. United Kingdom* only of inhuman or degrading treatment and *not* torture has significant implications regarding the issue of extra-territorial jurisdiction (as would the same finding in any new European Court of Human Rights cases). Under the 1984 U.N. Treaty Against Torture, (which ***post-dated*** *Ireland v. United Kingdom*), universal criminal jurisdiction (and arguably also universal civil jurisdiction) would apply in regards to actions by a foreign State constituting torture. *However, no such extra-territorial criminal (or civil) jurisdiction would apply in the case of inhuman or degrading treatment under the U. N. Treaty Against Torture provisions.* This is the case presumably due to the *allegedly* lesser suffering resulting from the application of inhuman and degrading treatment (as opposed to torture) and reduced or no stigma attaching to such State actions which are classed as something other than torture.[84,85] It may be that a classification of an activity as 'torture' has a very specific connotation, while the term 'inhuman or degrading treatments or punishments' may, for whatever reason, be somewhat more vague.

The European *Court* of Human Rights in classifying the five interrogation techniques in *Ireland v. United Kingdom* as 'inhuman and degrading' applied a much *less* stigmatizing descriptor as compared to the designation of 'torture' (recall that the Commission *did* classify the techniques as 'torture'). In using the classification of 'inhuman or degrading treatment' rather than 'torture' was the Court implicitly, *to a degree* at least, *in effect*, according the respondent government a wider 'margin of appreciation' in deciding upon what methods to use to restore order in times of emergency than the Commission was prepared to do? This result arising *not* by the Court condoning Article 3 Convention violations of any kind (which include also inhuman or degrading treatment or punishment), but rather by eliminating the threat of universal criminal, or arguably even universal civil jurisdiction. That threat would be eliminated based on the Court's holding that there is a distinction to be made between the Article 3 prohibition against torture v. the Article 3 prohibition against inhuman and degrading treatment. Recall also that

---

[83] *Ireland v. the United Kingdom* (Application 5310/71), European Court of Human Rights, 13 December 1977. http://www.unhcr.org/refworld/docid/3ae6b7004.html. Accessed 27 June 2009, para 12 of the Separate Opinion of Judge Fitzmaurice.

[84] *United Nations Convention Against Torture and Other Cruel, Inhuman or Degrading Treatment or Punishment.* UN General Assembly Resolution 39/46, 10 December 1984, entering into force 26 June 1987. http://www.unhchr.ch/html/menu3/b/h_cat39.htm. Accessed 17 June 2009.

[85] Roth (2008, pp. 215–239).

the United Kingdom abandoned these interrogation techniques even though the violence in Northern Ireland continued at the time.

8. **There is no proper distinction to be made under customary international humanitarian law between 'torture' and 'inhuman or degrading treatment or punishment' in Article 3 of the Convention and both, in reality, trigger universal criminal and civil jurisdiction**: The alleged distinction made by the European Court of Human Rights in *Ireland v. United Kingdom* between: (i) torture (as a special level of inhuman or degrading treatment involving the highest intensity of suffering and cruelty) *versus* (ii) a less severe form of inhuman or degrading treatment (not classified as torture and simply termed 'inhuman or degrading treatment') has implications, as mentioned, regarding extra-territorial jurisdiction. It is here argued, however, that such a distinction was *not* made in the 1949 *Geneva Conventions* (which had in fact become customary international humanitarian law by the time of the instant case). The 1949 Geneva Conventions read as follows on the non-derogable prohibition regarding torture or inhuman treatment or punishment:

> **Article 3**
> *In the case of armed conflict not of an international character occurring in the territory of one of the High Contracting Parties, each party to the conflict shall be bound to apply, as a minimum, the following provisions*:
> 1. Persons taking no active part in the hostilities, including members of armed forces who have laid down their arms and those placed hors de combat by sickness, wounds, detention, or any other cause, shall in all circumstances be treated humanely, without any adverse distinction founded on race, colour, religion or faith, sex, birth or wealth, or any other similar criteria.
> *To this end the following acts are and shall remain prohibited at any time and in any place whatsoever with respect to the above-mentioned persons:*
> (a) Violence to life and person, in particular murder of all kinds, mutilation, *cruel treatment and torture;*
> (b) Taking of hostages;
> (c) *Outrages upon personal dignity, in particular, humiliating and degrading treatment;*
> (d) The passing of sentences and the carrying out of executions without previous judgment pronounced by a regularly constituted court affording all the judicial guarantees which are recognized as indispensable by civilized peoples (emphasis added).[86]

The words "cruel treatment *and* torture" in Article 3(1)(a) of the 1949 *Geneva Convention* serve to *equate in severity* (i) various undefined forms of "cruel treatment" to (ii) "torture"; a specific form of cruel treatment (describing both generally as particular acts of "violence to life and person.") The 1949 *Geneva Convention* appears then to articulate the notion in Article 3(1) (a) that the same level of severity in suffering and equivalent cruelty is present for certain other forms of cruel treatment as may be present for torture. Hence, in the 1949 *Geneva*

[86]Geneva Conventions Relative to the Treatment of Prisoners of War (Numbers I–IV), 12 August 1949 (entry into force 21 October 1950). http://www.icrc.org/Web/Eng/siteeng0.nsf/htmlall/genevaconventions. Accessed 23 June 2009.

Convention "torture" and "cruel treatment" are both listed in Article 3(1) (a) along with other examples such as "murder of all kinds" and "mutilation" which most would agree constitute acts of great depravity and induce maximum suffering. The question of what other than torture, murder and mutilation constitutes 'cruel treatment' is undefined in Article 3(a) of the 1949 *Geneva Convention. Further, there is no indication in Article 3 that certain "Outrages upon personal dignity; in particular humiliating and degrading treatment" (Article 3(c)), might not also constitute 'cruel treatment' equivalent in severity to torture; depending on the specific facts of the case (i.e. who the victims were, their vulnerability, the nature of the acts, the duration of the treatment, etc.). On this analysis, customary international law provides for universal criminal jurisdiction in respect of both 'torture'* ***and*** *'inhuman or degrading treatment' of detainees in an armed conflict (non-international or international) where the facts warrant (i.e. the inhuman or degrading treatment is cruel and creates significant suffering)*:

> Whereas the 1949 Geneva Conventions' 'grave breaches' regime withheld universal criminal jurisdiction from non-international armed conflicts and from offences committed in international armed conflicts against same-state nationals, ***subsequent state practice and opinio juris appear to validate the exercise of universal criminal jurisdiction over 'serious violations' of IHL*** **[international humanitarian law]** ***norms governing non-international armed conflicts (i.e. norms set forth in Common Article 3 of the 1949 Conventions*** *and, in so far as binding on the states concerned, those contained in the Second Additional Protocol of 1977)* [i.e. the International Criminal Tribunal for the Former Yugoslavia (ICTY) held that violations of common Article 3 of the Geneva Convention and the ICTY Statute fell within the jurisdiction of the tribunal] (emphasis added).[87,88]

9. **Changes were made in the wording of Article 3 of the European Convention on Human Rights as compared to Article 3 of the 1949 Geneva Convention and this has profound implications**: The wording in the *European Convention on Human Rights and Fundamental Freedoms* concerning the prohibition against torture and inhuman or degrading treatment or punishment differed, however, from that of the 1949 Article 3 *Geneva Convention* prohibition in that the word 'cruel' was removed from the relevant Geneva Convention provision so that the relevant Article of the *European Convention on Human Rights* reads as follows:

> **Article 3 Prohibition of torture**
> No one shall be subjected to torture or to inhuman or degrading treatment or punishment.[89]

[87]See International Criminal Tribunal for the Former Yugoslavia Decision on the Defense Motion for Interlocutory Appeal on Jurisdiction in the Tadic case (IT-94-1-A) Appeals Chamber 2, 2 October 1994, para 94.

[88]Roth (2008, p. 218).

[89]*United Nations Convention Against Torture and Other Cruel, Inhuman or Degrading Treatment or Punishment.* UN General Assembly Resolution 39/46, 10 December 1984, entering into force 26 June 1987. http://www.unhchr.ch/html/menu3/b/h_cat39.htm. Accessed 17 June 2009.

This then left it open to the European Court of Human Rights (at least in the view of the Court) to hold, as it did in *Ireland v. United Kingdom*, that inhuman or degrading treatment which was not classed as torture is *by definition* of a lesser severity than torture in that such treatment allegedly *always* causes less serious suffering than does torture:

> *In order to determine whether the five techniques should also be qualified as torture, the Court must have regard to the distinction, embodied in Article 3 (art. 3), between this notion and that of inhuman or degrading treatment. In the Court's view, this distinction derives principally from a difference in the intensity of the suffering inflicted.*
>
> The Court considers in fact that, whilst there exists on the one hand violence which is to be condemned both on moral grounds and also in most cases under the domestic law of the Contracting States but which does not fall within Article 3 (art. 3) of the Convention, *it appears on the other hand that it was the intention that the Convention, with its distinction between "torture" and "inhuman or degrading treatment",* ***should by the first of these terms attach a special stigma to deliberate inhuman treatment causing very serious and cruel suffering*** (emphasis added).[90]

Recall, however, that Article 3 of the *European Convention on Human Rights* was intended to incorporate the Article 3 *Geneva Convention* jus cogens prohibition against certain grave offences. Further, recall that no reference to any alleged distinction between 'torture' versus other types of 'cruel' treatment (based on presumed differences in severity of suffering between the two) is reflected in the Article 3 wording of the 1949 *Geneva Convention. Hence, these other types of cruel treatment equivalent to torture in severity of suffering could include various forms of 'inhuman and degrading treatment or punishment' according to Article 3(1) (a) of the 1949 Geneva Convention (and, by extension, also according to the European Convention on Human Rights given that the European Convention was intended to incorporate article 3 of the Geneva Convention).*

10. **The arbitrary nature of the European Court of Human Rights' distinction in *Ireland v. United Kingdom* between 'torture' and 'inhuman or degrading treatment'**: Consider also that in its rationale in the instant case for making an absolute distinction between 'torture' *versus* 'inhuman and degrading treatment', (i.e. a distinction that is allegedly applicable in all circumstances), the European Court of Human Rights refers to torture as "deliberate inhuman treatment causing very serious and *cruel* suffering" (see the citation above at note 9). Hence, the notion of 'cruel suffering' has been incorporated by the European Court of Human Rights into the very definition of 'torture'. *As a consequence then; any activity the Court does not label as 'torture' is arbitrarily considered to be of lesser severity and considered to be an activity which does not cause "cruel suffering."* With respect, there is, however, no legal or factual basis provided by the Court in the instant case for the Court's rejection of the contention that the five interrogation techniques (as applied by the RUC to the IRA detainees) were inhuman and

[90]*Ireland v. the United Kingdom* (Application 5310/71), European Court of Human Rights, 13 December 1977. http://www.unhcr.org/refworld/docid/3ae6b7004.html. Accessed 27 June 2009, para 167.

degrading treatment of equivalent cruelty to torture such that they could, in fact, just as well be labeled torture (this is *not* to imply that maltreatment of any kind reaches to the level of inhuman or degrading treatment. Rather the issues here commented on are whether any meaningful non-arbitrary distinction can, or should be made between 'torture' versus 'inhuman or degrading' treatment or punishment, and what are the implications of any such distinction).

11. **The judicially crafted distinction between 'torture' and 'inhuman or degrading treatment or punishment' versus the subjective reality of the victims**: The European Court of Human Rights holding (in *Ireland v. United Kingdom*), in effect, that torture is *always exclusive* of those forms of activity labeled simply with the moniker 'inhuman or degrading treatment or punishment' is, as explained, legally insupportable. *The consequences of the Court's distinction, whether intended or not, is to restrict the scope of those State activities to which extra-territorial jurisdiction (universal criminal and/or civil jurisdiction) would apply.* Hence, activities classed as 'inhuman or degrading' (but not torture) might escape the application of universal criminal or civil jurisdiction despite every indication (from the victims themselves, psychologists, psychiatrists and other physicians, and other relevant witnesses) that the suffering endured, and the aftermath, both psychologically and physically, is as severe and cruel as caused by State techniques classified by the European Court of Human Rights as 'torture'. The alleged distinction between the two: torture *versus* inhuman or degrading treatment or punishment may, depending upon the specific facts, often be but an illusory judicially crafted one.

12. **On the lack of moral justification for restrictions in the scope of the term 'torture' motivated by concerns regarding universal criminal jurisdiction**: It is noteworthy that such an approach as taken by the European Court of Human Rights in *Ireland v. United Kingdom* is consistent with the same Court's later vigorous defense of State immunity in cases such as *Al-Adsani* (which on the view here was misguided and led to an unjust outcome for victims of torture and for international justice). The approach taken by the European Court of Human Rights in *Ireland v. United Kingdom*, as in *Al-Adsani*, reduces the possibility for extra-territorial jurisdiction (though the *Ireland v. United Kingdom* European Court of Human Rights ruling has implications for universal criminal jurisdiction and the *Al-Adsani* ruling for universal civil jurisdiction).

The restriction of universal *criminal* jurisdiction, (due to improperly classifying certain State actions as 'inhuman or degrading', but something other than 'torture'), adversely impacts on foreign States and national foreign courts considering, for instance, if there is a necessity for an extradition request. *Restriction of universal criminal jurisdiction, hence, impedes efforts to apprehend and prosecute perpetrators of inhuman or degrading treatment amounting to torture when the offending State is unwilling or unable to prosecute. Thus, when the Court has improperly classed actions as inhuman or degrading, but falling short of torture, this contributes to impunity for perpetrators of torture.* In effect, the risk is that universal criminal jurisdiction – under the 1984 Treaty Against Torture and under customary international humanitarian law (as contemporarily understood) – will be undermined; not just by certain States in particular instances, but by international courts such as the European Court of Human Rights (even when the State actions against its detainees at issue do in fact constitute torture). (Please refer also to Roth's description of U.S. motivation, under the Bush administration, *to avoid being subject to universal criminal jurisdiction under the 1984 U.N. Torture Treaty* as a factor in its classing the interrogation techniques used at Guantanamo Bay (i.e. water-boarding, sleep deprivation and others) against suspected members of Al-Qaida as something other than torture and hence consistent with U.S. obligations under the U.N. Torture Treaty.)[91] *When an international court such as the European Court of Human Rights wrongly classifies State actions as 'inhuman or degrading' treatment or punishment, but not 'torture', the improper restriction of universal criminal jurisdiction in such cases gains an air of legitimacy which is unwarranted.* This author, hence, vehemently *disagrees* with those academic experts and other legal authorities who contend that: "... there remain legitimate jurisprudential considerations that favor a more limited definition of torture than moral intuition alone might recommend."[92] Put differently, and arguably somewhat more transparently, the current author contends that the goal of limiting universal criminal jurisdiction is *not* a legal or moral justification for the States, or the national or international courts not calling it as they genuinely see it when it in fact what they see is State action amounting to torture. Recall also that there is *no* definitive definition of torture, and that the Courts decide whether certain State actions constitute torture based on their own interpretation and assessment of the facts such that various Courts may reach different conclusions on the same facts. In any case, notwithstanding the aforementioned points, inhuman and degrading treatment as referred to in Article three of the Geneva Convention is, as previously explained, equivalent to torture in cruelty and in the suffering it produces and hence must also trigger universal criminal jurisdiction.

13. **The margin of appreciation and under-inclusive definitions of 'torture'**: In a separate opinion in *Ireland v. United Kingdom* Judge O'Donoghue stated the following:

> I am a firm upholder of the doctrine frequently approved by the Court that a margin of appreciation should be accorded to a State for its action taken in an emergency and impugned as a contravention of the Convention. *In the present case, however, the invocation of this principle in favour of the respondent Government has been treated by the Court, in my opinion, as a blanket exculpation for many actions taken which cannot be reconciled with observance of the obligations imposed by the Convention.*[93]

The current author is in accord with Judge O'Donoghue's assessment above of how overbroad was the European Court of Human Rights application of the

[91]Roth (2008, p. 217).

[92]Roth (2008, p. 217).

[93]*Ireland v. the United Kingdom* (Application 5310/71), European Court of Human Rights, 13 December 1977. http://www.unhcr.org/refworld/docid/3ae6b7004.html. Accessed 27 June 2009, separate opinion of Judge O'Donoghue.

principle of "margin of appreciation" in the *Ireland v. United Kingdom* case. *The current author, however, in addition, suggests that this overbroad application of the 'margin of appreciation' is reflected also in the Court's under-inclusive definition of 'torture'*. That under-inclusive definition of torture *excluded* inhuman or degrading treatment which, by the Court's own admission, caused intense mental and physical suffering for the 14 IRA detainees victimized by the application of such techniques (*Please take note that nothing said here should be misconstrued as support for either the violent actions of the IRA or the opposing extremist Protestant forces which are referred to in the Ireland v. United Kingdom case*).

Roth makes the statement that:

> Guarding the line between 'torture' under Article 1 of the Torture Convention and 'cruel inhuman and degrading treatment' under Article 16 [of the same Treaty], for the purpose of limiting the reach of transnational criminal justice, is currently not a fashionable enterprise.[94]

It is here contended; however, that the issue is *not* one of what is currently 'politically correct', but rather what is civilized. If cruel inhuman or degrading means are used then, at the very least, it is imperative that they be classed as the torture that they do in fact represent. This, in order that the member States of the international community and their peoples may properly assess the issues of morality and accountability that their use create.

14. **On the role of the European Court of Human Rights in facilitating accountability for individual perpetrators of torture and other international crimes**: Note that the European Court of Human Rights in the instant case held:

> ... unanimously that it *cannot* direct the respondent State to institute criminal or disciplinary proceedings against those members of the security forces who have committed the breaches of Article 3 (art. 3) found by the Court and against those who condoned or tolerated such breaches.[95]

One may question whether, in reaching the conclusion referenced in the quote immediately above, the Court was in the instant case, giving the State a wider 'margin of appreciation' than that called for under the *European Convention of Human Rights*. The Court notes in the instant case that: "The domestic margin of appreciation is... accompanied by a European supervision."[96] What European supervision, however, is present when the European Court of Human Rights is unwilling *to order* the State to accord victims justice by: (i) the State investigating adequately and impartially and (ii) the State prosecuting those *found by the State* to have been responsible for what arguably is torture, or, at the very least, inhuman and

---

[94]Roth (2008, p. 227).

[95]*Ireland v. the United Kingdom* (Application 5310/71), European Court of Human Rights, 13 December 1977. http://www.unhcr.org/refworld/docid/3ae6b7004.html. Accessed 27 June 2009, para 246 (10).

[96]*Ireland v. the United Kingdom* (Application 5310/71), European Court of Human Rights, 13 December 1977. http://www.unhcr.org/refworld/docid/3ae6b7004.html. Accessed 27 June 2009, para 207.

degrading treatment which constitutes a grave Article 3 European Convention violation. Is such a directive not consistent with the Court's role of safeguarding the rights guaranteed in the European Convention and ensuring that States have met their positive obligations under the Convention and also that they will do so in future? *If* the Court can be said to have provided a wider margin of appreciation to the respondent State in *Ireland v. United Kingdom* than required under the Convention, did it do so because a practice many would regard as torture creates an especially sensitive situation for a State (such as the U.K.) which, in contemporary times at least, for the most part, is regarded as a champion of democratic values? In this regard, recall the words of Judge O'Donoghue who rendered a separate opinion in the *Ireland v. United Kingdom* case and who contended that the Court's majority in that case had, via an over-emphasis on the principle of 'margin of appreciation', offered "a blanket exculpation for many actions [of the respondent State]. . .which cannot be reconciled with observance of the obligations imposed by the Convention."[97]

15. **On the nature of an effective remedy for victims of international crimes**: Some may argue in fact that the failure of the European Court of Human Rights to order the respondent State to institute criminal or disciplinary hearings in the instant case (for the *uncontested* Article 3 ECHR violations) constitutes a failure to protect the victims' right to a full and effective remedy under Article 13 of the European Convention. Article 13 of the European Convention reads as follows:

> **Article 13 Right to an effective remedy**
> Everyone whose rights and freedoms as set forth in this Convention are violated *shall have an effective remedy* before a national authority notwithstanding that the violation has been committed by persons acting in an official capacity.[98]

Financial reparations may not be sufficient to restore the victims' dignity when the perpetrators potentially have impunity. Often as not the victims' prime, or additional key objective in bringing the case to the European Court of Human Rights is to attempt to have culpability assigned to the perpetrators, albeit indirectly, through an affirmation by the Court that there were Convention violations causing grave harms.

16. **The European Court of Human Rights' approach to the issue of non-pecuniary specific remedies**: Note that there have been cases in which the European Court of Human Rights has in fact *articulated a duty* of the respondent State to implement *specific* measures by way of *non-pecuniary* reparation.[99] For instance, in

---

[97]*Ireland v. the United Kingdom* (Application 5310/71), European Court of Human Rights, 13 December 1977. http://www.unhcr.org/refworld/docid/3ae6b7004.html. Accessed 27 June 2009, separate opinion of Judge O'Donoghue.

[98]*European Convention on Human Rights and Fundamental Freedoms* (as amended by Protocol Number 11 and with protocols 1, 4, 6, 7, 12 and 13), entry into force 1 November 1998 (original Convention adopted by the Council of Europe 1950 and entered into force 3 September 1953). http://www.echr.coe.int/NR/rdonlyres/D5CC24A7-DC13-4318-B457-5C9014916D7A/0/English Anglais.pdf. Accessed 20 June 2009.

[99]Colandrea (2007, pp. 396–411).

Assanidze v. Georgia,[100] the Court went further than simply: (i) issuing declarations regarding which articles of the European Convention on Human Rights had been violated and (ii) leaving it to the State to choose the appropriate measures to effect reparation (the latter reflecting its traditional view of its mandate in issuing orders). In the *Assanidze v. Georgia* case, Tengiz Assanidze (the applicant), a Georgian national, was held in custody for various crimes of which he had been convicted. However, he was not released despite having received a pardon by the then President of the Republic of Georgia. After the pardon, and while still in custody, he was convicted of further serious charges. He was later found not guilty by the Supreme Court of Georgia on the later charges, but still not released from prison. The European Court of Human Rights reiterated in the Assanidze case that the requirements of Article 41 of the European Convention of Human Rights stipulated that it was for the States themselves to select and implement the appropriate remedy, though that implementation was to be monitored by the Committee of Ministers of the Council of Europe:

> As regards the measures which the Georgian State must take, subject to supervision by the Committee of Ministers, in order to put an end to the violation that has been found, *the Court reiterates that its judgments are essentially declaratory in nature and that, in general, it is primarily for the State concerned to choose the means to be used in its domestic legal order in order to discharge its legal obligation under Article 46 of the Convention, provided that such means are compatible with the conclusions set out in the Court's judgment*...(emphasis added).[101]

Despite the above disclaimer, in the Assanidze case the European Court of Human Rights went on to articulate: (i) a positive obligation on the State in respect of the *specific non-pecuniary remedial measures* required given the particular circumstances of the case, and (ii) to expressly indicate that the respondent State was, *in the view of the Court, obligated to take those specific measures outlined by the Court as the appropriate remedy*; namely to release the applicant from custody. The Court put the matter thus:

> *However, by its very nature, the violation found in the instant case does not leave any real choice as to the measures required to remedy* it. In these conditions, having regard to the particular circumstances of the case and the urgent need to put an end to the violation of Article 5 § 1 and Article 6 § 1 of the Convention, *the Court considers that the respondent State must secure the applicant's release at the earliest possible date.*[102]

---

[100] *Assanidze v. Georgia* European Court of Human Rights (Application 71503/01), Grand Chamber judgment of 8 April 2004. http://cmiskp.echr.coe.int/tkp197/view.asp?action=html&documentId=699751&portal=hbkm&source=externalbydocnumber&table=1132746FF1FE2A468ACCBCD1763D4D8149. Accessed 1 July 2009.

[101] *Assanidze v. Georgia* European Court of Human Rights (Application 71503/01), Grand Chamber judgment of 8 April 2004. http://cmiskp.echr.coe.int/tkp197/view.asp?action=html&documentId=699751&portal=hbkm&source=externalbydocnumber&table=1132746FF1FE2A468ACCBCD1763D4D8149. Accessed 1 July 2009, para 202.

[102] *Assanidze v. Georgia* European Court of Human Rights (Application 71503/01), Grand Chamber judgment of 8 April 2004. http://cmiskp.echr.coe.int/tkp197/view.asp?action=html

The argument made here, (given the Court's reasoning in *Assanidze v. Georgia*), is that where there are known or suspected perpetrators of a Convention violation – *especially where the infringement rises to the level of an international crime such as, but not limited to a practice of torture, or other crimes against humanity* – the violation "by its very nature, does not leave any real choice as to the measures required to remedy it". *Hence, in such cases, the European Court of Human Rights, if it is to fully and authentically meet its Article 41 Convention mandate*, must *order* a specific non-pecuniary State remedial measure; namely, a fair and impartial investigation by the State and a criminal or other appropriate and relevant State proceeding (i.e. court martial where applicable, etc.) to hold perpetrators to account. The reality is, however, that the European Court of Human Rights, to date, has tended merely to articulate that there is a duty of respondent States to implement such specific non-pecuniary remedial measures in respect of defendants and Article 6 Convention violations, and other types of cases such as illegal seizure of property and right to family cases. However, the Court has tended not to articulate the duty of the State to provide specific non-pecuniary remedies in respect of State violations of Article 2 (right to life), Article 3 (prohibition against torture) and/or Article 4 (prohibition of slavery and forced labour) all of which may constitute international crimes in certain circumstances. For instance, in *Magomed Musayev and Others v. Russia*, the European Court of Human Rights specified that no effective criminal investigation into the murder of the applicants' relatives (whose bodies had been located in a mass grave) had been conducted:

> *It follows that in circumstances where, as here, the criminal investigation into the violent death was ineffective* and the effectiveness of any other remedy that may have existed, including civil remedies, was consequently undermined, *the State has failed in its obligation under Article 13 of the Convention* (emphasis added).[103]

Notwithstanding the foregoing, however, the order in *Magomed Musayev and Others v. Russia*: (i) did *not* stipulate that a proper criminal investigation was a necessary part of any remedy the State must offer, and (ii) did *not* stipulate that the State had a concomitant duty to provide such an investigation with a view to holding the perpetrator to account. Rather, the Court simply made a declaration regarding an Article 13 violation (no effective remedy) in relation to Article 2 (right to life) amongst other declarations and awarded financial sums in respect of pecuniary and non-pecuniary damages.

Hopefully, the Court' jurisprudence will continue to develop in this regard, and the day will come when specific non-pecuniary measures to be taken by the respondent State are *ordered* in respect, for instance, of the aforementioned

---

&documentId=699751&portal=hbkm&source=externalbydocnumber&table=1132746FF1FE2A468ACCBCD1763D4D8149. Accessed 1 July 2009, para 202–203.

[103]*Magomed Musayev and Others v. Russia* (Application 8979/02), Chamber judgment of the European Court of Human Rights, 23 October 2008. http://www.ius-software.si/EUII/EUCHR/dokumenti/2008/10/CASE_OF_MAGOMED_MUSAYEV_AND_OTHERS_v._RUSSIA_23_10_2008.html.

serious Convention violations. After all, impunity may contribute to a perpetuation of such grave Convention violations. Further, where the crimes perpetrated on behalf of the State constitute violations of customary international humanitarian or human rights law; the European Court of Human Rights – in not ordering specific non-pecuniary measures (i.e. directing the respondent State to take actions that would result in accountability for perpetrators) – indirectly helps to undermine the universal criminal jurisdiction that is triggered for States when the respondent State is unwilling or unable to take the necessary steps to hold perpetrators to account.

Article 41 of the *European Convention on Human Rights*, it is here contended, in contrast to authors such as Colandrea,[104] does *not* preclude the Court *ordering* specific non-pecuniary remedial measures. Recall that Article 41 of the Convention reads as follows:

> **Article 41 Just satisfaction**
> If the Court finds that there has been a violation of the Convention or the protocols thereto, and *if the internal law of the High Contracting Party concerned allows only partial reparation to be made, the Court shall, if necessary, afford just satisfaction to the injured party.*[105]

The point here is that the State providing anything less than full accountability for the perpetrators wherever reasonably feasible constitutes only "partial reparation" and falls far short of "just satisfaction" for the victims.

17. **The European Court of Human Rights ordering specific general measures to remedy underlying systemic problems that result in repetitive (identical or substantially similar) Convention violations**: The European Court of Human Rights has, in some recent cases, adopted what has been termed the 'pilot judgment procedure'. The latter term refers to the Court consideration of well-founded individual like (repetitive) cases as emblematic of a *systemic problem* in State legislation, or in some other structural aspect of State functioning. In considering such cases, the Court has sometimes ordered a change in the State legislation to have it better conform to the State's obligations under the European Convention, or ordered some other *specific general measure* which would remove the underlying systemic problem giving rise to persistent Convention violations of a certain type. In this way, the Court may advance the general protection of human rights, rather than concerning itself with the individual complaints alone.[106] However, in the pilot judgment procedure all individual complainants must themselves have been injured in some way by the State's actions.

---

[104]Colandrea (2007, pp. 396–411).

[105]*European Convention on Human Rights and Fundamental Freedoms* (as amended by Protocol Number 11 and with protocols 1, 4, 6, 7, 12 and 13), entry into force 1 November 1998 (original Convention adopted by the Council of Europe 1950 and entered into force 3 September 1953). http://www.echr.coe.int/NR/rdonlyres/D5CC24A7-DC13-4318-B457-5C9014916D7A/0/English Anglais.pdf. Accessed 20 June 2009.

[106]Compare Colandrea (2007, Sect. 5 "Individual and General Interests in the European System for the protection of Human Rights").

Despite the Court's proclaimed interest in advancing human rights generally, the European Court of Human Rights does *not* permit *individual complainants* to challenge specific State laws (i.e. as being contrary to the State's Convention obligations) if the individual complainants themselves have not been victimized in some way due to the law in question, or if the *mere existence* of the legislation does not disadvantage a certain individual or group of identified individual complainants. In contrast, challenges to domestic legislation as being incompatible with State Convention obligations is possible in all cases for inter-State petitions (i.e. in the *Ireland v. United Kingdom* case here discussed, Ireland contested certain U.K. so-called emergency legislation which Ireland held was completely inconsistent with various Convention guarantees regarding individual human rights). In this way also the Court gives deference to the State while, at the same time, the individual's ability to use the European Court of Human Rights to advocate for the public interest in regards to human rights concerns is seriously curtailed in the manner described. This is the case though the Convention clearly mandates the Court to take into consideration general human rights interests beyond the immediate victim (s) where necessary for justice, i.e. Article 37(c) of the Convention allows the Court to consider an otherwise inadmissible application where general human rights interests are implicated: "However, the Court shall continue the examination of the application *if respect for human rights as defined in the Convention and the protocols thereto so requires*."(emphasis added).[107] In considering what the Court may or may not order under the Convention rules, it is essential to keep in mind that the Convention is premised on the notion that "The jurisdiction of the Court under the Convention is a very important legal mechanism for the promotion and protection of human rights."[108]

D. The European Court of Human Rights' Deference to Domestic Legislation via Application of the "Margin of Appreciation" Principle: Another Potential Pathway to Impunity

Case 4: Thiemann and Others v. Norway (Application 18712/03)

The Thiemann case concerns Norwegian war children (children born to a German father and a Norwegian mother during World War II) as the result of the *Nazi Lebensborn project* (which we will discuss further in a later section). Note that

[107]*European Convention on Human Rights and Fundamental Freedoms* (as amended by Protocol Number 11 and with protocols 1, 4, 6, 7, 12 and 13), entry into force 1 November 1998 (original Convention adopted by the Council of Europe 1950 and entered into force 3 September 1953), Article 37(c). http://www.echr.coe.int/NR/rdonlyres/D5CC24A7-DC13-4318-B457-5C9014916D7A/0/EnglishAnglais.pdf. Accessed 20 June 2009.
[108]Malinverni (2008, p. 1).

many of the war children had, in the first instance, been the victims of the international crime of *forced removal* from Norway to Germany at the hands of the Nazis (since the plan was to have the children reinforce the alleged purity and genetic robustness of the German population and some of the children were sent to Germany by the Nazi regime). Further, all of the war children born as part of the Lebensborn project were victims of *enslavement* to the Nazi regime for its stated objective of building a so-called master race. The children's relationship with their mothers may, in many (though not all) instances, have been severely damaged given that the children were, in essence, the product of *sexual slavery* connected to the Lebensborn Nazi project. In fact, many mothers of these war children even after the war had arguably, on their own initiative, surrendered their children for adoption or foster placement (though just how voluntary were such surrenders is questionable given the enormous societal and economic pressures these women faced in post WW II Norway).

These children were subjected to harsh and discriminatory treatment in post WW II Norway as the Norwegian government itself concedes. We will consider: (i) the role of the Norwegian government in, unintentionally for the most part, creating a discriminatory and hostile environment for these war children in immediate post WW II Norway, and (ii) the failure of the Norwegian governments of various post WW II periods to provide protective measures to the Norwegian war children and their mothers. *It is essential to point out that nothing in the discussion of the Thiemann case which follows is intended to detract from the bold and innovative positive contribution to children's human rights that Norway has made, and continues to make.* Rather, this discussion focuses exclusively on what is here contended were: (i) key missteps by various post WW II Norwegian governments in regards to its treatment of the Norwegian war children, and (ii) the legally insupportable *inadmissibility* rulings by both the Norwegian courts and the European Court of Human Rights in the Thiemann case. *The objective here is to examine, in the context of the Thiemann case, in what way the European Court of Human Rights' application of the' principle of margin of appreciation' can be arbitrary and an impediment to the goal of providing a modicum of justice to the victims of fundamental human rights violations.*

We will consider whether these Norwegian war children were doubly victimized. More specifically, we will consider whether there was a post WW II period of victimization of war children in Norway lasting decades and resulting from, in effect, an apartheid system within that country directed at war children (that alleged apartheid system arising then as a function of the various Norwegian governments' inadequate and discriminatory legislative, policy and/or practice initiatives in response to the war children's economic and social plight in post WW II Norway).

An apartheid system, of course, has its concomitant discriminatory negative consequences for many areas of child development. Its adverse effects on one's quality of life can be long-lasting or even permanent. Apartheid, furthermore, whether explicit State policy, or implicit policy manifest in practice, is itself an international crime (i.e. a crime against humanity). In this regard, consider the startling historical fact that in the immediate post World War II Norway, prominent figures called for all the Norwegian war children to be deported to Germany thus further creating a marginalized status for war children in the public perception and consciousness. In fact, there was research evidence presented to the European Court of Human Rights in *Thiemann* that for a brief period in immediate post WW II Norway a law resulted in Norwegian war children (born to women who were *married to Germans*) losing their Norwegian citizenship and being deported to Germany along with their mothers (who also had lost their Norwegian citizenship). The law in question did *not* apply to war children born out of wedlock (which was the case for the majority of war children).

We will address the issue of whether the Norwegian war children's suffering was compounded by the alleged violation of their European Convention right to respect for their family life (Article 8), non-discriminatory treatment (Article 14) and protection from humiliating or degrading treatment (Article 3) (these violations arising due to the action and/or inaction of the various Norwegian governments in the post World War II period which failed to safeguard the aforementioned Convention guarantees for these children). We will consider whether the nature of the treatment the war children endured in Norway both immediately after the war in 1945 (but before 1953 when the Convention entered into force in Norway), and after the entry into force of the *European Convention of Human Rights* in Norway in 1953, gives rise to a legitimate civil compensation case. Importantly, we will examine also: (i) whether the *Thiemann* civil case was properly considered by the Norwegian courts to be time barred and hence inadmissible and (ii) whether the European Court of Human Rights' ruling the Thiemann case inadmissible by virtue of an alleged failure to exhaust domestic remedies (given the inadmissibility rulings of the Norwegian Courts which blocked any domestic judgments on the merits) was legally justified, or, instead, based on an inappropriate margin of appreciation accorded the State. We will address also the question of whether the Theimann case represents an ordinary civil action for personal injury, or something quite different and with unique implications for: (i) the matter of any potential time limitations on the civil action in the domestic courts, and for (ii) the admissibility of the case before the European Court of Human Rights.

Procedural History and Background

The case of *Thiemann and Others v. Norway* was heard by the Chamber (First Division) of the European Court of Human Rights as to admissibility on 8 March 2007.[109] There were in fact several distinct groups of applicants involved who stayed their actions pending the outcome of the case as pursued by an initial group of seven Norwegian complainants. The applicants were all persons born during

[109] Colandrea (2007, p. 406).

World War II of a Norwegian mother and a German father (the children are referred to in Europe as 'war children' or 'krigsbarn'). These children were the outcome of a Nazi maniacal scheme originated by Himmler based on fallacious assumptions which had as its objective to create a so-called 'master race' (a scientific fiction given what modern genetics teaches about the *human* species and reproductive probabilistic genetic outcomes). The scheme involved having women deemed desirable according to the objectives of the Nazi master race program; give birth in secret to the offspring of Nazi fathers. The mothers were to surrender the children to the SS organization which would be responsible for placing the children for adoption and allegedly ensuring that their educational and other needs were met. Such a reproduction centre was opened in Norway by the Nazis in 1941 and from late 1940 to 8 May 1949 between 10,000 and 12,000 children were born in Norway from a Norwegian mother and German father under the aforementioned Nazi program.

The European Court of Human Rights' *uncontested* findings of fact included the following:

1. The mothers and children were discriminated against in Europe and many of the mothers did not have the means to adequately care for the children since they could not obtain employment. Many of the children as a result ended up in institutionalized care or foster homes;
2. Many public officials, clergymen and even medical doctors publicly expressed concerns about the children; alleging the children were defective; carried poor genes and/or that they could not be considered loyal Norwegians and were likely fifth colonists [enemy spies];
3. On 9 July 1945 a War Children's Committee was set up by the Norwegian government to determine whether it was advisable that the war children and their mothers be deported to Germany and what measures could be taken to have the children be better integrated into mainstream Norwegian society. The Committee recommended against deportation and advised instead a massive public education campaign which would encourage non-discriminatory attitudes amongst the Norwegian public towards the war children born of German fathers (and also those born of non-Norwegian fathers of other foreign nationalities). The government decided *against* the public education campaign holding the situation did not require it;
4. The notion of a War Children's Act stipulating various other protective measures was also rejected in 1945 on the grounds that such was not needed. The claim of the government at the time in rejecting such proposals was that the children were allegedly being rapidly absorbed into Norwegian society and finding adequate placements with relatives or in adoptive or foster homes.

The Norwegian government has, in recent times, acknowledged the harms suffered by the Norwegian war children. For instance, in his New Year speech to the Norwegian people on 1 January 2000, then Prime Minister, Kjell Magne Bondevik stated:

> ... We cannot let the turn of the century pass without taking in the injustice suffered by many war children in the Post War area [era]. *On behalf of the State of Norway I should like*

to apologise for the discrimination and injustice to which they had been subjected (emphasis added).[110]

Judicial History of the Theimann Case Prior to the Application Before the European Court of Human Rights

(a) ***The Oslo City Court Inadmissibility Decision of 16 November 2001 Concerning the Norwegian War Children's Petition for*****: (i)** ***Declarations regarding Alleged European Convention Violations by Norway Affecting their Substantive Rights, and*** **(ii)** ***Financial Compensation:***

The seven applicants (the first group) filed a civil suit 10 December 1999 in the Oslo City Court alleging they had suffered harms due to Norway's violations of *European Convention on Human Rights* ('European Convention') Articles 3 (protection against torture or inhuman or degrading treatment); article 8 (respect for private and family life) and Article 14 (protection against discrimination) in the post WW II era. The applicants sought: (i) a declaration that the State of Norway had committed the Article 3, 8 and 14 European Convention violations hence infringing their fundamental human rights, and (ii) financial reparations not to exceed 2,000,000 NOK per applicant. The applicants contended that Norway was liable for the harms they had suffered at the hands of State employees in post WW II Norway and as a result of Norway's failure to protect them and take reasonable steps to ensure their rights as war children. The City Court ruled 16 November 2001 that Norway could *not* be held responsible for *European Convention on Human Rights* violations which occurred prior to the Convention being ratified by Norway (i.e. violations that occurred between 1945 and later, but which took place before September 1953). The Oslo City Court in ruling the war children's application inadmissible held that: (i) the applicants would have to be able to prove a 'continuing situation' (abuse that originated prior to 1953 but was ongoing and continued after the European Convention came into force in Norway in 1953), but that the complaints could not likely be considered related to an ongoing situation given the variety of types of abuse and harassment complained of, and the lengthy time period of 55 years involved, and (ii) each applicant would need to prove that he or she was the personal victim of the European Convention violations complained of, and that these violations were part of a continuing situation that originated in 1945 and continued thereafter, or occurred after September 1953 when Norway as a party to the European Convention on Human Rights was obligated to comply with the obligations set out in the *European Convention on Human Rights*:

> in the City Court's opinion, it *cannot* be assumed that we are dealing with a single ongoing situation, in the sense that abuses committed in 1945 are not time-barred as long as the

[110] *Thiemann and Others v. Norway* (Application 18712/03), European Court of Human Rights Decision regarding admissibility, Heard 8 March 2007. http://www.menschenrechte.ac.at/orig/07_4/Thiermann.pdf. Accessed 2 July 2009, Facts, p. 4.

> victim can today be subjected to a violation of a quite different character. As regards the relationship to the ECHR [European Convention on Human Rights], it is the individual abuses against which the Convention protects the citizens (emphasis added).[111]

The Oslo City Court ruled the case *inadmissible* then in part on the premise that the *claim for financial reparations was time barred* pursuant to a 1979 Act regarding time limitations for civil suits. That Act specified that: (i) civil suits petitioning for reparations regarding non-pecuniary damage were time-barred three years after the applicant was aware, or should have been aware of the damage he or she personally suffered, and knew the identity of the person responsible, or (ii) time barred, in any event, twenty years after the impugned act or other circumstances giving rise to the damages. Further, the Court held that a 10 year time limitation rule regarding civil suits that was instituted in 1996 in Norway was also applicable in the case. The Oslo City Court held, in regards to the issue of compensation, that: (i) all of the seven applicants' claims for damages were time barred by the 20 year time limitation period rule specified in the 1979 civil compensation legislation, and that (ii) in any event; each *individual* complainant would have to prove the *personal* harms they had suffered in post WW II Norway due to their status as a war child and the State's violations of the Convention in regards to the rights of war children.

The Oslo City Court also drew conclusions in regards to the applicants' petition for declarations (which will be challenged in a later section). Those judicial declarations would have asserted that the Norwegian government violated the European Convention Articles 3, 8 and 14 rights guarantees in respect of the Norwegian war children. The Court's conclusions were as follows: (i) given the time bar which the Court held applicable in *Thiemann* in regards to the claim for compensation, the applicants had no legal interest at stake in the issues at hand which would warrant the Court issuing declarations affirming State violations of the European Convention; (ii) the declarations the applicants sought concerned government *policy* matters in post World War II Norway (concerning how to deal with war children in that country) that were largely, if not completely, beyond what the Court could properly consider as pertains to the merits of the case; (iii) there were too few applicants (122) to provide declarations which speak to purported European Convention violations perpetrated on the relevant identifiable larger group (10,000 Norwegian 'war children'); (iv) the events took place more than 55 years previous and evidence was scant such that the individual claimants were unlikely to be able to prove any violations they themselves had suffered (i.e. with evidence that met the required civil law standard) again negating the applicant's legal interest in the issues and the basis for any declarations; (v) no similar legal proceedings seeking a declaratory remedy for war children had occurred in other countries which could serve as a model of sorts (i.e. there was no precedent anywhere for the Court affirming "historical truths" about the State's treatment of

[111]Opinion of the Oslo City Court in *Thiemann and Others v. Norway* (Application 18712/03), European Court of Human Rights Decision regarding admissibility, Heard 8 March 2007. http://www.menschenrechte.ac.at/orig/07_4/Thiermann.pdf. Accessed 2 July 2009, cited at p. 9.

war children); and (vi) evidence that Norwegian war children had been treated more harshly than were war children in other European countries in the post-World War II period required research and was *not* available to the Court, and hence could *not* form the basis for a declaration.

(b) ***Borgarting High Court Inadmissibility Decision of 21 June 2002 regarding the War Children's Financial Compensation Claim***

The seven Norwegian war child applicants (the first group) appealed to the Norwegian Borgarting High Court against the inadmissibility decision of the Oslo City Court in respect only of their claim for financial compensation. These first seven applicants had thus withdrawn their petition for declaratory relief and had reformulated their petition regarding the request for financial compensation in an attempt to challenge the time bar ruling of the lower court. The Borgarting High Court, however, dismissed the appeal and upheld the inadmissibility decision of the lower court on the compensation claim based on a time limitation. *Importantly, the High Court stated that:* (i) *it based its decision solely on the time limitation bar and* **not** *on the merits of the compensation case, and that* (ii) *the High Court took no position on the merits of the case.* The following additional points are of note also in the Borgarting High Court's decision and relevant to the commentary that follows:

1. The Borgarting High Court *rejected* the applicants' contention that since their petition related to violations of the *European Convention on Human Rights*, their case was not an ordinary tort action. The High Court held, instead, that: (i) the case concerned an *ordinary civil claim* for compensation respecting personal injury, and that (ii) it was time barred as per the Norwegian 1969 compensation statute and the 1980 time limitations act for such ordinary tort actions. (The High Court noted that the time limitation statute was later amended in a way not relevant to the Court's reasoning in the instant case).
2. The High Court suggested that:(i) Norwegian compensation law must be presumed to have been consistent with Norway's international law obligations even *prior* to incorporation of the *European Convention on Human Rights* into Norwegian domestic law; namely into Norway's Human Rights Act in 1999, and that (ii) therefore it must be presumed that the applicants' legal action for compensation – which the seven applicants launched in 1999 – could have been pursued much earlier before a time bar was operative "possibly relying on the Convention [to which Norway was a party on 15 January 1952 and which entered into force in Norway 3 September 1953] and [on] European Court of Human Rights case law";[112]
3. The High Court held that the action for damages in the instant case was time barred by the Norwegian statute setting out the 20 year time limitation on civil suits for compensatory damages;

[112]*Thiemann and Others v. Norway* (Application 18712/03), European Court of Human Rights Decision regarding admissibility, Heard 8 March 2007. http://www.menschenrechte.ac.at/orig/07_4/Thiermann.pdf. Accessed 2 July 2009, p. 11.

4. The Borgarting High Court made reference to the fact that the European Court of Human Rights case law finds that time bars are *not* automatically incompatible with certain European Convention rights such as the Article 6 right to access a court for an impartial hearing to determine one's civil rights in a disputed matter. The High Court itself noted, however, that: "*The timebarring rules must* ***not*** *be such as to make this* [*Convention*] *right in reality illusory...* (emphasis added)."[113] The High Court made reference also to the European Court of Human Rights jurisprudence holding that time bars to a civil action are reasonable, for instance, if there are alternate remedies available.
5. The High Court rejected the petitioners' claims of ongoing Convention violations which the applicants held were related to: (a) the ongoing psychological and physical ramifications of their abusive experiences as war children unprotected by the Norwegian government; (b) the ongoing injurious treatment they, as adults, continued to receive given their status as war children, and (c) the fact that they had received no remedy from the government to date (i.e. the High Court agreed with the lower Court that the violations were so diverse that they could *not* be considered to constitute an 'ongoing situation'). The High Court held, further, that even if Norway had a duty to act to protect Norwegian war children born of German fathers; this duty ended when the applicants reached the age of maturity. (In the instant case, the youngest of the applicants reached the age of majority in 1965). At the same time, the High Court accepted the notion that the ramifications of childhood abuse may arise later in life and can be long lasting (but held that this did not negate the operation of the time bar): "That the effects of the damaging acts are durable and arise late does *not* mean that the 20 years' time-limit does not start to run (emphasis added)."[114]

(c) ***Supreme Court of Norway***

The Appeals Selection Committee of the Supreme Court of Norway denied the seven applicants leave to appeal the judgment of the Borgarting High Court.

Commentary on Thiemann and Others v. Norway

1. **The 'margin of appreciation principle' (as *properly* applied by the European Court of Human Rights) is *not* supposed to function as a de facto absolute State immunity from civil liability regardless of the factual context of the case**: The European Court of Human Rights in *Thiemann* deferred to: (i) Norwegian domestic

---

[113] *Thiemann and Others v. Norway* (Application 18712/03), European Court of Human Rights Decision regarding admissibility, Heard 8 March 2007. http://www.menschenrechte.ac.at/orig/07_4/Thiermann.pdf. Accessed 2 July 2009, p. 11.

[114] *Thiemann and Others v. Norway* (Application 18712/03), European Court of Human Rights Decision regarding admissibility, Heard 8 March 2007. http://www.menschenrechte.ac.at/orig/07_4/Thiermann.pdf. Accessed 2 July 2009, p. 12.

civil compensation law, and the national time limitation statute and (ii) to the national courts' interpretation and application of that law. Hence, the European Court of Human Rights applied the 'margin of appreciation principle' in the instant case. That principle of 'margin of appreciation' is premised on the notion that the European Court of Human Rights has a restricted mandate; namely to ensure that the States Parties to the *European Convention on Human Rights* fulfill their obligations under the Convention. This the States do by upholding the rights and freedoms of individuals as articulated in the Convention: (i) by meeting certain positive obligations in this regard, and (ii) by not taking actions that directly or indirectly cause infringements of the rights and freedom guarantees of the Convention. The European Court of Human Rights is thus *not* in any sense another level of appeal in respect of the domestic court judgments. Hence, the notion of subsidiarity is operative in the European Convention human rights system. At the same time, however, the application of the 'margin of appreciation principle' in a particular case is *not* considered as an absolute given. Rather, the specific facts of the case are to determine if, and to what degree, the principle of margin of appreciation is applicable. *Hence, margin of appreciation is* ***not*** *to function as a de facto State immunity from civil liability arbitrarily applied.* The contention here is that in the Thiemann case, however, the margin of appreciation principle was just so arbitrarily applied so as to create an unjustified State immunity against any civil suit by the war children.

2. **The *European Convention on Human Rights*, through its various *renvoi* to earlier international law, is relevant to periods before its entry into force in Norway (and this is *not* retroactive application of the European Convention)**:

(a) ***The European Convention on Human Rights includes a renvoi to the 1948 Universal Declaration of Human Rights (UDHR)***: The preamble of the *European Convention on Human Rights* (ECHR) makes reference to the 1948 *Universal Declaration on Human Rights* (UDHR) *and its rights guarantees as infusing the spirit of the law in the ECHR*. The UDHR preamble makes clear that the UDHR was intended to set out: "a common standard of achievement for all peoples and all nations" in all future endeavors (presumably also in fashioning future international human rights treaties). Hence, the *European Convention on Human Rights* was intended to be consistent with the principles and values of the UDHR. Certain of the key provisions of the 1948 UDHR provide that all persons are equally deserving of respect for their human dignity and rights; that children and their mothers are entitled to special care and assistance; and that the family must be protected by the society and the State:

Universal Declaration of Human Rights:
Article 1
All human beings are born free and equal in dignity and rights.
Article 16(3)
The family is the natural and fundamental group unit of society and is entitled to protection by society and the State.

Article 25(2)
Motherhood and childhood are entitled to special care and assistance. All *children, whether born in or out of wedlock, shall enjoy the same social protection* (emphasis added).[115]

Consequently, the *European Convention on Human Rights* Articles which are at issue in the Theimann case [Article 3: the right to be protected from inhuman or degrading treatment or punishment or torture; Article 8: respect for private and family life, and Article 14: protection from discrimination] may be considered to incorporate the 1948 UDHR principles of: (i) special care and assistance and protection owing to children (whether born inside or outside of wedlock), and to their mothers, and (ii) the right of the family to societal and State protection. This in that there is an express renvoi to the UDHR made in the preamble of the Convention impacting how the European Convention articles should be interpreted, i.e. as consistent with the guarantees in the UDHR in regards to the higher standard of 'special care and assistance' owed to children and their mothers. Note that most of the Norwegian war children born during World War II to German fathers were the result of the Lebensborn Nazi 'program' and born out of wedlock. Thus, the guarantee of non-discrimination and special care and assistance contained in UDHR Article 25(2) is especially relevant in their case. *The renvoi to the 1948 UDHR makes the European Convention relevant then to the more immediate post World War II period in Norway prior to the Convention's entry into force in Norway in 1953 and its incorporation into Norwegian domestic law in 1999; though the reference to the UDHR in the ECHR preamble itself is not binding law.*

(b) ***The European Convention on Human Rights ('the European Convention') includes a renvoi to common Article 3 of the 1949 Geneva Conventions which sets out ongoing obligations to the war affected children***: Article 3 of the *European Convention on Human Rights* incorporates the principles of common Article 3 of the 1949 *Geneva Conventions* and uses almost identical wording as was used in Article 3 (c) of the 1949 *Geneva Conventions*. Those *Geneva Convention* principles include the right of persons not engaged in combat to be protected from violence to life and person; from cruel treatment of any kind and from inhuman or degrading treatment without discrimination based on any inherent or acquired characteristic (i.e. ethnicity, place of origin, nationality, colour, religion, etc.). Hence, Article 3 of the *European Convention on Human Rights* has a built-in renvoi, or reference to a body of law external to the European Convention; namely, international humanitarian law (the 1949 *Geneva Conventions*). (Note that Norway ratified the 1949 Geneva Conventions on 3 August 1951).

The 1949 *Geneva Conventions in turn incorporated much earlier notions of the non-derogable minimum standards of civilized treatment of persons which must be observed in both peace time and during times of armed conflict.* For instance, the

[115] *Universal Declaration of Human Rights*, adopted and proclaimed by the General Assembly of the United Nations, 10 December 1948. http://www.un.org/en/documents/udhr/#atop. Accessed 5 July 2009.

1907 *Hague Convention* (discussed in more detail at note 4 below) which was the precursor to the 1949 *Geneva Conventions* stated that the parties were "animated by the desire to serve, even in this extreme case, the interests of humanity."[116] Hence, the lines between international human rights versus international humanitarian law are blurred and the two bodies of law, in some aspects at least, converge (recall that in the Ireland case previously discussed, the European Court of Human Rights made reference to international humanitarian law – the 1949 Geneva Conventions – in reaching its decision as to whether or not the U.K. had, for instance, violated Article 3 of the *European Convention on Human Rights*). Further, the minimum standards of civilized conduct in peace time versus during periods of armed conflict also overlap. Thus, common Article 3 of the Geneva Convention is an international norm spanning all of these divides (though originally conceived as applicable primarily during non-international conflict),[117,118]

Application of Article 1 of the *European Convention on Human Rights* (dealing with the equal access to the European Convention rights for all persons within the State's jurisdiction) and Article 3 (dealing with the non-derogable right to be protected from torture and from inhuman or degrading treatment, etc.) to the Thiemann case is thus *not* retroactive application of the law (i.e. application of the European Convention to events that occurred before Norway became a party to the European Convention on Human Rights and the Convention came into force in Norway in 1953). This is the case given the fact that the European Convention on Human Rights expresses certain principles (i.e. of non-discrimination and humane treatment) that are part of international customary law reflected in law that predates WW II. The aforementioned view then is contrary to that of the European Court of Human Rights position on the issue (that the war child applicants in *Thiemann* could not raise the issue of *European Convention on Human Rights* (ECHR) violations for the period prior to 1953 even if not time-barred due to a statute of limitations); a ECHR position reflected in the following quote from the judgment:

> Moreover, as to the alleged causes of the grievances which the applicants considered imputable to the respondent State, it should be emphasised that the impugned statements made by certain public officials and *the contested political decisions and legislative measures* taken by the authorities occurred during the first years after the Second World War *and essentially predated the entry into force of the Convention with respect to Norway (3 September 1953)*. The same could be said about *the deliberate political choices made at that time not to follow the War Children Committee's 1945 recommendation to launch an attitude-building information campaign* (emphasis added).[119]

---

[116]Preamble, Convention IV respecting the Laws and Customs of War on Land, signed at The Hague, 18 October 1907, in Schindler and Toman (2004, p. 55).

[117]Kolb (1998, pp. 409–419).

[118]Heintze (2004, pp. 789–814).

[119]*Thiemann and Others v. Norway* (Application 18712/03), European Court of Human Rights Decision regarding admissibility, Heard 8 March 2007. http://www.menschenrechte.ac.at/orig/07_4/Thiermann.pdf. Accessed 2 July 2009, under "Assessment by the court".

(c) ***The European Court of Human Rights' emphasis on the Norwegian government's so-called discretionary policy decisions concerning Norwegian war children in post WW II Norway***: Note the reference in the above citation from the European Court of Human Rights Thiemann decision to "contested *political* decisions and legislative measures" and the "deliberate *political choices* made at that time not to follow the War Children Committee's 1945 recommendation to launch an attitude-building information campaign". The consistent reference to politics in the same statement as contains reference to legislative measures makes it appear that the war children's case concerns *but policy-making* of the Norwegian government in the post WWII period which escapes careful judicial scrutiny.

3. **More on renvoi in the *European Convention on Human Rights*:** Pinzauti[120] highlights the fact that: (i) many articles of the *European Convention on Human Rights*, like other bodies of international human rights law, contain *renvoi* (reference to other external bodies of law including international law), and that (ii) the effect is that the *European Convention* articles that make such an external reference must therefore be interpreted in light of these other bodies of law and the guidance they provide. *Such renvoi, Pinzauti explains, are to be expected in that they help to unify and harmonize international human rights law.* In this connection, Pinzauti points out further that: "A distinction should be made between [inadmissible] retroactive application of the law ..., and resort to instruments enacted later in time in order to *clarify* and *spell out* a notion that already existed at the time when the facts occurred" (an approach which is fully admissible even in a criminal law context).[121] This is true also, it is here suggested, for the built-in renvoi to international humanitarian law (i.e. to customary international humanitarian law and to the *Geneva Conventions* and additional protocol I) in Articles 3, 8 and 14 of the *European Convention on Human Rights* as they apply to war affected children.

4. **The 1907 *Hague Convention* and implications for analysis of the Thiemann case**: Note that the principles with regard to the treatment of war-affected children stipulated in the 1949 *Geneva Convention* can be considered to have been well-established international law (which *pre-dated* even the 1949 *Geneva Conventions*) and were simply codified in the *Geneva Conventions*. For instance, Article 46 of the 1907 *Hague Convention*[122] stipulates that "family honor and rights" are to be respected in respect of foreign nationals found within the territory of the State holding power during or after armed conflict. Recall that in post World War II Norway, at least for a period, the Norwegian war children were regarded by certain public officials, by many other high profile and influential persons, and by a segment of the general Norwegian public as *foreign nationals* rather than as persons with dual Norwegian–German nationality. Article 23 of the 1907 Hague Convention insures that the rights of foreigners in the occupied territory are to be respected

[120] Pinzauti (2008, pp. 1043–1060).

[121] Pinzauti (2008, p. 1054).

[122] Hague Convention (1907). http://www.icrc.org/IHL.NSF/WebList?ReadForm&id=195&t=art. Accessed 5 July 2009.

and they are to have access to the courts thus setting a standard for respect for fundamental human rights. Article 46 of the 1907 *Hague Convention* appears to be a precursor of sorts to Article 8 of the *European Convention on Human Rights* (ECHR) with the ECHR Article 8 guarantee of respect for private and family life *both* in peace time and during armed conflict.

Since these principles of international humanitarian law pre-dated the *European Convention*, and are simply articulated and codified in Article 3 and 8 of the European Convention; these European Convention articles must be considered applicable also to the period 1945–1953. Hence, the war child applicants' claims relating to European Convention violations are *not* precluded in respect of harms suffered that occurred, or at least originated prior to 1953.

Let us consider now in more detail – with reference to the 1949 *Geneva Conventions* and the additional Protocol I thereto – the controversy as to: (i) whether Norway violated the applicants' European Convention rights under Articles 3, 8 and 14 from 1945 on with ongoing violations of these articles that continued even up to the date of the claimants filing the legal action, and (ii) whether, even if such violations occurred, the case was justifiably ruled inadmissible before the European Court of Human Rights for failure to exhaust domestic remedies (i.e. the case was not filed with the Norwegian Courts until 1999 and ruled by the latter courts to be time barred under the national statute on time limitations in civil compensation cases).

5. **Under Geneva Convention IV, Norway had *ongoing* legal obligations to the Norwegian war children as 'protected persons' (persons with dual Norwegian–German nationality) which did not necessarily end at the time the children reached age of majority**:

(a) ***Norway's ongoing obligations to the war children***: Norway had an obligation under customary international humanitarian law dating from 1945 to 1949 and also under the 1949 Geneva Conventions Article 3 (later incorporated into the European Convention on Human Rights Article 3) to ensure that it did not perpetuate the suffering of the war children which had, in the first instance, originated in the Nazi war crimes deriving from the Lebensborn program (which Nazi program involved, for instance, enslavement of the children to the Nazi regime for the authorities of Nazi Germany to do with the children as they saw fit including forced removal to Germany). Article 3 of the *Geneva Convention IV* regarding protection of civilians within the State's jurisdiction or power (regardless of ethnic or national origin, etc.) specified that as protected persons (as certainly were the Norwegian and other war children as civilians) the war affected children had an absolute right to be protected from "violence to their life or person" (Article 3(a)), and from "outrages on their human dignity" including "humiliating and degrading treatment" (Article 3(c)). Under Article 27 of Geneva Convention IV, the Norwegian children as protected persons (persons who had a foreign nationality) were entitled to "respect for their person"; "Respect for their honour" and their "family rights" (among other rights) which would include protection for the family as a family unit.

(b) **The duty to ensure the war children's integration into mainstream Norwegian society**: It is important to note that the 1949 *Geneva Convention* IV specified under Article 6 that: "*Protected persons whose release, repatriation or* *re-establishment may take place after such dates* [*referring to the dates that marked the end of military hostilities*] *shall meanwhile continue to benefit by the present Convention*."[123] Hence, the Norwegian war children – perceived by many, if not most, in immediate post WW II Norway as if they were foreign nationals (given the German nationality of their fathers) – pursuant to Article 6 of Geneva Convention IV, were *legally entitled under international humanitarian law* to *ongoing* care and protection from mental or physical abuse, and from affronts to their human dignity for the period required for their "re-establishment" (i.e. successful re-integration into Norwegian society with their single mothers having been reasonably provided with the supports needed for such integration into mainstream Norwegian society).

It can be argued that the affront to the applicants' human dignity of not having adequate compensation provided and full accountability by the State constituted an ongoing separate Convention violation under Article 13 regarding the failure to provide an effective remedy for the violations of Article 3 and 8 of the European Convention. The State of Norway, it is uncontested, did *not* fulfill its obligations in that regard. The State thus violated Geneva Convention IV which stipulated *ongoing legal obligations* to children with foreign nationality affected by war as 'protected persons' who were under the State's jurisdiction. That Norway did not meet its obligations to the Norwegian war children – as was acknowledged by Prime Minister, Kjell Magne Bondevik of Norway in 2000 – *cannot* then be something simply and conveniently relegated to the category of a 'policy decision' beyond the purview of any Court (as was the claim, for instance, of the Oslo City Court).

6. **The protection of war affected children guaranteed under the 1949 Geneva Convention IV (Articles 24 and 38) was part of established international humanitarian law and the European Convention Articles 3, 8 and 14 were in part a codification of this earlier law. Hence, The European Convention is applicable to the period prior to the European Convention's entry into force in Norway and its incorporation into Norwegian law in 1999**: The war children as 'protected persons' and as war affected children were entitled to special protections under the *Geneva Convention* IV of August 1949 already treated as the norm in international humanitarian law long before the European Convention was incorporated into Norwegian domestic law in 1999. These special protections, as *Geneva Convention* IV articulates, were *not* to be undermined or negated due to the children's nationality or, by extension, the fact that the war children had dual nationality (as in the case of the Norwegian war children born to German fathers). The children were to receive the same State protections as did "aliens in time of peace" and their right to family preserved:

> **Geneva Convention IV Relative to the Protection of Civilian Persons in Times of War**
> **Art. 24**. The Parties to the conflict shall take the necessary measures to ensure that *children under fifteen, who are orphaned or are separated from their families as a result of the war,*

---

[123] Geneva Convention IV Relative to the Protection of Civilian Persons in Times of War, 12 August 1949, Article 6. http://www.icrc.org. Accessed 4 July 2009.

are not left to their own resources, and that their maintenance, the exercise of their religion and their education are facilitated in all circumstances. Their education shall, as far as possible, be entrusted to persons of a similar cultural tradition.

The Parties to the conflict shall facilitate the reception of such children in a neutral country for the duration of the conflict with the consent of the Protecting Power, if any, and under due safeguards for the observance of the principles stated in the first paragraph.

They shall, furthermore, endeavour to arrange for all children under twelve to be identified by the wearing of identity discs, or by some other means (emphasis added).[124]

Art. 38. With the exception of special measures authorized by the present Convention, in particularly by Article 27 and 41 thereof, *the situation of protected persons shall continue to be regulated, in principle, by the provisions concerning aliens in time of peace. In any case, the following rights shall be granted to them:*

(1) they shall be enabled to receive the individual or collective relief that may be sent to them.

(2) they shall, if their state of health so requires, receive medical attention and hospital treatment to the same extent as the nationals of the State concerned.

(3) they shall be allowed to practise their religion and to receive spiritual assistance from ministers of their faith.

(4) if they reside in an area particularly exposed to the dangers of war, they shall be authorized to move from that area to the same extent as the nationals of the State concerned.

(5) *children under fifteen years, pregnant women and mothers of children under seven years shall benefit by any preferential treatment to the same extent as the nationals of the State concerned* (emphasis added).[125]

Hence, the European Convention articles 3, 8 and 14 which were central to the Thiemann case must be considered as informed by the aforementioned Geneva Convention articles. The European Convention is thus applicable to the period from 1945 on and to the ongoing violations of which the applicants complained though the European Convention did not enter into force in Norway until 1953 and was not incorporated into Norwegian domestic law until 1999.

7. **Norway had ongoing obligations to the Norwegian war children under Additional Protocol I to the 1949 *Geneva Convention* to ensure their proper re-integration into Norwegian society and which extended, if necessary, beyond the age of majority:**

(a) ***The additional protocols to the Geneva Conventions of 1949 contain specific provisions for the protection of children from the effects of war in all its forms*****:** For instance, article 77 of Protocol I additional to the 1949 Geneva Convention (which concerns the protection of civilians in international armed conflicts) states that children affected by war are to be protected and respected and receive the care they require on account of their age or for any other reason. The hate speech directed toward war children in Norway by various prominent public figures and public officials in the period immediately after the war, and the various forms of physical and psychological abuse they suffered in post-World War II Norway over many years, are inconsistent with Article 77 which reads as follows:

[124]Geneva Convention IV Relative to the Protection of Civilian Persons in Times of War, 12 August 1949, Article 24. http://www.icrc.org. Accessed 4 July 2009.

[125]Geneva Convention IV Relative to the Protection of Civilian Persons in Times of War, 12 August 1949, Article 38. http://www.icrc.org. Accessed 4 July 2009.

> **Art 77. Protection of war affected children (Protocol I Additional to the 1949 Geneva Convention)**
> 1. Children shall be the object of special respect and shall be protected against *any form* of indecent assault. *The Parties to the conflict shall provide them with the care and aid they require, whether because of their age or for any other reason* (emphasis added).[126]

It is noteworthy that Article 77 of Protocol I *stipulates no age limit in regards to the definition of 'children'*, hence the implication is that such protection should extend until *their situation no longer required it* and *not* just until age of majority in contrast to what the European Court of Human Rights contended in *Theimann*.

(b) ***Article 78 of Protocol I to the 1949 Geneva Convention is particularly telling and relevant to the issues in the Theimann case***: *Article 78*[127] *makes it clear that all children affected by the war who are in the State' jurisdiction, or under its control who require protection are entitled to the same State protection regardless of their nationality.* (Article 78 of Protocol I makes it clear, for instance, that no child *of foreign nationality* was to be removed from the territory under the guise of 'evacuation' where this was in fact not necessary for their health or safety. Further, if this was to occur for some legitimate reason in the best interests of the child; even then it was to occur only with the consent of the parents or guardian when the latter could be located. In addition, Article 78 stipulated that while the child was away, the child's religious and educational upbringing consistent with the parent's or guardian's wishes became the responsibility of the State doing the evacuation. Further, Article 78 made it clear that the State had the duty to: (i) return the children to the original territory from which they were evacuated when the circumstances made this possible without threat to the well-being of the children, and (ii) return the children to their original family unit where this was possible). The point here is that *the ethic underlying Article 78 was one of non-discrimination* in affording war affected children within the State's jurisdiction the protection and care they required irrespective of nationality. This non-discriminatory principle in according everyone within the State's jurisdiction equal rights is codified also in Article I of the European Convention on Human Rights.

(c) ***Protocol I to the 1949 Geneva Convention hence affirmed that*: (i) *there were positive State duties in respect of children affected by war – regardless of the children's nationality – where the children were under the State's jurisdiction and control and* (ii) *these obligations could extend beyond the end of the conflict depending on the specific protection needs of the children***: The Article 78

[126] Protocol Additional to the Geneva Conventions of 12 August 1949 and Relating to the Protection of Victims of International Armed Conflict (Protocol I), Adopted 8 June 1977 by the Diplomatic Conference on the Reaffirmation and Development of International Humanitarian Law applicable in Armed Conflicts, and entry into force December 1979. http://www.unhchr.ch/html/menu3/b/93.htm. Accessed 4 July 2009, Article 77 (Protocol I).

[127] Protocol Additional to the Geneva Conventions of 12 August 1949 and Relating to the Protection of Victims of International Armed Conflict (Protocol I), Adopted 8 June 1977 by the Diplomatic Conference on the Reaffirmation and Development of International Humanitarian Law applicable in Armed Conflicts, and entry into force December 1979. http://www.unhchr.ch/html/menu3/b/93.htm. Accessed 4 July 2009, Article 78 (Protocol I).

(Protocol I to the 1949 Geneva Convention) focus then was on protection of children while respecting family life and the integrity and wishes of the original family unit. Consider then that the Norwegian war children were considered foreigners in that they had acquired German citizenship by virtue of having a German father and there were calls for their losing their Norwegian citizenship along with their mothers losing theirs (which did in fact occur in a number of cases for a short period after the war). The point here is not the exact number of deportations of Norwegian war children which occurred in immediate Post World War II Norway, but rather the underlying ethic that is articulated in Protocol I to the Geneva Convention in regards to the protection of children which is well-established international humanitarian law. *That ethic creates a positive obligation on the State not to discriminate against children affected by war who have any sort of link to a foreign State (such as did the Norwegian war children) so as not to adversely affect their ability to receive the protection and care of the State so many desperately require during and after armed hostilities.*

8. **The time bar affected the applicants' substantive rights under the European Convention as there was no alternate remedy**: In the Thiemann case, a civil remedy arising due to *State liability* for a failure to protect the Norwegian war children against various forms of abuse as war children in post World War II Norway was in all likelihood the only remedy which would have been effectively available. This is the case given that the evidence available was degraded with key documents missing in some instances. Individual perpetrators were difficult to identify, or no longer living such that criminal cases that met the 'beyond a reasonable doubt' standard were not feasible. Thus, a time bar to the civil action brought by the seven applicants against Norway was not just a procedural bar (i.e. one mandating a different venue for settling the dispute and receiving a remedy); but rather, the time bar affected their substantive rights, i.e. their right to an impartial judicial hearing to determine: (i) the merits of their suit for compensation for Norway's alleged violation of their right to have been protected from inhuman or degrading treatment and to have their right to family respected as well as (ii) the merits of their petition for various declarations[128] regarding Norway's alleged failure to adequately care and protect them as war children in the post World War II period. One could argue then that there was an ongoing violation of: (i) Article 6 of the European Convention on Human Rights regarding the right to access the courts in the determination of one's civil rights in a legal dispute (i.e. at every level of the domestic courts and at the European Court of Human Rights, the case was ruled inadmissible rather than dismissed on its merits), and (ii) an ongoing violation of Convention Article 13; the right to an effective remedy in respect of Article 3, 8 and 14 violations of the European Convention.

The European Court of Human Rights, however, deferred to the Norwegian Court's position on the time bar issue and held that the applicants, due to the time

---

[128] *Thiemann and Others v. Norway* (Application 18712/03), European Court of Human Rights Decision regarding admissibility, Heard 8 March 2007. http://www.menschenrechte.ac.at/orig/07_4/Thiermann.pdf. Accessed 2 July 2009.

bar, had not exhausted domestic remedies. There was no consideration of the fact that: (i) there were ongoing obligations to the war children under international humanitarian law that had never been met and would have made their case viable even after the alleged statutorily defined limitation period had expired (as here discussed in previous notes), or (ii) the fact that the applicants did not have access to any relevant documentary evidence (which was held in the State archives) until research reports on the Norwegian war children became available in the period from 1999 to 2004. The European Court of Human Rights did not explain why it considered the latter applicant contention unsubstantiated. In this regard, it is noteworthy that: (i) the authoritative research reports on Norwegian war children upon which the applicants relied in *Thiemann* were not issued until 2004 and that (ii) these researchers may have had access to archival documentary material on war children and the resources and academic expertise to investigate them that the applicants did not have.

9. **There is no time limitation period when seeking remedies for having suffered the imposition of 'apartheid'**:

(a) ***The legislative scheme that set Norwegian war children apart***: Consider that the systemic discrimination reflected in the legislation and practice of the Norwegian government in dealing with its Lebensborn war children in the *immediate* post WW II period essentially created an apartheid system, i.e. recall that the decree which deprived women who had married Germans after 9 April 1940 and their children of their Norwegian citizenship indefinitely was later incorporated into law, and that the children were not allowed to regain their citizenship until the law was amended in 1949. Note further that the respondent government, in its answer to the complaints in *Thiemann* in regards to child allowances, contended that it was not contrary to Article 14 of the European Convention that: (i) the Child Benefit Act of 1946 did *not* cover Norwegian war children who had lost their Norwegian citizenship, and that (ii) the Act in fact did *not* mention war children. It was not until April 1950 that war children who were not eligible to receive benefits under the 1946 Child Benefit Act became eligible for child allowance.

While the government correctly pointed out that none of the seven applicants in Thiemann were among the Lebensborn who had lost their citizenship, the point is that such discriminatory legislation serve to erroneously legitimize systemic discrimination against war children in the society at large thus creating an apartheid system. Coupled with public officials stating that such children and their mothers could not be trusted to be loyal to Norway, the legislative system fits the oppressive characteristics of an apartheid system which is institutionalized and designed to ensure that the identified group is suppressed. *There is no suggestion here, however, that this system of apartheid persisted once all of the remnants of this discriminatory legislation had been dismantled by about 1950.* Yet, the fact remains that many victims of this early apartheid had not yet received a remedy more than 50 years after the fact. *There is no statute of limitations on the civil liability that attaches to the State regarding the practice of apartheid.* Hence, the rationale for imposing a time bar on the Thiemann case in this respect also appears to be legally insupportable. Time bars are normally imposed to create a date certain when obligations end. However, as explained, if no remedy has been provided, obligations for human rights violations of the gravity of apartheid do not cease.

(b) ***The nature of apartheid***: Apartheid is a degrading practice which constitutes an affront to human dignity and is inconsistent with the tenets of customary international human rights law. In Norway's case, the system of apartheid can be said to have been present in the very early post WWII Norway years and instituted through discriminatory legislation as discussed and through polices that set the war children apart and deprived them of necessary protection (i.e. Recall that there was a failure to implement pro-active measures to ensure that these children were properly treated in school, orphanages and foster homes, etc., and treated with respect in the society at large; there was a refusal by the government to institute a public education campaign for the benefit of these children to counteract the ill-will against these children found in some segments of Norwegian society; a refusal to arrange for vocational training for the mothers so that they could provide for themselves and their children; and a refusal to remove the barriers to gaining financial assistance due to the children's paternity; all of which were recommended by the War Children's Committee in 1945 in order to protect this highly vulnerable group of children and their mothers). Even after the statutorily sanctioned discrimination against war children ended; discrimination persisted with little if any State protection provided to the war children.

(c) ***Norway's defense of the failure to take special protective measures for the war children and their mothers (at least in the period 1945–1950) as being in this group's best interests is unconvincing especially when coupled with the presence of discriminatory legislation in respect of this group in the same period***: It is as ironic as it is cynical that the government in the Thiemann case argued that it was determined by the Norwegian government of the day in the immediate post WWII period that it was *in the war children's best interest* not to institute a public education program and protective measures for the children and their mothers. The European Court of Human Rights summarized the government's position in this regard thus:

> The Government had been of the opinion that it would be more beneficial for the war children to fit into society *without special attention* being drawn to them through such a campaign. This assessment had been strengthened by the fact that the children were quite quickly absorbed into society. *Consequently, on the basis of the relevant knowledge at the time, the Government did not initiate an information campaign. It was not deemed necessary in the interest of either the children or their mothers to take special protective measures.* Thus, the decisions taken had not been based upon neglect of the children or even limited resources. On the contrary, *the Government's focus had been the interest of the war children and whether or not special measures,* including an information campaign, had been necessary to protect them.[129]

The attempt here by the Norwegian government appears to be one of sidestepping the accusation that the war children had been treated as separate and apart from other children in not being provided with the State protections and advocacy to which they were entitled. Note that in order to have an equal chance at

[129] *Thiemann and Others v. Norway* (Application 18712/03), European Court of Human Rights Decision regarding admissibility, Heard 8 March 2007. http://www.menschenrechte.ac.at/orig/07_4/Thiermann.pdf. Accessed 2 July 2009 (under The Law, discussion of the government's position).

a good life; sometimes individuals or groups of individuals are entitled to unequal treatment (special measures) to counteract certain disadvantages that they face at the outset for various reasons such as did the war children. The government went on to claim that the Norwegian war children had begun to integrate rapidly and well into Norwegian society obviating the need for the public education campaign. However, the 2004 research reports on Norwegian war children and their poor adjustment on average in later life as assessed on a variety of measures (i.e. income level, mental and physical health status, disability status, suicide rate, stability of family life, etc.) compared to a control reference group suggests that the respondent government's claims in this regard are inaccurate.

(d) ***Norway's recognition in contemporary times of the persistent need to provide more effective remedies for the Norwegian war children***: In addition, note that it was not until 2000 that an apology to the war children was issued by the then Prime Minister of Norway on behalf of the government (past and present) for the systemic adverse discriminatory treatment Norwegian war children had received in post WW II Norway. Further, the ex gratia compensation system was still being revised in 2005 and accepting applications from Norwegian war children on additional grounds (bullying) all of which demonstrates that the society was still coming to terms with the consequences of the government's treatment of the war children which had originated in events that occurred many decades previous in post WW II Norway. It is clear from these latter facts that the government of Norway itself recognized that justice had even in the millennium eluded these war child victims of systemic discrimination.

10. **The ex gratia compensation system for war children in Norway:** Note also that the ex gratia compensation system that the Norwegian government had put in place involved no time bar for war child applicants or any other. The ex gratia system in 2005 added a bullying ground and provided compensation of 20,000 NOK (in 2005) specifically for a bullying claim based on a *personal statement alone*. The latter sum works out to approximately 2,200 EUR at current rates. The ex gratia compensation system also allowed up to 200,000 NOK total compensation for various types of very significant other maltreatment. The applicant under the guidelines in respect of these other serious injury claims had to prove his or her case on the basis of probability (making out a "sufficiently probable" case to use the European Court of Human Rights description of the ex gratia criteria in respect of these latter claims) and establish individual damages; though the standards for proof were more relaxed and the type of acceptable evidence broader than the normal legal standards require. Some of the latter claims concerned damages due to such serious or even criminal harms as rape and other forms of sexual abuse; inadequate schooling; wrongful placement in institutions such as psychiatric institutions, placement in unsuitable or abusive foster homes, and other forms of abuse sometimes rising to the level of inhuman or degrading treatment.

The sum of 200,000 NOK, as mentioned, works out to about 22,000 Euros at current rates. These compensation sums, however, *could not address the applicant's desire for public legal declarations as to the Norwegian government's violation of certain European Conventions* which infringements arose due to the treatment of the Lebensborn war children in Post-World War II Norway. Further, the sums to be awarded were fairly nominal given the long-lasting and significant harms suffered by war children and their mothers essentially marginalized from the rest of Norwegian society. Most of these children were, furthermore, born out of wedlock and living with their ostracized single mothers in Norway with inadequate supports. Hence, the ex gratia compensation system was *not* an effective remedy in the eyes of the Thiemann applicants.

Further, there was no guarantee that an appeal for increased compensation through the ex gratia compensation system (which increase would have had to have been approved by the Norwegian Parliament) would have been successful and, even if it was, that there would be any meaningful increase in compensation awarded. The amount of compensation awarded through the ex gratia system to Norwegian war children treated as 'aliens in their own land' in post WW II Norway is likely a fraction of what potentially could have been awarded through the courts had the case not been ruled inadmissible by the Norwegian Courts (and the European Court of Human Rights).

11. **The European Court of Human Rights in Thiemann did *not* defer to Norwegian legislation setting up a relaxed standard of proof (in the ex gratia compensation system) regarding the grant of reparations to Norwegian war children**: The European Court of Human Rights describes the Norwegian ex gratia compensation in its Theimann judgment as follows:

> ***Even if an individual war child cannot prove that he/she fulfils the legal criteria for obtaining damages from an individual or the State, he/she can apply for ex gratia compensation (billighetserstatning)*** from the State with respect to injury suffered, either due to the acts or omissions of public authorities or for instance criminal acts by individuals. This is meant to be the last resort to obtain damages when a person has suffered harm or distress. *It is sufficient that the application describes the circumstances that form the basis for the claim*, and *if possible* document these with for instance a doctor's or psychologist's certificate, testimony from family, friends or others that have knowledge of the applicant's situation, etc. ***In particular if the events occurred quite some time back, as would be the case in relation to many war children, there are no strict requirements as to the evidence for the acts/omissions that form the basis for the claim***. Furthermore, the relevant Ministry has an obligation to look into and examine the case. ***The arrangement of ex gratia compensation is not subject to any statutes of limitation*** (**emphasis added**).[130]

Note further, that: (i) the standard of proof to be met by the war children under the ex gratia system, even before 2005, was one of "reasonableness" or "sufficient probability" and (ii) it was not required for an award that the identity of the wrongdoer be known or proved:

> *Whether the claim for compensation is granted is based on a test of reasonableness*. It is in particular relevant if the public authorities can be blamed for the harm. It is sufficient that a

[130] *Thiemann and Others v. Norway* (Application 18712/03), European Court of Human Rights Decision regarding admissibility, Heard 8 March 2007. http://www.menschenrechte.ac.at/orig/07_4/Thiermann.pdf. Accessed 2 July 2009, under "Recent Research on War Children" (discussion about the ex gratia compensation system).

public body is to blame; *the identification of the wrongdoer among the public officials is not a condition*. The amount of compensation awarded *ex-gratia* is based on an assessment of reasonableness.[131]

Instead of applying the same more relaxed standard of proof and eliminating the time bar as did the Norwegian government in the war children's case (i.e. in considering *ex gratia compensation* claims by Norwegian war children), the European Court of Human Rights (ECHR) held, *by insisting on direct compelling documentary proof* relating to individual cases, etc., and *upholding a time limitation*, that the applicants had not proven that they were individually victimized as war children and that their case was, in any event, inadmissible for failure to exhaust domestic remedies.

The Norwegian government itself as reflected in: (i) the original iteration of the ex gratia system (i.e. which did not require identification of the wrongdoer or documentary evidence where this was not reasonably available) and (ii) in the revisions to the ex gratia compensation system in 2005 (i.e. *the addition of the bullying ground and the requirement only for a credible personal statement rather than some sort of proof of individual harm suffered*) did *not* think it just to impose upon war child victims the normal legal standards required for a successful compensation claim through the Norwegian courts This is significant in that the government of Norway with its own archives of materials on the treatment it accorded the war children was ideally positioned to assess what would be the just resolution and mechanism of resolution for these victims.

12. **The very existence of Norway's ex gratia system demonstrates that Norway, in actuality, regarded the Lebensborn war children's claims to be something other than ordinary compensation claims**: It appears that Norway was prepared to acknowledge that war children were entitled to compensation if they could make out a reasonable case and that they should not have to endure the hardships of hiring a lawyer and going through an arduous court process. Recall that bullying was added as a ground to the ex gratia compensation system in 2005 where only a credible personal statement was required as proof thus greatly enhancing the chances of a successful claim via the ex gratia compensation system (though compensation on the latter ground was nominal). *Hence, Norway, as evidenced by the ex gratia system and its flexible approach* (*i.e. no time bar and the use of the standard of reasonableness for awarding reparations for certain serious types of abuse of war children, etc.*) *regarded these claims as in a class of their own rather than as ordinary personal injury claims.*

Recall that an ex gratia compensation system admits of no legal liability but offers the compensation gratuitously. This is something which any State rarely offers and may, in some sense, be regarded as a *de facto* out-of-court settlement

---

[131]*Thiemann and Others v. Norway* (Application 18712/03), European Court of Human Rights Decision regarding admissibility, Heard 8 March 2007. http://www.menschenrechte.ac.at/orig/07_4/Thiermann.pdf. Accessed 2 July 2009, under "Recent Research on War Children" (discussion about the ex gratia compensation system).

which serves the State's interests. For instance, an ex gratia compensation system may serve to facilitate reconciliation while also avoiding for the State the risks of an expensive court process where the outcome is not certain, and where that outcome may in fact be a court-ordered settlement of much greater magnitude than the ex gratia system provides. Consider in this regard that the first group of seven Lebensborn applicants in Thiemann represented but a test case and there were many others who had essentially the same complaint.

However, the Norwegian government took the opposite approach in Thiemann in arguing before the European Court of Human Rights. Norway argued to the European Court of Human Rights that: (i) the war child applicants had to meet a high legal standard (as in a normal civil suit through the courts) in proving individual harms and contended further that (ii) the case was, in any event, inadmissible due to the applicants' alleged failure to exhaust domestic remedies given the Norwegian courts' ruling of inadmissibility due to the time bar. These arguments were raised despite the fact that: (i) the European Court of Human Rights is a specialized court concerned with providing remedies for fundamental human rights violations relating to European Convention rights guarantees and (ii) there was no argument that Lebesnborn war children as a group had suffered insult to their human dignity given some of the actions and inaction of certain Norwegian governments in post WW II Norway. It appears then that Norway preferred to deal with this particular shameful past in regards to war children in-house rather than run the risk of bearing the stigma of having the European Court of Human Rights declare that certain Convention violations had and/or were still occurring in respect of the Lebensborn war children.

13. **The European Court of Human Rights was arguably selective and arbitrary in the manner in which it applied the 'principle of margin of appreciation' in *Theimann***: The Norwegian Courts approached the Thiemann case as an historical oddity involving past government policy decisions which were not properly before the court, and compensation claims that it anticipated could not be proved, i.e. The Oslo City Court (as cited by the European Court of Human Rights in its Thiemann admissibility decision) stated that "... it would be best for all the parties involved to leave these issues to historians and politicians, not lawyers."[132] It may be argued then that, to some degree at least, the Norwegian court decisions in Thiemann may have been a foregone conclusion based on two arguably incorrect inter-related assumptions: (a) that the case was an ordinary tort action, and (b) that it was time barred.

The European Court of Human Rights had no difficulty in applying a large 'margin of appreciation' in respect of Norway's time limitation statute on civil suits and holding this absolute time bar to be applicable in the Thiemann case (all of which was further grounded on the European Court's deference to the Norwegian Court's treatment of the Thiemann case as an ordinary civil compensation case).

---

[132]Opinion of the Oslo City Court in *Thiemann and Others v. Norway* (Application 18712/03), European Court of Human Rights Decision regarding admissibility, Heard 8 March 2007. http://www.menschenrechte.ac.at/orig/07_4/Thiermann.pdf. Accessed 2 July 2009, p. 10.

However, the European Court of Human Rights would ***not*** *show such deference to the government of Norway's legislated ex gratia compensation system and the implications of its existence and of its handling of war children's claims.* (That ex gratia compensation system was of course separate and apart from the normal civil compensation mechanism available through the courts and access to it was not time barred. In addition, the rules of evidence, as discussed, were much less stringent in the ex gratia compensation system than in the civil courts). *The Norwegian ex gratia compensation system, however, must be considered as central and as part of the larger context of the Theimann case in determining: (i) whether the Thiemann case was in fact an ordinary tort case, or something quite different; (ii) whether a statute of limitations should be applicable if in fact the case was something other than a normal compensation claim, and (iii) whether the normal standard of proof required in an ordinary personal injury civil suit should also be met to make out the war children's case.* However, the European Court of Human Rights essentially treated the information on the ex gratia compensation system as a side note rather than as central to an analysis of whether the Norwegian Courts were correct or incorrect in regarding the Lebensborn war children's case as a personal injury case as any other and subject to the same constraints. There is a hint, however, that the European Court of Human Rights implicitly recognized the implication of treating the Thiemann case as something other than an ordinary tort civil case (i.e. a case alleging massive systemic discrimination of a targeted and identifiable highly vulnerable group of children and their mothers): "There can be no doubt that if a State were to be found liable under the Convention for a large number of people being subjected to such treatment [as described by the Thieman applicants and as reflected in the 2004 research reports on the Norwegian Lebensborn war children], this would constitute a very serious matter."[Apartheid?][133]

14. For the European Court of Human Rights to assess the issues in *Thiemann* while considering the Norwegian ex gratia compensation system as context was relevant even though the seven applicants in Thiemann did not avail themselves of the system. This since, for the reasons explained in note 10 above, the ex gratia system did not provide an effective remedy. (Recall that applicants to the European Court of Human Rights are *not* expected to pursue ineffective remedies in order to attempt to exhaust domestic remedies). It is important also to note that it was not until 2005 that the Norwegian government further relaxed the rules as to standards of proof required for war children to prove harms as war children and added a bullying ground where only a credible personal statement (supported by documents and other evidence if possible) was required as to the injuries suffered. As mentioned the awards under that bullying provision, however, were nominal at best. *This amendment to the ex gratia system, however, points out the fact that the Norwegian government itself recognized that justice demanded an extremely*

---

[133] *Thiemann and Others v. Norway* (Application 18712/03), European Court of Human Rights Decision regarding admissibility, Heard 8 March 2007. http://www.menschenrechte.ac.at/orig/07_4/Thiermann.pdf. Accessed 2 July 2009, under 'Court's Assessment'.

flexible system in assessing the war children's claims. The applicants in Thiemann held that prior to 2005 few (Lebensborn) war children were successful in their compensation claims under the Norwegian ex gratia compensation system even with its relatively relaxed rules

15. **The European Court of Human Rights improperly downplayed evidence of the poor life outcomes for Norwegian war children as relevant to the seven applicants' (the first group's) claims in Thiemann**:

The Thiemann applicants presented evidence of a practice (though not at all material times an 'official' policy in Norway in post-World War II), of discriminatory and harsh treatment of Norwegian war children. *The evidence indicated that the Norwegian government did not provide protection against this maltreatment* (some of this harsh or abusive treatment was accorded the war children by private individuals and some by government employees such as those running State orphanages). *In addition, the evidence showed that the government did not take pro-active steps to prevent the maltreatment.*

Evidence was presented to the European Court of Human Rights in two research reports regarding the discriminatory Norwegian legislation and practice that adversely affected the Norwegian war children in the immediate five years following the war. One report was titled *The State and the War Children, a historic survey of the war children's treatment by the State authorities during the first Post War years* by Mr Lars Borgersrud and a second research report was titled: *War Children's Conditions of Life, a Register Based Survey* by Mr Dag Ellingsen. As to the discriminatory legislative history, recall that there was a 17 August 1945 decree that deprived women who had *married* Germans after 9 April 1940 and their children of their Norwegian citizenship. Most of these women with their children were deported though these deportations had stopped by 12 October 1945. The provisions of the August 1945 decree resurfaced in an Act of 13 December 1946 thus becoming law. That Act was amended 1 January 1949 and provided that Norwegian war children born to German fathers and Norwegian mothers and who had lost their Norwegian citizenship could re-acquire it; though their mothers, even if living in Norway, could not. The new citizenship Act of 1950 repealed these provisions and permitted both mothers and children to regain their Norwegian citizenship (the children either as of right at age 18 or by application to the Norwegian government). The respondent government rationalized the stripping of Norwegian citizenship by telling the Court that other States also had legislation such as the 1946 Act in Norway and stated that:

> After the war it was deemed as offensive to the general sense of justice if Norwegian women, married to Germans, who therefore had become German citizens, should retain their Norwegian citizenship if they still lived in Norway.[134]

[134] *Thiemann and Others v. Norway* (Application 18712/03), European Court of Human Rights Decision regarding admissibility, Heard 8 March 2007. http://www.menschenrechte.ac.at/orig/07_4/Thiermann.pdf. Accessed 2 July 2009, under "Recent Research on War Children" (discussion of the legislative history in Norway regarding war children).

The European Court of Human Rights, however, undermined the import of such evidence by noting that none of the seven applicants from the first group in Thiemann had been deported. However, such evidence of discriminatory legislation goes to the issue of the government's attitude toward Norwegian war children and the poisoning of the climate in the country for these children in Norway which lasted for years to come. After all, it was a *positive obligation* of the Norwegian government to set a tone which would have been conducive to fostering the children's positive well-being and equitable treatment. Note also in this regard the evidence regarding the Norwegian Child Benefit Act adopted on 24 October 1946 which excluded the Lebensborn war children, a situation that continued until the *Bread Winner Insurance Act* and *Advance Payment Act* came into force on 1 April 1958 and allowed the war children who had previously been excluded to then receive the benefits.

The reports also (as described in the Thiemann European Court of Human Rights decision), detailed the fact that there was a significantly higher rate of suicide, physical and mental health problems and disability amongst the Norwegian war children as compared to control groups of the same period. Further, the war children had a lower standard of living as adults, less education and among female war children, a higher divorce rate as compared to the control reference group. Of course the report stated that these facts did not apply to each and every Norwegian war child but rather represented the comparative outcome statistics in relation to non-war children of the time.

That there was significantly higher poverty and there were also health problems which persisted throughout life among Norwegian war children (as compared to a control reference group) was a completely foreseeable consequence of the harms they experienced due to their status as Lebensborn (though other factors may also have played a role). Hence, there was abundant evidence of a discriminatory practice (direct and/or indirect) toward Norwegian war children in post WWII Norway which practice the State itself acknowledged and evidence of which was presented to the European Court of Human Rights in Thiemann. *The European Court of Human Rights, however, undermined the import of this evidence by requiring that the applicants prove that they as individual war children had been harmed.* First, the evidence in the 2004 research reports on Norwegian war children showed that as a group they were overrepresented among those with mental health and physical problems, and poverty as well as other outcomes commonly associated with early trauma and difficult life circumstances growing up. The burden should have been on the government to demonstrate that in fact these applicants were the exception and not the rule in having suffered harms as war children. We will consider the proper procedure in a systemic discrimination case next.

16. **The European Court of Human Rights did not apply a reasonable procedure in assessing the validity of the individual applicant's claims in the context of a systemic discrimination case**: As in the Ireland case here previously discussed, the European Court of Human Rights (ECHR) in *Thiemann* held that proving a practice was not sufficient when individuals or a group of individuals brought forward a claim (i.e. they would have to prove individual damages unlike the situation in inter-State petitions to the European Court of Human Rights where

one State complained of another State's practice allegedly amounting to a Convention violation). Recall that the European Court of Human Rights holds, as was mentioned in our discussion of Ireland, that evidence of a practice means that the State will be held accountable for knowing the practice exists or for the fact that the State should have known but this becomes relevant in Thiemann (according to the ECHR) only if the individual complainants can show personal damages.

It can be argued, however, that the proper procedure in a systemic or practice complaint brought by a group of individuals, as in *Thiemann*, is that the complainants establish a *prima facie case* that there is a practice (whether part of official policy or not) that constitutes a Convention violation or numerous violations and that significantly adversely affects a certain identifiable group of which the complainants are members. *The burden then shifts to the respondent to challenge the evidence* of such an alleged practice and any systemic adverse effects on the identified target group or the individual applicants.[135] *In Thiemann, the government did not provide evidence of the excellent integration of most war children into Norwegian society and their good life outcomes. Indeed, the 2004 research reports presented to the European Court of Human Rights speak to the opposite being the case. Further, there was no question that the adverse treatment the war children received at least in the early post WWII years was based in part on legislated discrimination.* The very existence of the ex gratia compensation system belies the government's contention that those war children who suffered long-term harms as the result of the actions or inaction of the governments of the time were very few. It can also be argued that the standard of proof in demonstrating their individual injuries which the government argued to the European Court of Human Rights (and which the European Court accepted as the proper standard) was much higher than should have been the case in a systemic discrimination case with shifting burdens (and much higher than Norway usually expects under their ex gratia system given the challenges the war children face in accessing the relevant information concerning their personal history).

17. **Summary of the issue regarding the European Court of Human Rights' discretionary approach to the application of the principle of margin of appreciation**: The Theimann case was, furthermore, held to be time barred according to the European Court of Human Rights (ECHR) applying the widest margin of appreciation to the Norwegian statute of limitations. Hence, because the case was time barred according to the Norwegian Courts, the European Court of Human Rights held that the applicants had not exhausted the domestic remedies when they had the chance (before the time bar became operative). This even though war children's compensation claims were *not* time barred under the ex gratia compensation system in Norway, and hence regarded by the Norwegian government (consistent with the contention of the ECHR applicants in Thiemann), as something

[135] Written Comments of Interrights in *Nachova and Others v. Bulgaria* (application 43577/98 and 43579/98), 2 November 2004. http://www.interrights.org/app/webroot/userimages/file/Nachova%20 Written%20comments%202%20November.doc. Accessed 7 July 2009.

other than ordinary tort (personal injury) compensation claims. The ECHR, in contrast, agreed with the Norwegian Courts and relegated the applicants' case to the category of an ordinary tort claim; one that was time barred by the Norwegian statute of limitations on civil claims for personal injury. *It appears then that the European Court of Human Rights (ECHR) application of the principle of margin of appreciation in Thiemann is discretionary and, to a degree at least, arbitrary (i.e. deference to the Norwegian Statute of Limitations but not to the Norwegian ex gratia compensation system and its rules which were designed especially for cases such as those of the war children). It would appear that the ECHR concluded that the applicants had not exhausted domestic remedies as essentially a foregone conclusion based on complete deference to the State's courts on the question of the time bar and whether or not the case was an ordinary tort case.*

The European Court of Human Rights (ECHR) accepted the Norwegian High Court's holding that the applicants could have raised the issue of European Convention violations before the court *in the context of a normal compensation claim under Norway's 1969 Damage Compensation Act which claim would be subject to the limitation period.* This, the Norwegian High Court held, was the case since Norwegian law is presumed to be consistent with international human rights law. These violations then would have been those which occurred from 1953 on. The European Court of Human Rights thus deferred to the State's legislation and the Court's interpretation of the applicable legislation: "In this connection the Court recalls that it is primarily for the national authorities, notably the courts, to resolve problems of interpretation of domestic legislation."[136] However, given that an ex gratia compensation system existed that was intended to address cases such as that of the Lebensborn war children (and would have been available even after the Norwegian court rulings), clearly theirs was not a normal tort action despite the contentions in this regard of the Norwegian courts and the European Court of Human Rights. The European Court of Human Rights, however, deferred to the Norwegian courts' assessment of Thiemann as a normal compensation case to which time limitations were applicable on the contention, as noted, that the Norwegian court's interpretation of Norwegian law must take priority. *However, this relegation of the case to the category of a normal compensation case is not consistent with the Norwegian law which set up the ex gratia system that handles war child claims for compensation as a special category of claim. Hence, the European Court of Human Rights arguably had no basis in law for the deference it showed the Norwegian courts in regarding Theimann as a time barred regular run-of-the-mill tort civil case since Norwegian law itself allows for special treatment of war child cases.* This is an essential point in that it should have impacted the European Court of Human Rights' consideration of whether a time bar was applicable and whether the applicants could be held to have exhausted the domestic

[136] *Thiemann and Others v. Norway* (Application 18712/03), European Court of Human Rights Decision regarding admissibility, Heard 8 March 2007. http://www.menschenrechte.ac.at/orig/07_4/Thiermann.pdf. Accessed 2 July 2009, under "Recent Research on War Children", under subtitle "Court's Assessment".

remedies as well as the court's assessment of what would be considered sufficient evidence of the alleged individual harms suffered.

References

Colandrea V (2007) On the power of the European Court of Human Rights to order specific non-monetary measures: some remarks in light of the Assanidze, Broniowski and Sejdovic cases. Hum Rights Law Rev 7:396–411

de Oliveira Moll L (2003) Case note *Al-Adsani v. United Kingdom*: state immunity and the denial of justice with respect to violations of fundamental human rights. Section IV (4): "The forfeiture of sovereignty approach". Melbourne J Int'l L 4:561–591

Galicki Z (Special Rapporteur) (2006) United Nations General Assembly, Preliminary report on the obligation to extradite or prosecute ("aut dedere aut judicare"). http://daccessdds.un.org/doc/UNDOC/GEN/N06/379/01/PDF/N0637901.pdf?OpenElement. Accessed 26 June 2009

Glueck S (1946) The Nuremberg trial and aggressive war. Harv Law Rev 59:396–456

Greenspan M (1959) The modern law of land warfare. University of California Press, Berkeley

Hall CK (2008) The duty of States Parties to the Convention against Torture to provide procedures permitting victims to recover reparations for torture committed abroad. EJIL 18:921–937

Heintze HJ (2004) On the relationship between human rights law protection and international humanitarian law. Int Rev Red Cross (IRRC) 86:789–814

Higgins R (1982) Asser Institute lectures on international law: certain unresolved aspects of the law of state immunity. Neth Int'l L Rev 29:265–276

Kolb R (1998) The relationship between international humanitarian law and human rights law: a brief history of the 1948 Universal Declaration of Human Rights and the 1949 Geneva Conventions. Int Rev Red Cross (IRRC) 324:409–419

Malinverni G (Judge at the European Court of Human Rights) (2008) Ways and means of strengthening the implementation of the European Convention on Human Rights at [the] national level, 9–10 June 2008, Stockholm Colloquy, p. 1. http://www.echr.coe.int/NR/rdonlyres/A1F9E54E-B257-4C1B-81CA-8A477110B80C/0/StockholmdiscoursMalinverni09 10062008.pdf. Accessed 2 July 2009.

McGregor L (2007) Torture and state immunity. EJIL 18:903–919

Pinzauti G (2008) The European Court of Human Rights' incidental application of international criminal law and humanitarian law: a critical discussion of *Kononov v. Latvia*. J Int'l Crim Just 6:1043–1060

Roth BR (2008) Just short of torture: Abusive treatment and the limits of international criminal justice. J Int'l Crim Just 6:215–239. http://jicj.oxfordjournals.org/cgi/reprint/6/2/215. Accessed 30 June 2009

Schindler D, Toman J (eds) (2004) The law of armed conflicts: a collection of conventions, resolutions and other documents, 4th edn. Nijhoff, Leiden

Spinedi M (2002) State responsibility v. individual responsibility for international crimes: Tertium Non Datur? EJIL 13:895–899

Watts, Sir Arthur (1994) The legal position in international law of heads of states, heads of government and foreign ministers. 247 RdC (1994-III), p. 82

Wirth S (2002) Immunity for core crimes? The ICJ's judgment in the Conga v. Belgium case. EJIL 13:877–893

PART II: The European Court of Human Rights' Reluctance to Classify European Convention Violations as International Crimes Even When Those Violations Likely Constitute 'Genocide' or 'Crimes Against Humanity' in Times of Peace or in Immediate Post-conflict Periods

Abstract Part 2 considers the adverse implications for (a) the protection and advancement of international human rights, and for (b) accountability for international crimes; of the European Court of Human Rights' reticence to acknowledge that certain peacetime violations of the *European Convention on Human Rights* may constitute 'genocide' or 'crimes against humanity'. Cases are considered which include: (a) forced sterilization of Roma women in Czechoslovakia and Slovakia in the 1990s and in the early years of the millennium; (b) deaths and injuries of civilians in post-conflict Kosovo under the civil administration of the United Nations Mission in Kosovo due to the failure of KFOR and/or UNMIK to remove unexploded cluster bombs from the area that they were charged with keeping safe and secure; and (c) lead poisoning of Roma and other minorities (labelled as "gypsies") in Kosovo due to their placement by the United Nations Mission in Kosovo in U.N. highly lead contaminated refugee (IDP) camps.

I. De Facto Abrogation of Potential International Crimes Due to the European Court of Human Rights' Rulings Classifying Such Acts Exclusively as European Convention Human Rights Violations

A. *Introduction*

The cases presented in this part attempt to demonstrate that the European Court of Human Rights' rulings generally frame potential international crimes, (as defined under the Rome Statute), not as what prima facie are likely international crimes, but

S.C. Grover, *The European Court of Human Rights as a Pathway to Impunity for International Crimes*,
DOI 10.1007/978-3-642-10799-3_2, © Springer-Verlag Berlin Heidelberg 2010

rather *exclusively* as violations of the human rights and freedom guarantees of the *European Convention on Human Rights.* Hence, the European Court of Human Rights treats such potential international crimes – the most grave of the fundamental human rights violations – as but ordinary, though often serious, human rights violations. There is generally then no comment from the European Court of Human Rights, even as obiter dictum, about the likelihood that a certain act is an international crime and should be investigated and prosecuted as such if the evidence substantiates that an international crime was likely committed. The silence on this point from the European Court of Human Rights in most such relevant cases occurs despite the fact that the prima facie apparent international crimes at issue (i.e. conspiracy to contribute to, or contributing to attempted genocide, crimes against humanity, war crimes) are considered to be an affront to the conscience and dignity of the international community and to be offences against humanity itself. The question is here then explored as to whether the approach of the European Court of Human Rights in this regard serves to create the erroneous impression that the aforementioned fundamental human rights violations do *not* create sufficient alarm in the international community to warrant prosecution of the individual perpetrators of the apparent international crimes in question, i.e. before the International Criminal Court (ICC), or the domestic courts, or even before foreign courts (under a theory of universal criminal jurisdiction) should all case admissibility requirements be met. The extent of indignation from the international human rights community in response to fundamental human rights violations is, it should be recalled, one criterion amongst several others relied upon by the ICC prosecutor for the purpose of (i) determining the perceived gravity of the international crimes alleged and (ii) in assessing admissibility of the case before the ICC. The cases in this part are divided according to various classifications of international crimes under the ICC statute (the Rome Statute). This then allows for consideration of: (i) whether the facts in each case potentially meet the ICC elements of the crime for the various categories of international crime discussed; and (ii) whether the European Court of Human Rights took note of the potential international crime context of the facts of the case, and of the implications thereof for proper assessment of the case and determination of a just remedy.

II. Forced Sterilization of Roma Women as Part of a Widespread Systemic Discrimination Against, and Persecution of the Roma People: Are the Elements Present for the ICC Crimes of "Genocide by Causing Serious Bodily or Mental Harm" (Article 6(b)); "Genocide by Imposing Measures Intended to Prevent Births" (Article 6(d)) and the Crime Against Humanity of "Enforced Sterilization" (Article 7(1)g-5)?

A. *Overview of the Plight of Roma Women in Contemporary Europe*

Case 1: K.H. and Others v. Slovakia (Application. 32881/04) European Court of Human Rights Chamber Judgment, 28 April 2009

Background to K.H. and Others v. Slovakia Regarding Actions in the Domestic Courts

K.H. and Others v. Slovakia[1] involves a group of eight female applicants to the European Court of Human Rights all of them having Roma ethnic identity and holding Slovakian citizenship. The applicants alleged that they had undergone forced sterilization by agents of the State as the result of discrimination related to their Roma ethnicity. The forced sterilization procedures, they alleged, had occurred *without the applicants' knowledge* while the women were in hospital to deliver their babies which in each case had to be delivered by caesarean. *Several of the women, prior to the delivery, or on discharge from the hospital, had been instructed by hospital personnel to sign certain documents and had done so, but the signature did not, they alleged, reflect informed consent* (i.e. *they contended that they had been and continued to be unsure of what the documents actually stated*). On the contrary, the women maintained that at the time they had no idea what they were signing but went ahead and did sign anyway based on the information they received from hospital personnel regarding why they should sign. The women had all come to realize that since leaving the hospitals in question, they had been unable to conceive again and wondered if they had been the victims of forced sterilization. At that time then the women were uncertain as to exact reproductive status and this caused them great mental distress.

In an effort to discover their reproductive status (i.e. whether they had undergone forced sterilization, and just what medical procedures were performed on them at the hospitals in question), the women attempted to gain effective access to their hospital medical records. The women had given powers of attorney to the Centre for

[1] *KH and Others v. Slovakia* (Application 32881/04), European Court of Human Rights (Chamber, Fourth Section), Judgment of 28 April 2009.

Civil and Human Rights, an NGO working from Kosice, to act on their behalf in attempting to gain access to their hospital medical records. The lawyers from the Centre were authorized by the women to review and photocopy the women's medical records at the women's own financial expense using a portable photocopier from the Centre. Photocopying the material was intended to ensure that the hospital medical records of these women applicants would not be lost or destroyed. Further, the purpose of gathering this material was ultimately to determine the cause of the women's apparent infertility (i.e. by having independent medical experts review the medical records to determine just what procedures the women had been subjected to and whether any of these procedures might have rendered the women infertile). The foregoing was in contemplation of possible civil suits.

The lawyers were unable to obtain authorization from the hospital administrations to consult or photocopy the women's hospital medical records. Furthermore, on 11 October 2002, the Ministry of Health communicated to the legal representatives of the applicants that the Ministry took the position that section 16(6) of the 1994 Slovakian Health Act did *not* permit a patient to authorize another to person consult the patient's medical records on their behalf (with the exception that the legal representative of a minor child; namely the parents or legal guardian, *or* someone appointed as a legal guardian for an adult without legal capacity may consult the medical records of the person for whom they are the legal representative). In other words, the hospitals and the Ministry of Health took the view that the women's lawyers were not 'legally authorized persons' as defined under the 1994 Health Act and hence were not permitted to consult the women's medical records or to photocopy them.

The Presov Hospital Case: Six of the women sued J.A. Reiman University Hospital in Presov ('the Presov Hospital') on 13 January 2003. The women were successful at the Presov District Court in having the court grant them the opportunity via an *interim order to consult their medical records and make handwritten excerpts thereof as well as photocopy* their hospital medical records (all via their legal representatives). Thus, the Presov District Court held that the term legal representative in the 1994 Health Act included persons authorized by any patient to consult the patient's medical records and was not restricted to the legal representatives of minors and others without legal capacity. That decision, however, was *reversed* in part by the Presov Regional Court on 7 July 2003 which ruled that the 1994 Health Act did *not* permit the women to obtain photocopies of these records through their legal representatives. The Court held that the hospital would have to turn over the portions of medical records to competent authorities which they were court-ordered to do in the context of any judicial proceedings (i.e. a civil or criminal case) which materialized. The *final decision* of the Presov District Court entered into force 19 August 2003 and allowed the applicants (through their legal representatives) only to consult their hospital medical records and to make handwritten excerpts of those records but not to photocopy them. The Presov District Court contended that the medical records were owned by the hospital and that allowing the applicants to photocopy them might allow the applicants to abuse the use of these records. The latter decision not to allow the applicants the right to photocopy their own hospital medical records was upheld by the Regional Court of Presov on 17 February 2004. The Presov Regional Court did *not* consider meritorious the applicants' arguments that: (i) their inability to obtain photocopies of their hospital medical records disadvantaged them in terms of hindering their ability to properly determine whether they had a viable basis for a civil suit and/or criminal complaint while the medical institution had such access to the applicant's medical records and that (ii) the denial of the opportunity for the legal representatives to photocopy the medical records on behalf of the applicants resulted in a violation of their right to effective access to the courts for determination of their civil rights (a violation of Article 6(1) of the European Convention on Human Rights).

The applicants appealed to the Constitutional Court on 24 May 2004. The Constitutional Court on 8 December 2004 rejected the first six applicants' appeal in which the applicants had alleged European Convention on Human Rights violations regarding Article 6(1) (right to access the court for determination of civil rights), 8 (right to private and family life) and 14 (right to non-discriminatory treatment) due to the Presov Hospital granting them only restricted access to their hospital medical records.

The Krompanchy Hospital Case: The two remaining applicants brought the same civil suit against the Health Care Centre in Krompachy ('the Krompachy Hospital') on 13 January 2003. The women argued that their European Convention rights respecting Articles 6 (right to access the courts) and 8 (right to private and family life) had been violated due to their being given only restricted access to their medical records. The District Court ordered the Krompachy Hospital to allow the two women to consult their medical records and make handwritten excerpts but denied them the right to photocopy the records based on the same section of the 1994 Health Care Act relied on in the previous case concerning the other six applicants who had filed their case in the Presov courts. On appeal, the Regional Court of Kosice: (i) upheld the lower court ruling regarding the prohibition on photocopying the hospital medical records; and (ii) ruled that there was no evidence that the Hospital had actually denied the two applicants' right of access to their own medial records given that the women's legal representatives had not submitted documents to the hospital regarding their authority to access the files on behalf of their clients. (The latter ruling was made even though *the Hospital had, in any event, stated it would not allow any authorized representative of any of their patients to photocopy medical files.*) The Supreme Court dismissed the appeal on 31 May 2005 as premature and unsubstantiated in that the women had not, through their legal representatives, actually tried to access their records from the Hospital (*even though such access had been routinely denied to the legal representatives of other patients of the hospital based on the 1994 Health Act*).

The two Krompanchy Hospital applicants filed a complaint to the Constitutional Court on 25 June 2004 also alleging violation of European Convention articles 6(1), 8 and 14. Their complaint was dismissed 27 October 2004 as on the same grounds as in the Presov Hospital case.

New Slovakian heath care legislation of 1 January 2005: The amended Health Care Act allowed for photocopying of medical records by an authorized representative of the patient.

Findings of the women's legal representatives after consulting the hospital medical records: Of the first six applicants concerned with the Presov Hospital, the legal representatives discovered that V.D. (the sixth applicant) had been sterilized in 1997 and J.Ce. (the fifth applicant) had undergone a hysterectomy during the caesarean delivery of her baby in 1997. No information on sterilization of the third and fourth applicants could be located in the medical records by the lawyers for the applicants. The notes from the "surgery book" did *not* indicate that the first and second applicants (K.H. and J.H. respectively) had been sterilized. The lawyers informed the Court in July 2005 that they had viewed and made photocopies (in accord with the new legislation) of the medical records of applicant six. The medical records of applicants one, three, four and five had also been accessed but only in March 2005 after several requests even after the domestic court orders granting access. On 22 May 2006, the Director of the Presov Hospital informed the second applicant (J.H.) that she had in fact been sterilized and provided her only with a simple record of the fact of the surgical procedure but claimed that the detailed medical record on her had been lost due to "erroneous manipulation in the past" (to use the European Court of Human Rights description of what was communicated to her lawyer by the Presov Hospital).[2] The Ministry of Health in May 2007 acknowledged that the second applicant's rights under the 2004 Health Care Act had been violated by the hospital's failure to keep her detailed medical records secure.

With regard to the remaining two applicants, their lawyers were finally able to consult and photocopy their clients' medical records on an unspecified date in the first half of 2005.

Procedural History and Outcome of K.H. and Others v. Slovakia Before the European Court of Human Rights

The complaints: The eight applicants complained to the European Court of Human Rights that: (i) *their Article 8 Convention* rights had been violated by the two Hospitals' refusal to allow them expeditious access to their medical records and the Hospitals' refusal for an extended period to allow them to photocopy the records; (ii) *their Article 6(1) Convention right to access the courts* had been violated by the Hospitals' refusal to permit them (through their legal representatives) full access to their personal medical records which put them at a distinct disadvantage in determining the strength of any potential civil suit and in filing a civil suit dependent on unrestricted access to the records including being able to make photocopies that could be examined by independent medical experts; (iii) *their Article 13 right to an*

[2] *KH and Others v. Slovakia* (Application 32881/04), European Court of Human Rights (Chamber, Fourth Section), Admissibility Decision of 9 October 2007, under 4(a) "subsequent developments as regards the records in the Presov Hospital."

effective remedy had been infringed in regards to the Article 6(1) and Article 8 Convention violations and lastly that (iv) *their Article 14 Convention right to non-discriminatory treatment* had been violated by the discriminatory treatment they had received in regards to enjoyment of their Article 6(1) and Article 8 Convention rights due to their sex (gender), race, colour, association with a national minority and ethnicity.

The European Court of Human Rights admissibility decision: The case was ruled: (i) admissible by the Chamber of the European Court of Human Rights as to the alleged violations of Articles 6(1)(access to the court), 8 (right to private and family life) and 13 (right to an effective remedy) *resulting from the failure (until 2005 when a new Heath Care Act came into effect) of the public authorities to allow the applicants (through their legal representatives) to photocopy their medical records*; (ii) inadmissible as to the Article 14 discrimination claim; (iii) inadmissible on the facts on the issue of Convention 6(1) and 8 violations relating to simple access to the files and (iv) inadmissible in regards to the Article 6 (1) Convention right to a fair hearing in the domestic courts proceedings that had already occurred.

The inadmissibility decision on the Convention Article 6(1) fair hearing issue: The European Court of Human Rights Chamber – addressing admissibility with respect to the issue of the right to a fair hearing in the domestic courts (another aspect of the Article 6(1) Convention rights) – contended that: (i) the proceedings in the domestic courts which had already taken place were not clearly for the purpose of receiving redress for any improper medical treatment the applicants may have received at the hospitals in question during their deliveries and thus (ii) that no determination could be made on the fairness of the domestic proceedings:

> *It has not been argued in the present case that the applicants concerned actually initiated proceedings with a view to receiving redress in respect of any shortcomings in their medical treatment. In these circumstances, their complaints about the unfairness of such proceedings* [in the domestic courts] *are hypothetical.* It is not for the Court to speculate about the evidential situation in domestic proceedings which the applicants may envisage introducing or about the outcome of such proceedings (emphasis added).[3]

We will consider in the commentary which follows whether the Chamber erred in ruling inadmissible the question of whether the applicants had received a fair hearing by the domestic courts given the underlying issues in the case that drove the necessity for unrestricted access to the applicants' medical records (including the ability to make photocopies of the records) in the first instance.

The inadmissibility decision on the Convention Article 14 right to non-discriminatory treatment relating to respect for private and family life and access to the courts: The European Court of Human Rights Chamber in its admissibility decision held that the case was inadmissible regarding the claim of discriminatory

[3]*KH and Others v. Slovakia* (Application 32881/04), European Court of Human Rights (Chamber, Fourth Section), Admissibility Decision of 9 October 2007, under "The court's assessment 2(b) right to a fair hearing."

treatment by the hospital staff and in the domestic proceedings with regard to the applicants' enjoyment of their Convention Article 6(1) and Article 8 rights.

The applicants had submitted to the European Court of Human Rights (ECHR) Chamber considering admissibility several studies regarding sterilization practices on Roma women in Europe. Those reports, including a 2003 report authored by the Commissioner of Human Rights of the Council of Europe, suggested that the sterilization practices as performed on Roma women were motivated often as not by ethnic discrimination and intolerance. The ECHR Chamber, however, disregarded this larger social context stating the following:

> The Court first notes that the present case relates to impediments which the applicants complain of having experienced while attempting to have effective access to their medical records through their authorized representatives. It has not been its task to examine the circumstances of the applicants' stay and treatment in the hospitals concerned, several years before the introduction of the present application, an issue which the applicants apparently have not submitted to the ordinary courts and ultimately, the Constitutional Court.[4]

We will consider in the commentary on the case which follows whether in fact the European Court of Human Rights Chamber was duty bound to consider the larger social context of the treatment of Roma women's reproductive health by public authorities in Slovakia given its responsibility to judicially and fairly consider the admissibility of every aspect of the case as presented. We will also consider whether the fact that the legislation applicable at the time – the 1994 Health Act – prohibited access to patient medical files by the authorized legal representative of those patients defeated the claim of discrimination as the prohibition applied to all persons (with the only exception relating to persons without legal capacity who could have their medical files accessed by their legal representative).

Additional holdings of the European Court of Human Rights Chamber considering admissibility: Also note that the European Court held that since the public authorities had not acknowledged the Convention violations or provided redress, the applicants retained their victim status even though they (with the exception of applicant two whose file was "lost") were eventually able to photocopy their medical records. The Court also ruled that the applicants had raised claims with potential merit in relation to allegedly being disadvantaged in any possible civil suit due to their inability to photocopy their medical records and provide these to independent experts (a violation of the access to court right provided for in Convention article 6(1)).

The Court considered that applicant two (J.H.) should seek redress through the domestic courts for the Presov Hospital's mishandling of her file. The Court held that as a consequence of the late discovery that her file had been lost it could not be concluded that the hospital had denied her access to her records but rather that she

[4] *KH and Others v. Slovakia* (Application 32881/04), European Court of Human Rights (Chamber, Fourth Section), Admissibility Decision of 9 October 2007, under "The court's assessment complaint under Article 14 of the Convention."

did not have access for another reason (i.e. the losing of the medical record). Hence, her complaint was dismissed for failure to exhaust domestic remedies. The Court also considered that the sixth applicant (V.D.) who had been able to consult her file in May 2004 before the application to the European Court of Human Rights application of August 2004 did not retain victim status as to the issue of access to her records.

The European Court of Human Rights Judgment on the Merits:

The European Court of Human Rights held that:

(a) **Convention Article 8**: the women's Article 8 Convention right to respect for private and family life had been violated by the hospitals' refusal to grant full access to their medical records as well as the right to photocopy those records. That Convention right, the Court held, entailed certain positive obligations being placed on the State, namely to provide an effective and accessible procedure to the applicants for their obtaining the personal information which the State held about them which the applicants considered relevant in the circumstance. Hence, the European Court of Human Rights (ECHR) held it could *not* agree with the government's reliance on the principle of the State's margin of appreciation i.e. in setting legislative policy and practice in this instance as a basis for the claim that the State had complied with Article 8. The Court found no justifiable reason for the denial to the women's authorized legal representatives of full access to the hospital medical records and of the opportunity to photocopy those records;

(b) **Convention Article 6(1)**: the ECHR held that it was essential for the applicants to obtain photocopies of their file: (i) as some significant portions of the file could not be reproduced otherwise (i.e. medical diagrams, their signature, etc.); (ii) this was important for the applicants' sense of mental and physical integrity and (iii) the photocopies were essential in the applicants being able to determine the strength of any civil claim they might have. For these reasons, the ECHR held that the applicants Convention article 6(1) right to access the court had been violated by the overly restrictive provisions of the 1994 Slovakian Health Act with respect to ability to have one's authorized legal representatives photocopy one's personal hospital medical records.

(c) **Convention Article 13**: The ECHR held that there had been no Convention Article 13 violation in relation to Article 8. The ECHR maintained in this regard that the Article 13 right to a remedy does *not* include the right to challenge before a domestic court a law (such as the 1994 Health Act of Slovakia in regards to certain of its provisions). The ECHR found it unnecessary to determine whether there had been a violation of Article 13 in relation to the rights guaranteed under Convention Article 6(1).

Reparations were awarded in the amount of about 3,500 Euros to each applicant as non-pecuniary damages and about 8,000 Euros jointly to all of the applicants for costs and expenses of bringing the case to the European Court of Human Rights.

B. *Case 1: Commentary on K.H. and Others v. Slovakia*

1. **The importance of the larger social context – the treatment of Roma women's reproductive health and rights in Slovakia – in determining the facts and issues in *K.H. and Others v. Slovakia***: A central issue in *K.H. and Others v. Slovakia* is to what extent this case should have been assessed by the European Court of Human Rights with reference to the larger social context in which the facts occurred; those facts being: (i) the forced sterilization of several of the applicants without their knowledge, and (ii) the denial to the patients (via their authorized legal representative) of full access to their hospital medical records, and of the right to photocopy their hospital medical records (which the applicants wished to access in order to determine whether in fact they had been sterilized, without their knowledge or informed consent, by means of some surgical procedure while in hospital ostensibly only to deliver their babies). It is here respectfully contended that the failure of the European Court of Human Rights to consider the larger social context (especially the treatment of Roma women's reproductive health and health-related human rights generally in Slovakia): (i) distorts the Court's proper understanding, to a degree, of the nature of the issues involved in the case, and (ii) ultimately militates against providing the victims of such a grievous harm as forced sterilization the full measure of justice they deserve.

2. **A potential *systemic pattern of forced sterilization of the Roma women applicants in K.H. and Others* as a factor in their need to access their medical records**: In *K.H. and Others v. Slovakia*, the larger social context of the treatment in Slovakia of Roma people, and of Roma women in particular in regards to their reproductive health and rights, as mentioned, was specifically excluded from consideration by the European Court of Human Rights. It is essential, however, to consider this larger social context as it goes to the heart of what actually occurred in the case. It is *not* just that these women wanted access to routine medical records that may or may not have shown instances of medical neglect, and/or reckless or incompetent medical care or treatment that amounted to what is considered 'medical malpractice' (of varying severity depending on the individual applicant's case). The applicants, instead, wanted access to hospital medical records that could potentially show a systemic pattern of *forced sterilization of Roma women* without the patients' knowledge. Recall that the applicants filed their complaints as a group. Thus, not only could their individual medical records show which, if any, of the particular applicants had been victimized by being subjected to a sterilization procedure without their knowledge or informed consent, but, cumulatively, the records would show if there had been a *systemic pattern* of such abuse at the hospitals in question. If the latter were the case, the gravity of the offences could potentially be of a different order of severity altogether; namely acts that could be considered as intended to contribute to the genocide of the Roma. That is, acts constituting "genocide by causing serious bodily or mental harm" (as defined under Article 6(b) of the Rome Statute); "genocide by imposing measures intended to prevent births" (as defined under Article 6(d) of the Rome Statute) and/or the crime

against humanity of "enforced sterilization" (as defined under Article 7(1)g-5 of the Rome Statute).[5]

The *domestic courts* also essentially *disregarded* this systemic aspect of the forced sterilization of Roma women in the broader Slovakian society and apparently also in regards to the *K.H. and Others* applicants. The domestic courts held that the hospital's denial of adequate access to their medical files had *not* affected the women's European Convention Article 6(1) right (to access the courts and receive a fair hearing in determination of potential civil claims). In fact, however, adequate access to the medical records might have shown a systemic pattern of forced sterilization. Such a demonstration would presumably provide a more solid basis for a high claim for damages. This in that it could then be argued that the women were the targets of *systemic discrimination and ethnic hatred* as Roma, rather than simply being random individual victims of a particular physician's intentional or unintentional mistreatment. Further, the evidence of a systemic pattern would have assisted the women in potentially proving that the forced sterilization was in fact based on intent to do this harm rather than on unintentional medical incompetence. To the extent that the domestic courts did *not* consider the systemic discrimination aspect (evident in the fact that Roma women were being targeted for forced sterilization), the European Court of Human Rights appears to have erred in ruling inadmissible the applicants' claim of a violation of Article 6(1) of the European Convention due to alleged unfair hearings in the domestic courts.

We will consider in a later note whether the elements of various genocidal crimes may have been met in the instant case. (This of course can only be definitively determined after a full criminal investigation.) Note that there is no suggestion here that the aforementioned international crimes, if they did occur, would have been prosecutable before the International Criminal Court (ICC) given that the forced sterilization took place in the late 1990s before the ICC Rome Statute entered into force in Slovakia on 11 April 2002.

3. **Interpreting the unique significance, given the larger social context, of the denial to the applicants' authorized legal representatives of full access to the Roma women's hospital medical records**: If the denial (to the authorized legal representatives of these women) of full access to the women's hospital medical records took place in the context of international crimes, this shades the interpretation of the meaning of the hospital's denial (of unrestricted access to the hospital medical records for these lawyers). If such international crimes as genocide or crimes against humanity were committed (as defined under Rome Statute Articles 6(b), 6(d) and 7(1)g-5 respectively), it would have relevance to the Court's assessment of why the medical records were kept from the authorized legal representatives of these Roma women applicants and to the Court's assessment of what would constitute a full, effective and just remedy in the instant case.

---

[5]*Rome Statute* (enabling statute of the International Criminal Court), entered into force 1 July 2002. http://untreaty.un.org/cod/icc/index.html. Accessed 15 July 2009.

Indeed, the hospital depriving the female Roma victims of forced sterilization of the information that they had in fact been subjected to this 'medical procedure' (i.e. by denying their legal representatives access to the medical records) could potentially be considered itself to be part of the mental harms inflicted as part of one or more of the aforementioned international crimes relating to the attempt to destroy in part or in whole a particular ethnic group (if in fact such crimes occurred). Assuming that the forced sterilizations which occurred in the instant case were part of a wider pattern of like behaviour by physicians and other medical personnel in Slovakia directed at Roma women of child bearing age, (as will be discussed in a later note appears to be the case according to some well-respected NGO and U.N. reports), the refusal of access for the women's lawyers to the Roma women applicants' medical records, (so that they could discover whether or not they had been sterilized), in these circumstances, could also amount to: (i) inhuman or degrading treatment (an Article 3 European Convention of Human Rights violation) and (ii) an act causing great mental harm and suffering (a crime against humanity under Article 7(1)(k) of the Rome Statute given that it was directed toward a particular ethnic group and part of a systemic pattern of such abuse). The financial reparation in such an instance then would presumably reflect the gravity of the entire circumstances of the case and the framing of the denial of adequate access for the women to their medical records as part of a systemic pattern of serious mental and physical abuse that may rise to the level of an international crime.

4. **The implication of the larger social context for determining the issue of an Article 14 European Convention on Human Rights violation pertaining to discrimination**: The European Court of Human Rights in the admissibility decision held that it was restricted to considering only the narrow issues of the applicants' right (via their authorized legal representative) to unrestricted access to their medical records and to photocopy the records. The Court thus declined to consider: (i) the implications for the case of the applicants' status as victims of forced sterilizations, or (ii) the larger Slovakian social context at the time with regard to the occurrence of forced sterilization of Roma women and the fact of their frequently receiving discriminatory substandard medical treatment by health care providers. In fact, however, consideration of the larger social context was essential to determining whether discrimination had occurred with respect to the applicants' enjoyment of their Article 6(1) and Article 8 European Convention rights. If the evidence of forced sterilization of the Roma women applicants in the instant case coincided with: (i) a systemic pattern of disregard for the reproductive and other health rights of Roma women in the broader society, and with (ii) a systemic pattern of forced sterilizations generally in Slovakia in other hospital or medical settings targeting Roma women, then the hospitals in the instant case could more readily be presumed to have participated in this discriminatory practice also (given the occurrence of forced sterilization of at least several of the Roma women applicants). The denial to the applicants in the instant case of unrestricted access to their medical records and its consequences for the applicants' Article 6(1) and 8 Convention rights would thus be intricately tied to discriminatory factors in these circumstances. This in that lack of full access to the medical records and inability to copy

the records (via their authorized legal representative) had a disproportionately greater adverse impact on Roma women (an identifiable group characterized by ethnicity or cultural heritage) as they were the ones being selectively targeted for forced sterilization. Such restricted access to their medical file thus, as discussed, put them at a particular disadvantage (i.e. prevented them from determining whether or not they had been the victim of a forced sterilization). The fact that: (i) a policy (such as the hospital policy not to allow anyone's authorized legal representative to access medical files unless the person represented lacked legal capacity) or (ii) a statutory provision (the provision of the 1994 Health Act prohibiting photocopying of medical records) creates a greater adverse effect on one group than on another is itself discriminatory whether or not the differential impact was intentional or not. In K.H. and Others, the hospital policy, and the 1994 Health Act provisions concerning access to medical records both had such a differentially adverse impact on Roma women who were targeted for forced sterilization and could only confirm their status through full access to their hospital medical records.

Thus, though the hospital policy and the photocopying prohibition clause of the 1994 Health Act appear neutral on their face (i.e. applicable to all patients), they were in fact discriminatory for Roma women in Slovakia at the time of the instant case for the reasons explained. Hence, the European Court of Human Rights ruling that the applicants' complaint regarding an Article 14 Convention violation (discrimination) in regards to their enjoyment of certain Convention rights was inadmissible appears legally insupportable. Note that the U.S. Helsinki Commission has concluded that to date the European Court of Human Rights has not answered the following question: "What threshold must be crossed before the court will actually determine that alleged discrimination takes a case out of the discretion of the States party to the Convention and brings it within the reach of the Court?"[6]

5. **An Article 13 Convention violation in connection with the right to non-discriminatory treatment**: The disproportionately greater adverse impact of the 1994 Health Act in Slovakia upon Roma women would (for the reasons explained in note 4 above) be a sufficient legal basis for allowing the women to make a complaint before the European Court of Human Rights (ECHR) regarding an Article 13 violation of their right to a remedy regarding discrimination (since the domestic courts upheld the statutory prohibition of photocopying of medical records under the 1994 Health Act (until its amendment entered into force in 1005) and this created a disproportionately greater adverse impact for Roma women). However, the ECHR ruled that individual complainants did *not* have the right to challenge a domestic law in relation to Article 13. [Recall that in *Ireland*, previously discussed, the ECHR held that: (i) complaints to the ECHR challenging a domestic practice (associated with a particular set of laws) are permissible only in the context of an inter-State petition and not in relation to individual complaints and (ii) that the rules of exhaustion of domestic remedies are *not* applicable when

[6]Slager (2006).

a State brings a complaint about another State's statutorily authorized or unauthorized practice.] The Convention Article 13 provision, however, does not contain any exclusion clause for individuals challenging domestic law or practice as the source of the rights violation:

> **Article 13 Right to an effective remedy**
> Everyone whose rights and freedoms as set forth in this Convention are violated shall have an effective remedy before a national authority notwithstanding that the violation has been committed by persons acting in an official capacity.[7]

There would appear to be no supportable legal rationale for allowing such challenges to domestic law for inter-State petitions but ruling the same such complaints brought to the ECHR by individuals or groups of individuals inadmissible (even where the greater adverse implications of the domestic law for a particular group are proven prima facie). This would seem to be even more so the case where the alleged Convention violations stemming from the operation of the domestic law (i.e. the 1994 Slovakian Health Act) are widespread and related to other grave European Convention violations (as in the case of Roma women victims of forced sterilization who faced State legislative barriers to full and effective access to their hospital medical records which lack of access caused the women great mental harm by leaving them unsure of their fertility status). Alternatively, if the ECHR is correct – if there is a legal basis to deny Article 13 violations where a domestic law is being challenged through the individual complaints process – then this aspect of the ECHR procedure should be changed. That is, the individual complaints process should be modified to allow for Article 13 Convention claims which relate to a particular domestic statute and its negative consequences for enjoyment of various European Convention rights (where the domestic courts have failed to provide a remedy and have declined to rule some or part of the domestic statute unlawful and inconsistent with European Convention rights).

6. **The issue of whether the 1994 Slovakian Health Act served as a convenient smokescreen for discriminatory treatment of the Roma women applicants**: The legislation at issue in the case, the 1994 Health Act, prohibited photocopying of patient files by anyone. In addition, the hospitals misinterpreted the 1994 Health Act as articulating a prohibition against providing authorized legal representatives of patients access to medical files unless the patients were lacking in legal capacity. It is suggested, however, that the 1994 Health Act may have served, in this instance, as but a convenient smokescreen for blocking access to such medical records as did exist on forced sterilization in respect of the Roma women applicants in K.H. and Others. As a result of this blocked access to their medical records, the women were unable to confirm or disconfirm that they had been the

[7] *European Convention on Human Rights and Fundamental Freedoms* (as amended by Protocol Number 11 and with protocols 1, 4, 6, 7, 12 and 13), entry into force 1 November 1998 (original Convention adopted by the Council of Europe 1950 and entered into force 3 September 1953). http://www.echr.coe.int/NR/rdonlyres/D5CC24A7-DC13-4318-B457-5C9014916D7A/0/EnglishAnglais.pdf. Accessed 17 July 2009.

victims of forced sterilization (until they filed civil suits in the domestic courts and gained access, via their authorized legal representatives, to their medical records as a result of court orders). Note that the hospitals in question in *K.H. and Others* were reluctant to divulge information *quite apart from any perceived legislative restrictions* as evidenced by several uncontested facts; among which are the following: (i) even after the Presov Courts had ordered that access to the medical files be permitted, the Presov hospital was very resistant and it took quite some time before the hospital acquiesced to the court order and permitted the first, third, fourth and fifth applicants access to their medical records (in March 2005) through their legal representatives; (ii) the surgery notes for applicant two did *not* reveal that she had been sterilized and it was not until some time after her legal representative had consulted the surgery notes that she was told by the Director of the Hospital that in fact she had been sterilized. In addition, the hospital notified the second applicant that it had 'lost' her detailed medical records (which is a fact inconsistent with the hospital's purported concern for protecting the security of the medical records, and with its rationale for prohibiting the authorized legal representatives of the Roma women applicants unrestricted access to the women's medical records i.e. for fear, according to the hospital, that the information would be "abused").

The loss of applicant two's detailed medical record is especially disturbing in that it may have contained information on the considerations which went into the decision to perform a forced sterilization procedure on applicant two and whether there was any discriminatory element involved. Given the aforementioned, it would appear, that the denial of full access to the records for the women applicants in *K.H. and Others* by the Presov Hospital was not just a matter of any perceived legislative restrictions since hospital barriers to accessing the records persisted for the women's authorized legal representatives even in the face of court orders to provide that access. (In the case of the Krompanchy Hospital, the two remaining applicants also did not gain access to their medical records until very late in 2005 and though their legal representatives had not immediately filed the authorization papers, it was uncontested that such legal representatives were routinely refused access to their clients' files.)

Note that the European Court of Human Rights in the judgment on the merits could find no basis for the hospitals' contention that the applicants might abuse their own medical record information were they able to photocopy the records (as opposed, for instance, to being forced to make handwritten excerpts while omitting those materials that could not be properly copied in handwriting such as charts or certain other technical materials). The question arises as to whether the hospitals considered such *alleged* 'abuse' of the medical records was more likely where the women could make photocopies of the material and potentially provide the copies to independent experts who could then confirm, based on the contents of the photocopied file materials, whether a forced sterilization had occurred.

> The originals of the records contained information which the applicants considered important from the point of view of their moral and physical integrity. In particular, the applicants feared that they had been subjected to an intervention affecting their reproductive status. The records would convey not only information about any such intervention, but also

> whether the applicants had given consent to it and in what circumstances. A typed or handwritten transcript of the records could not faithfully represent the particular features of the original records bearing, in some cases, the applicants' signatures. With photocopies of the records the applicants would not only be able to establish a basis for civil litigation but also to demonstrate to their families and communities, where appropriate, that their infertility was not a result of any deliberate action on their part.[8]

It appears (*though it is not proven*) that the fact of the forced sterilization having been performed on the Roma women may have been a critical factor in denial of access to the medical records to the women's authorized legal representatives; especially given that the struggle continued for some time even after the hospitals were court-ordered to provide reasonable unrestricted access to the records for the applicants' lawyers. That the aforementioned likely possibility is not proven is due to the fact that such questions were not addressed at any level of the domestic courts and also not at the European Court of Human Rights. This is the situation though the question of intent in the hospitals and the Ministry of Health in Slovakia depriving the women of full access to their hospital medical records is in fact central to an analysis of the issues in the case.

7. **Implications of (i) the pattern of forced sterilization of Roma women in Slovakia generally (at the times relevant in the case), and (ii) in respect of the women applicants in *K.H. and Others* for assessment of the issues in the instant case**: The larger social context demonstrated that there was a pattern of forced sterilization of Roma women in Slovakia.[9,10] In the instant case, V.D. (the sixth applicant) had undergone a forced sterilized in 1997 without her knowledge; J.Ce., the fifth applicant had undergone a hysterectomy during the caesarean delivery of her baby in 1997 it appears without her knowledge or informed consent while J.H. had also been sterilized without her knowledge or informed consent. The surgery book with regards to the first applicant did not indicate that she had been sterilized but this had also been the case for J.H. and it later was revealed that in fact J.H. had been sterilized. J.H. was eventually provided by the Presov hospital with a simple record of the fact that she had been sterilized. Hence, three of the eight applicants in *K.H. and Others* were able to confirm, through the hospital medical records their lawyers had accessed, or through the hospital's revelations via the Director, that they had been subjected to forced sterilization; while the remaining applicants could not find confirmation through the records or otherwise. The fact that the other five women did not have confirmation of being the victims of forced sterilization at the hospitals in question, however, does not completely rule out that possibility. This given the situation with the other three applicants and the apparent absence of detailed medical records in some cases and evidence of lost medical documents in others.

---

[8] *KH and Others v. Slovakia* (Application 32881/04), European Court of Human Rights (Chamber, Fourth Section), Judgment of 28 April 2009, para 39.

[9] European Rights Centre (2006).

[10] Zampas et al. (2003).

In each of the aforementioned cases, the basic fact pattern was the same: (i) all of the women affected (harmed) were Roma; (ii) they had gone to the hospital to deliver their babies; (iii) all had experienced fertility problems since their stay at hospital; (iv) all had to struggle through the courts to gain access to their hospital medical records; and (v) the hospital medical records, or in some cases admissions by the hospital involved, revealed that the reason for at least three of the eight women's infertility (subsequent to leaving the hospital after the birth of their child) was the fact that they had been subjected to forced sterilization without their knowledge. Whether the other applicants were also victims of forced sterilization was not reflected in their medical documents

The 2003 research study report by the European Roma Rights Centre (ERRC) titled *Body and soul: Forced sterilization and other assaults on Roma reproductive freedom in Slovakia* (listed in the references for this part) is based on a fact finding mission conducted between August to October 2002 in Eastern Slovakia. The fact finding involved, in part, interviews of 230 women from 40 Romani settlements in Eastern Slovakia on topics including sterilization practices, treatment by health-care professionals in maternal health-care facilities and access to reproductive health-care information. Also interviewed on the same topics were Slovak hospital directors, doctors, nurses, patients, government officials, activists, and non-governmental organizations. The interviews were conducted by persons with expertise in the area of women's human rights and health care who were affiliated with various highly respected independent human rights NGOs working jointly on this research.

The *Body and Soul* 2003 ERRC report findings were that of:

1. Coerced and forced sterilization
2. Misinformation in reproductive health matters
3. Racially discriminatory access to health-care resources and treatment
4. Physical and verbal abuse by medical providers
5. Denial of access to medical records[11]

The finding of such widespread or systemic violation of a targeted ethnic group's reproductive rights appears to satisfy the required elements of the crime under Article 7(1)g-5 of the Rome Statute articulating the "crime against humanity" of enforced sterilization. Further, recall the fact that there had been a long history of persecution against the Roma including: (i) forced sterilization under the Nazis and (ii) legislation and programs that mandated forced sterilization of Roma under the communist Czech regime when that was in place.[12] This latter fact appears to suggest that the occurrence in more contemporary times of forced sterilization of Roma women in Slovakia (as relates also to the women applicants of K.H. and Others) was an unofficial continuation of former such systemic practices aimed at the destruction, in whole or in part, of the Roma population. These latter facts then

[11]European Rights Centre (2006, executive summary, p. 13).

[12]European Rights Centre (2006, executive summary, p. 13).

meet the elements of the crime of genocide as defined under Articles 6(b) and 6(d) of the Rome Statute:

> *The Slovak government claims these programs were dismantled following the fall of communism in 1989. However, our fact-finding reveals that serious human rights violations continue despite the official change in the most obviously problematic law.* Indeed, our fact-finding clearly indicates that discrimination against Romani women remains deeply and disturbingly entrenched in Slovak society. Government officials and health-care providers today openly condone attitudes and practices that violate the bodily integrity, health rights and human dignity of Romani women in need of reproductive health-care services. Romani women are particularly vulnerable to multiple forms of discrimination because they bear the double burden of both race and gender stereotypes (emphasis added).[13]

The occurrence of the aforementioned forced sterilization and the historical context then was also the larger context of the denial of adequate access to the Roma women's medical records (and, as discussed, the greater adverse impact on this group in regards to denial of such proper access). The refusal of the European Court of Human Rights thus to find an Article 13 Convention violation in respect of the Roma women's article 6(1) and (8) rights under the European Convention on Human Rights in *K.H. and Others* would appear to be insupportable given the unique significance of the statutory block to proper access to medical records in the case of the Roma women (i.e. as members of a targeted ethnic population whose reproductive rights had historically been violated as somewhat a matter of routine and where this systemic abuse appeared to be ongoing) (recall that the constitutional court in Slovakia also had dismissed the Roma women applicants' challenge to the 1994 Health Act bar against their authorized legal representatives photocopying the women's hospital medical records). The European Court of Human Rights, it is here contended, was duty bound as an international human rights court, and the court of last resort for a civil remedy for these applicants, to: (i) take note of the larger social context of forced sterilization and it implications in the instant case, (ii) provide a remedy for the Article 13 Convention violations which, it is here suggested, did occur, for instance, in relation to European Convention Article 14 given the disproportionate impact of the 1994 Slovakian Health Act on this particular ethnic group and the lack of a civil remedy through the domestic courts (given the domestic courts' ruling to uphold the alleged legitimacy of the 1994 Health Act prohibition on photocopying ones own personal medical records), (iii) award higher non-pecuniary damages than were awarded given this unique context of forced sterilization as part of an ongoing historical pattern victimizing Roma women which included also harming them mentally by the refusal to provide proper access to medical records and adequate and accurate medical records which might confirm or disconfirm their sterilization, and (iv) advise the State to properly investigate the forced sterilizations and take any and all proper civil and criminal law measures to ensure that the women received justice (given that there is no time bar in respect of consideration of international crimes such as forced sterilization).

[13]European Rights Centre (2006, executive summary, p. 14).

In regard to the issue of criminal prosecution of individual perpetrators for the crime of forced sterilization (committed as part of a systemic crime against a particular or distinct cultural/ethnic group such as the Roma) recall that Slovakia had declared on 28 May 1993 that it would be bound by the terms of the *United Nations Convention on the Prevention and Punishment of the Crime of Genocide*.[14]

Note, in any event, that in other European Court of Human Rights cases, such as *Cahal v. United Kingdom* where Article 3 European Convention rights had been, or might be violated, the European Court of Human Rights held that ensuring the State provided as effective a remedy as can be in light of various State-imposed constraints (i.e. based on important State interests and concerns, statutory restrictions, etc.) may ***not*** be sufficient to create compliance with the requirements of Article 13 of the European Court of Human Rights:

> ... given the irreversible nature of the harm that might occur if the risk of ill-treatment materialised and *the importance the Court attaches to Article 3 (art. 3), the notion of an effective remedy under Article 13 (art. 13) requires independent scrutiny of the claim that there exist substantial grounds for fearing a real risk of treatment contrary to Article 3 (art. 3)* (emphasis added).[15]

In the instant case, there were Article 3 European Convention violations regarding access to the medical records relating to the forced sterilizations that had occurred several years prior to the women's civil suits. The State blocking access to the applicants' lawyers regarding the women's hospital medical records in this circumstance (such that the women would not have the opportunity of possibly confirming, through the medical records, whether or not they had been sterilized) constituted further mental harms under the Article 6(b) Rome Statute definition of genocide. The severe mental harms and anguish associated with the issue of having delivered a baby in hospital and possibly having undergone forced sterilization while hospitalized for delivery of a baby and inability to confirm this through the medical records (due to lack of access to the records or their insufficiency), might lead other Roma women not even to attempt to receive adequate pre and postnatal hospital or other medical care, proper maternity and delivery services or perhaps even encourage many Roma women to avoid pregnancy altogether; all of which could endanger the reproductive capacity in the Roma population in Slovakia. The context of Article 3 European Convention violations (inhuman or degrading treatment) in the instant case could not then properly be ignored by the ECHR on the view presented here, and should have led to the finding in *K.H. and Others* of Article 13 violations in regards to the European Convention rights guaranteed under

---

[14]*United Nations Convention on the Prevention and Punishment of the Crime of Genocide*, Approved and proposed for signature and ratification or accession by General Assembly resolution 260A(III) of 9 December 1948, entry into force 12 January 1951, in accordance with article XIII. http://www.unhchr.ch/html/menu3/b/p_genoci.htm. Accessed 19 July 2009.

[15]*Cahal v. United Kingdom*, European Court of Human Rights Chamber judgment (Case 70/1995/576/662), 15 November 1996. http://cmiskp.echr.coe.int/tkp197/view.asp?action=html&documentId=695881&portal=hbkm&source=externalbydocnumber&table=F69A27FD8FB86142BF01C1166DEA398649. Accessed 17 July 2009.

Article 6(1), 8 and Article 14. It is noteworthy that nowhere in the European Court of Human Rights admissibility decision or judgment on the merits in *K.H. and Others* does the court make reference to the pattern of systemic forced sterilization of women in Slovakia in the post-Communist era as possibly being the informal continuation of a practice of genocide that was legislated by the State in previous times.

8. **The cases pertaining to access to medical records were brought before the courts years after the women were subjected to the forced sterilization procedures in hospital but yet the quality of care and treatment they had received in hospital was highly probative to the issues in the medical records cases**: The apparent pattern of forced sterilization – though it occurred for the women applicants in *K.H. and Others* several years before the application to the domestic courts and to the European Court of Human Rights regarding access to their hospital medical records – was still highly relevant to the issues in the instant access to medical records case. Recall that a pattern of forced sterilization of a particular ethnic group – such as, for instance, Roma women – to the extent that it meets the elements for genocide or a crime against humanity is not time barred in terms of its relevance in determining criminal law remedies. That the cases concerning access to medical records were brought several years after the applicants' hospital stay is quite understandable and related to the very nature of the alleged victimization the women had endured. It took several years trying to conceive before the women came to realize that they may have been forcibly subjected to some sort of sterilization procedure while at the hospital to deliver their babies. This then would account for their sudden inability to conceive over the last number of years since their hospital stay. In any case, the time for filing a civil suit would likely not begin to toll until the women realized that they may have been harmed at the hospital which realization did not occur for a number of years.

9. **Inconsistency in the European Court of Human Rights consideration of the larger social context in determining the proper holding in a case**: It is important to note that in fact the European Court of Human Rights is quite inconsistent when it comes to the issue of considering the larger social context. For instance, in the case of *D.H. and Others v. Czechoslovakia*,[16] the conditions for Roma in Czechoslovakia generally were intentionally omitted from consideration by the *Chamber* in assessing the merits of the case. However, the *Grand Chamber* did in fact consider the larger social context in determining the merits of the appeal case leading a dissenting justice to make the following comment:

> 4. The approach:
> After noting the concerns of various organisations about the realities of the Roma's situation, the Chamber stated: "The Court points out... it is not its task to assess the overall social context. Its sole task in the instant case is to examine the individual applications..." (at paragraph 45).

---

[16]*DH and Others v. Czechoslovakia* (application 57325/00), Grand Chamber judgment, 13 November 2007. http://www.asil.org/pdfs/ilib071214.pdf. Accessed 17 July 2009.

> 5. Yet the Grand Chamber does the exact opposite... the entire judgment is devoted to assessing the overall social context... Thus, to cite but one example, the Court states at the start of paragraph 182: "The Court notes that as a result of their turbulent history and constant uprooting the Roma have become a specific type of disadvantaged and vulnerable minority". Is it the Court's role to be doing this?[17]

Clearly, it is the current author's view that a proper assessment of the facts and the law in ECHR cases in which a discriminatory context is present requires careful consideration of the historical and contemporary larger social context affecting the targeted group. (The answer to Judge Borrego Borrego's question: "Is it the Court's role to be doing this?" – on the view expressed here – is 'Yes'.) Any arbitrary or discretionary decision by the Court as to whether or not to consider the larger social context – especially in relation to European Convention Article 2 and 3 grave violations – would appear to undermine the correctness and legitimacy (for the applicants and the respondents) of the European Court of Human Rights' decision and/or judgment; at least in certain respects (i.e. a dismissal of potentially viable Article 13 Convention complaints among others).

10. **U.N. Committee on the Elimination of Racial Discrimination (CERD) conclusions and recommendations on the issue of forced sterilization of Roma women in the Czech Republic**: Note that the U.N. Committee on the Elimination of Racial Discrimination (CERD) in March 2007 concluded (based on various reports and a review of the Czech Republic sixth and seventh reports) that coerced sterilization of Roma women had been occurring in the State as late at least as 2004; though not part of official policy. The Committee found that the State had not adequately acknowledged the harms done to Roma women in the State both before and after 1991 due to forced sterilization, and had not taken strong enough measures to prevent the practice. CERD stated in its conclusion:

> The State Party should take strong action, without further delay, to acknowledge the harm done to victims [of forced sterilization]... It should take all necessary steps to facilitate victims' access to justice and reparation, *including through the establishment of criminal responsibilities* and the creation of a fund to assist victims in bringing their claims....[18]

Clearly, the CERD was forthright in the need for State accountability regarding forced sterilization. The CERD mentioned the duty of the State to prosecute individual perpetrators; something the European Court of Human Rights to date has not done in such cases as have been before it i.e. from former Czech Federation States such as the now independent Slovakia. The CERD also stipulated in its conclusions a positive obligation on the State to provide adequate reparations and financial and other assistance to help these often impoverished Roma victims of forced sterilization with filing civil claims. To date the European Court of Human Rights, in contrast, has not made an order regarding systemic remedies in cases of forced sterilization such as those brought by Roma women.

---

[17] *DH and Others v. Czechoslovakia* (application 57325/00), Dissenting opinion of Judge Borrego Borrego (translation) at para 4 and 5 of the dissenting opinion.

[18] CERD/C/CZE/CO/7, para 14.

C. *Other Cases of Interest Regarding Forced Sterilization of Roma Women*

Case 2: V.C. v. Slovakia (Application 18968/07) European Court of Human Rights Chamber Admissibility Decision 16 June 2009

There is, at the time of writing, a case of forced sterilization of a Roma woman of Slovakian nationality (V.C., born in 1980) which is pending before the European Court of Human Rights (ECHR) for a judgment on the merits. The case was ruled admissible by the European Court of Human Rights in a decision dated 16 June 2009 (*V.C. v. Slovakia*, application 18968/07).[19] V.C. had been sterilized 23 August 2000 while in Presov Hospital where she was having a caesarean section to deliver her second child. Her first child had also been delivered by caesarean. (Note that Presov Hospital was at the time under the management of the Ministry of Health.)

V.C. alleges that she underwent a forced sterilization via tubal ligation; that is, sterilization without her informed consent. When the caesarean section was *imminent* and she was having severe labour pains, V.C. was asked to sign a consent form for sterilization. The applicant maintains that she did not know what the term 'sterilization' meant and that she had been told by the medical personnel that she would die if she had more children after this second child. The applicant's position is that she signed the consent form while in the stage of advanced labour and suffering great pain such that her cognitive abilities at the time were impaired. Further, she maintained that at the time she believed (based on what she understood of what the medical personnel had explained to her while she was in a state of advanced labour) that in addition to the C-section, the physicians were going to perform a procedure that was 'life saving'. That is; that they would perform a procedure which would prevent her from dying during the delivery of a third and any subsequent children. V.C. contended that she did not understand that tubal ligation is not a life – saving procedure but rather sterilization and that she had told the medical personnel, when asked if she wanted more children that she did want more. According to the applicant, that conversation took place just before she signed the consent.

V.C. submitted to the ECHR that she had suffered significant psychiatric symptoms (an hysterical pregnancy in which she displayed all the outward signs of pregnancy though she was infertile) due to her resultant infertility; that she had been ostracized by the Roma community due to her inability to conceive and that her husband had left her several times due to her infertility.

After the release of the Body and Soul report in January 2003, the applicant said she realized that she had been misled by the medical personnel at the hospital who

[19] *V.C. v. Slovakia* (application 18968/07), European Court of Human Rights Chamber admissibility decision, 16 June 2009. http://cmiskp.echr.coe.int/tkp197/view.asp?item=69&portal=hbkm&action=html&highlight=slovakia&sessionid=26869279&skin=hudoc-en. Accessed 20 July 2009.

had told her that the procedure (tubal ligation) was life saving surgery. She was only able to get access to her hospital medical file in May 2004 after receiving a judicial order that required she be provided such access through her lawyer.

Her complaint was dismissed at all levels of the domestic civil courts as it was at the Slovakian Constitutional Court (the latter court is responsible for the protection of the constitutional and European Convention rights of the individual). While the court of first instance (the Presov District Court) agreed that V.C. had signed the consent form just before the C-section (in an unsteady hand while in a "lying position" and that she had signed with her maiden name; incorrectly dividing the name into two words), they held the procedure and the consent to be lawful (decision of 28 February 2006). Note that the District Court held, almost *as if* this were a mitigating factor, that the sterilization procedure performed on V.C. was not irreversible as she still had the option of in vitro fertilization. The District Court also held that the fact that V.C.'s sterilization procedure had not been approved by a sterilization committee first; created only an infringement of formal administrative rules and that it allegedly did *not* constitute a violation of V.C.'s substantive rights under the *European Convention on Human Rights*. The Presov Regional Court (the appeal level), upheld the lower court's ruling maintaining that the procedure had been medically indicated (allegedly necessary due to the risk of rupture of the uterus); that the applicant had allegedly been duly informed of the need for sterilization and that she allegedly provided informed consent (decision of 25 October 2006). The appeal court also held that prior approval by a sterilization committee was not necessary in V.C.'s case as her reproductive organs were allegedly not healthy and that the determination that sterilization was medically necessary in such a case lay with the head physician. The applicant appealed to the Constitutional Court alleging that: (i) she had been subjected to violations of her fundamental constitutional rights via discrimination and cruel, inhuman or degrading treatment, as well as a violation of her right to protection of her private and family life and her right to family as well as (ii) violations of the European Convention Articles 3, 8, 12, 13 and 14. The Constitutional Court dismissed her complaint as "manifestly ill-founded" (decision of 14 February 2008). The Constitutional Court held that the domestic courts were only bound to uphold the procedural guarantees of the Constitution and those provided under international law to which Slovakia was a party and that therefore the lower courts could not be held liable for any violation of the applicant's substantive rights under Articles 3, 8, and 12. The Constitutional Court held it purportedly lacked jurisdiction to examine alleged errors of fact or law made by the domestic courts and hence could not rule on the Article 13 Convention claim regarding lack of an effective remedy.

V.C. as an applicant to the European Court of Human Rights alleged violations of the *European Convention of Human Rights* Articles 3 (right to be protected from inhuman or degrading treatment), 8 (right to respect for private and family life), 12 (right to found a family), and 14 (right to protection from discrimination). The case was ruled admissible and is pending.

D. *Case 2: Commentary on V.C. v. Slovakia*

1. **The Slovakian Constitutional Court and its erroneous attempt to dissociate procedural from substantive rights in the forced sterilization cases**: Consider the fact that in *V.C v. Slovakia*, the Constitutional Court declined to consider V.C.s contention that the Regional Court and the lower courts by declining to offer her redress had violated her substantive human rights under Article 3, 8, 12, 13 and 14 of the Convention. The Constitutional Court held that it could consider her case only if she alleged an Article 6(1) European Convention violation in relation to the other Convention rights. In other words an alleged procedural defect (Article 6(1) infringement to a fair trial of her civil claims) in the manner in which the ordinary civil courts had dealt with her complaint of Article 3, 8, 12, 13 and 14 violations. The Constitutional Court held that otherwise it would be considering whether the regional and lower courts had themselves violated the applicant's substantive rather than procedural European Convention rights. The European Court of Human Rights Chamber in its admissibility decision, however pointed out that Article 3 and 8 of the Convention encompass both substantive and procedural rights guarantees and that the applicant was not obligated to allege a violation of Article 6(1) in order to have her case heard by the Constitutional Court. (One can also consider whether, in actuality, in order to decide if domestic court rulings are constitutional; issues of fact and law are integral to such determinations contrary to the claims of the Slovakian court regarding the jurisdictional constraints under which it operates.)

2. **Inadequate criminal investigations into the systemic pattern of forced sterilizations of Roma Women in Slovakia**: V.C. did *not* initiate any individual criminal proceedings. However, the Office for Human Rights and Minorities of the Government of Slovakia initiated criminal investigations of other such alleged cases of forced sterilizations in January 2003. The latter was in response to the Centre for Reproductive Rights' and the Centre for Civil and Human Rights' release of their report *Body and soul: Forced sterilization and other assaults on Roma reproductive freedom.*[20] Note that the Office for Human Rights and Minorities of the Government of Slovakia, however, also issued a press release dated 28 January 2003 threatening to start criminal proceedings against the authors of the *Body and Soul* report under the Slovak Criminal Code for either: (i) failure to inform law enforcement authorities of criminal activities (if the findings of the *Body and Soul* report were found by the criminal investigators to be true) or alternatively (ii) "spreading of false rumours and creating panic in society." (if the alleged findings of fact in the *Body and Soul* report were found to be false). The threats, regarding criminal prosecutions of the *Body and Soul* authors were ultimately never acted upon.[21] The fact that: (i) such threats could be officially and publically made

---

[20]Zampas et al. (2003).

[21]Joint statement of Amnesty International (London, U.K.), Centre for Reproductive Rights (New York, U.S.A.), European Roma Rights Centre (Budapest, Hungary), Human Rights Watch (New York, U.S.A.), International Helsinki Federation for Human Rights (Vienna, Austria),

by agents of the government against Roma human rights defenders (who had a right under international law to report on their findings of human rights violations and to advocate on behalf of vulnerable groups such as the Roma) and that (ii) the threats were not acted upon would seem to suggest that the government was not loathe to attempt to undermine the credibility and integrity of these human rights advocates with threats of criminal prosecutions that were not viable in the first instance. This speaks to the societal reluctance in Slovakia, (as in most European countries where such is occurring), to: (i) deal forthrightly and vigorously with the issue of a pattern of forced sterilization of Roma women which has occurred in the very recent past (and which, in some instances, may still be occurring), in that country, and (ii) to acknowledge and address the possibility that such forced sterilizations may amount to the crime of genocide or crimes against humanity given the surrounding facts of the post 1991 Slovakian forced sterilizations.

It is noted by the European Court of Human Rights Chamber in *V.C. v. Slovakia* that the criminal proceedings regarding the alleged forced sterilization of several Roma women in Slovakia (not V.C.) were discontinued on the contention that no offence had been committed (this after also a decision on the matter by the Constitutional Court).[22] Notwithstanding the need not to prejudge the aforementioned criminal cases which were discontinued, it is important, at the same time, to acknowledge the fact that the criminal investigations may not have been adequate. In this regard note that 'The European Commission Against Racism and Intolerance' (ECRI), (in its periodic report on Slovakia of 26 May 2009, fourth monitoring cycle), stated the following in regards to the recent Slovakian criminal investigations of the alleged forced sterilization of Roma women:

> ECRI notes with concern that the problems as regards investigations into allegations of sterilizations of Roma women without their full and informed consent noted in its third report remained. *The authorities continued to investigate these allegations under the **crime of genocide** rather than, for example, under the crimes of assault or of inflicting grievous bodily harm. The angle under which these allegations were investigated thus rendered proof of a crime having been committed virtually impossible and the possibility for redress through the courts almost null.* The investigations also continued to focus on the issue of consent forms being signed rather than on whether full prior information was provided. Due to these flaws, in most cases, the courts decided that the allegations were unproven. ECRI wishes to stress that at the very least, the authorities should secure legal aid to victims so that they can seek compensation through civil law... ECRI regrets that due to the above-mentioned problems in the investigations of allegations of sterilisations of Roma women without their full and informed consent, no redress has been possible for the majority of women involved.[23]

Consortium 'Let's Do It, People Against Racism', Centre for Civil and Human Rights, Slovak Helsinki Committee on the forced sterilization of Romani women in Slovakia (2003). Press release of the European Roma Rights Centre, 22 July 2003. http://www.errc.org/cikk.phpcikk=326.

[22]Romea Press Release (2009).

[23]*V.C. v. Slovakia* (application 18968/07), European Court of Human Rights Chamber admissibility decision, 16 June 2009, citation of paras. 111and 113 of the ECRI report on Slovakia, under D. in the admissibility decision subtitled "The ECRI Report on Slovakia". http://cmiskp.echr.coe.int/tkp197/view.asp?item=69&portal=hbkm&action=html&highlight=slovakia&sessionid=26869279&skin=hudoc-en. Accessed 20 July 2009.

It is quite remarkable, and telling that the European Commission Against Racism and Intolerance (ECRI) essentially implies in the quote above that prosecutions of the perpetrators of forced sterilization of Roma women (part of an apparent systemic pattern of such abuse) will be successful only if the cases are framed as "crimes of assault" or of inflicting "grievous bodily harm" as opposed to cases of 'genocide'. That is, the Commission is not denying that the cases may in fact meet the criteria for genocide, but rather suggesting that a downgrading of the crime to a simple, or alternatively an aggravated assault is a precondition for any chance of prosecutorial success in the domestic courts. The ECRI maintains that this is because the proof is not sufficient for a claim of genocide. While the chances for prosecutorial success may indeed be less in the domestic courts if genocide is the exclusive claim (as opposed to also lesser and included offences regarding simple or aggravated bodily assault) this is not in itself support for the notion that a genocide claim is insupportable in principle in the Roma forced sterilization cases. It is here contended, in contrast, that several available, methodologically sound research reports by credible independent NGOs which are based on first hand fact finding missions (i.e. "Body and Soul" report produced by the Centre for Reproductive Rights) provide ample evidence of a systemic pattern of forced sterilization of Roma women which appears on its face to meet the criteria for genocide. Note also, in this regard, the following factors correlated with the contemporary forced sterilizations of Roma women in Slovakia and in the Czech Republic (according to NGO and Council of Europe reports, etc.) that appear consistent with the crime of genocide or at the very least the crime against humanity of enforced sterilization and speak to the issue of intent:

(i) **Roma women treated with disdain and in a humiliating and degrading fashion while in hospital to deliver their babies**: Most, if not all Roma women victims of alleged forced sterilization allege, as did V.C., that they were placed in a special hospital "Gypsy room" for the delivery, and that they were not permitted to share toilet facilities with non-gypsy patients. (The hospital disputed this claim.) Most, if not all, Roma women victims of alleged forced sterilization further claim that: (a) they were asked about their Roma identity by the medical personnel while in hospital and (b) discouraged from having more children via various arguments presented by the hospital medical personnel while they, the patients, were in the throes of advanced labour and in great pain and that (c) the information they were given was more often than not factually/medically incorrect and/or did not reveal the infertility implications of the procedure additional to the C-section about to be performed (i.e. V.C. alleges that she was told that the procedure which was to be performed on her – in addition to the C-section – was life saving; while in fact tubal ligation is *not* intrinsically a life saving procedure, and, as V.C. argued to the European Court of Human Rights, had tubal ligation in fact been life saving in her specific case, her signing the consent form or providing oral consent would not have been required). In fact during domestic civil proceedings in V.C.'s case, the doctor who performed the sterilization on V.C. conceded that the sterilization had not been life saving in her case;

(ii) **Roma women facing discrimination in contemporary Slovakian society at large** in respect to medical services, housing, employment, education of their children and virtually all other areas of life;

(iii) **The disproportionately high rate of sterilization of women belonging to the Roma ethnic/cultural group (compared to their percentage makeup in the Slovakian population as a whole), and the fact that the majority of complainants in Slovakia and the Czech Republic regarding forced sterilization are Roma rather than non-Roma women**: The disproportionately higher rate of complaints regarding forced sterilization in Slovakia coming from Roma women as opposed to non-Roma women is probative. It is probative given the fact that this long persecuted ethnic/cultural group (the Roma) places an extremely high value on fertility, and that the complainants wanted to have more than one or two children. This is not surprising given that the Roma are traditionally an oppressed group that in the past, historians agree, has been subjected to genocide. Recall, regarding the issue of the premium the Roma place on fertility, the fact that V.C, as many other Roma women who have been sterilized after having one or two children, reported being ostracized by the Roma community due to her infertility. This marginalization of the Roma woman by her community is likely to occur, it appears, where the community, most often incorrectly, perceives the woman's sterilization as having been voluntary, or perceives the woman's infertility as something inherent to her genetic makeup (i.e. the latter perception occurring, for instance, if the sterilization information has not been shared by the woman with her local Roma community). Thus, the fact that a particular ethnic/cultural group that places such a high value on fertility should have comparatively high rates of sterilization complaints (high considering the percentage of the larger population that the ethnic group comprises) is consistent with the likelihood that the sterilization was in fact forced (i.e. a sterilization involving: (i) coercion; such as threats or misinformation designed to encourage the women to undergo the sterilization, and/or (ii) lack of informed consent);

(iv) **The consistency in the reported circumstances in which the alleged forced sterilization or hysterectomy took place; namely, *in the context of receiving a caesarean section for delivery*** compared to the rate amongst non-Roma women in Slovakia of forced sterilization complaints where the sterilization is alleged to have occurred during a caesarean section;

(v) **The contemporary and historical evidence of a systemic pattern of sterilization of Roma women in Slovakia** (a former State member of the Czech Federation where the latter had had a system of State-sponsored sterilization of Roma women): The sterilization State sponsored legislative scheme of the former communist Czechoslovakia provides a context for the more contemporary Roma forced sterilization phenomenon now occurring as an informal but yet systemic practice in Slovakia. V.C. presented evidence that in Presov District, 60% of the sterilization operations performed from

1986–1987 were on Roma women though they made up only 7% of the population in the District. She also presented a 1983 study revealing that 26% of sterilized women in Eastern Slovakia (where V.C. resides) were Roma and that by 1987 this figure had risen to 36.6%.[24] That this pattern had not dissipated after 1989 was evidence by various NGO reports and the findings of the Council of Europe Human Rights Commissioner as well as the European Commission Against Racism and Intolerance (ECRI) 2009 report on Slovakia.[25]

3. **Evidence of a contemporary systemic pattern of Roma women in Slovakia and the Czech Republic undergoing forced sterilization during a caesarean**: It appears from independent NGO, European Council and U.N. human rights committee reports that even in contemporary times: (i) The incidence of forced sterilization complaints is much higher for Roma than non-Roma women and there is evidence regarding forced sterilization at disproportionately higher rates for Roma women (including minors) compared to non-Roma women at some or many Slovakian hospitals, (ii) there is a disproportionately higher incidence for Roma women (including minors) as compared to non-Roma women of consent forms not signed at all, or signed during times of great stress, or without proper and accurate information provided in a reasonable period before the procedure to allow for informed consent, or signed under duress caused by providing the woman with medical misinformation and of sterilizations occurring without the prior approval of a sterilization committee (i.e. it is uncontested that in *V.C. v. Slovakia*, the complainant was asked to sign the consent while she was in advanced labour and just about to have a C-section just as is so commonly reported in most Roma forced sterilization cases according to various human rights NGOs).[26] The aforementioned factors are consistent with forced sterilization.

---

[24]*V.C. v. Slovakia* (application 18968/07), European Court of Human Rights Chamber admissibility decision, 16 June 2009, under point 7 "Accounts of sterilization practices in Slovakia". http://cmiskp.echr.coe.int/tkp197/view.asp?item=69&portal=hbkm&action=html&highlight=slovakia&sessionid=26869279&skin=hudoc-en. Accessed 20 July 2009.

[25]European Commission Against Racism and Intolerance (ECRI) 2009 report on Slovakia cited in *V.C. v. Slovakia* (application 18968/07), European Court of Human Rights Chamber admissibility decision, 16 June 2009, under point C "The ECRI report on Slovakia". http://cmiskp.echr.coe.int/tkp197/view.asp?item=69&portal=hbkm&action=html&highlight=slovakia&sessionid=26869279&skin=hudoc-en. Accessed 20 July 2009.

[26]The League of Human Rights in the Czech Republic (2007). Shadow report to the Committee on the Elimination of Racial Discrimination for the Czech Republic, under "Coerced and unlawful sterilizations of Romani women", 19–27. http://www2.ohchr.org/english/bodies/cerd/docs/ngos/liga.pdf. *See also* Comments to the Fourth Periodic Report of the Slovak Republic on performance of the obligations arising from The Convention on the Elimination of All Forms of Discrimination Against Women Submitted to the Committee on Elimination Against Women for its 41st session June–July 2008 by the Centre for Civil and Human Rights, May 2008. http://www2.ohchr.org/english/bodies/cedaw/docs/ngos/CFIDH_Slovakia_41.pdf. Accessed 24 July 2009.

The government submitted to the European Court of Human Rights in *V.C. v. Slovakia*, however, that that its expert advisory group had reported that Roma women in Slovakia actually had a lower rate of caesarean section and sterilization than did non-Roma women. If the hospital records did not reflect high rates of sterilization and C-sections of Roma women, the question arises as to whether or not the hospital records upon which the expert committee primarily relied were accurate (i.e. recall that in *K.H. and others v. Slovakia*, previously discussed, not all of the instances of forced sterilization of Roma women which the hospitals concerned finally acknowledged were in fact found to have been recorded in the patients' detailed hospital medical records or in the surgery notes). The question also arises as to why most of those women alleging that they had been subjected to a forced sterilization during a C-section in Slovakia and the Czech Republic were Roma rather than non-Roma (i.e. see the League of Human Rights 2007 Shadow Report to the U.N. Committee on the Elimination of Racial Discrimination [CERD] (for the Czech Republic)).[27] Note that the Czech Ombudsman's report – in response to complaints from a victims' group formed in 2005 to advocate for the basic human rights of Romani women ("The Group of Women Harmed by Sterilization") – indicated that medical files revealed that doctors and social workers throughout the Czech Republic tended to recommend caesareans to Romani women. The report concluded that this was apparently done "to manufacture 'indicators,' through which sterilisation would appear necessary and legitimate." Hence, the Ombudsman's report reveals, in effect, that ironically the alleged 'best interests' of the victims (Roma women) was being used as a rationale for various fundamental human rights abuses as not uncommonly occurs in other factually diverse human rights violation cases. If such was occurring in the Czech Republic, it is not unlikely that the same factors underlie the over-representation of Slovakian Roma women complaining of forced sterilizations having occurred during their caesareans.[28]

It is noteworthy that the Slovakian government – sponsored expert advisory group (their independence open for debate) also concluded that "no genocide or segregation of the Roma population had occurred".[29] Note that the government struck expert group relied on government (i.e. Ministry of Health) documents for rates on sterilization and C-sections and that the expert group stated that there were

[27]The League of Human Rights in the Czech Republic (2007). Shadow report to the Committee on the Elimination of Racial Discrimination for the Czech Republic, point 5.23, p. 21. http://www2.ohchr.org/english/bodies/cerd/docs/ngos/liga.pdf.

[28]The League of Human Rights in the Czech Republic (2007). Shadow report to the Committee on the Elimination of Racial Discrimination for the Czech Republic, point 5.29, p. 2. http://www2.ohchr.org/english/bodies/cerd/docs/ngos/liga.pdf.

[29]Conclusions of the Slovakian expert group investigating allegations of forced sterilizations of Roma women in hospital as paraphrased by the European Court of Human Rights in its 16 June 2009, admissibility decision in *V.C. v. Slovakia* (application 18968/07), under point 7(b) Accounts of Sterilization Practices in Slovakia: Information submitted by the respondent government. http://cmiskp.echr.coe.int/tkp197/view.asp?item=69&portal=hbkm&action=html&highlight=slovakia&sessionid=26869279&skin=hudoc-en. Accessed 20 July 2009.

no *official* statistics on the ethnicity of the patients available upon which the group could rely in compiling its report.

4. **The Council of Europe Commissioner of Human Rights' 29 March 2006 report on Slovakian Roma women and their forced sterilization post 1991**: In response to the report of the Council of Europe Commissioner of Human Rights' of 29 March 2006[30] confirming a pattern of forced sterilization of Roma women; especially in Eastern Slovakia post 1991, the Slovakian government introduced a number of legislative measures which included the following provisions among others; effective and full access to their own medical records and further: (i) a guaranteed right of informed consent; (ii) a requirement that patients be given adequate information about the sterilization procedure and its ramifications before undergoing the procedure, and as a precondition to assumptions being made that informed consent had in fact been given and (iii) a thirty day waiting period *after* informed consent is given; a "cooling off" period if you will, allowing sufficient time for the woman to consider and reconsider her sterilization decision and change her mind to abandon the planned sterilization if she wishes. Recall that in *V.C. v. Slovakia*, the medical records reveal that there was no approval for the sterilization by a sterilization committee and that V.C. was sterilized a number of hours after entering hospital on the same day while undergoing a caesarean section and after signing a consent form when the C-section operation was imminent.

Note, however, that the above mentioned legislative changes go to the heart of minimum ethical medical practice and would have been part of the ethical requirements applicable to the hospitals and medical personnel providing maternity and delivery services to these Roma women at the outset (i.e. under International law and international ethical guidelines for medical practice such as the European Convention on Human Rights and Biomedicine [ECHRB]).[31] There is then no justifiable excuse for a lower standard of care (amounting as discussed possibly to a violation of fundamental human rights) having been provided before these legislative changes were introduced.

The facts of these cases prima facie appear to meet certain of the key elements of the Rome Statute crime of genocide. Of course, the knowledge and intent of the accused, as well as his or her specific actions or inaction, are further issues to be considered in regards to whether the crime of genocide has actually been committed by *a particular i*ndividual perpetrator. However, recall also that in a case before the European Court of Human Rights, there is no individual perpetrator or group of perpetrators against whom the complainant has filed the action. Rather, in the

---

[30]Council of Europe Commission for Human Rights report, para 32–38, cited in *V.C. v. Slovakia* (application 18968/07), European Court of Human Rights Chamber admissibility decision, 16 June 2009, under "C. The Council of Europe Commission for Human Rights." http://cmiskp.echr.coe.int/tkp197/view.asp?item=69&portal=hbkm&action=html&highlight=slovakia&sessionid=26869279&skin=hudoc-en. Accessed 20 July 2009.

[31]Council of Europe treaty, *European Convention on Human Rights and Biomedicine*, entered into force in Slovakia 1 December 1999. http://conventions.coe.int/Treaty/Commun/QueVoulezVous.asp?NT=164&CL=ENG. Accessed 22 July 2009.

European Court of Human Rights, the respondent is the State. In order to make out a *human rights complaint* against *the State* of, for instance, an Article 2 or 3 European Convention violation that may also amount to genocide or crimes against humanity, the complainant, it would seem, should *not* need to meet the standard of 'beyond a reasonable doubt', but rather a civil law standard of proof (this is a point we will consider here in a later note below).

5. **The reluctance of the domestic courts and the European Court of Human Rights to frame the Roma forced sterilizations cases as instances of genocide**: it is not at all clear why, as the *European Committee Against Racial Intolerance* seems to suggest, it should allegedly be more difficult for Slovakian prosecutors to prove forced sterilization of a Roma woman as part of a systemic pattern of such abuse (genocide) (given that it is agreed by highly respected independent human rights NGOs and U.N. bodies that a systemic pattern of forced sterilization of Roma women persisted, for instance, in Slovakia and the Czech Republic in the post-Communist era[32]), than to prove isolated incidents of forced sterilization unrelated to any systemic pattern. In the latter case, the physician's intent to cause infertility and the patient's lack of informed consent and/or the presence of coercion by hospital medical personnel to obtain compliance must still be proven as would motive related to ethnic prejudice and discrimination. What are the implications then of the Slovakian courts apparently: (i) not being amenable to the possibility of a systemic pattern of forced sterilizations as an indicator of genocide or a crime against humanity perpetrated against these Roma women and (ii) their declining to consider the implications of the same for the society at large (i.e. the need for a public apology for *systemic* abuses (forced sterilizations of Roma women) amounting potentially to international crimes and the need for systemic institutional changes and proper monitoring, a compensation fund for victims, assistance for victims in filing civil and criminal complaints, etc.) and the implications for the alleged perpetrators (i.e. in regards to the probability of the criminal prosecutions perhaps for commission of an international crime, the severity of the criminal law penalties imposed, the probability that substantial civil remedies will be paid by the individual perpetrators and the hospitals involved, etc.)? Consider that even in certain recent cases of forced sterilization of Roma women (i.e. the case of Helena Ferencikova in the Czech Republic), the case was held by the domestic courts (District Court and Appeal level High Court) to be statute-barred in respect of any possibility of the victim receiving financial compensation for the harms caused and the lower domestic courts have ruled that the victims were owed only an apology. Recent Czech Supreme Court jurisprudence in non-sterilization cases in the Czech Republic involving claims for reparations for non-financial harms incurred, in contrast, held that there is no time bar on compensation claims for

[32]Bureau of the Council of Government of the Czech Republic (2007). Report on the Situation of Roma Communities in the Czech Republic (2006). (Under the discussion of the lower court rulings in the case of the Roma woman Helena Ferencikova who was illegally sterilized.) http://www.vlada.cz/assets/ppov/zalezitosti-romske-komunity/aktuality/Report-on-the-situation-of-Roma-Communities-in-the-Czech-Republic-2006.pdf. Accessed 20 July 2009.

certain non-pecuniary damages or losses where there are substantive rights violations. This may increase the chance that the Czech Supreme Court may rule that no time limitation exists in cases of forced sterilization as well though this is of course uncertain until rulings in such cases are issued by that Court. *Of course, no such time bar would exist if forced sterilization cases involving ethnic targeting are considered to be instances of a pattern of systemic abuse amounting to genocide, or a crime against humanity.*

It should be recognized, however, that there is a real State interest in having these cases declared as something *other than* genocide or a crime against humanity given: (i) the gravity of such offences and the stigma in the international community of States which attaches to the State where such international crimes have occurred, and (ii) the victims' concomitant entitlement to substantial reparations from the State for having been the victims of such a grievous crime as forced sterilization as part of a pattern of actions that potentially constitute 'crimes against humanity' targeting the Roma, or as 'genocide', which if not State sponsored, occurred, in part or in whole, due to the State's failure to take the steps necessary to protect this highly vulnerable national ethnic population (which was well known to be high risk for serious victimization of various sorts). In regards to the State's reluctance to admit the possibility of genocide having occurred and/or occurring (i.e. in the form of forced sterilization) the Slovak government's 2005 submission to the U.N. Committee for the Elimination of Discrimination Against Women (CEDW) (in response to a complaint from the Roma Rights Centre) provides a case in point. The Slovak government submission to the CEDW incredulously stated that "medical interventions [i.e., sterilizations] had no influence on the reproductive ability of the Roma ethnic minority."[33] The latter statement appears (in futile fashion) to try to eliminate the possibility of a charge of *genocide* by suggesting that though *individual* Romani women may have undergone forced sterilization, this did not in any way serve to destroy the *Roma population* itself in part or in whole. The Slovak government suggested further that the forced sterilizations involved but procedural (technical) violations of Slovak law involving inadequate procedures for obtaining informed consent and other procedural irregularities rather than actions constituting a form of genocide.[34]

The question arises whether the European Court of Human Rights (ECHR) will demonstrate the same reluctance as did the Slovakian Courts in classifying these

[33]Statement from the Slovak government 2005 submission to the U.N. Committee for the Elimination of Discrimination Against Women in response to the Roma Rights Centre complaint to the Committee regarding forced sterilizations occurring in Slovakia, cited at p. 17 of the 2006 report "Accountability and impunity: Investigations into sterilizations without informed consent in the Czech Republic and Slovakia" prepared by the Commission on Security and Cooperation in Europe (CSCE). The CSCE report available through a link at http://www.america.gov/st/washfile-english/2006/August/200608171045451CJsamohT0.678158.html. Accessed 24 July 2009.

[34]Commission on Security and Cooperation in Europe (CSCE) (2006) Accountability and impunity: Investigations into sterilizations without informed consent in the Czech Republic and Slovakia, under "Illegal Sterilizations Dismissed as Mere 'Procedural Shortcomings'", pp. 13–14.

systemic patterns of forced sterilization of Roma women (in the post-Communist era of an independent Slovakia) as genocide or a crime against humanity (i.e. in *D.H. and Others v. Slovakia*, there is no comment (even additional to the judgment proper) on the forced sterilization of one or more of the applicants perhaps being part of a systemic pattern which constitutes genocide, or of such acts as possible crimes against humanity). Whether in *V.C. v. Slovakia*, where the applicant alleges also an Article 3 European Convention violation (inhuman or degrading treatment), the European Court of Human Rights addresses the issue of whether forced sterilizations of Roma women constitutes genocide (as an integral part of its analysis of the case, findings of fact, and determination of what constitutes just satisfaction in the circumstance) remains to be seen. Consider in this regard that the European Court of Human Rights has traditionally been reluctant to find that violations of Article 3 – inhuman or degrading treatment – have been linked to discrimination based on ethnicity (or on any other ground) as commented upon by Judge Bonello of the European Court of Human Rights offering a partly dissenting opinion in *Anguelova v. Bulgaria* in regards to the Court's rejection of the Article 14 discrimination complaint in relation to the applicant's claim of an Article 3 violation of the right to be protected from torture or inhuman or degrading treatment or punishment:

> *I consider it particularly disturbing that the Court, in over fifty years of pertinacious judicial scrutiny, has not, to date, found one single instance of violation of... the right not to be subjected to... degrading or inhuman treatment or punishment (Article 3) induced by the race, colour or place of origin of the victim.* Leafing through the annals of the Court, an uninformed observer would be justified to conclude that, for over fifty years democratic Europe has been exempted from any suspicion of racism, intolerance or xenophobia. The Europe projected by the Court's case-law is that of an exemplary haven of ethnic fraternity, in which peoples of the most diverse origin coalesce without distress, prejudice or recrimination. The present case energises that *delusion* (emphasis added).
>
> *Frequently and regularly the Court acknowledges that members of vulnerable minorities are deprived of life or subjected to appalling treatment in violation of Article 3; but not once has the Court found that this happens to be linked to their ethnicity.* Kurds, coloureds, Muslims, Roma and others are again and again killed, tortured or maimed, but the Court is not persuaded that their race, colour, nationality or place of origin has anything to do with it. Misfortunes punctually visit disadvantaged minority groups, but only as the result of well-disposed coincidence (emphasis added).[35]

Recall then that the crime of genocide requires the intent to destroy a targeted ethnic or other identifiable group in whole or in part. Unless the European Court of Human Rights recognizes that the systemic pattern of forced sterilization of Roma women in Slovakia or in the Czech Republic in recent years is linked to discrimination against the Roma, the Court will make no finding, and will issue no obiter comments, affirming that the European Convention Article 3 violations in such

[35]*Anguelova v. Bulgaria*, European Court of Human Rights Chamber judgment (Application 38361/97), 13 June 2002, Opinion of Judge Bonello at para 2 and 3 of his partly dissenting opinion. http://www.coe.int/t/dg3/romatravellers/jurisprudence/caselaw/ANGUELOVA_en.asp. Accessed 21 July 2009.

cases are in fact or are likely simultaneously instances of genocide committed against the Roma. If the facts warrant a holding that genocide against the Roma has occurred in the context of a pattern of forced sterilization, let us hope that the European Court of Human Rights will have the courage to suggest that at least prima facie this appears to be the case. While it goes without saying that the European Court of Human Rights is not a criminal court, the fact of genocide or likely genocide having occurred is properly an essential aspect of the Court's finding of fact in forced sterilization cases where there is an occurrence of a systemic and/or widespread pattern of this fundamental human rights abuse targeting a certain ethnic/cultural group such as the Roma. *V.C. v. Slovakia* may answer the question as to whether the European Court of Human Rights declines to comment on the issue of genocide in forced sterilization cases apparently involving discrimination, or mentions it, but minimizes the need for a finding of fact on the issue such as did, according to the League of Human Rights for the Czech Republic, the Ombudsman for the Czech Republic calling any conclusion on the matter "premature":

> . . . despite the examination of extensive evidence, which proves that certain forces conspired in order to compel Romani women to forfeit their ability to give birth through extreme, invasive, coercive sterilisation practices, and furthermore that these were racially motivated considerations, the Ombudsman stopped short of concluding that these issues were racially discriminatory. Apparently, this conclusion remains too controversial. . . .
>
> *The Ombudsman also dismisses the possibility that the crime of genocide may have been perpetrated, believing that although facts in certain areas give rise to relevant concerns, the conclusion may be premature* (emphasis added).[36]

Wherever there is a downgrading of the crime of genocide to ordinary European Convention Article 3 violations (regardless of the fact that the latter are also grievous human rights violations), it compromises the potential prosecution of the crime which actually occurred which is of a different order of gravity and offends all of humanity. Further, if all International Criminal Court admissibility requirements are met (i.e. in cases other than those referred by the U.N. Security Council, admissibility requirements such as the crime having occurred after the entry into force of the Rome Statute in the domestic state, the State being a Party to the Rome Statute, etc.), and the government involved is unwilling or unable to prosecute the crime of genocide, (assuming the crime is one of genocide), then a European Court of Human Rights decision treating the cases as exclusively involving European Convention violations (rather than instances of possible or actual genocide) may improperly mitigate against the possibility of a legitimate prosecution by the International Criminal Court (given that the ICC Prosecutor considers the outrage of the international community about the crime to be one indicator of the gravity of the crime which is in turn one of the prime considerations regarding admissibility). It is essential then for the interests of justice that the European Court of Human

[36]The League of Human Rights in the Czech Republic (2007). Shadow report to the Committee on the Elimination of Racial Discrimination for the Czech Republic, point 5.31–5.32, p. 2. http://www2.ohchr.org/english/bodies/cerd/docs/ngos/liga.pdf.

Rights, where the facts warrant, does not avoid linking article 14, and i.e. Article 2 and/or Article 3 European Convention violations, for fear of invoking the spectre of possible genocide, or crimes against humanity if, in fact, this is the reality of what occurred.

6. **The 'beyond a reasonable doubt' standard of proof used by the European Court of Human Rights introduces arbitrariness and excessive judicial discretion in reaching conclusions in cases brought by individuals or groups of individual complainants**: The European Court of Human Rights elaborates on the Court's application of a 'beyond a reasonable doubt' standard of proof as follows:

> In assessing evidence, the Court adopts the standard of proof "beyond reasonable doubt"... *However, such proof may follow from the co-existence of sufficiently strong, clear and concordant inferences or of similar unrebutted presumptions of fact.* Where the events in issue lie wholly, or in large part, within the exclusive knowledge of the authorities, as in the case of persons within their control in custody, strong presumptions of fact will arise in respect of injuries and death occurring during that detention. Indeed, the burden of proof may be regarded as resting on the authorities to provide a satisfactory and convincing explanation... (emphasis added).[37]

The European Court of Human Rights' interpretive framework for applying the 'beyond a reasonable doubt standard' leaves excessive room for judicial discretion and arbitrariness. For instance, in any particular admissible case, it is largely discretionary whether or not the Court holds that there exists a: "co-existence of sufficiently strong, clear and concordant inferences or of similar unrebutted presumptions of fact" which meets the standard of "beyond a reasonable doubt." There is thus no indication provided by the Court as to what precisely is the European Court of Human Rights' criterion for deciding whether the pattern of inferences that may be drawn from the facts, or the pattern of uncontested facts is sufficiently strong and clear to meet the test for proof 'beyond a reasonable doubt'. Not surprisingly then, in a case such as *Angelova v. Bulgaria*, (involving the death of a 17-year-old Roma boy at the hands of Bulgarian police while in detention), the European Court of Human Rights (ECHR) did *not* find that the European Convention violations (of the Article 2 right to life and Article 3 right to be protected against torture or inhuman or degrading treatment or punishment) guarantees was 'racially motivated' (to use the ECHR's term). This was the Court's conclusion as to discrimination, (*no* violation of the European Convention Article 14 guarantee of non-discriminatory treatment), despite various reports by: (i) the Council of Europe and the United Nations (i.e. The Special Rapporteur on Extrajudicial, Summary or Arbitrary Executions to the United Nations Commission on Human Rights) and (ii) independent international human rights bodies such as Amnesty International all attesting to widespread systemic violation by Bulgarian law enforcement authorities of Roma rights under Articles 2 and 3 of the *European Convention on*

[37] *Anguelova v. Bulgaria*, European Court of Human Rights Chamber judgment (Application 38361/97), 13 June 2002, Opinion of Judge Bonello at para 111. http://www.coe.int/t/dg3/romatravellers/jurisprudence/caselaw/ANGUELOVA_en.asp. Accessed 21 July 2009.

Human Rights.[38] It would appear then that the Court is wittingly or unwittingly reluctant to admit of systemic discrimination claims where these link to European Convention violations that may also constitute international crimes (i.e. systemic police brutality of a targeted ethnic/cultural group, including torture and/or inhuman or degrading treatment and sometimes leading to death of the apprehended individuals as the 'crime against humanity' of 'persecution' as defined under Article 7(1)(h) of the *Rome Statute*[39]).

7. **Implications of the mismatch between the criminal law standard of proof demanded by the ECHR and the civil procedure employed regarding shifting burdens**: The European Court of Human Rights states, (in the above quote from *Anguelova v. Bulgaria*), that where the events in question lie exclusively or largely within the knowledge of the government, and where the injuries or death occurred while the victim was in the custody of the State, then the State must carry the burden to explain what happened and establish why the State should not be considered to have violated i.e. Article 2 and/or 3 of the European Convention (and/or some other Convention Articles) and be held accountable. Note that this shift of burden from the applicant (complainant) to the State is characteristic of a civil case where the applicant, for instance, establishes a claim through a preponderance of the evidence, not to the criminal law standard of 'beyond a reasonable doubt' (The applicant in a civil case first establishes a prima facie case on a preponderance of the evidence and then the burden shifts to the respondent to defeat the applicant's claims, etc.). Hence, the procedure (shift of burden) when employed, and the standard of proof ('beyond a reasonable doubt') that the European Court of Human Rights demands from the applicant, are a mismatch.

Since the applicant is, according to the European Court of Human Rights, expected to meet the standard of proof of 'beyond a reasonable doubt', it would appear that almost any excuse the State provides for the victimization of the complainant would serve to undermine the ability of the applicant to reach the 'beyond a reasonable doubt' standard of proof. This is the case since the State's 'explanation/rationale' may create the *erroneous illusion* of a reasonable doubt in the applicant's *individual* case no matter that the explanation is unlikely given the systemic pattern of abuse (i.e. the pattern of forced sterilization of Roma women occurring during the same time period as did the forced sterilization of V.C.). *To the extent then that the Court undermines systemic evidence of discrimination relating to, for instance, Article 3 violations, the individual applicant is unlikely to be able to defeat* ***any*** *explanation the respondent State proffers save for the most outrageous or implausible*.

It remains to be seen whether in the Roma alleged forced sterilization case of *V.C. v. Slovakia* (the State disputes that the sterilization was forced), the European Court will consider that the State: (i) for a time had exclusive control of the victim's

---

[38] *Anguelova v. Bulgaria*, European Court of Human Rights Chamber judgment (Application 38361/97), 13 June 2002, Partly Dissenting Opinion of Judge Bonello at point 5–6. http://www.coe.int/t/dg3/romatravellers/jurisprudence/caselaw/ANGUELOVA_en.asp. Accessed 21 July 2009.

[39] *Rome Statute* (enabling statute of the International Criminal Court), entered into force 1 July 2002, Article 7(1)(h). http://untreaty.un.org/cod/icc/index.html. Accessed 15 July 2009.

medical records; (ii) has exclusive knowledge of what, in reality, happened to cause medical *mis*information to be provided to V.C. (regarding the erroneous information communicated to her by the hospital medical personnel that tubal ligation was, in her case, a life saving operation) and whether this was related to her Roma ethnicity; and (iii) has exclusive knowledge of what factors, in reality, instigated the decision to obtain a consent from V.C. while she was in advanced labour and about to undergo a C-section, and then to perform a sterilization procedure during her caesarean, and whether these events were a function of her being of Roma ethnicity. If the Court does consider the above factors as a whole as something within the exclusive purview of the State, then, on its own description, the proper procedure is to shift the burden to the State to explain and justify its actions as something other than actions constituting European Convention violations (and require of the State in this regard a genuinely "satisfactory and *convincing* explanation."). Consider also that though V.C. was not detained, she was essentially, in practice, under the custody and control of the hospital and medical personnel during the administration of anesthesia and the performance of the caesarean. This is when the injuries occurred (the alleged 'forced' sterilization occurred during the caesarean while the applicant was anesthetized and had no control or legal capacity). This, too, then should (on the Court's own analysis) place a very heavy burden on the State to justify how and why V.C. lost her fertility due to sterilization during the C-section when, for instance: (i) it is uncontested that she suffered great mental harms and societal marginalization as a result, (ii) it is well known by Roma that being ostracized by that community is foreseeable when one is infertile as a young woman and it is therefore likely that V.C. would not wish to be sterilized, and (iii) it is uncontested that V.C. told the medical personnel in the hospital just before her C-section, when she was asked, that indeed she wanted to have more children after this delivery (though she agreed to what she thought, according to her, was a lifesaving procedure and not one that would cause her to be infertile).

The European Court of Human Rights standard of proof of 'beyond a reasonable doubt' is likely then, it appears: (i) to introduce an unacceptable degree of judicial arbitrariness and discretion into the Court's process for reaching conclusions as to whether or not systemic discrimination relating to violations of various of the European Convention rights such Article 2 and 3 has occurred and hence (ii) undermine the likelihood of the Court making comments or reaching conclusions about whether or not certain international crimes such as, but not limited to, crimes against humanity, persecution, and/or genocide may also have been committed (whether State sponsored or not) and whether this possibility ought to be acknowledged and investigated by the State.

8. ***The European Convention on Human Rights* Article 32 does *not* require proof "beyond a reasonable doubt"; yet the European Court of Human Rights demands just such a standard to establish that ethnic discrimination was the factor underlying other violations of the European Convention**: Judge Bonello in *Anguelova v. Bulgaria* points out that the European Court of Human Rights insistence on a 'beyond a reasonable doubt' standard of proof is *not* based on European *Convention on Human Rights* requirements:

> *Nowhere does the Convention mandate the "proof beyond reasonable doubt" standard today required of the victim to convince the Court that death or ill-treatment were induced by ethnic prejudice. Article 32, on the contrary, gives the Court the widest possible discretion as to the interpretation and the application of the Convention.* What the Convention does mandate is quite the opposite: that its provisions should be given thorough implementation. Any exercise in interpreting the Convention must be geared to "securing the universal and effective recognition and observation" of the guarantees enumerated, unless it is to turn into a betrayal of the spirit and the letter of its momentous preamble.
>
> The Convention has to be applied by the Court in such a way as to guarantee "not rights that are theoretical or illusory, but rights that are practical and effective" [*Artico v. Italy*, judgment of 13 May 1980, Series A (issue 37)]. *No more effective tool could be devised to ensure that the protection against racial discrimination becomes illusory and inoperative than requiring from the victim a standard of proof that, in other civil-law disputes, is required of no one* (emphasis added).
>
> *So long as the Court persists in requiring in human rights disputes a standard of proof that fifty years experience has shown to be as unreal as it is unrealistic and unrealisable, it will, in effect, only continue to pay lip-service to the guarantees it then makes impossible to uphold.*[40]

Judge Bonello holds that: (i) where there are European Convention violations against an ethnic or other minority occurring in a context of widespread and/or systemic discrimination; and/or (ii) where criminal investigations are generally inadequate for such violations, and/or (iii) where State offenders responsible for this ethnic persecution have generally not been prosecuted, the burden in the European Court of Human Rights case should shift to the respondent State to prove that the violations were not due to discrimination.[41]

9. **The lack of justification for the European Court of Human Rights' reliance on the 'beyond a reasonable doubt' standard of proof**: Judge Bonello comments in *Anguelova v. Bulgaria* that the European Court of Human Rights has never explained or justified why it relies on a 'beyond a reasonable doubt' standard of proof. He also notes that "This doctrine [the reliance on a 'beyond a reasonable doubt' standard] only rewards those the Convention would fain not see rewarded" [i.e. by impunity for ethnic persecution].[42]

To recap then; the suggestion is made by the current author that the reliance by the European Court of Human Rights on a 'beyond a reasonable doubt' standard of proof applied to Article 14 European Convention claims (i.e. ethnic/cultural discrimination) in relation to, for instance, violations of the minority's Article 2 (right to life) and/or Article 3 (right to be protected from torture and from inhuman or degrading treatment or punishment) acts, in effect, as a shield against the Court

---

[40] *Anguelova v. Bulgaria*, European Court of Human Rights Chamber judgment (Application 38361/97), 13 June 2002, Partly Dissenting Opinion of Judge Bonello at points 9 and 13 http://www.coe.int/t/dg3/romatravellers/jurisprudence/caselaw/ANGUELOVA_en.asp. Accessed 21 July 2009.

[41] *Anguelova v. Bulgaria*, European Court of Human Rights Chamber judgment (Application 38361/97), 13 June 2002, Partly Dissenting Opinion of Judge Bonello at point 18. http://www.coe.int/t/dg3/romatravellers/jurisprudence/caselaw/ANGUELOVA_en.asp. Accessed 21 July 2009.

[42] *Anguelova v. Bulgaria*, European Court of Human Rights Chamber judgment (Application 38361/97), 13 June 2002, Partly Dissenting Opinion of Judge Bonello at point 10. http://www.coe.int/t/dg3/romatravellers/jurisprudence/caselaw/ANGUELOVA_en.asp. Accessed 21 July 2009.

making findings that support the interpretation that certain international crimes may or likely have been committed (i.e. genocide or crimes against humanity for instance). This since the Article 14 evidence presented by the applicant is generally not considered by the Court to have been sufficient to meet the standard for proving the discrimination (in relation to Article 2 or 3 violations) to the Court-mandated standard of 'beyond a reasonable doubt'. This then helps to: (i) foster impunity for ethnic persecution, and (ii) greatly reduces the likelihood of any follow-up proper criminal investigation by the State of possible international crimes, or (iii) the likelihood of criminal prosecution of perpetrators of any international crime that may have been committed (i.e. prosecution domestically, or by the International Criminal Court even if all ICC admissibility requirements have been met). This as the facts of the case have been artificially downgraded by the European Court of Human Rights (through its reliance on a 'beyond a reasonable doubt' standard) from: (a) facts supporting the occurrence of a possible international crime to (b) facts supporting the occurrence only of certain European Convention violations *unrelated to widespread and/or systemic ethnic discrimination. That is, the gravity of the situation has effectively been undermined due to the applicants' foreseeable inability to meet the European Court of Human Rights criminal law standard of proof in a discrimination case.* The European Court of Human Rights places an impossibly high burden upon the applicant for proving ethnic discrimination through reliance on what Judge Bonello terms a "legally untenable" standard of proof used here *in the context of a human rights as opposed to a criminal judicial proceeding.*[43]

III. A Systemic Pattern of Severe Physical Harm to Roma Living in Lead Contaminated United Nations IDP Refugee Camps in Northern Kosovo: Are the ICC Elements Present for the ICC Crimes of Genocide by Causing Serious Mental or Bodily Harm (Rome Statute Article 6(b)), and the Crimes Against Humanity of Apartheid (Rome Statute Article 7(1)(j)) and Persecution (Rome Statute Article 7(1)(h))?

A. *Introduction*

In the next section, we consider the European Court of Human Rights' refusal to adjudicate on the merits of two cases concerning victims of alleged European Convention human rights violations which occurred due to the action and/or

[43] *Anguelova v. Bulgaria*, European Court of Human Rights Chamber judgment (Application 38361/97), 13 June 2002, Partly Dissenting Opinion of Judge Bonello at point 10. http://www.coe.int/t/dg3/romatravellers/jurisprudence/caselaw/ANGUELOVA_en.asp. Accessed 21 July 2009.

inaction of States *operating under a mandate provided by a United Nations Security Council resolution* authorizing a peacekeeping and a security mission in Kosovo (UNMIK was the U.N. body responsible for the interim civil administration of Kosovo replacing the authorities of the Former Republic of Yugoslavia; while KFOR (a multinational force under State and NATO *operational* command) was responsible for the security mission). The European Court of Human Rights in these cases has either refused at the outset to review the case for alleged lack of jurisdiction (i.e. the 2006 case brought by the Roma Rights Centre against the U.N. Interim Administration Mission in Kosovo (UNMIK) pertaining to the lead contaminated U.N. Northern Kosovo refugee camps),[44] or, in a publicly issued decision, ruled the case inadmissible for alleged lack of jurisdiction (*Behrami and Behrami v. France*)[45] (a case involving death and grievous other injury to children who unwittingly played with an unexploded cluster bomb that it was KFOR's responsibility to clear from the area).

The European Court of Human Rights' claim of lack of jurisdiction in these cases is based on its contention that though the States themselves either acted in a certain manner, and/or failed to act at times, and this is what caused the harms to civilians and violation of their fundamental human rights, these actions and/or inactions were, in the final analysis, ultimately attributable to the United Nations (we will consider the Court's reasoning in detail on this point in the commentary on the instant cases). The Court's conclusion regarding who is the accountable party (i.e. the United Nations) poses an insurmountable difficulty for the complainants in that: (i) the United Nations has absolute immunity against civil suits, and (ii) the European Court of Human Rights' position is that it has jurisdiction only to address those complaints (relating to violations of the European Convention on Human Rights) brought against States, and not those brought against the United Nations, or against any other international organization.

This presumption about attribution of ultimate responsibility to the United Nations (which entity was beyond the reach of the European Court of Human Rights) was *inferred* by the European Court from the fact that UNMIK (the U.N. interim administration mission in Kosovo) and KFOR (Kosovo Security Force under NATO command) were *allegedly* acting lawfully *in all respects* and under the auspices/authority of the United Nations (pursuant to U.N. Security Council resolution 1244). The commentary on the two aforementioned cases will: (i) challenge the European Court of Human Rights' claim of lack of jurisdiction in the two cases, and (ii) provide an argument that rather than being in the position of lack of jurisdiction; the Court instead improperly *declined its jurisdiction* in these cases. The European Court of Human Rights in declining its jurisdiction or, depending on one's perspective, refusing to adjudicate the merits for actual lack of

---

[44]Roma Rights Centre (2007).

[45]*Behrami and Behrami v. France* (Application 71412/01) [heard in conjunction with *Saramati v. France, Germany and Norway* (Application 781/01)], 2 May 2007. European Court of Human Rights, Grand Chamber decision on admissibility. http://hei.unige.ch/~clapham/hrdoc/docs/ECHRBehrami.doc. Accessed 25 July 2009.

jurisdiction in such cases has, according to Justice Arbour, left many unanswered questions, in particular as to what the consequences are – or should be – for acts or omissions "in principle attributable to the U.N."[46] The question, on the analysis here, in respect of such cases is instead: 'When will the European Court of Human Rights cease declining its proper jurisdiction over complaints brought against States (i.e. the cooperating States of UNMIK and KFOR) which – *notwithstanding the fact that they act under the official authority of the United Nations* – have acted through their agents to commit, or have been complicit through various actions or inaction in committing unlawful European Convention fundamental human rights violations?'

It should be noted at the outset that the European Court of Human Rights does *not* in actuality take a clear, unequivocal position on whether or not the actions or inactions of States participating in U.N. peacekeeping (UNMIK) and security missions (KFOR) are attributable to the United Nations not just in principle but in fact. In regard to this point, Justice Arbour notes that in *Behrami and Behrami v. France* that:

> The Grand Chamber unanimously [held] that both in respect of KFOR – an entity exercising lawfully delegated Chapter VII powers of the Security Council – and UNMIK – as a subsidiary organ of the U.N. created under Chapter VII – the impugned acts and failure to act were "***in principle***, attributable to the U.N." *At another point, the Court states that the actions in question were "**directly attributable** to the U.N."* (emphasis added).[47]

This equivocation of the European Court of Human Rights itself on this critical point, (in respect of who is responsible for the European Convention violations in these instances; the U.N. or the individual States that acted or failed to act), reveals also that there is no solid legal basis for the Court's claim of lack of jurisdiction in the above cases as is discussed in detail in what follows. Note that the nature of UNMIK is highly complex. It comprised diverse combined functions such as demilitarization (coordinated with KFOR under NATO command), humanitarian functions such as the return of refugees, civil administration, establishing democratic institutions and the like. UNMIK is headed by the Special Representative of the U.N. Secretary General in Kosovo and four deputy international Special Representatives. In addition, there are several international organizations involved aside from the U.N. (UNHCR; the United Nations High Commission for Refugees involvement ended in June 2001): OSCE (Organization for Security and Cooperation in Europe which includes States from Europe, North America and Central Asia), and the European Union (concerned with economic reconstruction of Kosovo). Hence, individual European States which were a party to the *European Convention on Human Rights* were heavily involved in the administration and operations of UNMIK. The situation involving international governance continued through, for instance, the European Union Rule of Law Mission (ELUX) in Kosovo deployed in 2008 to take over certain UNMIK civil administrative functions (i.e. by

[46]Arbour (2008).

[47]Arbour (2008).

providing policing and judicial services using European Union State resources in this regard).

The discussion which follows is intended to reveal that: (i) the European Court of Human Rights' *de facto* exoneration of the individual cooperating States (involved in the U.N. peacekeeping and security mission in Kosovo) for the human rights abuses in the aforementioned cases is *inconsistent* with established international law on assignment of responsibility for unlawful acts (i.e. violations of fundamental human rights), and that (ii) the United Nations' peace and security mandate does *not* serve as a shield providing immunity against liability (for European Convention on Human Rights violations) to States operating under the U.N.'s authority (the European Court of Human Rights in the aforementioned cases claimed it lacked jurisdiction against individual States given the importance of the U.N.'s security and peace objectives and the Court's concern that its adjudicating such human rights cases as mentioned would interfere with the U.N.'s ability to effectively carry out its international peace and security objectives). The two Kosovo cases; *Behrami and Behrami v. France* and the Roma U.N. lead contaminated refugee camps case are described separately below in respect of their respective facts and procedural background. However, the commentary on both cases is combined as the key issue in both is whether individual States rather than the U.N. can be held accountable when cooperating States are acting under the auspices of the U.N.

B. Case 3: The U.N. Kosovo Lead Contaminated Roma Refugee Camps Case (The 2006 Case Brought by the European Roma Rights Centre Against the United Nations Interim Administration Mission in Kosovo (UNMIK) on Behalf of 184 Residents Living in U.N. Refugee Camps (Near Contaminated Abandoned Lead Smelters and Mines in Northern Kosovo) and the European Court of Human Rights' Decision Declining Review of the Case Based on the Court's Alleged Lack of Jurisdiction Over the Case)

Background and Procedural History of the Case Concerning U.N. Northern Kosovo Lead-Contaminated Refugee Camps Occupied by Roma

Beginning in June 1999, (at the cessation of NATO bombing of the former Yugoslavia and upon the signing of an agreement between Serbia and NATO by which Serbia agreed to withdraw its forces from Kosovo), Roma and other minorities also regarded as "gypsies", were violently expelled by ethnic Albanians from their homes in Kosovo in the context of 'ethnic cleansing'. This forced removal (involving also killings, "disappearances," and other extreme violence against these minorities) was carried out under the *smokescreen* of retaliation against the Serbs and *alleged* Serb collaborators for their international crimes in the Former Yugoslavia. The Roma settlement of Roma Mahalla which had housed about 8,000 Roma was routed and burned by the Albanians while KFOR troops stationed in Mitrovica stood by without intervening to stop the destruction and pillage. About four-fifths of Kosovo's pre-1991 Romani population, roughly 120,000 persons, were forced from their homes and became internally displaced persons. About 600 of these internally displaced persons (IDPs) (Roma, Ashkali, and Egyptian ('RAE')), expelled from communities in South Mitovica (i.e. the 'Roma Mahala' also referred to as 'Fabrika' or 'Mitorvica/Mitrovice Mahala'), were placed by the United Nations in 1999 in IDP refugee camps in Northern Mitrovica which camps posed a significant hazard to their health as the camps were located in most instances on highly lead contaminated land in towns in fairly close proximity to the Trepca Mines factory complex.[48] The IDP camps in question are as follows: (a) the Zitkovac/Zhikoc Camp; operational from 1999 to 2006; (b) *the Cesmin Lug/ Cesminluke Camp; operational in 1999 and still operational to this date*, (c) the Kablare Camp operational from 2001 to 2006; (d) *the Osterode Camp operational from 2006 and currently still operational*; and (e) *the Leposavic/Leposaviq Camp operational from 1999 and at least until 2008*. Zitkovac/Zhikoc, Cesmin Lug/ Cesminluke, and Kablare camps were located within 3 km of the Trepca smelter, and within 300 m of two mine work sites. Leposavic/Leposaviq was built about 45 km from the Trepca mines. Osterode was also dangerously close to the Trepca mines. By 2004, the World Health Organization (WHO) had "declared a health emergency on the camp grounds" and recommended the immediate removal of children and pregnant women from the camps.[49]

The camps for the internally displaced Romani and other minorities were supposed to provide only temporary sanctuary. International pressure from human rights activists, U.N. human rights bodies and various NGOs led UNMIK in 2006 to close two of the Roma lead contaminated IDP camps; namely the camps at Zitkovac and at Kablare, with some of the inhabitants helped to relocate to their original area of residence in Mitrovica, (but with no assistance from the U.N. in re-establishing themselves, many were unable to stay and survive), and some moving to a new temporary camp in Osterode (a former French military base). The Osterode camp is only a short distance away from the Trepca Mines area, and also heavily lead contaminated. The inhabitants of Cesmin Lug camp refused to move to what was supposed to be the "temporary" Osterode IDP camp as the latter camp was in fact not, contrary to the claims of UNMIK, "lead safer". As of June 2009, a decade after the camps were established, about 670 Roma still live in the remaining lead contaminated camps near the abandoned Trepca lead mine complex.[50] This, despite the dire health warnings the World Heath Organization issued as early as 2000

[48]Roma Rights Centre (2006, p. 4).

[49]Roma Rights Centre (2006, p. 7).

[50]Human Rights Watch (2009a).

regarding the foreseeable, and inevitable adverse impact of the extremely lead poisoned camp environments on the health of the inhabitants. That lead poisoning can and has caused irreversible brain damage and stunted growth in some of the camp children according to Human Rights Watch researchers monitoring the camps. In addition, there have been other serious adverse health effects for the refugee children and adults alike due to the chronic exposure to the highly toxic lead poisoned environment. Such prolonged lead exposure can cause kidney failure, and, further, very high levels of lead in the blood can also lead to coma and death. Indeed, there have been deaths in the camp, including of children, according to Roma Rights Reports and some of these are thought by medical experts to be likely due to lead poisoning.[51]

The World Health Organization ('WHO') report in 2000 found that all children, and most adult 'RAE' living in the IDP camps around the Trepca industrial site had lead blood levels much beyond the permissible level, and that the lead blood levels for the Romani were even higher than for the non-Romani population of the camps. In 2004, the WHO declared the IDP camps *uninhabitable* using as evidence, for instance, their finding that the lead concentration in the soil at the Zitkovac camp (now closed) was 100.5 times higher than the recommended levels, while the lead in the soil at the Cesmin Lug camp (still operational) was 359.5 times what was considered safe for human health. According to the European Roma Rights Centre, children in the camps who required urgent medical care due to their high lead blood levels [up to at least February 2006] did *not* receive that care, and, for the most part, pregnant women were not removed from the IDP camps despite pressure from WHO and international advocacy groups such as the German based human rights group "Society for Threatened Peoples." The latter group, in 2005, sent a doctor with expertise in environmental toxin health effects, Dr. Klaus-Dieter Runow, to test for lead poisoning in blood and hair samples to be taken from the persons housed at the Osterode IDP camp.[52] Dr. Runow found extraordinarily high levels of lead in the blood and in the 66 hair samples he collected from the occupants of the camp. He concluded in his report that the Osterode camp inhabitants were suffering from heavy metal poisoning and that their suffering would continue, (notwithstanding any improvement in living conditions at the Osterode camp relative to the other camps), as long as they stayed in the camp. He stressed that detoxification would require removal of the refugees from the camp and could **not** simply be accomplished via on-the-spot medical treatment. (Apparently, treatment, in any case, cannot be safely conducted in a lead contaminated environment.) Hence, the exceedingly small medical staff that tried from February 2006 to provide medical service to the refugees at the Osterode IDP camp could not in fact eliminate the lead poisoning of the refugee victims. This since the camp refugees were being exposed to high levels of lead on an ongoing basis. All doctors who examined the situation agreed that the children especially needed to be treated in hospital but neither

[51]Roma Rights Centre (2006, p. 9).

[52]Roma Rights Centre (2007).

WHO nor UNMIK took the responsibility to bring them to hospital in Belgrade. Dr. Runow found that "the lead values of the refugees [at the Osterode camp] exceeded the reference value by at least 20, [and] in the case of several children the values were 1,200 times the permissible level. Many tests displayed also very high cadmium and arsenic values."[53]

In July 2005, the European Roma Rights Center (ERRC) sent a letter to UN Secretary General Kofi Annan urging him to waive immunity for any U.N. personnel who had violated the human rights of Roma by keeping these refugees in the life-threatening lead contaminated Kosovo IDP camps and failing to relocate them to safe areas. However, there was no such action taken by the Secretary General. Rather, the Under-Secretary-General for Peacekeeping Operations simply responded to the ERRC by requesting more information on the immunity question and suggesting that UNMIK was trying to resolve the lead contaminated refugee camp issue as best it could.[54] In September 2005, a *criminal* complaint was filed by the ERRC with the Kosovo Prosecutor concerning criminal negligence against unspecified perpetrators in allowing the Roma to be exposed to toxic lead levels in the IDP camps, but there was *no investigation* initiated by that office.

According to Human Rights Watch:

> Small-scale testing for lead contamination and... treatment designed to remove lead from blood, carried out by doctors and nurses, took place a few times between 2004 and 2007, focusing on children... *But no comprehensive testing and treatment has ever been carried out. In 2007, the UN Mission (UNMIK) decided to halt treatment, and testing was discontinued after the erroneous conclusion (based on the assumption that the Roma would soon be moved out of the camps) that it was no longer required.* Subsequent testing by the North Mitrovica Hospital, requested by the camp residents, indicated that some children continued to have dangerously high levels of lead in their blood (emphasis added).[55]

The remaining operational Kosovo lead contaminated IDP camps, (which are located in an area which is ethnically Serb), have been under the control of the 'Kosovo Ministries of Communities and Returns' since the May 2008 hand-over of the camps by UNMIK. The IDP camp inhabitants are still left to languish in the remaining operational lead contaminated camps (Cesmin Lug/Cesminluke Camp, Osterode Camp, and Leposavic/Lepsaviq Camp), while those domestic and international bodies that could resolve the situation have failed to do so. It appears that first UNMIK (and the individual cooperating States that comprise UNMIK), and now certain other authorities are, *in practice*, treating the Roma and other so-called 'gypsy' minorities (men, women and children) as if they are expendable and un-entitled to European Convention protections.

[53]Causevic and Singula (2006, p. 3).

[54]Roma Rights Centre (2006, pp. 9–10).

[55]Human Rights Watch (2009a).

Procedural History

The European Roma Rights Centre (ERRC) filed an application to the European Court of Human Rights on 20 February 2006 on behalf of 184 Romani residents of U.N. camps for internally displaced persons (IDPs) in Northern Kosovo. The complaint was filed against UNMIK as "the acting government or 'state' in Kosovo."[56] In its application, the European Roma Rights Centre stressed the fact that UNMIK was not acting in Kosovo only as an international organization, but also acting as the "surrogate state authority" during the interim post-conflict transition period. The ERRC perspective communicated to the Court is reflected in the following ERRC position statement:

> It [UNMIK] administers the territory, enters into international contracts, appoints judges, and makes law. As the "government" it cannot avail itself of wholesale immunity but rather, as every sovereign, must be answerable for its conduct under the law... Residents of Kosovo are citizens of Serbia and Montenegro, a party to the Convention [European Convention on Human Rights]. At present, however, the authorities of Serbia and Montenegro do not have authority over the territory of Kosovo, and thus their ability to guarantee implementation of the Convention on the territory of Kosovo is limited. Individuals in Kosovo cannot be denied their human rights because a different government is in charge.[57]

The European Roma Rights Centre took the position that the application fell within the jurisdiction of the European Court of Human Rights for the following reasons (notwithstanding any immunities alleged by UNMIK or the U.N.): (i) UNMIK had itself agreed to be subject to the *European Convention on Human Rights* (ECHR), and hence could be held accountable for ECHR violations; (ii) the U.N. could *not* claim immunity for violations of the *jus cogens* international norms concerning right to life and the prohibition against torture and inhuman or degrading treatment which were clearly implicated in the instant case, and (iii) the U.N. had itself maintained that it was bound by international human rights law as were U.N. personnel (i.e. such as those comprising UNMIK carrying out U.N. directives in Kosovo).[58]

The European Roma Rights Centre alleged European Convention violations of Article 2: right to life; Article 3: right to be protected from torture and inhuman or degrading treatment; Article 6: right to a fair hearing; Article 8: right to respect for private and family life; Article 13: right to an effective remedy and Article 14: right to be protected from discrimination. The Centre also asked for interim or emergency measures which called on the Court to order the immediate removal of the inhabitants from the lead contaminated IDP camps to safe locations and provision of medical treatment for the lead poisoning and other health problems of those affected. *On 21 February 2006, the very next day after the European Roma Rights*

---

[56] Roma Rights Centre (2007).

[57] Roma Rights Centre (2007).

[58] Roma Rights Centre (2007).

Centre filed the application to the European Court of Human Rights, the Court faxed a letter back to the European Roma Rights Centre declining to review the case on the contention that the Court allegedly had no jurisdiction to do so. The Court maintained that UNMIK, a U.N. legal entity, was not a Party to the European Convention and therefore not subject to the Court's jurisdiction; the Court being charged as it was with assessing extent of *State* compliance with the *European Convention on Human Rights.*[59]

It is very troubling; both from a human rights perspective, and in considering the need for transparency of the Court, that the case was not heard by a judicial panel of the Court as to admissibility and that, at least as far as this author has been able to determine, no public admissibility decision was issued. (This is contrary to the situation in the Behrami case discussed in a later section which also concerned issues of U.N. involvement in Kosovo and the alleged implications for jurisdiction of the Court.) To date, there does not appear to be an explanation from the European Court of Human Rights as to why the decision of the Court regarding the lead contaminated Kosovo U.N. refugee camps and involving this most vulnerable population (Roma internally displaced persons in Kosovo) should not be made widely available to the general public through a publicly issued admissibility decision allowing the general public and academic legal scholars to scrutinize the Court's reasoning in the matter and also to become better aware of the facts of the case.

What was so different about the Behrami case as compared to the Kosovo U.N. lead contaminated refugee camps case that it was only in the first that an admissibility decision was publicly issued by the Court? The answer to that question, of course, lies with the Court. However, the following differences are notable and provide food for thought on the issue: (i) the Behrami case involved two victims, while the lead contaminated U.N. IDP camps case involved systemic and ongoing human rights violations which threatened the health and lives of the camps' inhabitants numbering in the many hundreds (this is not at all to diminish the gravity of the inhuman treatment accorded the Behrami children; one of whom was killed and the other grievously injured due to a callous disregard for their life and well-being arising from the intentional failure to remove unexploded mines from the area where they resided): (ii) in *Behrami* the impugned acts of UNMIK and KFOR (and their individual State constituents) occurred prior to the entry into force of the Rome Statute on the territories of the States that comprise UNMIK (the UN interim civil authority in Kosovo) and KFOR (the NATO multinational force providing security in Kosovo during the transition period). The U.N. lead contaminated refugee camps case, in contrast, involved violations that persisted over a very lengthy period from June 1999 and continued after July 2002 when the Rome Statute entered into force on the territories of the States that comprise UNMIK and KFOR until 2006 (and continues to this day for a segment of the Roma still left in the remaining U.N. camp with its highly toxic lead contaminated environment); and (iii) In *Behrami*, there was no request for interim measures from the Court,

[59]Roma Rights Centre (2007).

while in the IDP U.N. camps case the European Roma Rights Centre had requested that the European Court of Human Rights order interim emergency measures to remove the camp inhabitants from what was known to be a highly toxic lead contaminated and health threatening environment. Of course, such interim measures could be ordered only in the context of a pending or actual case. In the U.N. Kosovo IDP camps case, however, as mentioned, there was a refusal by the European Court to have a judicial panel hear the case as to the issue of admissibility hence sidestepping the request for interim measures which could have saved these victims from further serious adverse health impacts due to chronic high lead exposure.

Next we consider whether international crimes ripe for prosecution by the International Criminal Court may have been perpetrated against the Roma and other minorities left to suffer in the U.N. Kosovo lead contaminated IDP camps. Those perpetrators then may include certain agents of the States and of governmental international organizations cooperating with UNMIK. *Note, however, that there is no suggestion here in this regard pertaining to any specific person as any such conclusions would require a thorough criminal investigation as to any particular person's specific involvement, knowledge and intent.*

C. Commentary on the Lead Contaminated UN Kosovo Roma Refugee Camps and the Failure to Prevent or End Harms to the Roma and Other Minorities Due to Extraordinarily High Lead Exposure for Those Inhabiting the Camps: Are Those Responsible Potentially Guilty of Genocide by Causing Serious Physical or Mental Harm and/or the Crimes Against Humanity of Persecution and Apartheid?

The European Roma Rights Centre suggests that UNMIK (responsible for managing the IDP camps in Northern Kosovo from June 1999 until May 2008) knew about the lead contamination and its great threat to the health of the camp inhabitants especially children (who are the most vulnerable to the effects of lead exposure) from at least 2000 when the World Health Organization ('WHO') issued its report on the risks to the inhabitants of the camps due to the very high levels of lead in the camp soil which exceeded many times WHO standards regarding safe levels. Subsequent blood tests by WHO and other medical authorities confirmed that the camps' inhabitants had exceedingly high blood lead levels, especially the children, and that the health of the camps' residents was being seriously imperilled both by the high levels of lead poisoning, and the general substandard living conditions in the U.N. IDP camps.[60] Indeed, the fact that the area around the abandoned lead

[60] Human Rights Watch (2009b).

mines and heavy metals smelters was highly toxic and dangerous to human health was well know even prior to the WHO studies.[61] To date, there has been no criminal justice remedy or compensation for the Roma and other IDP camp victims. Human Rights Watch takes the position (with which this author and various highly respected international human rights NGOs and U.N. human rights bodies are agreed) that:

> The years of continuous failure of UNMIK and its international partners to find a durable solution for the inhabitants of the camps constitute multiple human rights violations, including of the right to life; the prohibition of cruel, inhuman and degrading treatment; the right to health, including medical treatment; the right to a healthy environment; and the right to adequate housing.[62]

The question of *individual State responsibility* and concomitant State civil liability (as opposed to accountability attributed to UNMIK, KFOR or the U.N. as legal entities in and of themselves) for grievous international human rights abuses occurring in the context of a U.N. peacekeeping and security mission is addressed in the commentary following the description of the *Behrami* case below. The question we will consider at this point then is rather the following: Assuming it is possible to attribute responsibility to individual persons for the U.N. Kosovo IDP lead contaminated camp situation, do the facts regarding the international human rights abuses against the Roma and other minorities left in highly lead contaminated IDP camps in Kosovo potentially support a classification of the violations as: (i) ***genocide*** *by causing serious physical or mental harm to members of the group* (Rome Statute Article 6(b)), and/or (ii) *the crimes against humanity of*: (a) ***persecution*** *against any identifiable group or collectivity on... racial, national, ethnic, cultural,... grounds... in connection with... any crime within the jurisdiction of the Court* (Rome Statute Article 7(h)); (b) ***apartheid*** (Rome Statute Article 7(j)) and (c) *other inhumane acts... intentionally causing great suffering, or serious injury to body or to mental or physical health* (Rome Statute Article 7(k)).[63] If so, this would then result in: (i) civil liability for the individual States whose agents were involved in these grave human rights abuses and (ii) criminal and civil liability for the particular State agents who initiated, or were in any way intentionally and knowingly complicit in these violations of international human rights and international criminal law. Prosecution of these persons would then, in principle, if not in practice, be possible domestically and, as will be discussed, potentially also possible by the International Criminal Court or, under a theory of universal jurisdiction, by a forum State other than that where the crimes occurred.

---

[61]Human Rights Watch (2009b).

[62]Human Rights Watch (2009b).

[63]*Rome Statute of the International Criminal Court.* Text of the Rome Statute circulated as document A/CONF.183/9 of 17 July 1998 and corrected by procès-verbaux of 10 November 1998, 12 July 1999, 30 November 1999, 8 May 2000, 17 January 2001 and 16 January 2002). The Statute entered into force on 1 July 2002. http://www.un.org/children/conflict/keydocuments/english/romestatuteofthe7.html. Accessed 1 August 2009.

In order to address the above question, we must consider the elements of each of these crimes as defined under the Rome Statute and general rules of interpretation regarding assessment of the elements of the crimes as stipulated in the Rome Statute. Let us begin with selected general rules of interpretation and certain Articles of the Rome Statute regarding accountability that are relevant here. We will then address intent and actions or inaction in relation to the Kosovo IDP camps case, and consider whether the elements of the specific aforementioned international crimes are present. We will consider in that assessment the specific factual context and surrounding circumstances in which this conduct occurred (relating to the lead contaminated refugee camps in Kosovo which house Roma and other minorities).

Rules of Interpretation (Rome Statute)

The following points are especially relevant in considering whether international crimes may have been committed in the Kosovo IDP lead contaminated camp case:

1. "*Existence of intent and knowledge can be inferred* from relevant facts and circumstances."[64]
2. "A particular conduct may constitute one or more crimes."[65]
3. The mental element is satisfied if the person commits the material elements of the crime with "intent and knowledge." Intent is inferred when "the person means to engage in the conduct" and "means to cause that consequence or is aware that it will occur in the ordinary course of events."[66]
4. "Immunities which may attach to the official capacity of a person under... international law, shall *not* bar the Court from exercising its jurisdiction over such a person."[67]
5. "The fact that a crime within the jurisdiction of the Court has been committed by a person pursuant to an order of a... superior, whether military or civilian, shall not relieve that person of criminal responsibility unless: (a) The person was under a legal obligation to obey orders of the... superior in question; (b) The person did not know that the order was unlawful; and (c) *The order was not manifestly unlawful. For the purposes of this article, orders to commit genocide or crimes against humanity are manifestly unlawful.*"[68]

---

[64]Rome Statute, Elements of the Crime, General Introduction at point 2. http://www.icc-cpi.int/NR/rdonlyres/.../Element_of_Crimes_English.pdf. Accessed 1 August 2009.

[65]Rome Statute, Elements of the Crime, General Introduction at point 9. http://www.icc-cpi.int/NR/rdonlyres/.../Element_of_Crimes_English.pdf. Accessed 1 August 2009.

[66]*Rome Statute of the International Criminal Court*, Article 30 ("Mental Element").

[67]*Rome Statute of the International Criminal Court*, Article 27(2) ("Irrelevance of Official Capacity").

[68]*Rome Statute of the International Criminal Court*, Article 33 ("Superior Orders and Prescription of Law").

6. The Court shall have jurisdiction over natural persons... A person who commits a crime within the jurisdiction of the Court shall be individually responsible and liable for punishment... if that person (a) commits such a crime, whether as an individual, jointly with another or through another person regardless of whether that other person is criminally responsible... in any other way contributes to the commission or attempted commission of such a crime by a group of persons acting with a common purpose. Such contribution shall be intentional and shall... (d)(ii) *be made in the knowledge of the intention of the group to commit the crime*... (Note that all emphasis in the above six points was added)....[69]

The Question of ICC Jurisdiction

We turn now then to consideration of whether or not specific international crimes may have been committed in relation to the Kosovo lead contaminated IDP camps and if so whether they fall under the International Criminal Court's (ICC) jurisdiction. The harms that the Roma and other minorities (all regarded as "gypsies" by the Albanians) suffered as inhabitants of U.N. lead contaminated refugee camps occurred with respect to two of the camps from 1999 until 2006 and for the remaining camps (Osterode and Cesmin Lug) is still ongoing as they have not yet been closed. Hence, while any international crimes that may have been committed in relation to the Roma IDP camps (i.e. by those in charge of managing the camps, and those who were involved with the camps in diverse ways and to various extents) may have begun before the Rome Statute entered into force in 2002, they persisted after that date. As an ongoing crime persisting after 2002 then these actions or inactions if they do constitute international crimes fall under the *temporal jurisdiction* of the ICC. The international crimes if committed were committed by persons who are nationals of States that are a party to the Rome Statute (among others) and on a territory that also is a party to the Rome Statute (Serbia ratified the Rome Statute 6 September 2001). While Kosovo unilaterally declared independence in 2008, even if such is eventually recognized internationally, the fact that nationals that are from States Parties to the Rome Statute would be the alleged defendants provides the Court with *geographic jurisdiction* as per Article 12 of the Rome Statute.

In addition, the fact that any such person alleged to have committed international crimes in regards to the U.N. IDP camps in Kosovo was working under the auspices of the United Nations pursuant to Security Resolution 1244 would *not* offer any immunity from prosecution by the ICC for nationals of States Parties to the Rome Statute (and perhaps also not for nationals of non-State Parties to the Rome Statute in certain instances depending on the interpretation regarding whether Kosovo may be considered to have ratified the Rome Statute as it was previously part of Serbia which ratified the Rome Statute 6 September 2001). This is the case in that

[69] *Rome Statute of the International Criminal Court*, Article 25 ("Individual criminal responsibility").

immunities that attach to a person under international law are *not* a bar to prosecution by the ICC as per Article 27(2). The fact that the acts or omissions constituting any international crimes that may have been committed in relation to the Kosovo IDP camps were made pursuant to orders from UNMIK, an alleged subsidiary organ of the United Nations, would not eliminate the potential culpability of the individual defendant(s) if the alleged crimes involved are 'genocide' and 'crimes against humanity' which are, under the Rome Statute, considered "manifestly unlawful." Hence, the individual is required to disobey orders as per Article 33 of the Rome Statute to commit or in any way participate or assist in the commission or attempted commission of such manifestly unlawful acts.

If such alleged international crimes were committed by: (i) those individuals who made decisions regarding the placement of IDP refugee camps and their continued existence on highly lead contaminated soil and/or by (ii) those who managed the camps without due regard for the health and well being of the refugees, then it could potentially be argued that, insofar as such acts or lack of action, created grave harms for the refugees, the conduct of these defendants contributed to the attempted genocide and crimes against humanity which the extremist Albanians had initiated and which caused the Roma, in the first instance, to be internally displaced persons in need of temporary housing and protection. According to Article 25(3)(d)(ii) of the Rome Statute, any contribution to international crimes committed by a group of persons acting with a common purpose (i.e. the extremist Albanians acting against the Roma and other minorities regarded as gypsies to effect killings, disappearances and ethnic cleansing, etc.) does *not* require that the individual defendant intended to further the group's criminal purpose. It is sufficient for culpability to attach to that individual defendant if he or she acted knowing that those acts *would* further the intentions of the group with the common purpose (i.e. by facilitating chronic exposure of the Roma to lead poisoning which inevitably causes severe physical harm and can cause death, the individual defendant would understand that this outcome would be consistent with the objectives of the extremist Albanian mob that had implemented a campaign of ethnic cleansing against the Roma and other so-called "gypsy" minorities which included killings and other harms perpetrated on the Roma and other minorities in Kosovo).

Evidence Relevant to the Issue of Possible Genocide and Crimes Against Humanity in Relation to the U.N. Kosovo Lead Contaminated Refugee Camps Housing Roma and Other "Gypsy" Minorities

While it is not possible to prejudge any case, it is not unreasonable to consider what type of evidence in relation to the lead contaminated U.N. IDP camps in Kosovo could potentially be used by a Prosecutor to determine probable cause, based on prima facie evidence, to believe that certain international crimes may have been committed and that the facts should be thoroughly criminally investigated for that possibility. Those potential international crimes then would have been committed against: (i) those persons currently living in the remaining U.N. lead contaminated

IDP camps in Kosovo (Osterode and Cesmin Lug) and (ii) against those persons who lived in the other such camps from 1999 until they were able to leave or until those particular camps were closed.

First let us consider the issue of the mental element required for the crime of genocide by causing serious physical or mental harm. As mentioned, it is *not* necessary under the Rome Statute Article 25(3)(d)(ii) that agents of those States cooperating with UNMIK themselves directly intended to destroy the 'RAE'; only that they knew that their actions or inaction would further the intent of those extremist Albanians attempting ethnic cleansing by all means necessary including killing and other forms of violence such as were documented by Amnesty International, Human Rights Watch and other independent NGOs. Clearly, there is ample evidence that: (i) these multinational State agents (contributing to UNMIK) were well aware of the dire consequences of leaving the RAE in the highly lead contaminated IDP camps and, more specifically, that they knew that the risk of permanent serious physical harm and even death was a foreseeable consequence of doing so and (ii) they were well aware of the genocidal intent of the extremist Albanian elements in regards to the RAE should any of that population remain despite the Albanian ethnic cleansing efforts (that intent of the extremist Albanians being evidenced by the fact that killings and 'disappearances' were part of the so-called ethnic cleansing campaign of the Albanian extremist element which went much beyond just forcing 'gypsy' peoples out of their homes (settlements) in Kosovo). That evidence of UNMIK knowledge in this regard previously discussed and summarized here includes, but is not limited to, the following:

1. Those State agents cooperating with UNMIK (i.e. including, but not limited to delegates from States belonging to the OSCE) deciding on plans for managing the IDP camps in Kosovo were provided with information in a health report (*UNMIK itself commissioned in 2000*) with information about the extraordinarily high blood lead levels especially in Roma children inhabiting the camps and informed of the consequences of chronic high lead level exposure. Yet, despite dire warnings in the health report about the risks to the persons living in the camps very little, if anything, was done from 2000 to 2004 by UNMIK to address the problem. UNMIK's alleged lack of funds was cited as a barrier to closing the lead contaminated IDP camps and resettling the inhabitants in new settlements;
2. In 2004, WHO declared the Kosovo IDP camps to be sites that posed a health emergency and recommended that at a minimum all children and pregnant women be removed from these sites on an urgent basis (a higher than average number of miscarriages and stillbirths at the camps have also been reported by medical personnel);
3. In 2006, only after much pressure from the international community two of the IDP camps housing the RAE were closed based on the high lead levels in the soil and the resultant lead poisoning of the inhabitants;
4. Some of the Roma were moved to Osterode camp which was known to be just metres away from the Trepca lead mines. UNMIK instituted some alleged untried and unverified precautionary measures in respect of the lead

contamination which measures were later found to be inadequate as the reported blood lead levels in the children and others remained high for those in Osterode (as determined by a physician with environmental expertise from the "Society for Threatened Peoples" who did extensive testing on hair and blood samples from the inhabitants of the camp in 2005). Yet, the camp to this date is still operational and occupied by RAE victims of both Albanian extremism and UNMIK disregard;

5. Cesmin Lug camp remains open despite the fact that soil lead levels there were determined to be 359.5 times what is considered safe for human health (according to independent testing by WHO in 2004) as does the extremely lead contaminated Osterode Camp;
6. Testing in 2006, by medical personnel from Northern Mitrovica Hospital confirms that blood lead levels are dangerously high for inhabitants at Osterode and many camp inhabitants have suffered severe physical consequences and a certain number have died; according to physicians, likely as a result of chronic high lead exposure;
7. Diagnostic testing was done on a sporadic basis by WHO and physicians attached to independent NGOs and ordered stopped in 2007 by UNMIK due to the presumption that all IDP camp inhabitants would be returned to the Mahalla (which has not occurred). Furthermore, medical treatment has been exceedingly limited for the victims of the U. N. lead contaminated camps over the many years of operation of these lead toxic camps as previously discussed;
8. The living circumstances in the Roma IDP camps have been assessed by independent observers from NGOs such as the European Roma Rights Centre and Human Rights Watch to be so poor, even aside from the lead contamination that these observers consider the situation to amount to inhuman and degrading circumstances.

The UNMIK personnel and those outside State nationals working with them, on the above analysis, had the duty under Article 33 of the Rome Statute to disobey UNMIK orders or directives that would cause them to leave the Kosovo Roma and other minorities in highly lead contaminated IDP camps just as they would have such a duty not to leave those persons to be physically injured or even killed by extremist Albanians or in any other situation under their control which posed a significant health hazard to this group. Such orders would be manifestly unlawful insofar as they would be known to result in systemic severe physical harm to civilians (and, furthermore, to civilians perceived as belonging to a particular ethnic minority or cultural group). It is uncontested that these internally displaced persons were entirely dependent on UNMIK personnel for their survival and safety and that the U.N. was duly informed of the high lead levels in the IDP camps and their correlated extreme health hazard. Hence, UNMIK personnel had a high fiduciary duty toward these vulnerable persons in their care and that duty was not only not fulfilled, but actively undermined. Further, recall that the camps were kept open despite enormous pressure to close them coming from international human rights organizations, the World Health Organization and others. Hence, the harms which were caused to the Roma and other minority inhabitants of the Kosovo IDP camps (and which for some continue) involved the active engagement of UNMIK personnel from various States directed, *in effect*, to perpetuate the hazardous living conditions for these persons (by virtue of keeping the lead-contaminated camp(s) operational) and cannot be said to be attributable simply to passive neglect and ignorance of the situation.

Intent can be inferred then from the above facts and circumstances given the continued placement of the Roma in highly lead contaminated IDP camps with the full knowledge of the consequences; namely (i) knowledge of the grave hazard to the physical and mental health of the camps' inhabitants, and (ii) the knowledge that the inevitable severe physical harms which would ensue for the camps occupants would further the objectives of the extremist Albanian element which wanted to eliminate the RAE from the region by all means necessary. Note that under Article 6 of the Elements of the Crime of the Rome Statute; the Court decides matters of intent (i.e. such as also inferred from the defendant's knowledge of the circumstances) in regards to genocide on a case-by-case basis taking into account the totality and gravity of the facts.

The fact, that Roma and other minorities perceived as "gypsies" were the inhabitants of the U.N. lead contaminated camps in Kosovo gives rise to the possibility also of the crime of persecution of an identifiable cultural or ethnic group and apartheid. Persecution requires the deprivation of one or more fundamental human rights as defined under international law. In this instance, one can argue that the Roma and the other camp inhabitants were treated in a degrading and inhuman manner which posed a significant threat to their lives contrary to the European Convention on Human Rights (Article 3) and other international treaties. The State agents of UNMIK knew that such harms as were being inflicted on the 'gypsies' in the U.N. camps would simply be a *de facto* extension of the widespread and systematic attacks that had been directed toward this group by the Albanian radicals and would not at all be consistent with mitigating the harms of those attacks. Given that (i) medical treatment was not readily forthcoming to these U.N. camp victims, and that (ii) the Kosovo IDP lead contaminated camps were kept open despite the health warnings and opposition from international human rights groups and others such as the WHO, it is not unreasonable to conclude that there was little concern about the contribution that lead poisoning of the RAE (gratis U.N. housing in the IDP camps) was making to the ethnic cleansing objectives of the extremist Albanians. Hence, the elements of the crime of persecution set out in Article 7(i)(h) may have been met. Likewise the inhuman nature of the living circumstances of the RAE in the Kosovo U.N. camps and the denial of adequate diagnostics and medical care, directed as it was to this identifiable ethnic/cultural group, may well satisfy the elements of the crime of apartheid under Article 7(1) (j) of the Elements of the Crime. The RAE U.N. crafted ghettos (in the form of U.N. IDP camps in Kosovo) were entirely consistent with the forced segregation and institutionalized discrimination already imposed on the group by the extremist Albanians, but with the added feature of intolerable and life threatening substandard living conditions arising from highly lead contaminated soil.

One would be hard pressed to think of another situation in which such an historically oppressed group suffering also contemporary widespread discrimination in both Western and Eastern European States, would knowingly be placed and left for a decade or more in such hazardous segregated conditions by the UN. Of course, the above is a rendition without the defence side of the story, but surely the grievous injury visited upon these persons by the U.N. knowingly housing them in high lead toxic camps and declining adequate medical care rises to the level of probable cause for an investigation by the ICC Prosecutor. The reality is, however, that the European Court of Human Rights declining to review the case and downplaying the case in the extreme (by sending its refusal to hear the case, even as to admissibility, by faxed letter to the European Roma Rights Centre, rather than issuing a public admissibility decision after a hearing) may lead the ICC Prosecutor (should any such case be brought to the ICC) to miscalculate the level of international outrage at such abuse of this minority group. This is critical in that the level of international concern is one indicator in the assessment of the gravity of the alleged offences which the ICC Prosecutor considers in making an ICC admissibility decision for that Office (i.e. decisions regarding whether the Prosecutor will initiate an investigation and possibly bring forward cases to the ICC Pre-Trial Chamber).

IV. Death and Injury to Civilians Due to the Failure of KFOR and/or UNMIK to Remove Unexploded Cluster Bombs in Post-conflict Kosovo

A. *Case 4: Behrami and Behrami v. France (Application 78166/01), European Court of Human Rights Grand Chamber Judgment (Heard together with Saramati v. France, Germany and Norway, 2 May 2007)*

Background and Procedural History of Behrami and Behrami v. France

Mr. Agim Behrami (an Albanian who was living in Northern Kosovo in Metrovica in the Republic of Serbia) brought a complaint on his own behalf and on behalf of his deceased son Gadaf Behrami born 1988 under Article 2 (right to life) of the European Convention on Human Rights (while Bekir Behrami complained of his serious injury due to an unexploded mine that had been left in the area). Gadaf Behrami was killed by an unexploded cluster bomb (dropped during NATO bombardment of the area in January 1999 during the Serb–Albanian Kosovo conflict to pressure the former territory of Yugoslavia to comply with the demands of the international community). That bomb and the others were all supposed to have been cleared from the Northern Kosovo area in the post-conflict period by KFOR (NATO forces acting under U.N. Security Council (UNSC) resolution 1244 of 10 June 1999 and responsible for security in the area). Another son, Bekir Behrami, was gravely injured by the aforementioned explosive device but survived. A special U.N. interim administration in Kosovo (UNMIK) was also deployed to the area under UNSC resolution 1244. In addition, a special representative reporting to the U.N. Secretary General was appointed to head and implement UNMIK (i.e. the interim administration in Kosovo). *UNMIK was to coordinate closely with KFOR* regarding de-mining operations, a point which is significant in the analysis of the accountability issue in the case as will be discussed.

The UNMIK police investigated the incident concerning the grave harms that befell the two Behrami boys. In interviewing witnesses, the UNMIK police obtained testimony from a French KFOR officer that KFOR had been aware for months of the unexploded cluster bombs in the area, but did not act on the information since, in KFOR's view, it was *not* a high priority concern. In their 18 March 2000 report, the UNMIK police classified the incident involving the death of the young child Gadaf Behrami as an "unintentional homicide due to imprudence",[70] but the case was *not* prosecuted by the District Public Prosecutor's office. The KFOR command rejected the complaint made by Mr. Behrami (that KFOR had not complied with its obligations under UNSC resolution 1244) on the grounds that the U.N. (UNMIK) had been responsible for mine clearing since 5 June 1999 and that KFOR had performed such a function only until UNMIK took over (the incident with the Behrami boys and the unexploded mine had occurred 11 March 2000).

The European Court of Human Rights held that the complainants were owed protection of their European Convention rights by the individual States contributing to the U.N. mission in Kosovo. The Court suggested further that it appeared that the complainants were under the jurisdiction of those States cooperating with the U.N. mission in Kosovo (UNMIK and KFOR were entirely responsible respectively for the public administrative powers and the security in the region) (the previous administration having been dismantled). The question the Court held it must consider then was not the issue of extraterritoriality, but rather whether the conduct of the *individual States* in contributing to UNMIK and KFOR (which were States Parties to the European Convention) was subject to the Court's scrutiny with respect to the issue of their compliance with the European Convention.

The Court found that UNMIK had taken over from KFOR the task of de-mining (as a humanitarian task) *prior* to the detonation which killed one Behrami boy and seriously wounded the other. However, the Court contended that the U.N. maintained 'ultimate control' of both UNMIK and KFOR through a chain of command where certain levels had been delegated U.N. operational authority (i.e. NATO command had operational authority over the KFOR troops). *For that reason, the Court held that the respondent in the Behrami case was the U.N. and the Court*

---

[70]*Behrami and Behrami v. France* (Application 71412/01) [heard in conjunction with *Saramati v France, Germany and Norway* (Application 781/01)], 2 May 2007. European Court of Human Rights, Grand Chamber decision on admissibility, p. 5. http://hei.unige.ch/~clapham/hrdoc/docs/ECHRBehrami.doc. Accessed 25 July 2009.

hence (allegedly) lacked jurisdiction given that the U.N. was not a State let alone a State Party to the European Convention on Human Rights. The Court held that UNMIK was a subsidiary organ of the U.N. and that both KFOR and UNMIK were ultimately responsible to the U.N. Security Council pursuant to the UNSC resolution under which they were exercising authority in Kosovo.

The European Court of Human Rights in *Behrami* did not contest the notion that European Convention violations had occurred in the case which were grave enough to potentially outweigh the States' right to engage in those acts or omissions consequent to carrying out their international obligations to participate in the directives of an international organization of which they were members (i.e. the United Nations). Rather, the Court held that the acts or omissions which caused these violations of European Convention guarantees were *not* attributable to the individual member States contributing to UNMIK or KFOR as far as accountability was concerned (for those which were also States Parties to the European Convention) since (i) the U.N. *allegedly* had 'ultimate control' over the activities of these bodies, and (ii) the acts and omissions occurred extraterritorially *under U.N. auspices* and were not allegedly the result of decisions ultimately attributable to the State authorities. The Court held then that while the individual States had an obligation to comply with Article 1 of the U.N. Charter (i.e. the duty in carrying out any operation pursuant to international obligations to respect and protect fundamental human rights such as those incorporated in the *European Convention on Human Rights*), any violations of the European Convention by the individual States participating in UNMIK were *not* subject to the Court's scrutiny and the Court could not order just reparations for the harms resulting from these violations.

Milanovic and Papic[71] point out that in fact the complainants in *Behrami* had *not* asked the European Court of Human Rights to decide whether KFOR or UNMIK or both (or individual State constituents of the aforementioned legal entities) *had violated U.N. Security Resolution 1244*, but rather whether the individual States had violated the *European Convention on Human Rights* which requires States Parties to secure European Convention rights and freedoms to everyone within their jurisdiction. Hence, the question of State extraterritorial jurisdiction was central to the way in which the case had actually been presented to the Court. Milanovic and Papic thus suggest that the Court *reframed* the case so as to avoid answering the questions actually posed to the Court namely; whether or not there was *individual State accountability under the European Convention* for failure to de-mine and whether or not there existed *State jurisdiction* over the persons harmed. The aforementioned legal scholars put the matter succinctly thus:

> However, the question presented both in *Behrami* and *Saramati* was not whether Resolution 1244 was violated, but whether the *ECHR* was violated... whether or not KFOR had the duty under Resolution 1244 to de-mine areas that NATO itself saturated with cluster bombs is not the point. The issue is whether *France* had the obligation to do so *under the ECHR*, in the same way as France would undoubtedly have had such a positive obligation to secure

[71] Milanovic and Papic (2009, p. 275).

> human rights, namely the right to life, of persons within its own territory if, say, a fighter aircraft dropped a few cluster bombs on a vineyard in Champagne. The distribution of duties of the civil and military international missions in Kosovo under Resolution 1244 would only be relevant to answering the merits question of whether France acted with due diligence in fulfillment of its positive obligations.[72]

We examine in the commentary that follows how the Court focused instead on delegation of powers of the Security Council under resolution 1244 to UNMIK and (via NATO) to the KFOR troops and assess whether in fact *individual States* are accountable also under the *European Convention* for the harms caused by the failure to de-mine.

Commentary on the Issue of the Accountability of Individual States Participating in U.N. Peacekeeping or Security Missions for Complicity in U.N. Fundamental Human Rights Violations Arising from a Failure to Prevent or Stop the Abuse

1. **The European Court of Human Rights' assignment of accountability for international wrongdoing to the United Nations *versus* the individual States involved in U.N. peacekeeping missions or in security operations**: The central issue in the Kosovo U.N. lead contaminated refugee camps case and in *Behrami* is whether: (i) State personnel which were placed at the disposal of an international organization (i.e. the United Nations) for *peacekeeping o*perations, (i.e. the operations carried out by UNMIK) *and their home States*, and/or KFOR troops and *their respective individual countries of origin* (member States of NATO), acting in Kosovo under the authority of a U.N. security council resolution to ensure security, can be held accountable for their international wrongdoing or complicity in the same which occurred during these operations conducted under the auspices of the U.N. (regardless whether the wrongdoing was the result of actions or inaction or a combination of the two by KFOR troops and/or UNMIK personnel contributing to the mission), *or* (ii) whether the international organization (the United Nations) is responsible for the international wrongdoing, or (iii) whether both the U.N. and the *individual States* involved in UNMIK and/or in KFOR are accountable for the international human rights violations. The consensus in the academic international law literature appears to be that which body is to be held accountable for the wrong doing depends on which body had *effective* and *exclusive actual operational control* day-to-day and with respect to the specific misconduct alleged (as opposed to which body had *theoretical ultimate* control *in principle o*ver UNMIK and KFOR).[73]

The U.N. regards *peace-keeping missions* (constituted by personnel from the various cooperating States as in UNMIK) as subsidiary organs of the United

---

[72]Milanovic and Papic (2009, p. 275).

[73]Commentary of the International Law Commission (ILO) on Draft Article 5 of the ILO *Draft Articles on Responsibility of International Organizations* at para 8, Cited in Larsen (2008, p. 516).

Nations since, according to the U.N., this personnel is under the U.N.'s ultimate control.[74] However, this appears to be a claim that is based more on form than on substance as was recognized by the International Law Commission:

> While it is understandable that, for the sake of efficiency of military operations, *the United Nations insists on* ***claiming*** *exclusive command and control over peacekeeping forces, attribution of conduct should also in this regard be based on* ***a factual*** *criterion* (emphasis added).[75]

As to the ***factual*** indicator of who has effective and exclusive *operational* control of: (i) personnel from the cooperating States in a U.N. peacekeeping mission (UNMIK) and (ii) operational control of security forces (KFOR), note that these agents of the State (UNMIK personnel and KFOR forces) contribute to the United Nations' peace and security mission at the behest of their own governments. They act as agents for their own governments in order to realize their government's decision to place contingents of that State's personnel and/or troops at the disposal of the U.N. and cooperate in the peace and security mission (as required under the U.N. Charter). Whether it is (a) the *individual States* which contributed to a U.N. peacekeeping and security mission under a U.N. Security Council resolution as in Kosovo, or (b) *the United Nations* which is accountable for any international wrongdoing by the U.N. mission (or perhaps both) is elucidated by Article 5 of the International Law Commission's *Articles on the Responsibility of States for Internationally Wrongful Acts and* Draft Article 5 of the ILC *Draft Articles on the Responsibility of International Organizations which read respectively as follows:*

> ***Responsibility of States for Internationally Wrongful Acts***
> **Article 5: Conduct of persons or entities exercising elements of governmental authority**
> The conduct of [an]... entity which is *not* an organ of the State [i.e. UNMIK]... but *which is empowered by the law of that State to exercise elements of the governmental authority shall be considered an act of the State under international law*, provided the... entity is acting in that capacity in the particular instance [i.e. the State's personnel participating in UNMIK are acting on behalf of their country of origin/home State as well as on behalf of UNMIK as an entity such that UNMIK is exercising member State authority as well as acting under U.N. authority](emphasis added as well as portions in square brackets added).[76]

> ***Responsibility of International Organizations***
> **Draft Article 5**
> The conduct of an organ of a State... that is placed at the disposal of [an]... international organization shall be considered under international law *an act of the latter organization* [*the international organization*] ***if*** **[and only if]** ***the*** **[*international*]** ***organization exercises***

[74]Larsen (2008, p. 513).

[75]Larsen (2008, p. 516).

[76]Article 5 of the ILC Articles on the Responsibility of States for Internationally Wrongful Acts, http://untreaty.un.org/ilc/texts/instruments/.../draft%20articles/9_6_2001.pdf. Accessed 26 July 2009.

> ***effective control over that conduct*** (emphasis added as well as portions in square brackets added).[77]

The States that agree to participate in U.N. peacekeeping missions (or security missions under U.N. auspices) do so by making certain of their personnel available for participation in the U.N. mission and *delegating to them the authority to act on behalf of the State* as part of the mission (Compare Article 5 of the *Articles on the Responsibility of States for Internationally Wrongful Acts*). Thus, while the peacekeeping mission (i.e. UNMIK) may be doing the U.N.'s work, it does *not* necessarily follow that the individual State personnel which constitute UNMIK are, *in practice*, acting as part of a subsidiary organ of the U.N. in doing that work (contrary to the claims of the United Nations). This is reflected also in the fact that it is each of the cooperating States in the peace-keeping mission, and *not* the United Nations, that has disciplinary and criminal prosecutorial jurisdiction over its respective personnel contributing to the U.N. mission as well as day-to-day effective operational control. Thus, (using UNMIK as an example), it is certainly the case that: (i) UNMIK as an entity in and of itself is perceived formally, and claimed by the U.N. to be, a subsidiary organ of the international organization; and (ii) it is under U.N. authority/auspices that the UNMIK personnel were deployed and situated outside their home territories to run the interim administrative functions in Kosovo. Notwithstanding the foregoing, however, such missions are, in practice, comprised of a collection of entities exercising their respective State's governmental authority in a coordinated effort, *but under the effective and exclusive control in day-to-day operations of their respective States and the special representative appointed by the U.N. for UNMIK* (compare draft Article 5 of the ILC *Draft Articles on Responsibility of International Organizations* regarding the issue of "effective control").

Note also, (in regards to the issue of State versus U.N. accountability for international wrongdoing during security operations), the advisory opinion of the Venice Commission on accountability issues relating to KFOR. (The 'Venice Commission' is a name more commonly used to refer to the 'European Commission for Democracy Through Law' which is the advisory body to the Council of Europe on constitutional matters.) The Venice Commission's opinion regarding the accountability of KFOR forces contemplates the possibility of accountability being attributed to the *respective individual home States of the KFOR (NATO) forces* for international human rights abuses committed while those forces were acting under the auspices of the United Nations pursuant to Security Council resolutions:

> KFOR... is not a UN peacekeeping mission... *Its acts are not attributed in international law to the United Nations as an international legal person. This includes possible human rights violations by KFOR troops.* It is more difficult to determine whether acts of KFOR troops should be attributed to the international legal person NATO (in which case the jurisdiction of the ECHR could not be established against the impugned act) or whether

[77] Draft Article 5 of the ILC *Draft Articles on the Responsibility of International Organizations*, Cited in Larsen (2008, p. 514).

> they must be attributed to their country of origin (which means that the jurisdiction of the ECHR could be established if the state whose troops acted is a member of the Council of Europe). *Not all acts by KFOR troops which happen in the course of an operation under the unified command and control of a NATO Commander must be attributed in international law to NATO but* ***they can also be attributed to their country of origin***... (emphasis added).[78]

It is striking to note that the United Nations intervened in *Behrami* at the request of the Court and contended that if accountability for international wrongdoing were to be assigned by the European Court of Human Rights in the case, it should go to KFOR (under NATO command), which is not considered by the UN as a subsidiary organ, as opposed to UNMIK which is a UN peacekeeping mission regarded by the U.N. as a subsidiary organ of the U.N. Thus, in *Behrami*, the U.N. appeared to be steadfastly resistant to the notion of assuming any responsibility even though UNMIK played a key role in coordinating with KFOR and supervising removal of cluster bombs in Northern Kosovo. The U.N. *alleged* that the body designated by UNMIK to remove the unexploded mines could not effectively do so as KFOR had allegedly not provided the necessary mine location data to UNMIK for accomplishing this objective. Note that the U.N. position in *Behrami* does *not* appear to be consistent with the Venice Commission's view that the U.N. is obligated to allow for the attribution of responsibility to individual U.N. peacekeeping mission personnel for international human rights abuses they have committed during their participation in the mission (*thus implicating also their home State*) where the interests of justice demand it:

> Immunity of international organizations does not express the judgment that everything which an international organization does can be presumed to be legal and well-founded. This can also be inferred from Section 6.1 of... UNMIK Regulation no. 2000/47 of 18 August 2000 which provides that the immunity is in the interests of KFOR and UNMIK ***and not for the benefit of the individuals themselves. The Secretary-General shall have the right and the duty to waive immunity of any UNMIK personnel in any case where, in his opinion, the immunity would impede the course of justice and can be waived without prejudice to UNMIK*** (emphasis added).[79]

It is, to say the least, ironic and seems contrary to the values underpinning the U.N. Charter (as well as specifically Articles 1 and 25 of the U.N. Charter) to suggest by implication, as does the Venice Commission in the above quote, that impunity of individuals for international human rights violations committed during U.N. peacekeeping operations (and concomitant civil immunity for their home States against any related liability) should, at times, be tolerated even if this is not in the interests of justice. The abuses should be tolerated, according to the

[78]Opinion 280/2004 on Human Rights in Kosovo: Possible Establishment of Review Mechanisms, adopted by the Venice Commission on 8–9 October 2004, CDL-AD (2004) 033 at para. 76. http://www.venice.coe.int/docs/2004/CDL-DI(2004)004rev-e.asp. Accessed 28 July 2009.

[79]Opinion 280/2004 on Human Rights in Kosovo: Possible Establishment of Review Mechanisms, adopted by the Venice Commission on 8–9 October 2004, CDL-AD (2004) 033 at para 63. http://www.venice.coe.int/docs/2004/CDL-DI(2004)004rev-e.asp. Accessed 28 July 2009.

Venice Commission, where the Secretary-General deems it to be necessary so as not to prejudice UNMIK. The argument can be raised, however, that it is the very impunity accorded to the individuals responsible for the international human rights abuses and the civil immunity provided to their respective home States that undermines the perceived credibility and the good works of U.N. peacekeeping missions such as UNMIK.

The immunity of the States was affirmed by the European Court of Human Rights in *Behrami* via its attribution of responsibility for international wrongdoing during a U.N. peacekeeping mission (UNMIK) to an entity-namely the U.N.-which allegedly lawfully enjoys absolute immunity rather than holding to account the home States of the individual perpetrators. It is entirely unclear how this ruling in any way furthers the objectives of the United Nations as expressed in the U.N. Charter.

2. **Accountability may be shared between the U.N. and the individual States involved in peacekeeping and security operations**: Larsen points out that even if it could be said that the United Nations is accountable for certain international wrongdoing, this would *not* preclude the possibility, according to ILC State and international organization responsibility principles, that the State is also accountable:

> Although it may not frequently occur in practice, dual or even multiple attribution of conduct cannot be excluded. *Thus, attribution of a certain conduct to an international organization does not imply that the same conduct cannot be attributed to a State*, nor does vice versa attribution of conduct to a State rule out attribution of the same conduct to an international organization (emphasis added).[80]

Hence, in the context of the case involving Kosovo inhabitants of lead contaminated U.N. refugee camps, and of the Behrami case (concerning the killing of one child and maiming of another from the same family in Kosovo by cluster bombs that were supposed to have been cleared), the responsibility in these instances *may* in fact be shared by the United Nations and the individual States involved (the States which had effective and exclusive operational control of the personnel responsible for managing the U.N. refugee camps and/or for supervising and monitoring the mine clearing operation under the auspices of the U.N.).

It would appear – *given the consensus that effective and exclusive control over U.N. peacekeeping and security forces is the criterion for deciding which entity (State or the U.N.) has accountability for international wrongdoing* – that there was no legally tenable basis for the European Court of Human Rights' holding that the United Nations *exclusively* was accountable for any alleged international wrongdoing in *Behrami a*nd the Kosovo lead contaminated refugee camp cases (*as opposed to the individual States which had effective and exclusive control over those situations in actual practice, or accountability being assigned to both the individual States involved in UNMIK and/or KFOR and the U.N.*). The Court did

[80]ILO commentary on the issue of dual responsibility shared between the State and an international organization, Cited in Larsen (2008, p. 517).

not at all consider the possibility of *shared responsibility* for international wrongdoing in Northern Kosovo between (a) the individual cooperating States *and* (b) the U.N. and/or the U.N. Security Council (SC) (the latter two as entities with juridical personality of their own). Note in this regard, however, that assigning legal responsibility to the U.N. Security Council as a legal entity in and of itself may be quite difficult given the wording of the U.N. Charter which, according to some legal scholars, leaves the Council a "wide margin of *political discretion*, especially in the context of Chapter VII when it acts for the maintenance and restoration of international peace and security (emphasis added)."[81] It is here suggested, however, that human rights violations are *not* a matter of 'political discretion' and that therefore the U.N. Security Council, too, ought to be held liable for significant international human rights violations occurring under its authority though under current practice this is most unlikely.

Larsen notes that in *Behrami* "*the Court* [*the European Court of Human Rights*] *does* ***not*** *explicitly make clear what legal basis it applies in the decision* [based as it is on the contentious and arguably legally unsupported view that the U.N. is *exclusively* accountable for the alleged international wrongdoing and not the individual State(s) such that the case is therefore inadmissible given that the U.N. is not a party to the *European Convention on Human Rights* and the Court therefore lacks jurisdiction when the complaint is against the U.N. as a legal entity] (emphasis added)."[82] The situation is ripe then for the Court to rethink and revise its position on State versus U.N. accountability in future cases such as the instant cases of international wrongdoing perpetrated by State agents participating in a peacekeeping and security mission under U.N. auspices pursuant to a Security Council resolution.

3. **Individual States as accountable when they knowingly and intentionally allow U.N. human rights violations to occur or persist (Individual State accountability despite U.N. delegated authority under Chapter VII of the U.N. Charter)**: States are accountable for human rights abuses under, for instance: (i) customary humanitarian law and the 1950 Geneva Convention which sets out explicitly, or by implication, *positive obligations in respect of protecting and assisting* civilians also in immediate post-conflict situations,[83] and (ii) as States Parties to various international human rights treaties such as the *European Convention on Human Rights*. Arguably the *European Convention on Human Rights* is applicable extraterritorially as a constraint on the behaviour of personnel and troops from States that are a Party to the Convention (i.e. compare the Canadian court rulings holding that the *Canadian Charter of Rights and Freedoms*: (i) constrains Canadian forces and security agents from engaging in human rights abuses on

---

[81]Giegerich (2009), under Legal constraints on Security Council action, para 1.

[82]Larsen (2008, p. 512).

[83]Geneva Convention relative to the Protection of Civilian Persons in Time of War, 75 U.N.T.S. 287, entered into force 21 October 1950. http://www1.umn.edu/humanrts/instree/y4gcpcp.htm. Accessed 28 July 2009.

foreign soil and (ii) imposes a positive obligation upon them to respect the human rights of persons under their custody and/or control also when those State agents are operating extra-territorially).[84,85] States, under international customary law and under various treaty instruments, and, as reflected in the ILC articles on State responsibility, have a *positive obligation* to: (i) show due diligence in attempting to prevent international human rights abuses from occurring, and (ii) to end such human rights violations when aware of them. Some authors, however, hold that the aforementioned positive obligations under international law do *not* inculpate individual States (which are acting under the authority of U.N. Security Council resolutions) for failing to prevent or to end international human rights violations by the United Nations should these occur in the course of a peacekeeping and/or security operation:

> I do not claim on this basis that a state can be held responsible under human rights instruments for having 'supported or tolerated' human rights violations by the UN. . . .[86]

The current author, however, takes the opposite position; namely, that individual States are, under international human rights law, liable for participating directly or indirectly in any international human rights violations perpetrated by the United Nations, or in being complicit therein by supporting or tolerating such abuses. Clearly, intentional action or intentional lack of action that knowingly causes or perpetuates international human rights violations is beyond the jurisdiction of the United Nations. This as the U.N. as an organization, is, of course, (especially given its mandate), bound by international human rights law and by its Charter which incorporates human rights principles at Article 1(3) and which lists among other purposes of the United Nations the fostering and protection of human rights: "The purposes of the United Nations are... *encouraging respect for human rights and for fundamental freedoms for all* without distinction as to race, sex, language, or religion (emphasis added)."[87]

Furthermore, recall that the United Nations is regarded under international law as having legal (juridical) personality. Hence, the view of the Inter-American Court that individual States can be considered accountable for international human rights abuses actually committed by another legal entity (that entity being recognized as having legal personality under international law) *where the State has knowingly and intentionally failed to prevent or end the abuse by that other legal entity* seems to apply also in the Behrami and the Kosovo lead contaminated U.N. refugee camp cases:

> An illegal act which violates human rights and *which is initially not directly imputable to a State... can lead to international responsibility of the State, not because of the act itself, but*

---

[84]Grover (2008, pp. 40–53).

[85]Grover (2009, pp. 42–48).

[86]Larsen (2008, p. 519).

[87]Charter of the United Nations (Article 1). http://www.un.org/en/documents/charter/index.shtml. Accessed 27 July 2009.

> *because of the lack of due diligence to prevent the violation or to respond to it as required by the Convention* (emphasis added).[88]

States then cannot be legally authorized by the U.N. (i.e. given delegated power by the U.N. Security Council) to engage in actions or to refrain from engaging in actions that would interfere with the prevention of, or termination of human rights violations (i.e. such as: (i) declining to move to a safe place Roma refugees living in U.N. refugee camps in Northern Kosovo where the camps are known to be lead contaminated and where such an environment is known to be seriously hazardous to the health and longevity of the refugees, or (ii) failing to remove cluster bombs in the post-conflict situation in Northern Kosovo where the bombs are known to be present and known to pose an imminent risk to civilians of grievous injury or even death). Note in this regard, further, that Article 25 of the U.N. Charter specifically requires of States to carry out the decisions of the Security Council "*in accordance with the present* [UN] *Charter*". Hence, it is implicit also in the text of Article 25 of the U.N. Charter that the individual State members of the United Nations are *not* required to accept and carry out any U.N. decisions that are not consistent with the U.N. Charter (i.e. not consistent with Article 1 requirements for the respect of human rights and freedoms)

> **Article 25 of the United Nations Charter**
> The Members of the United Nations agree to accept and carry out the decisions of the Security Council *in accordance with the present Charter.*[89]

Hence, accountability accrues to the cooperating individual States of UNMIK given violation of Article 25 of the U.N. Charter arising from their: (i) knowingly and intentionally failing to properly oversee removal of cluster bombs which foreseeably would, and did kill and injure civilians in Northern Kosovo (i.e. the Behrami young boys as a case in point) as this does *not* constitute carrying out U.N. Security Council decisions (i.e. regarding peacekeeping missions) "in accordance with the present [U.N.] Charter", and (ii) leaving Roma refugees in lead contaminated U.N. refugee camps in Northern Kosovo to have their health and even longevity seriously compromised as this, too, is *not* consistent with acting in accord with Article 1 and Article 25 of the U.N. Charter. Further, it was clearly within the power of the individual States involved in UNMIK to remove the Roma refugees from lead contaminated U.N. refugee camps in Northern Kosovo to safe locations, and to properly supervise and/or organize the removal of cluster bombs in the region (i.e. and to demand from KFOR any necessary information to accomplish this latter goal when the duty was entirely transferred to UNMIK). *The cooperating individual States of UNMIK are accountable in these instances then as these States in practice had effective operational control over their respective UNMIK*

---

[88]Velásquez Rodríguez case, Inter-American Court Judgment of 29 July 1988, para. 172. http://www1.umn.edu/humanrts/iachr/C/4-ing.html. Accessed 28 July 2009.

[89]Charter of the United Nations (Article 25). http://www.un.org/en/documents/charter/index.shtml. Accessed 27 July 2009.

personnel who allowed international human rights abuses to occur or continue. Put differently, Article 25 of the U.N. Charter dictates a general norm regarding how U.N. Security Resolution decisions involving peacekeeping and security operations are, in practice, to be realized in concrete and specific day-to-day terms and that is *with due consideration for the fundamental human rights of the persons affected* (Article 25 of the U.N. Charter does *not* contemplate a margin of appreciation to member States in implementing SC resolutions which allows for, for instance, serious and/or systemic human rights violations occurring in the context of U.N. authorized peacekeeping and security operations). *The individual States (i.e. of UNMIK and KFOR) must therefore take responsibility for such international human rights violations which were knowingly and intentionally allowed to occur or allowed to continue in the course of the actual operations involved in the peacekeeping (peace-building) and/or security mission as these violations fall outside the scope of delegated U.N. authority.*

Note further that the European Court of Human Rights in *Behrami* held that the U.N.'s authority was delegated to NATO which was to take operational control of KFOR while the U.N. retained so-called 'ultimate control' of the KFOR operations via NATO (according to the U.N.'s perspective). Hence, it is here contended that insofar as the failure of KFOR to remove cluster bombs (and protect civilians known to be at risk because of these unexploded bombs) constitutes a violation of fundamental human rights under international law, KFOR forces and NATO's individual member States themselves (as well as NATO as an entity) are also accountable (i.e. the fact of acting under U.N. auspices or authority provides no shield from liability given the Article 25 U.N. Charter requirement for the conduct of member States).

Even if one were to agree with the European Court of Human Rights in *Behrami* that the cooperating States contributing to UNMIK were acting on authority delegated by the U.N. Security Council; that the Security Council at all times held 'ultimate control' over UNMIK, and that hence accountability was held only by the U.N. given its ultimate control over the peace-keeping and security mission, *it is here contended that that responsibility shifts (entirely, or at least in part) to the individual State once the State delegate acts, or fails to act knowingly allowing a substantive human rights violation or systematic human rights violations to occur or to persist*:

> ... the [U.N.] Charter fares better with regards to the accountability function. The SC [Security Council] being a body created by the UN Charter, derives its powers from and subjects their exercise to the constraints imposed by this document [the UN Charter]. ***Pursuant to Article 25 of the UN Charter, only those SC decisions which are in accordance with the Charter must be carried out by the member states***. The Council can therefore be held legally accountable for its actions at least in theory.[90]

One cannot just speak then in general terms about lawfully delegated authority by the U.N. (under Chapter VII of the U.N. Charter) to UNMIK and to NATO (with NATO taking command of KFOR), as did the Court, since the failure to de-mine

[90]Giegerich (2009), under Legal constraints on Security Council action, para 1.

and the failure to remove refugees from lead contaminated IDP camps is beyond the scope of any such lawfully delegated powers. For the above reasons then the current author disagrees with the view that the effect of the European Court of Human Rights' *Behrami* admissibility decision is that "the ECHR [European Convention on Human Rights] is, in effect, rendered irrelevant during international peace operations" [given the Court's assigning accountability to the U.N. which is not a State and not a party to the ECHR].[91] Instead, it is maintained that the individual States cooperating in UNMIK were accountable for the aforementioned international human rights violations in *Behrami* and in the UN Northern Kosovo lead contaminated refugee camps cases given the implications of *Article 25 of the U.N. Charter which renders international human rights abuses to be beyond any lawfully delegated U.N. authority*. (Whether, the United Nations Security Council as a legal entity in and of itself is also legally accountable is a topic beyond the scope of this book, but it seems likely that this is the case given the implications of Article 25 of the U.N. Charter.)

Note that the European Court of Human Rights in *Bosphorus v. Ireland* ruled that where European Convention rights have in fact been seriously compromised by a State Party (notwithstanding the fact that this occurred due to the State's participation in an international organization that purports to provide equivalent rights guarantees) the interest of international co-operation would be *outweighed* by the Convention's role as a "constitutional instrument of European public order in the field of human rights"[92] (hence allowing for attribution of accountability to the individual State Party to the European Convention for the international human rights abuses rather than attribution to the international organization whose directives the member State was following or cooperating with). While the latter case involved State cooperation with European Council directives, this principle regarding the accountability of individual States is, it is argued, equally applicable when States violate international human rights by tolerating or supporting U.N. international human rights violations as allegedly occurred in *Behrami*.

4. **Individual state accountability under the European Convention on Human Rights for States exercising extraterritorial jurisdiction while acting under U.N. delegated authority**: The fact that the individual States cooperating as part of UNMIK or KFOR (some of which are States Parties to the *European Convention on Human Rights*) were acting extraterritorially does *not* eliminate their accountability for the international human rights violations they perpetrated through their actions or inaction under U.N. auspices. This is the case since these individual States, in actuality, had jurisdiction over the persons affected by the harms they perpetrated. That is, the individual States comprising UNMIK and KFOR respectively had *effective control* over the *territory* in question (Kosovo)

---

[91] Larsen (2008, p. 531).

[92] Press release dated 30 June 2006 of the registrar concerning the European Court of Human Rights Grand Chamber judgment in *Bosphorus Airways v. Ireland*. http://www.echr.coe.int/.../HearingGCBosphorousAirways290904.htm. Accessed 28 July 2009.

in terms of civil administration and security. In the case of the Roma and other minorities in Kosovo housed in IDP camps, there was, in effect, furthermore, *effective control over these persons* in terms of dictating where they lived, the standard of their living conditions, their health status, their security, whether they would be assisted to resettle outside the country as refugees etc., since these persons, though not in detention, realistically had no other place to go and could not readily fend for themselves in the circumstance of ethnic cleansing being visited upon them by extremist elements of the Albanian community:

> ... the notion of jurisdiction in human rights treaties... is a question of fact, of effective control that a State has over a territory, or of authority or control that it has over a particular person.[93]

Hence, it was the individual States cooperating with U.N. Security Council resolution 1244 that actually exercised jurisdictional authority in Kosovo through their effective control over the territory and over particular persons within that territory (and not the fictional legal persons of UNMIK, KFOR or the U.N. proper that did so). Since these individual States exercised jurisdiction in this way, those that were States Parties to the *European Convention on Human Rights* then as per Article 1 of the Convention were obligated to provide to the persons in that territory under their jurisdiction the rights and freedom guarantees in the Convention and their actions or lack of action in this regard were subject to judicial scrutiny by the European Court of Human Rights.[94]

5. **U.N. Charter objectives regarding fostering peace and security are irrelevant to the issue of the accountability of individual States for international wrongdoing committed while participating in a U.N. authorized peacekeeping mission**: There is a strong objection to be made to the European Court of Human Rights' *Behrami* decision being grounded, in the final analysis, on the Court's stated desire *not* to rule in such a way that States participating in U.N. peacekeeping and/or security missions might be held accountable for international human rights violations occurring just prior to or during the mission. The Court's expressed fear was that accountability for international wrongdoing being attributed to the States members (i.e. of a peacekeeping or security mission) would cause those individual States to be reluctant to participate in future U.N. peacekeeping/security initiatives (thus allegedly reducing the likely accomplishment of U.N. peace and security objectives). On this point the Court states the following:

> Since operations established by the UNSC [United Nations Security Council] Resolutions under Chapter VII of the UN Charter are fundamental to the mission of the UN to secure international peace and security and since they rely for their effectiveness on support from member states, the Convention [European Convention on Human Rights] cannot be interpreted in a manner which would subject the acts and omissions of Contracting Parties which are covered by UNSC Resolutions and occur prior to or in the course of such missions, to the scrutiny of the Court [the European Court of Human Rights]. To do so would be to

[93]Milanovic and Papic (2009, p. 272).

[94]Milanovic and Papic (2009, p. 272).

> interfere with the fulfillment of the UN's key mission in this field... including with the effective conduct of its operations. *It would be tantamount to imposing conditions on the implementation of a UNSC Resolution which were not provided for in the text of the Resolution itself* (emphasis added).[95]

While the U.N.'s goals (as expressed in its Charter) are intended to enhance the interests of all of humanity, this objective is clearly *not* consistent with: (i) leaving Roma children and adults living in lead contaminated U.N. refugee camps such that their blood lead levels are off the chart and amongst the highest ever recorded, or (ii) KFOR or UNMIK leaving cluster bombs to kill one small child and seriously maim and blind another belonging to the Behrami family. The U.N. peace and security mandate is then *not* a legitimate rationale for the European Court of Human Rights' (ECHR) legal interpretation (as reflected in the quote above from the decision) of the issues in *Behrami* given the member States positive obligation to respect fundamental human rights in implementing U.N. resolutions. The Court's interpretation in *Behrami* is crafted to allow for individual State impunity, and hence total lack of accountability (given also the U.N.'s absolute immunity). With respect, there is, as a result of *Behrami*, European Court of Human Rights' artificially judicially-created lack of individual State accountability for international wrongdoing when States act as part of a U.N. peacekeeping (peace-building) and security operation. The implication of the European Court of Human Rights' decision in *Behrami*, (ruling the case inadmissible), is total immunity civilly for all concerned (i.e. individual States as well as the legal entities UNMIK, KFOR, NATO, the UNSC and the U.N. proper). If the U.N. is responsible as the European Court claims then unless and until the U.N. itself decides to exercise its '*discretionary* compassion' and (i) voluntarily pay just reparations to the Behrami family and to the Roma victims of the lead contaminated U.N. refugee camps (taking into account the gravity of the harms suffered), (ii) rectify the situations that gave rise to the harms in the first instance (i.e. by moving the Roma refugees to safe locales with decent housing and facilities, etc.), and (iii) waive immunity against criminal prosecution for individual perpetrators, there may be no justice for these victims.

It is respectfully suggested that it is clearly contrary to both Article 1 of the U.N. Charter (dealing with the positive obligations of cooperating States to honour their human rights obligations under the Charter), and Article 25 of the U.N. Charter (concerning the requirement that member States act in accord with the U.N. Charter including Article 1 in carrying out operations under U.N. resolutions) to suggest (as did the ECHR in *Behrami*) that: (i) meeting the U.N.'s peace and security objectives may, at times, lawfully come at the expense of human rights for some, and (ii) by means of immunity (i.e. not just for the U.N. itself, but also for individual States responsible for international wrongdoing during a U.N. peacekeeping/security operation and their agents). Article 103 of the U.N. Charter is of no assistance in

---

[95] *Behrami and Behrami v. France* (Application 71412/01) [heard in conjunction with *Saramati v. France, Germany and Norway* (Application 781/01)], 2 May 2007. European Court of Human Rights, Grand Chamber decision on admissibility, para 149. http://hei.unige.ch/~clapham/hrdoc/docs/ECHRBehrami.doc. Accessed 25 July 2009.

establishing immunity for individual States Parties to the *European Convention on Human Rights* that cooperated with the U.N. resolution 1244 relating to Kosovo and in carrying out the U.N. directives allowed U.N. international human rights violations to occur or persist. Article 103 of the U.N. Charter stipulates that:

> *In the event of a conflict* between the obligations of the Members of the United Nations under the present Charter and their obligations under any other international agreement, their obligations under the present Charter shall prevail (emphasis added).[96]

In the lead contaminated Kosovo U.N. refugee camp case and in *Behrami*, there is *no* conflict between the obligations of the cooperating individual States to U.N. resolution 1244 and their obligations under the *European Convention on Human Rights* (both impose the positive obligation to take all possible steps to secure and protect every person's fundamental human rights who may be affected by the States' actions or inaction). There was no conceivable security reason in either of the aforementioned cases that would have justified compromising, to any extent, the rights of the civilian victims in the instant cases let alone allowing such grave human rights violations as leaving Roma children and adults to suffer lead poisoning in U.N. refugee camps or failing to remove unexploded mines which could and did kill and maim children. Further, as previously discussed, Articles 1 and 25 of the U.N. Charter, taken together, establish the legal basis for accountability for individual States that engage in international wrongdoing (i.e. by failing to prevent or end U.N. human rights abuses) while operating under the auspices of the U.N. Hence, it is, with respect, fallacious to suggest, as does the European Court of Human Rights in *Behrami*, that "It would be tantamount to imposing conditions on the implementation of a UNSC Resolution which were not provided for in the text of the Resolution itself"[97] [to hold individual States accountable for wrongdoing committed just prior to, or while participating in U.N. peacekeeping and security operations such as those conducted under U.N. resolution 1244]. Those "conditions" referred to in the previous quote from the admissibility decision in *Behrami* are in fact already incorporated in the UNSC resolution through Articles 1 and 25 of the U.N. Charter.

Despite the rather technical and philosophical legal issues embedded in *Behrami*, it is important to always keep in mind the realities which the European Court of Human Rights plays a part in maintaining or altering:

> Most important. . . is the real-life implications that *Behrami* has for the protection of human rights in Kosovo. The Court has already used *Behrami* to dismiss several claims brought against European States for purported human rights violations in Kosovo. Indeed, Kosovo

[96]Charter of the United Nations (Article 103). http://www.un.org/en/documents/charter/index.shtml. Accessed 27 July 2009.

[97]*Behrami and Behrami v. France* (Application 71412/01) [heard in conjunction with *Saramati v. France, Germany and Norway* (Application 781/01)], 2 May 2007. European Court of Human Rights, Grand Chamber decision on admissibility, para 149. http://hei.unige.ch/~clapham/hrdoc/docs/ECHRBehrami.doc. Accessed 25 July 2009.

> has now truly become the only lawless land of Europe, a legal black hole over which there is no independent human rights supervision.[98]

It can be argued that affording immunity from civil liability to individual States for international wrongdoing when that wrongdoing occurred just prior to, or during U.N. peacekeeping missions: (i) undermines the faith of the most vulnerable and of the international community as a whole in the U.N. mission in question (as does affording immunity against civil and criminal liability to agents of the States cooperating with the U.N. mission), and (ii) erodes, within the international community, the perceived moral integrity of the U.N. as an international organization with a peace and security mandate founded on respect for fundamental human rights. The latter effects then do nothing in furtherance of the U.N.'s peace and security mission. In addition, when such lack of accountability for international wrongdoing is afforded to both to the UNSC member States and to the U.N. proper in various such recurrent situations globally, this ultimately is also likely to work against achievement generally of U.N. peace and security objectives. Ultimately then the European Court of Human Rights in *Behrami* holding individual States Parties to the European Convention (who cooperated with UNMIK and KFOR) to be immune from civil liability (a position set out in the Court's ruling that the case was inadmissible) is: (i) inconsistent with the Court's mandate to monitor compliance with the European Convention and, for the reasons explained above, (ii) represents in fact the Court ***declining*** its jurisdiction rather than an instance of the Court's lack of jurisdiction.

V. Interim Measures Requested by the European Court of Human Rights in Mamatkulov and Askarov v. Turkey Versus the Court's Denial of a Request for Interim Measures by Roma Victim Applicants Living in U.N. Lead-Contaminated Refugee Camps in Kosovo

A. *Introduction*

This commentary considers in-depth the refusal by the European Court of Human Rights to indicate to the respondent Party (i.e. those member States of UNMIK who are States Parties to the European Convention on Human Rights) a request by the Court for interim measures in the U.N. Kosovo lead contaminated refugee camps case (those camps, as discussed, housing Roma internally displaced persons who had fled their homes due to ethnic cleansing attacks by extremist Albanians). The issues are considered in the context of the European Court's established principles regarding the distinct role and significance of urgent interim measures for the

[98] Milanovic and Papic (2009, p. 295).

protection of human rights and freedoms as provided for in the European Convention. Those principles are discussed with reference to the European Court of Human Rights' *Mamatkulov and Askarov v. Turkey* Grand Chamber judgment where interim measures were granted.[99] Comparisons are made between the *Mamatkulov and Askarov v. Turkey* case and the facts in the U.N. lead contaminated IDP Kosovo camps case where the applicants requested the Court to indicate to the respondent a requirement for emergency interim measures but were denied by the Court. This comparison is made in order to demonstrate, with respect, that: (i) there was no supportable legal basis for the European Court of Human Rights' denial of emergency interim measures which would have required relocating the Roma to safe locations (i.e. outside the highly lead contaminated and squalid U.N. Kosovo refugee camps that were their homes); and that (ii) this decision by the Court (faxed to the European Roma Rights Centre by letter the day after the application to the Court was filed), in no way exculpates the Sates or their agents participating in UNMIK who were responsible (either directly or indirectly) for leaving the Roma in the lead contaminated camps either before and/or after the Court's decision was issued. We begin then with an examination of the European Court of Human Rights' Grand Chamber judgment in *Mamatkulov and Askarov v. Turkey* case and the Court's discussion of its views regarding the import of interim measures in that case and more generally in respect of the preservation of Convention rights.

B. Case 5: European Court of Human Rights' Grand Chamber Judgment in Mamatkulov and Askarov v. Turkey (Applications 46827/99 and 46951/99)

Background and Procedural History

The instant case *Mamatkulov and Askarov v. Turkey* concerns two Uzbek nationals; Mr Rustam Sultanovich Mamatkulov, and Mr Zainiddin Abdurasulovich Askarov; both members at the time of Erk (Freedom), an opposition party in Uzbekistan. The applicants had been arrested in Turkey on an international warrant pursuant to a bilateral extradition treaty between Turkey and Uzbekistan. The allegation was that the applicants had engaged in, and were planning further to engage in terrorist activity against the then sitting government of Uzbekistan. The applicants challenged their impending extradition from Turkey to Uzbekistan as allegedly constituting a violation of their European Convention rights under Article 2 (right to life), Article 3 (prohibition against torture and inhuman or degrading treatment or

[99] *Mamatkulov and Askarov v. Turkey* (Applications nos. 46827/99 and 46951/99). European Court of Human Rights, Grand Chamber judgment of 4 February 2005. http://www.unhcr.org/refworld/publisher,ECHR,UZB,42d3ef174,0.html. Accessed 8 August 2009.

punishment); Article 6 (right to a fair trial) and Article 34 (the right to file individual applications to the Court without hindrance from a State Party). On 18 March 1999, the President of the Chamber of the European Court of Human Rights that was to hear the case on the merits on 23 March 1999 requested that Turkey not extradite the applicants prior to the Chamber hearing the case (an interim measure). This request was made pursuant to Article 39 of the European Convention on Human Rights regarding interim measures. However, on 19 March 1999, Turkey issued a decree ordering the extradition of the applicants to Uzbekistan. On 23 March 1999, the European Court of Human Rights extended the time frame for the operation of the Court requested interim measure (not to extradite the applicants) to a date uncertain until further notice. Notwithstanding that fact, Turkey, however, handed custody of the applicants over to Uzbekistani authorities on 27 March 1999. In a letter dated 19 April 1999, Turkey transmitted to the Court various written assurances it had received from the Public Prosecutor of the Republic of Uzbekistan to the effect that: (i) the applicants' property would not be confiscated; (ii) the applicants' would not be subjected to torture or sentenced to capital punishment and (iii) Uzbekistan would honour all of its obligations under the U.N. Convention Against Torture.

On 11 June 1999, the Government of Turkey transmitted to the Court a diplomatic note dated 8 June 1999 from the Uzbek Ministry of Foreign Affairs setting out the evidence against the applicants pertaining to alleged terrorist activity; the provisions that had been made for their security, the fair process that had been allegedly offered to the defendants and information on the status of the court proceedings. In a letter dated 8 July 1999, the Government of Turkey informed the Court that by a judgment of 28 June 1999; the Supreme Court of the Republic of Uzbekistan had found the applicants guilty of various terrorist acts and had sentenced them to terms of imprisonment. In a letter to the Court dated 15 September 1999, the applicants' representatives reported, among other things, that they had not been able to contact their clients, that their clients had been subjected to a secret trial; that conditions in Uzbek prisons were inconsistent with acceptable international standards, and that prisoners were routinely subjected to torture. On 15 October 2001, Turkey was informed via the Uzbek Ministry of Foreign Affairs that Mr. Mamatkulov was sentenced to twenty years and Mr. Askarov to eleven years of imprisonment.

The government of Turkey informed the European Court of Human Rights at the hearing on 23 October 2001 that its representatives had visited the two men on 19 October 2001 and allegedly found them to be in good health with no complaints about the prison conditions. On 3 December 2001, the Turkish government received medical certificates drawn up by military doctors who had allegedly examined the two men and rendered them whatever medical care they needed. The Turkish government maintained and communicated to the Court that the men had received several visits from close relatives in the period January 2002–2004 as allegedly evidenced from the visiting lists at the prison. No evidence was presented to the Court, however, that the applicants had had contact with their counsel since their extradition.

The Chamber of the European Court of Human Rights ruled 6 February 2003 on the merits that the alleged violation of ECHR Article 3 was not supported since the Court had insufficient and inconclusive factual evidence to rely on and could not make further inquiries of the applicants since their extradition to Uzbekistan had been effected. The Chamber further ruled that European Convention Article 6 was not applicable to the extradition process in Turkey; and that, furthermore, there was no additional issue with respect to Article 6 as there was no conclusive evidence to suggest the trial process for the applicants in Uzbekistan was unfair. However, the Chamber ruled in favor of the applicants in respect of their complaint concerning Article 34 holding (by six votes to one) that Turkey had infringed the applicants' rights which were guaranteed under Article 34 of the Convention (the right of individual petition to the Court concerning European Convention violations).

> ... any State Party to the Convention to which interim measures have been indicated in order to avoid irreparable harm being caused to the victim of an alleged violation must comply with those measures and refrain from any act or omission that will undermine the authority and effectiveness of the final judgment.
>
> *Consequently, by failing to comply with the interim measures indicated by the Court under Rule 39 of the Rules of Court, Turkey is in breach of its obligations under Article 34 of the Convention* (emphasis added).[100]

The case was referred to the Grand Chamber on appeal at the request of the Turkish government.

The Grand Chamber Judgment and Reasoning in Mamatkulov and Askarov v. Turkey Regarding Interim Measures

The Grand Chamber *in Mamatkulov and Askariv v. Turkey*, as did the Chamber, held that it could not assess whether there had been a violation of Article 3 of the European Convention with respect to these particular applicants at the time they were extradited by Turkey to Uzbekistan in March of 1999 as it had insufficient evidence upon which to base a conclusion in this regard. Hence, the Grand Chamber ruled that there was no violation of Article 3 (the Court held further that there was no need for a separate examination regarding Article 2). Likewise the Grand Chamber also ruled that there had been no violation of Article 6(1) in that there was insufficient evidence in 1999 at the time of the extradition to reach a conclusion on: (i) whether extradition would pose a real risk to the applicants of torture or inhuman and degrading treatment or punishment, or (ii) whether there was a real risk the applicants would receive an unfair criminal trial in Uzbekistan. Hence, the Grand Chamber ruled there was no violation of Article 6(1) with respect to the extradition by Turkey or the criminal proceedings in Uzbekistan. The Grand

[100] *Mamatkulov and Askarov v. Turkey* (Applications nos. 46827/99 and 46951/99). European Court of Human Rights, Grand Chamber judgment of 4 February 2005, para 93 citing the *Mamatkulov and Askarov v. Turkey* Chamber judgment, para 110–111. http://www.unhcr.org/refworld/publisher,ECHR,,UZB,42d3ef174,0.html. Accessed 8 August 2009.

Chamber found that "Turkey's failure to comply with the indication given by the Court under Rule 39 of the Rules of Court [regarding the Court's request for interim measures]... prevented the Court from obtaining additional information to assist it in its assessment of whether there was a real risk of a flagrant denial of justice...".[101]

The Grand Chamber held that determinations regarding the implications of Turkey preventing the Court from properly assessing, based on sufficient factual evidence obtained from the applicants, etc., whether or not extradition of the applicants to Uzbekistan posed a real risk of torture and/or inhuman or degrading treatment and/or injustice via an unfair criminal trial in Uzbekistan (due to Turkey implementing the extradition decree in defiance of the European Court of Human Rights' indication of its requiring interim measures) are properly addressed under Article 34 of the European Convention. Article 34 sets out the European Court's authority to request interim measures to ensure the preservation of the parties' rights so as not to render any potential or pending case devoid of purpose or consequence:

> Consequently, the interim measure is sought by the applicant, and granted by the Court, in order to facilitate the "effective exercise" of the right of individual petition under Article 34 of the Convention in the sense of preserving the subject matter of the application when that is judged to be at risk of irreparable damage through the acts or omissions of the respondent State.[102]

The Grand Chamber held that the rights the applicants' were asserting under Articles 2 and 3 of the European Convention were potentially irreparably harmed due to Turkey failing to institute the Court requested interim measure (i.e. the failure to stay the applicants' extradition until and unless the European Court of Human Rights (ECHR) gave notice that the interim measure could be lifted). The European Court of Human Rights held that there was, therefore, a violation of Article 34 of the European Convention in that Turkey's failure to implement the interim measure interfered with the applicants' right of individual petition. This since the European Court of Human Rights found that once the applicants had been extradited to Uzbekistan: (i) the Court could not provide the applicants the Court's protection regarding their right to life and right to protection from torture or inhuman or degrading treatment and, in addition, (ii) the Court could not obtain further needed information from the applicants relevant to the applicants' assertion of their Article 2 and Article 3 Convention rights (i.e. once the applicants had been extradited and placed in a Uzbekistani prison, the men were unable to make contact with their lawyers). The European Court of Human Rights hence could not carry out

[101] *Mamatkulov and Askarov v. Turkey* (Applications nos. 46827/99 and 46951/99). European Court of Human Rights, Grand Chamber judgment of 4 February 2005, para. 91. http://www.unhcr.org/refworld/publisher,ECHR,UZB,42d3ef174,0.html. Accessed 8 August 2009.

[102] *Mamatkulov and Askarov v. Turkey* (Applications nos. 46827/99 and 46951/99). European Court of Human Rights, Grand Chamber judgment of 4 February 2005, para 108. http://www.unhcr.org/refworld/publisher,ECHR,UZB,42d3ef174,0.html. Accessed 8 August 2009.

its normal procedure in making determinations regarding the applicants' assertion of Article 2 and 3 European Convention on Human Rights violations.

Commentary on the European Court of Human Rights' Denial of the Applicants' Request for Interim Emergency Measures for the Protection of the Right of Individual Petition and Other European Convention Rights of Roma Housed in Highly Lead Contaminated U.N. Kosovo IDP Camps

1. **The Court's refusal in the Kosovo IDP camp case to indicate interim measures, and to hear the case for admissibility, created an indirect systemic adverse discriminatory impact on the Roma**: The refusal of the European Court of Human Rights to empanel a judicial bench to review the Kosovo U.N. lead contaminated IDP camps case for admissibility, and to indicate (to the respondent State members of UNMIK) the need for interim measures (relocating the Roma and other minorities who occupied the camps to safe locations), *in effect*, on the reasoning of the Court that it had *no jurisdiction*, created the illusion that the gypsy victims of high lead exposure in these refugee camps were not subjects of international human rights law. This is an unacceptable *discriminatory result* from any legal or moral perspective and cannot be justified. It is a discriminatory result in that only those perceived as 'gypsies' were housed in these lead contaminated camps (Roma, Ashkali, and Egyptian peoples) (the 'RAE').

That UNMIK instituted a comprehensive non-discrimination statute in Kosovo[103] is irrelevant given the reality of the lead toxic IDP camp situation the participating UNMIK States allowed to persist with those IDP camps housing members of particularly vulnerable ethnic populations perceived as 'gypsies'. The fact is that: (i) the United Nations either moved too slowly for most of the victims in closing certain camps to prevent or mitigate the serious adverse impacts on the health of these occupants stemming from the high lead exposure in the contaminated IDP camps (particularly with respect to children and unborn children both of which groups are most vulnerable to the effects of high lead exposure), or (ii) in the case of U.N. lead contaminated 'gypsy' refugee camps still open in Kosovo near the Trepca lead mines, did not take meaningful remedial steps at all in terms of securing relocation to safe uncontaminated areas with decent housing and adequate basic facilities. Indeed, by 2000, the RAE peoples suffering in the highly lead contaminated U.N. refugee camps were, based on the fact that UNHCR pulled out of UNMIK, apparently *not* at all a priority for UNMIK, and their plight *not* considered a humanitarian crisis requiring urgent remedial intervention:

> In order to implement its mandate, UNMIK [headed by the Special Representative for Kosovo of the U.N. Secretary-General] initially brought together four pillars under its leadership. *At the end of the emergency stage, Pillar I (humanitarian assistance), led by the*

[103] Roma Rights Centre (2006, p. 16).

Office of the United Nations High Commissioner for Refugees (UNHCR), was phased out in June 2000 (emphasis added).[104]

It is noteworthy also in this regard that UNMIK did not act on the 2004 World Health Organization report which, based on empirical medical evidence, concluded that the highly lead contaminated camps were *uninhabitable*.

This author must, given all of the aforementioned facts, disagree strongly with the rosy and, with respect, erroneous view that despite the virtual lack of legal accountability of UNMIK as an entity to the people of Kosovo including the RAE (notwithstanding its having full administrative authority over the territory at the time the European Roma Rights Centre brought the Kosovo Roma IDP camps case to the European Court of Human Rights in 2006), we can be reassured by the alleged safeguarding of fundamental human rights afforded all the peoples governed by the international administration established in Kosovo under U.N. authority:

> The international administrations of our times,... in Kosovo... operate in a rather sophisticated and developed international environment with consolidated democratic values and institutions, a developed international legal machinery, an advanced political and human rights culture, and international institutions, including strong media and civil society – *all of which indirectly provide considerable checks and balances against abuses*... This does not mean that the international administration should not strive to bridge this gap of accountability and to promote transparency and compliance with human rights in the exercise of its mandate (emphasis added).[105]

Clearly, the situation of the RAE trying to survive in highly lead contaminated refugee camps run by UNMIK with the inhabitants often relying on improvised housing created from scavenged boards, tin, sticks and plastic, no proper heating, dirt floors, etc., (such as was the case, for instance, at the Zitkovac/Zhikoc IDP camp[106]) does *not* reflect "a rather sophisticated and developed international environment with... an advanced... human rights culture," or evidence of an international environment providing "considerable checks and balances against [human rights] abuses...".

2. **On the culpability and liability of the individual States cooperating in UNMIK for the international human rights violations (i.e. European Convention violations) relating to the U.N. lead contaminated IDP camps in Kosovo**: We turn now to consideration of the obligation of the individual States cooperating in UNMIK to protect the human rights of the internally displaced RAE peoples in Kosovo and refer in our analysis to the *Vienna Convention on the Law of Treaties* (VC).[107] We will consider also the implications of the VC in our assessment of the

---

[104]European Commission for Democracy Through Law (Venice Commission) (2004). The human rights situation in Kosovo: Background information and issues for discussion (under: "Background" point 7). Opinion 280/2004. http://www.venice.coe.int/docs/2004/CDL-DI(2004)001-e.asp. Accessed 7 August 2009.

[105]Yannis (2004, p. 72).

[106]Roma Rights Centre (2006, p. 9, footnote 28).

[107]*Vienna Convention on the Law of Treaties*, adopted 22 May 1969 by the United Nations Conference on the Law of Treaties and open for signature and ratification in Vienna 23 May 1969;

validity or lack of validity of the European Court of Human Rights' decision to: (i) decline to adjudicate (in a public hearing of the Court) the admissibility of the U.N. Kosovo 'RAE' refugee camps case (which had been brought forward to the Court by the European Roma Rights Centre in February 2006), and to (ii) decline the applicants' request for an interim measure which would have removed the RAE from the U.N. lead contaminated IDP camps to a safe area, and presumably also to at least minimally adequate housing (thus preserving their European Convention rights under Article 2 and 3). *These denials were premised on the Court's view that it was UNMIK and not individual States that were accountable in Kosovo and hence the Court allegedly had no jurisdiction to hear the case or to request interim measures.* Let us begin then with an examination of the factors creating the obligations of *individual States* cooperating in UNMIK to the RAE internally displaced peoples of post-conflict Kosovo:

Facts and Law Relevant to the Issue of Individual State Accountability for Harms Caused the 'RAE' by Lead Exposure in the U.N. IDP Kosovo Camps

- Many of the States involved in UNMIK were States Parties to the *European Convention on Human Rights* (ECHR) at the relevant times (i.e. when involved in managing the U.N. lead contaminated IDP camps in Kosovo housing so-called 'gypsy' peoples [Roma, Ashkali, and Egyptian peoples 'RAE'] or participating in decision-making by UNMIK). It is here argued that the European Convention obligations of these individual States extended to protecting the rights and freedoms of the 'RAE' peoples in the IDP camps, as per Article 29 of the *Vienna Convention* which holds that treaties are binding on States regarding the territory and persons over which they have effective jurisdiction. The European Court of Human Rights accepted that the States participating in UNMIK had effective jurisdiction of the Kosovo region in that the Former Republic of Yugoslavia had transferred its sovereign authority to the international bodies UNMIK and KFOR;
- As has been discussed, and as was in fact uncontested by the European Court of Human Rights in *Behrami*, the peoples of Kosovo were under the extra-territorial jurisdiction and effective day-to-day control of those individual States participating in UNMIK during the relevant time. (UNMIK was the civil authority in Kosovo from 1999 up until about May 2008). The U.N. conceded in *Behrami* that while UNMIK was headed by a Special Representative of the U.N. Secretary General for Kosovo (a State national who reported to the Secretary General (SG) and the S.G. who then in turn reported directly to the U.N. Security Council); it was the individual member States cooperating in UNMIK and international representatives of various international bodies from diverse States who gave effect to the U.N.'s very general Kosovo mandate in the course of the "realities of their [the individual States'] daily operations." For instance, in

entered into force on 27 January 1980. http://untreaty.un.org/ilc/texts/instruments/.../conventions/1_1_1969.pdf. Accessed 9 August 2009.

2005, the Organization for Security and Cooperation in Europe, (comprised of numerous States including European States), *was part of a UNMIK task force* along with UNHCR, WHO, and KFOR contingents which developed the plan to move some of the IDP Roma and other so-called gypsy minorities to the Osterode IDP Camp claiming it was more lead safe. That the Osterode Camp would be a relatively lead free, safe environment, as discussed, turned out to be far from the truth. Further, rather than the IDP camps housing the RAE minorities being a temporary solution until the old settlements in Roma Mahalla could be rebuilt, two Roma IDP camps remained for over a decade and two of the three most lead contaminated camps, Osterode and Cesmincamp, are still operational. Hence, though the U.N., to use the Court's wording, may ***"in principle"*** have had so-called 'ultimate control' (at least in theory) of the activities performed under the auspices of UNMIK; it did *not* have effective control. There was then an express acknowledgment by the U.N. that it was the various UNMIK cooperating States and international governmental organizations that exercised actual real-life jurisdiction of the RAE in the IDP camps. Countless day-to-day decisions were, and are being made adversely affecting the RAE in the lead contaminated IDP camps and made on the basis of the prerogative of the individual State agents, and of international representatives and others (i.e. private contractors) working for UNMIK. These operational decisions regarding the U.N. lead contaminated IDP camps, furthermore, involve a largely discretionary interpretation of the U.N. very general mandate:

> The UN recalled the relevant provisions of UNSC Resolution 1244 which outlined the main responsibilities of the civil and security presences, *noting that the general and at times "imprecise" mandate was, for the most part, left to be concretised and agreed upon in the realities of their daily operations.*[108]

In making these very specific day-to-day concrete operational decisions on the State's own initiative (i.e. which operational decisions, for the most part, seriously adversely affected the inhabitants of the lead contaminated Kosovo IDP camps), the individual States cooperating in UNMIK were and are fully accountable and liable. *That is, accountability accrues to the individual States since the actual operationalization of the very broad and general U.N. mandate was carried out as a State sovereign function in meeting international obligations.* Though leaving the RAE in lead contaminated IDP camps was a violation of international human rights law, and presumably unlawful also under international criminal law, these acts were yet official State sanctioned acts by individual States participating in UNMIK (though beyond the jurisdiction of State sovereignty);

[108] *Behrami and Behrami v. France* (Application 71412/01) [heard in conjunction with *Saramati v. France, Germany and Norway* (Application 781/01)], 2 May 2007. European Court of Human Rights, Grand Chamber decision on admissibility, para 118 (European Court's summary of the U.N. submission). http://hei.unige.ch/~clapham/hrdoc/docs/ECHRBehrami.doc. Accessed 25 July 2009.

- In contrast to the position taken here on individual State accountability regarding the lead contaminated IDP camps in Kosovo, the suggestion was made in *Behrami* by the United Kingdom in its submission in that case that the individual States present in Kosovo under the authority of U.N. Security Council Resolution 1244 were not responsible for securing European Convention rights for the people of Kosovo:

  > the effect of UNSC Resolution 1244 was that, at the relevant time, the UNSC exercised the powers of government in Kosovo through an international administration supported by an international security presence to which the respondent States and other non-Contracting States had provided troops. None of the respondent States were therefore in a position to secure the rights and freedoms defined in Article 1 of the Convention to any of the inhabitants of Kosovo... the respondent States had neither the power nor the responsibility to secure the rights and freedoms defined in Article 1 since that responsibility was specifically vested in UNMIK.[109]

  It is here suggested, in contrast, that the individual States cooperating in UNMIK and KFOR had the power to secure the European Convention rights of the inhabitants of the lead contaminated U.N. camps *given that it was these States that made the day-to-day operational decisions regarding these camps, regarding security measures to protect the inhabitants of the area and decisions pertaining to other issues such as humanitarian concerns affecting minorities in the region.* They thus had the power and responsibility as States Parties to the European Convention to: (i) close the camps and relocate the occupants to safe and decent facilities or settlements, and to (ii) provide the medical assessments and care needed by those inhabitants of the camps already suffering from lead poisoning. It is, furthermore, legally indefensible to suggest, it is here argued, as did the U.K. in *Behrami*, that the *responsibility* to secure the European Convention rights to the people of Kosovo was *entirely* vested in UNMIK (a fictional legal person). UNMIK after all was not a party to the Convention as the European Court of Human Rights correctly pointed out in *Behrami*. However, that responsibility was vested, at least in large part, in those States cooperating in UNMIK who were also parties to the *European Convention on Human Rights*. Note also that, according to the U.N., the operation of the *European Convention on Human Rights* was *not* suspended in Kosovo under the international administration in the post-conflict period;
- There was *no new preemptory 'jus cogens' international law norm* relating to international peace and security missions carried out by the U.N. that would override the requirement of the individual States to meet their obligations under the European Convention as permitted according to Article 64 of the

[109] *Behrami and Behrami v. France* (Application 71412/01) [heard in conjunction with *Saramati v. France, Germany and Norway* (Application 781/01)], 2 May 2007. European Court of Human Rights, Grand Chamber decision on admissibility, para 114 (European Court's summary of the U.K. submission). http://hei.unige.ch/~clapham/hrdoc/docs/ECHRBehrami.doc. Accessed 25 July 2009.

Vienna Convention.[110] *In fact, on the contrary, meeting the Convention obligations in post-conflict Kosovo must be viewed as integral to the U.N.'s express mission of fostering democracy, peace and respect for fundamental human rights in the region*;

- The U.K. and other third party State interveners in *Behrami*, (and the European Court of Human Rights itself in *Behrami* and in the lead contaminated IDP Kosovo camps case), ***erroneously*** assessed the situation in which grave harms befell civilians under a U.N. orchestrated international administration in post-conflict Kosovo due to State actions ***as if***: (i) the individual States participating in UNMIK were in circumstances that made it impossible for them to meet their European Convention obligations given the context of an international authority presence in Kosovo (UNMIK) handling civil administration and security matters in coordination with KFOR, and (ii) those circumstances allegedly removed from the individual States participating in UNMIK, as per Articles 61 and 62 of the Vienna Convention (VC), any accountability and liability for European Convention violations that the acts of commission or omission by individual States cooperating in UNMIK had caused. Firstly, there was no change in circumstances that was unforeseen, as required under Article 62 of the VC[111] that could have allowed for the excuse of 'impossibility of performance' of the European Convention obligations by the individual States Parties to that Convention participating in UNMIK in post-conflict Kosovo. Furthermore, Article 61(2) and 62(2)(b) of the *Vienna Convention* stipulate that alleged 'impossibility of performance' of treaty obligations cannot be invoked for failure to meet convention/treaty obligations if the circumstances complained of are a result of the *State Party's own breach* of the treaty in question, or of obligations owed under international law. *Here, the individual State Parties themselves breached European Convention and jus cogens international law obligations by leaving persons in highly lead contaminated IDP camps. The States then relied on their own failure to meet their European Convention and other international obligations as justification for attributing the power and responsibility to remedy the situation to the U.N.*;
- *Note also, in consideration of the legal spirit and values underlying Article 60(5) of the Vienna Convention,*[112] (which stipulates that treaty obligations relating to

[110] *Vienna Convention on the Law of Treaties*, adopted 22 May 1969 by the United Nations Conference on the Law of Treaties and open for signature and ratification in Vienna 23 May 1969; entered into force on 27 January 1980, Article 64. http://untreaty.un.org/ilc/texts/instruments/.../conventions/1_1_1969.pdf. Accessed 9 August 2009.

[111] *Vienna Convention on the Law of Treaties*, adopted 22 May 1969 by the United Nations Conference on the Law of Treaties and open for signature and ratification in Vienna 23 May 1969; entered into force on 27 January 1980, Article 61(2) and 62(2)(b). http://untreaty.un.org/ilc/texts/instruments/.../conventions/1_1_1969.pdf. Accessed 9 August 2009.

[112] *Vienna Convention on the Law of Treaties*, adopted 22 May 1969 by the United Nations Conference on the Law of Treaties and open for signature and ratification in Vienna 23 May 1969; entered into force on 27 January 1980, Article 60(5). http://untreaty.un.org/ilc/texts/instruments/.../conventions/1_1_1969.pdf. Accessed 9 August 2009.

humanitarian concerns cannot be avoided based on a breach by another Party), that while the U.N. is not a party to the European Convention, breaches of humanitarian obligations by the U.N. do **not** remove European Convention obligations from the individual States Parties coopering in UNMIK relating to respect for basic jus cogens rights founded on humanitarian considerations;

- A 'good faith' reading of the European Convention does *not* permit abandonment of State obligations particularly as they relate to the *jus cogens* obligations under Articles 2 and 3 of the European Convention and as were implicated in the U.N. IDP Kosovo camps case. This view is contrary to the suggestion of the U.K., for instance, in *Behrami* as cited below:

> To avoid this result, Article 1 should be interpreted to mean that, where officials from States act together within the scope of an international operation authorised by the UN... *their acts did not bring those affected within the jurisdiction of the States* ***or engage the Convention responsibility of those States*** (emphasis added).[113]

Note, in this regard, that the European Court of Human Rights' position in *Behrami* and the IDP Kosovo camps case is that the U.N. (at least 'in principle'), and not the individual States actually making the concrete day-to-day decisions in post-conflict Kosovo as part of UNMIK, is accountable for the harms resulting from State decisions made under the auspices of UNMIK. The Court held in *Behrami* that individual States cooperating with the U.N. as U.N. member States may be assumed to be meeting their European Convention obligations given the presumption that the U.N. offers human rights protections at least equivalent to the *European Convention on Human Rights* guarantees. In the *Behrami* case (involving both UNMIK and KFOR) and the case of the lead contaminated U.N. Kosovo refugee camps, this is, of course, a questionable presumption at best. We will return to this point shortly. In any case, recall that nothing in the U.N. mandate emanating from U.N. Security Council resolution 1244 authorized the violation of the fundamental human rights of any population within Kosovo (in fact UNMIK was expected by the U.N. to operate within the framework of the *European Convention on Human Rights* and other international human rights treaties). Thus such violations as took place in the course of operational individual State day-to-day decision making must be said to have occurred under State and not U.N. authority (or perhaps under shared authority), and as such, any State that caused such violations to occur or continue (even if under alleged UNMIK auspices/authority) is accountable and liable in whole or in part;

- Articles 26 and 27 of the *Vienna Convention* are particularly relevant as to the issue of accountability of the individual States and their agents for: (i) the physical and mental harms inflicted on the RAE inhabitants of the lead

[113] *Behrami and Behrami v. France* (Application 71412/01) [heard in conjunction with *Saramati v. France, Germany and Norway* (Application 781/01)], 2 May 2007. European Court of Human Rights, Grand Chamber decision on admissibility, para 116 (European Court's summary of the U.K. submission). http://hei.unige.ch/~clapham/hrdoc/docs/ECHRBehrami.doc. Accessed 25 July 2009.

contaminated IDP camps in Kosovo and (ii) the undermining of the victims' non-derogable rights (such as, but not limited to, those under Article 3 of the ECHR which prohibits torture and inhuman and degrading treatment). Articles 26 and 27 of the VC read as follows:

> **Article 26**: Every treaty in force is binding upon the parties to it and *must be performed by them in good faith* (emphasis added).[114]
> **Article 27**: *A party may not invoke the provisions of its internal law as justification for its failure to perform a treaty*. This rule is without prejudice to article 46 (emphasis added).[115]

The States Parties to the *European Convention on Human Rights* (ECHR) which were participating in UNMIK, (such as the member States of the EU addressing economic reconstruction of Kosovo), knew as early as 2000, as mentioned, if not before that date, that the highly lead contaminated IDP camps would result in: (i) serious harms to the health of the RAE camp occupants, and (ii) grave violations of the non-derogable fundamental human rights of the camps' inhabitants as well as erosion of certain of their other European Convention rights. Yet, these States through their agents, were complicit on an ongoing basis from at least 2000 to May 2008 in knowingly and intentionally perpetuating, or being complicit, directly or indirectly, in perpetuating these harms thus violating: (i) their *European Convention on Human Rights* (ECHR) treaty obligations (for those States Parties to the European Convention participating in UNMIK), and (ii) for most, if not all the cooperating States in UNMIK, their treaty obligations under the *International Covenant on Civil and Political Rights*[116] as is clear given Articles 26 and 27 of the *Vienna Convention* (i.e. there was no justification for these States to fail to execute their obligations under the ECHR and ICCPR in good faith).

In the final analysis, it is the internal law of the individual States which, at the outset, allowed for individual States to freely involve themselves in U.N. peace keeping missions such as UNMIK and put their personnel at the disposal of the U.N. However, nothing in that internal State law, according to the VC Articles 26 and 27, will be considered (under the international law of treaties) to allow for the perpetuation of unlawful violations of fundamental human rights under the ECHR or the ICCPR (or under any other international human rights

[114]*Vienna Convention on the Law of Treaties*, adopted 22 May 1969 by the United Nations Conference on the Law of Treaties and open for signature and ratification in Vienna 23 May 1969; entered into force on 27 January 1980, Article 26. http://untreaty.un.org/ilc/texts/instruments/.../conventions/1_1_1969.pdf. Accessed 9 August 2009.

[115]*Vienna Convention on the Law of Treaties*, adopted 22 May 1969 by the United Nations Conference on the Law of Treaties and open for signature and ratification in Vienna 23 May 1969; entered into force on 27 January 1980, Article 27. http://untreaty.un.org/ilc/texts/instruments/.../conventions/1_1_1969.pdf. Accessed 9 August 2009.

[116]International Covenant on Civil and Political Rights, adopted and open for signature and ratification by the U.N. general Assembly, 16 December 1966, entered into force 23 March 1976. http://www.hrweb.org/legal/cpr.html. Accessed 9 August 2009.

instruments to which particular States participating in UNMIK are parties). Yet, such unlawful violations of treaty obligations ensued due to the existence of the highly lead contaminated IDP camps for the RAE peoples in Kosovo managed by these States participating in UNMIK;

- Consider also the implication of Article 31 of the *Vienna Convention* regarding the general interpretation of treaties for our understanding of *individual State accountability* (for States participating in UNMIK) regarding particular acts of commission and omission relating to the U.N. lead contaminated IDP Kosovo camps. Article 31 stipulates the following:

> 1. *A treaty shall be interpreted in good faith in accordance with the ordinary meaning to be given to the terms of the treaty in their context and in the light of its object and purpose.*
> 2. The context for the purpose of the interpretation of a treaty shall comprise, in addition to the text... *its preamble*... (emphasis added).[117]

According to a "good faith" reading of the *European Convention on Human Rights* (ECHR), (including its preamble which speaks to its stated express purpose, and as contemplated under Article 31 of the *Vienna Convention*), the States Parties to the ECHR were, under international treaty law, (i) obliged to honour the guarantees of rights and freedoms in the *European Convention*, and (ii) obliged to extend protection of these rights and freedoms to all peoples over whom they had jurisdiction (extraterritorially or not) regardless of whether the State Party acted alone or in cooperation with other States (i.e. in an international peacekeeping and security mission). The latter position regarding UNMIK *individual State* obligations in post-conflict Kosovo is consistent with the purpose of the *European Convention on Human* Rights as set out in its preamble which alludes to the objectives of: (i) collective enforcement of the principles of the *Universal Declaration of Human Rights*, and (ii) the Council of Europe objective of unifying members through further realization of fundamental human rights and freedoms in the territories of the member States *and as a means to securing justice and peace in the region.*

C. Conclusion: Individual State Responsibility and Accountability Relating to the Kosovo U.N. Lead Contaminated IDP Camps

It is here contended that given the aforementioned involvement in UNMIK of individual States Parties to the *European Convention on Human Rights* and their respective responsibility for the nature and consequences of that involvement, the

[117] *Vienna Convention on the Law of Treaties*, adopted 22 May 1969 by the United Nations Conference on the Law of Treaties and open for signature and ratification in Vienna 23 May 1969; entered into force on 27 January 1980, Article 31. http://untreaty.un.org/ilc/texts/instruments/.../conventions/1_1_1969.pdf. Accessed 9 August 2009.

European Court of Human Rights was in fact in a position, though it declined to do either, to hear the Kosovo lead contaminated IDP camps case as to admissibility and to rule the case admissible based on: (i) the victim status of the applicants, (ii) the time frame and location in which the alleged violations of the ECHR occurred (1999–2008 and with respect to certain camps still open), (iii) the nature and gravity of the European Convention violations alleged and (iv) the involvement of individual States Parties to the ECHR in failing to prevent and/or perpetuating the European Convention violations alleged. *That is, it is here contended that the case was within the jurisdiction of the European Court of Human Rights.*

It is, amongst others, the agents of those States that had direct jurisdiction and effective control over the RAE peoples in the lead contaminated IDP camps (and who thus had direct involvement in any violation of the RAE's non-derogable and other fundamental human rights under the European Convention related to the operational decisions about the camps) that must be held accountable in part or in whole as well as their home States (along with UNMIK and the U.N.) though UNMIK and the U.N. are immune regarding civil liability.

Article 26 and 27 of the *Vienna Convention* (as well as Articles 61(2), 62(2)(b) and 31) make it clear that individual States Parties (i.e. to the ECHR) must meet their treaty obligations even when participating in a U.N. international peacekeeping and security mission. In this instance, the *States Parties* to the European Convention participating in UNMIK were under an obligation to act in good faith in meeting their *European Convention on Human Rights* obligations to the RAE peoples of Kosovo and *not* to ignore their plight of living in highly lead contaminated U.N. IDP camps (especially since it was the individual States that had effective control over the situation). Note also in this regard that the U.N. framework for UNMIK in fact specified that the interim civil administration was to exercise public authority in manner, among other things, consistent with: (i) respect for human rights, non-discrimination, the rule of law, and democratic principles, and (ii) ***in accord with various international human rights treaty instruments including the European Convention on Human Rights***.[118] Hence, the U.N. itself tacitly acknowledged, through the UNMIK general framework for operation, that European Convention obligations were the responsibility of the individual UNMIK cooperating States. This, in that, as is uncontested, only individual States are parties to the ECHR not the international legal entity 'UNMIK'.[119]

State agents, it is suggested, are *not* simply agents of UNMIK and, according to the U.N. therefore protected by immunity (unless such immunity is waived by the U.N. Secretary-General), but also of their respective governments and hence arguably not covered by immunity for human rights treaty violations in their latter role. In any case, ECHR treaty violations are acts beyond the jurisdiction of the

[118] European Commission for Democracy Through Law (Venice Commission) (2004). The human rights situation in Kosovo: Background information and issues for discussion, at point 15 under Background (constitutional framework and human rights). http://www.venice.coe.int/docs/2004/CDL-DI(2004)001-e.asp. Accessed 7 August 2009.

[119] Yannis (2004, p. 71).

U.N. and hence arguably not subject to U.N. immunity provisions; especially when they rise to the level of potentially being international crimes.

Commentary on the Issue of Interim Measures

It follows then from the aforementioned also that the victims of lead poisoning in the lead contaminated IDP camps in Kosovo were entitled to interim measures indicated by the European Court of Human Rights. Those interim measures (i.e. relocation of the RAE to a safe area) would have: (i) preserved the Roma camp victims' right to life and protection from torture and inhuman treatment (guaranteed under the *European Convention on Human Rights*), and (ii) prevented any further irreparable harms to the mental and physical health of the applicants. These interim measures would further have helped to ensure that the case not be rendered moot in its most important aspect insofar as the health and lives of surviving camp occupants was still salvageable to a degree (as opposed to the consequence of not having interim measures (as in fact did occur) and having the RAE remain in the camps only to have their health further irrevocably and significantly harmed by chronic high levels of lead poisoning and their lives threatened or ended). Let us examine next then the European Court of Human Rights' views on the right to individual petition under Article 34 of the European Convention, and the relation of that Convention right to interim measures. We will examine whether the general views of the Court on the significance and relevance of interim measures, as expressed in the Grand Chamber judgment in *Mamatkulov and Askarov v. Turkey*, are or are not consistent with the denial of such measures in the lead contaminated Kosovo IDP camps case.

1. **The Grand Chamber in *Mamatkulov and Askarov v. Turkey* noted the following key aspects of interim measures**:

> **Article 34**... *is one of the fundamental guarantees of the effectiveness of the Convention system of human rights protection.* In interpreting such a key provision, the Court must have regard to the special character of the Convention as a treaty for the collective enforcement of human rights and fundamental freedoms (emphasis added).[120]
>
> *The object and purpose of the Convention as an instrument for the protection of individual human beings require that its provisions be interpreted and applied so as to make its safeguards practical and effective, as part of the system of individual applications.* In addition, any interpretation of the rights and freedoms guaranteed has to be consistent with "the general spirit of the Convention, an instrument designed to maintain and promote the ideals and values of a democratic society" (emphasis added).[121]

---

[120] *Mamatkulov and Askarov v. Turkey* (Applications nos. 46827/99 and 46951/99). European Court of Human Rights, Grand Chamber judgment of 4 February 2005, para 100. http://www.unhcr.org/refworld/publisher,ECHR,,UZB,42d3ef174,0.html. Accessed 8 August 2009.

[121] *Mamatkulov and Askarov v. Turkey* (Applications nos. 46827/99 and 46951/99). European Court of Human Rights, Grand Chamber judgment of 4 February 2005, para 101. http://www.unhcr.org/refworld/publisher,ECHR,,UZB,42d3ef174,0.html. Accessed 8 August 2009.

> The undertaking not to hinder the effective exercise of the right of individual application precludes any interference with the individual's right to present and pursue his complaint before the Court effectively... It is of the utmost importance for the effective operation of the system of individual application instituted under Article 34 *that applicants or potential applicants should be able to communicate freely with the Court without being subjected to any form of pressure from the authorities to withdraw or modify their complaints*.... For present purposes, the Court concludes that the obligation set out in Article 34 in fine requires the Contracting States to refrain not only from exerting pressure on applicants, but also from any act or omission which, by destroying or removing the subject matter of an application, would make it pointless or otherwise prevent the Court from considering it under its normal procedure (emphasis added).[122]

2. **The failure of the European Court to issue public decisions regarding admissibility and interim measures in the lead contaminated U.N. IDP camps case**: The European Court of Human Rights in declining interim measures in the IDP camps case denied to the Roma victims of U.N. lead contaminated IDP camps in Kosovo one of the fundamental Convention vehicles for the protection and preservation of their European Convention rights. This denial of interim measures interfered with the right of individual petition for those RAE IDP camp applicants on whose behalf the European Roma Rights Centre had filed an application to the Court in 2006 and, most likely, also the right of such petition for any future potential applicants who had been, or are in the lead contaminated U.N. Kosovo refugee camps given the chilling effect of the 2006 denial. The Court denied the interim measures *not* in the context of a publicly issued admissibility decision subsequent to a Chamber hearing, or a pubic decision on interim measures alone, but rather in the form of a letter faxed to the European Roma Rights Centre the day after the application and request for interim measures was sent by the Centre to the Court. The denial of interim measures (apart from the refusal to schedule the complaint for an admissibility hearing) in itself surely would have discouraged any further individual petition from the IDP camp victims given what likely was perceived by the applicants and their representatives as the Court's apparent disregard for the gravity of the RAE victims' plight.

There would appear to have been no obviously apparent basis for the failure to issue a public admissibility/interim measures decision in the Kosovo IDP camps case any more so than would have been the case had the Court failed to issue a public decision in *Behrami* (which also involved the Court in attributing accountability for UNMIK harms in Kosovo to the U.N. rather than to individual States participating in UNMIK and alleging lack of jurisdiction by the Court).

3. **The European Court of Human Rights' Rules of Court and interim measures**: It is important to realize that *there was no European Court of Human Rights' rule of court which precluded the Court from indicating a request for interim measures in the IDP camps case:* "The grounds on which Rule 39 may be

---

[122] *Mamatkulov and Askarov v. Turkey* (Applications nos. 46827/99 and 46951/99). European Court of Human Rights, Grand Chamber judgment of 4 February 2005, para 102. http://www.unhcr.org/refworld/publisher,ECHR,,UZB,42d3ef174,0.html. Accessed 8 August 2009.

applied are not set out in the Rules of Court".[123] Rule 39 of the European Court of Human Rights Rules of Court provides that:

> 1. The Chamber or, where appropriate, its President *may, at the request of a party* or of any other person concerned, or of its own motion, *indicate to the parties any interim measure which it considers should be adopted in the interests of the parties* ***or*** of the proper conduct of the proceedings before it.
>
> ...
>
> 3. The Chamber may request information from the parties on any matter connected with the implementation of any interim measure it has indicated (emphasis added).[124]

Rule 39 of the Rules of Court of the European Court of Human Rights (ECHR) appears *not* to require that interim measures only be indicated where the decision has already been made to hold an admissibility hearing since Rule 39 permits the Court to indicate such measures on the basis that it considers such measures to be in the interests of the Parties to do so (hence the use of the word "or" in the text of Rule 39 suggesting that it is an alternative circumstance to the aforementioned where interim measures are indicated as the Court considers them necessary for the "proper conduct of the proceedings before it."). This interpretation is consistent with the fact that item 3 of Rule 39 allows the Court to request more information relating to the need for the implementation of the interim measures *after* it has indicated a request *from the Court* for such measures i.e. in order to ensure the applicant's rights are preserved while it gathers that information (in the IDP camps case this further information might have been related to, for instance, the current level of lead poisoning for the camps' inhabitants, who was currently responsible for each of the camps, the level of UN involvement versus individual State involvement in decision-making and effective and/or ultimate control of the camps, etc. In the *Mamatkulov and Askarov v. Turkey* case, interim measures barring extradition would have allowed the Court to seek further specific information from the applicants' (through their representatives) on why they in particular were allegedly likely to suffer torture or an unfair trial in Uzbekistan).

Note also that Rule 39 of the Rules of Court of the ECHR allows that even before a Chamber is constituted, the President of the Chamber that *may* hear the case may request interim measures. It is entirely possible that after receiving the additional information during the period of the interim measures that the case does not proceed for any number of reasons. Hence, whether the Court deems interim measures necessary is an issue that is not necessarily always entirely contingent on the case

[123] *Mamatkulov and Askarov v. Turkey* (Applications nos. 46827/99 and 46951/99). European Court of Human Rights, Grand Chamber judgment of 4 February 2005, para 103. http://www.unhcr.org/refworld/publisher,ECHR,,UZB,42d3ef174,0.html. Accessed 8 August 2009.

[124] Rules of Court of the European Court of Human Rights (2009) (Rule 39), new edition with the amendments adopted by the Plenary Court 29 June 2009, entered into force 1 July 2009. http://www.echr.coe.int/NR/rdonlyres/D1EB31A8-4194-436E-987E-65AC8864BE4F/0/RulesOfCourt.pdf. Accessed 9 August 2009.

having already been accepted for an admissibility hearing and/or already scheduled for an admissibility hearing.

4. **The implications of the European Court of Human Rights' declining interim measures and an admissibility hearing in the IDP camps case**: The failure of the European Court of Human Rights to indicate to *the individual States that were cooperating with the UN peacekeeping mission in Kosovo* (UNMIK) the need for the interim measure (of removing the RAE inhabitants from the lead contaminated IDP camps and relocating them to a nontoxic environment) *interfered with: (i) the applicants' right of individual petition by essentially failing to preserve the applicants' asserted rights*; and (ii) interfered with the applicant's Convention right to be protected from irreparable (further) harm to their health. By ignoring, through the failure to request interim measures, the Roma's urgent situation pertaining to their ill heath and potential life threatening living conditions (relating to continued chronic exposure to extremely high levels of lead contamination in the IDP camps), the Court created a situation in which sadly any further individual petitions from this group were unlikely.

Note that unlike the situation in *Mamatkulov and Askarov v. Turkey* where the risk to the applicants' Article 2 and 3 Convention rights (should they be extradited) was yet to be determined, in the lead contaminated Kosovo U.N. IDP camps case, the risk to the applicants' Article 2 and 3 Convention rights (due to chronic exposure in the camps to extremely high lead levels) was well-established (by medical experts from WHO and other groups and uncontested by the Convention States Parties participating in UNMIK). Yet, it was in the latter case that the request for interim measures by the European Roma Rights Centre on behalf of a group of Kosovo IDP camp inhabitants was denied by the European Court of Human Rights

The failure of the Court to request interim measures and *what amounted to a forgone conclusion regarding the alleged inadmissibility* of the application is *not consistent*, it is here respectfully suggested, with: (i) the "object and purpose of the Convention as an instrument for the protection of individual human beings"; (ii) the right of individual petition under the Convention; nor with (iii) an interpretation of the Convention consistent with "the general spirit of the Convention, [as] an instrument designed to maintain and promote the ideals and values of a democratic society." The failure of the European Court of Human Rights to request the urgently needed interim measure of removing the RAE from the remaining IDP camps (urgently needed for their survival as determined by the World Health Organization and other medical experts) would in all likelihood nullify any positive outcome for any proceedings before the Court which might occur in due course should the Court relent and revise its position on admissibility. This, as entire families are left in the lead contaminated camps, and if the delay is long enough no member may survive to see the day, should it come, when the Court concedes their right to individual petition before the European Court of Human Rights.

5. **More on interim measures and the admissibility question as independent issues**: Note that in *Mamatkulov and Askarov v. Turkey*, interim measures were requested by the European Court of Human Rights, (a request for a stay of extradition by Turkey), *before* the Court had determined whether in fact there was any risk

to these particular applicants physically or mentally, or to their ability to receive a fair criminal trial in Uzbekistan. If no such risk existed, *even on a prima facie basis*, should these particular applicants' extradition be effected, then the case would not be appropriate for an admissibility hearing. Interim measures were, hence, requested by the Court in *Mamatkulov and Askarov v. Turkey before* any potential prima facie basis for an admissibility hearing could be determined in anticipation that while the interim measure was in place (the extraditions stayed) information could be collected regarding the risks associated with extradition to Uzbekistan for these particular applicants to the European Court of Human Rights. *Thus, in Mamatkulov and Askarov v. Turkey, the issue of interim measures was dissociated from the issue of whether there was a prima facie basis for an admissibility hearing.* In contrast, in the Kosovo U.N. lead contaminated Roma refugee camps case, the interim measures issue was linked by the Court to the admissibility issue (i.e. the Court's alleged lack of jurisdiction to monitor State compliance with the European Convention in regards to the IDP camps given the role of UNMIK). With respect, there would appear to be no defensible basis in law that would support this inconsistency in the Court's approach to indicating interim measures.

D. The Failure of the U.N. to Effectively Exercise Its Humanitarian and Human Rights Mandate Regarding the Kosovo U.N. Roma IDP Camp Situation and the Implications for Individual State Accountability

Note that after 2000, the UNHCR was no longer involved in UNMIK and hence the actual level of U.N. 'effective' or even 'ultimate' theoretical or formal control or even high priority humanitarian concern over the IDP camps and their 'gypsy' inhabitants may have been more illusory than real. There were numerous governmental international organizations and international representatives and individual States involved in UNMIK; none of which were willing to take action to ensure the safe relocation of *all* of the lead contaminated IDP camps' inhabitants to locations within or outside of Kosovo. There appeared to be no clear and unified plan or well orchestrated decision-making unified process under the ultimate control of the U.N. or any other body regarding the lead contaminated IDP camps. Rather, the management and decision-making regarding the lead contaminated IDP camps was chaotic and likely conflicting opinions on the proper course regarding the IDP camps and relocation were prevalent within UNMIK (i.e. only small numbers of camp inhabitants were tested for lead poisoning on a sporadic basis then the process stopped for alleged lack of funds); camp relocation occurred for some to areas just as lead contaminated if not more (Osterode Camp); there was no adequate provision of medical treatment on any meaningful scale; reports by the World Health Organization and even internal health reports were commissioned by UNMIK on lead poisoning of the IDP camp inhabitants but the recommendations in these reports (i.e. regarding regular monitoring of blood lead levels in the camps inhabitants; removal of children and pregnant women from the camps; later calls for closing the camps on an urgent basis, etc.) were not acted on in a timely manner or, in many cases, not at all (i.e. the highly lead contaminated Osterode and Cesmin Lug camps are still operational to this date). Under these circumstances (when the U.N. fails to fulfill its international human rights/humanitarian obligations in a specific case), according to the Court's own analysis (in *Behrami*), individual States must then ensure that they meet their European Convention obligations *and the States cannot be presumed to have done so simply by virtue of their cooperation as a member with the international organization (i.e. the U.N.) in respect of its missions*:

> In its Bosphorus judgment... the Court held that, while a State was not prohibited by the Convention from transferring sovereign power to an international organisation in order to pursue cooperation in certain fields of activity, the State remained responsible under Article 1 of the Convention for all acts and omissions of its organs, regardless of whether they were a consequence of the necessity to comply with international legal obligations, Article 1 making no distinction as to the rule or measure concerned and not excluding any part of a State's "jurisdiction" from scrutiny under the Convention. The Court went on, however, to hold that *where such State action was taken in compliance with international legal obligations flowing from its membership of [in] an international organisation and where the relevant organisation protected fundamental rights in a manner which could be considered at least equivalent to that which the Convention provides, a presumption arose that the State had not departed from the requirements of the Convention.* ***Such presumption could be rebutted***, *if in the circumstances of a particular case, it was considered that the protection of Convention rights was manifestly deficient: in such a case, the interest of international cooperation would be outweighed by the Convention's role as a "constitutional instrument of European public order" in the field of human rights...* (emphasis added).[125]

Hence, even according to the European Court of Human Rights' own jurisprudence: (i) individual States are responsible for meeting their treaty obligations (i.e. *European Convention on Human Rights* obligations) even when acting to meet their international obligations and acting under the auspices of international authority rather than completely under State sovereignty/authority, and (ii) individual States *can be held individually accountable in a situation where the international body (i.e. the United Nations) is failing to secure basic fundamental human rights guaranteed under the European Convention and the State is taking actions or failing to take actions as a member of that international organization that are counterproductive to securing Convention rights for persons under the State's effective control* (i.e. leaving refugees in highly lead contaminated IDP camps in post-conflict Kosovo). Since the individual States participating in UNMIK were aware of the U.N.'s failure in this regard at least as early as 2000, their obligation and accountability for the European Convention violations with respect to the RAE peoples living in highly lead contaminated IDP camps ensued at the latest from that date.

---

[125] *Behrami and Behrami v. France* (Application 71412/01) [heard in conjunction with *Saramati v. France, Germany and Norway* (Application 781/01)], 2 May 2007. European Court of Human Rights, Grand Chamber decision on admissibility, para 145. http://hei.unige.ch/~clapham/hrdoc/docs/ECHRBehrami.doc. Accessed 25 July 2009.

Given the *uncontested* facts in the U.N. Kosovo IDP Roma camps case brought to the attention of the European Court of Human Rights (i.e. the high levels of lead contamination in the Roma IDP camps which levels are highly dangerous to health and life threatening), the European Court of Human Rights should have, based on its own analysis in *Bosphorous*, concluded that the individual States participating in UNMIK could not, in such an instance, use UNMIK as a shield against their own accountability for the violation of the RAE peoples' European Convention rights. Yet, the Court insisted in this case that the systematic and ongoing disregard *in practice* by the U.N. for the fundamental human rights of the RAE who were stuck in life threatening toxic IDP camps was still not enough to trigger individual State responsibility. *The decision whether to leave the RAE in this situation or to remove them from the lead contaminated camps was, however, within the power of the individual States. The fact that UNMIK, as an entity, was "in principle" or in theory but* ***not*** *operationally and effectively in control supports that view.* In any case, it is here contended, that the States had a jus cogens obligation not to comply with any directive from UNMIK (such as keeping the RAE in the lead contaminated camps) which would seriously adversely affect the health of the RAE when those adverse effects were preventable.

Note that not only did UNMIK not take steps to protect *all* the RAE in the IDP camps for many years (two camps, as discussed, to this date are still operational), but it tried to conceal from camp inhabitants in 2000 the dangerous lead contamination situation:

> ... during 2000, UNMIK and KFOR contingents based in northern Mitrovica/Mitrovice conducted assessments of the soil toxicity in and around the camps which indicated a high level of lead contamination in the camps. *KFOR implemented measures to protect their personnel, including removing personnel with high lead levels from the area.* ***UNMIK did not provide information about the high levels of lead concentrations in the camp to the Roma residents of the camps*** (emphasis added).[126]

After three reports by the World Health Organization (WHO) about the extremely dangerous high toxic lead soil levels in the camps, and WHO reports that the lead blood levels of the camp inhabitants well exceeded accepted permissible standards as well as a fourth report in November 2004 by WHO that recommended the camp inhabitants be immediately removed to a safe location *on an emergency basis*, UNMIK took no remedial action based on WHO's recommendations.[127] It was only from independent medical health professionals who carried

[126]Decision of the Human Rights Advisory Panel of 5 June 2009, Case 26/08, NM and Others v. UNMIK heard by Mr. Marek Nowicki, Mr. Paul Lemmens, and Ms. Snezhana Botusharova under UNMIK regulation 2006/12 of 23 March 2006 on the establishment of the Human Rights Advisory Panel, para 5. http://www.toxicwastekills.com/downloads/Decision_eng_060609.pdf. Accessed 11 August 2009.

[127]Decision of the Human Rights Advisory Panel of 5 June 2009, Case 26/08, NM and Others v. UNMIK heard by Mr. Marek Nowicki, Mr. Paul Lemmens, and Ms. Snezhana Botusharova under UNMIK regulation 2006/12 of 23 March 2006 on the establishment of the Human Rights Advisory Panel, para 6. http://www.toxicwastekills.com/downloads/Decision_eng_060609.pdf. Accessed 11 August 2009.

out testing in 2005 that the Roma discovered that the camps were highly lead contaminated and that this posed a grave danger to their health.[128] In addition to the issue of lead contamination, UNMIK allowed these camp inhabitants to live, and, for some, to continue to live to this date in 2010, in inhuman and degrading circumstances in other respects as well as is uncontested:

> In addition, to the problems of lead contamination, living conditions in the Roma IDP camps were and are extremely poor. On account of the frequent lack of water and poor drainage, hygiene in the camps is described as appalling, resulting in frequent illnesses amongst the residents. The camps often had no running water, electricity, heating, health care or access to food inside the camp. The conditions are particularly dangerous for pregnant women. (emphasis added)[129]
>
> At least three persons are alleged to have died as a consequence of the harmful levels of lead in their bodies. Others are suspected to have died from lead-contamination related illnesses, but on account of the lack of proper medical testing and/or autopsies these claims have been difficult to verify. Lead poisoning has formally been diagnosed as a cause of illness in many of the complainants.[130]

The complicity of at least certain of the individual State delegates participating in UNMIK in: (i) keeping the RAE camp populations in this life threatening environment for years, some even to this date, rather than relocating them to safe environments; (ii) withholding from the camp residents vital information needed for these camp inhabitants to make decisions, if at all possible, that could potentially better safeguard their health and lives, (iii) the failure to provide comprehensive medical testing for lead poisoning, and medical treatment where needed, as well as the failure to provide safe and decent living conditions; (iii) the failure to do autopsies on those who had lived in the Roma IDP camps but died of suspected lead poisoning at some point after leaving the camps, or on those who died due to suspected lead poisoning while still in the camps, and to be transparent and open about the cause of death in all cases *may* rise to the level of international crimes as discussed *depending on what they knew, and when, intent and the specifics of their actions.*

---

[128]Decision of the Human Rights Advisory Panel of 5 June 2009, Case 26/08, NM and Others v. UNMIK heard by Mr. Marek Nowicki, Mr. Paul Lemmens, and Ms. Snezhana Botusharova under UNMIK regulation 2006/12 of 23 March 2006 on the establishment of the Human Rights Advisory Panel, para 7. http://www.toxicwastekills.com/downloads/Decision_eng_060609.pdf. Accessed 11 August 2009.

[129]Decision of the Human Rights Advisory Panel of 5 June 2009, Case 26/08, NM and Others v. UNMIK heard by Mr. Marek Nowicki, Mr. Paul Lemmens, and Ms. Snezhana Botusharova under UNMIK regulation 2006/12 of 23 March 2006 on the establishment of the Human Rights Advisory Panel, para 9. http://www.toxicwastekills.com/downloads/Decision_eng_060609.pdf. Accessed 11 August 2009.

[130]Decision of the Human Rights Advisory Panel of 5 June 2009, Case 26/08, NM and Others v. UNMIK heard by Mr. Marek Nowicki, Mr. Paul Lemmens, and Ms. Snezhana Botusharova under UNMIK regulation 2006/12 of 23 March 2006 on the establishment of the Human Rights Advisory Panel, para 12. http://www.toxicwastekills.com/downloads/Decision_eng_060609.pdf. Accessed 11 August 2009.

There are ongoing violations of the right to life and humane treatment in the remaining operational two Roma lead contaminated IDP camps in Kosovo. However, the human rights violations in the camps now closed, in addition, insofar as they caused physical and/or mental harms to many, if not all, of their occupants may also be regarded as involving 'ongoing violations'; especially since: (i) these persons may have their lives shortened due to lead poisoning resulting from their stay in the camps and (ii) many have ongoing psychological and physical symptoms due to chronic high lead exposure.

VI. The Implications of the European Court of Human Rights' Refusal to Hold an Admissibility Hearing on the Roma Lead Contaminated IDP Camps Case and to Indicate Interim Measures Requiring the Camp Inhabitants Be Relocated to Safe Areas on an Urgent Emergency Basis

A. *Fostering a Climate of Impunity Regarding the Victimization of the Kosovo Gypsy Minorities Placed in U.N. Lead Contaminated IDP Camps*

The European Court of Human Rights' refusal in 2006 (in response to the European Roma Rights Centre application on behalf of a group of Roma IDP camp victims) to request interim measures be taken by the UNMIK personnel (including, for instance, appointed international representatives and other State delegates from international government organizations participating in UNMIK, etc.) who had operational control over the camps (i.e. interim emergency measures such as relocation of the RAE out of the camps to safe locations) has facilitated two highly lead contaminated Roma IDP camps still being operational in North Mitrovica in 2010. Further, to this date, the United Nations has *not* responded to a 2005 request to waive immunity[131] for those responsible for these grievous human rights violations against the RAE internationally displaced who did, or currently do inhabit the highly lead contaminated U.N. IDP camps in Kosovo. The European Court of Human Rights, by refusing to hear the Roma IDP case, or to indicate emergency interim measures, contributed to: (i) undermining, within the European and international community, the perceived gravity of these ongoing human rights violations against the RAE IDP in Kosovo, hence fostering complacency in this

[131]Decision of the Human Rights Advisory Panel of 5 June 2009, Case 26/08, NM and Others v. UNMIK heard by Mr. Marek Nowicki, Mr. Paul Lemmens, and Ms. Snezhana Botusharova under UNMIK regulation 2006/12 of 23 March 2006 on the establishment of the Human Rights Advisory Panel, para 44. http://www.toxicwastekills.com/downloads/Decision_eng_060609.pdf. Accessed 11 August 2009.

regard, and to: (ii) the climate of silence and impunity for perpetrators as well as providing *de facto* immunity against civil liability for States that did or are cooperating with UNMIK in managing the lead contaminated Roma IDP camps. Hence, persons under international administration, as in Kosovo, according to the European Court of Human Rights' (in this author's respectful view) *misguided reasoning* in *Behrami*[132] and the Roma U.N. lead contaminated IDP camps case, are to be improperly left to the mercy and *discretionary* decision-making of the United Nations.

These RAE IDP victims, to date, have been afforded no recourse to any independent court concerning the grave human rights violations they have suffered while being governed by the international authority (UNMIK) operating under the auspices of the U.N. (or now; while being governed by local domestic institutions newly created or constituted but under the supervision and monitoring of the international authority UNMIK). The lack of access to a ***fully*** *independent and impartial tribunal* regarding claims for just reparations is in fact inconsistent with, for instance: (i) the *Rome Statute*[133] and the European Convention which endorse the principle of just reparations to victims of grave human rights violations such as violations which cause a systemic threat to life, and with (ii) international human rights requirements that victims have access to independent fair hearings of their claims by bodies that have no ties to either party.

Recall that the European Court of Human Rights in the lead contaminated U.N. Roma IDP camps case held that the Court had no jurisdiction as UNMIK as an entity, and allegedly not individual States, were responsible for the violation of the camp victims' European Convention rights. Yet, *individual States did participate in UNMIK and contributed to decision-making at the highest levels including in regards to the issue of the return of internally displaced persons* as reflected in the framework set out in Security Resolution 1244 that created UNMIK:

The Security Council...

> 13. Encourages *all Member States and international organizations* to contribute to economic and social reconstruction ***as well as to the safe return of refugees and displaced persons***, and emphasizes in this context the importance of convening an international donors' conference... at the earliest possible date... (emphasis added)[134]

---

[132] *Behrami and Behrami v. France* (Application 71412/01) [heard in conjunction with *Saramati v. France, Germany and Norway* (Application 781/01)], 2 May 2007. European Court of Human Rights, Grand Chamber decision on admissibility. http://hei.unige.ch/~clapham/hrdoc/docs/ECHRBehrami.doc. Accessed 25 July 2009.

[133] *Rome Statute of the International Criminal Court*. Text of the Rome Statute circulated as document A/CONF.183/9 of 17 July 1998 and corrected by procès-verbaux of 10 November 1998, 12 July 1999, 30 November 1999, 8 May 2000, 17 January 2001 and 16 January 2002). The Statute entered into force on 1 July 2002. http://www.un.org/children/conflict/keydocuments/english/romestatuteofthe7.html. Accessed 1 August 2009.

[134] U.N. Security Council Resolution 1244 (S/Res/1244), Adopted by the Security Council on 10 June 1999 at its 4011th meeting. http://www.unmikonline.org/regulations/unmikgazette/02english/Res1244ENG.pdf. Accessed 12 August 2009, para 13.

Furthermore, different *State delegates* from various States over the years of UNMIK operation have acted as the head of UNMIK exercising day-to-day operational control over the IDP camps while, in addition, the OSCE (Organization for Security and Cooperation in Europe) State delegates have participated in the development and implementation of UNMIK management and operational plans for the lead contaminated RAE IDP camps. Currently, the OSCE is charged with monitoring human rights and rule of law issues in Kosovo in areas that affect the right of return for *internally displaced* RAE peoples and the right of safe return of RAE from other countries.

Certainly UNMIK, *at least insofar as the RAE (so-called 'gypsy') peoples in the U.N. lead contaminated IDP camps were concerned*, in most respects, appeared to operate with an agenda quite distinct from, and inconsistent with, the stated goals of Security Council (SC) Resolution 1244. SC resolution 1244 in its preamble mentions that the intent of the U.N. Security Council via the resolution was, amongst other things, "to resolve the grave humanitarian situation in Kosovo, Federal Republic of Yugoslavia, and to provide for the *safe and free return of* ***all*** *refugees and displaced persons to their homes.*"[135] Not only did UNMIK, and the individual States that participated in UNMIK, for the most part, not solve the humanitarian crisis for the RAE victims of the U.N. lead contaminated IDP camps (i.e. by arranging returns in a timely and safe fashion; and providing the necessary support for re-establishing these IDPs successfully in the area of their old settlements); they arguably may be said to have significantly contributed to their suffering by gravely harming some or all of these persons physically and/or mentally through their IDP camp experience. Note in this regard, that in 2000, UNMIK had the following to say regarding the need for the IDP camps housing the RAE built near the Trepca lead mine complex:

> In view of continued killings of members of the Roma/Ashkali community in Kosovo, the time does not appear ripe to launch the forced returns of such vulnerable individuals. Furthermore, the forced return of individuals at risk, such as members of ethnic minorities, potentially violates Article 33 of the 1951 Refugee Convention. *In addition, according to the jurisprudence of the European Court of Human Rights, such forced returns could constitute a violation of Articles 2 and 3 of the European Convention for the Protection of Human Rights and Fundamental Freedoms (ECHR).... The fundamental protection enshrined in the ECHR – that people at serious risk of death or suffering inhuman or degrading treatment must not be forcibly returned.*[136]

Hence, in 2000, UNMIK expressed a concern about fundamental human rights violations (i.e. violations of Articles 2 and 3 of the European Convention and violations of the Refugee Convention) against the RAE should UNMIK institute 'forced return' of that minority population to Roma Mahalla at that time. Yet, at the same time, despite knowledge acquired by UNMIK (via internally commissioned

---

[135]U.N. Security Council Resolution 1244 (S/Res/1244), Adopted by the Security Council on 10 June 1999 at its 4011th meeting. http://www.unmikonline.org/regulations/unmikgazette/02english/Res1244ENG.pdf. Accessed 12 August 2009, preamble.

[136]UNMIK (2000, p. 3).

health reports as early as 2000) about the life threatening conditions in the lead contaminated U.N. RAE IDP camps, UNMIK would appear to have demonstrated a consistent disregard for the rights of the RAE guaranteed under European Convention Articles 2 (right to life) and 3 (right to be protected against inhuman or degrading treatment). This, given: (i) the operation and maintenance of highly lead contaminated RAE IDP camps in Kosovo from 1999 to 2008 and the continued operation of two of the most highly lead contaminated camps to the current date in 2010; (ii) the lack of regular medical assessment and comprehensive medical treatment for all RAE affected, and (iii) the grossly substandard and degrading living conditions in the RAE IDP Kosovo camps even aside from the lead contamination issue. Alternative safe locales within or outside the country were, for the most part, not forthcoming for over a decade for most of the RAE IDPs, and, for many, have still not come to fruition.

Note further that the individual States members of the U.N. contribute to the U.N. Peacekeeping Mission (established in 2005). In working groups set up by the U.N. Peacekeeping Mission, individual State delegates have and had ample opportunity to insist on the closing of the remaining operational U.N. Roma lead contaminated IDP camps in Kosovo and ensure that such is accomplished. At present, the Peace Keeping Commission has: (i) seven individual State members selected by the U.N. Security Council: Burkina Faso, China, France, Mexico, the Russian Federation, the United Kingdom of Great Britain and Northern Ireland, and the United States of America; (ii) seven individual State members selected by the U.N. Social and Economic Council: Algeria, El Salvador, Guinea-Bissau, Luxembourg, Morocco, Poland and Republic of Korea; (iii) five members selected on the basis of being the five top contributors to U.N. budgets and in terms of voluntary contributions: Canada, Germany, Japan, the Netherlands and Sweden; (iv) Five members selected on the basis of being the top providers of military personnel and civilian police to United Nations missions: Bangladesh, India, Nepal, Nigeria and Pakistan; and the seven members elected by the U.N. General Assembly: Benin, Chile, Georgia, Jamaica, South Africa, Thailand and Uruguay.[137] There is simply no supportable basis for suggesting that this large number of States and their nationals participating directly in U.N. decision-making regarding so-called peace missions which include a humanitarian aspect: (i) do not have the power to effect the relocation of the Roma and other minorities to safe areas with decent housing in Kosovo or outside Kosovo and out of their current life threatening locale in the two remaining operational U.N. lead toxic IDP camps, or (ii) that these States should not be held civilly liable by international courts (i.e. with respect to the European States, by the European Court of Human Rights) under international human rights law for not doing so.

[137]Organization Committee Membership of the United Nations Peace-building Commission. For a list of the 31 member States see the Commission link at http://www.un.org/peace/peacebuilding/mem-orgcomembers.shtml. Accessed 12 August 2009.

B. *The Kosovo Human Rights Advisory Panel to UNMIK: Is This a Vehicle for Just Reparation and Public Acknowledgement of Fundamental Human Rights Violations Against the RAE Inhabitants of U.N. Lead Contaminated IDP Camps Managed by UNMIK, or But an 'Alice in Wonderland' Version of an Independent Forum for Achieving Justice?*

B.1 *About the Human Rights Advisory Panel to UNMIK*

Recall that the European Court of Human Rights: (i) declined to provide the RAE IDP camp victims with emergency lifesaving relief via a Court request for interim measures (i.e. urgent request by the Court directed to the powers managing the U.N. IDP camps to relocate the Roma out of lead contaminated camps to safe areas), and (ii) declined to hold an admissibility hearing. It is an especially ironic and cruel twist to the continuing tragic saga of the RAE victims of the U.N. lead toxic IDP camps that, despite their essentially being shut out by the European Court of Human Rights, attempts on their part to obtain justice via the alternate route of the Human Rights Advisory Panel to UNMIK has resulted in their being subjected to certain of the legal niceties of the European Court of Human Rights' Rules of Court and to its jurisprudence after all. This in that the Advisory Panel established under UNMIK regulation 2006/12 relies on the *European Convention on Human Rights* procedural rules, and is guided by European Court of Human Rights' case law.

The Human Rights Advisory Panel's mandate is proclaimed by the Panel to be to consider alleged violations of: (i) the *European Convention on Human Rights*; (ii) the *Universal Declaration of Human Rights*, (iii) *the International Covenant on Civil and Political Rights*; (iv) the *International Covenant on Economic, Social and Cultural Rights*; (v) the *Convention on the Elimination of All Forms of Racial Discrimination*; (vi) the *Convention on the Elimination of All Forms of Discrimination Against Women*; (vii) the *Convention Against Torture and Other Cruel, Inhuman or Degrading Treatment or Punishment* and (viii) the *Convention on the Rights of the Child*. The Panel may receive complaints from individuals, groups of individuals, non-governmental organizations, a family member on behalf of a victim or by a trade union. The Panel may also appoint a representative to act on behalf of suspected victims where the victims have none and violations are thought by the Panel to have occurred (i.e. given the reliable information available to the Panel in a particular case). The Panel can also consider complaints against UNMIK from *indirect victims*; that is, persons who suffered harm due to the human rights violations inflicted by UNMIK on their close relative. However, all complaints must pertain to violations that occurred after 23 April 2005 (the date the Advisory Panel is held to have assumed temporal jurisdiction), or violations that stem from facts/situations that existed prior to that date, but constitute '*ongoing violations*'.

All complaints must be filed no later than six months after departure from the IDP camps unless the violations are ongoing. As will be discussed, the Advisory

Panel has ruled inadmissible claims relating *to IDP camp conditions* for those who left the camps more than six months before filing their complaint to the Panel, but ruled admissible complaints from these same former IDP camp residents relating to UNMIK's breach of their positive obligation to protect the applicants' human rights under various European and ICCPR and other international human rights law. UNMIK's alleged justification for the distinction was that only the breach of positive obligations constituted an ongoing violation; a contention that this author challenges in the discussion that follows. One can speculate that, in regards to the camp conditions, the complainant, if successful, could show great physical and mental harms due to the camp conditions which would justify substantial pecuniary reparation. In contrast, proving a breach of UNMIK's positive obligation to protect the applicants' Convention rights might bring only nominal reparations if the Advisory Panel regards the reparations as simply a symbolic acknowledgement of the fact that the breach occurred and unrelated to the level of actual harm resulting from the breach.

The Panel's information leaflet outlines the fact that the Panel is comprised of three members appointed by the Special Representative for the U.N. Secretary General on the nomination by the President of the European Court of Human Rights. Hence, the Kosovo Human Rights Advisory Panel to UNMIK hearing the human rights complaint of the RAE U.N. IDP camp victims is appointed by the head of UNMIK – the latter being the very body alleged to have perpetrated the gross human rights violations against the RAE IDPs relating to, for instance, life threatening living conditions and inhuman and degrading treatment over more than a decade arising due to the lead contaminated IDP camps. If that were not unsettling enough; UNMIK's head appoints the Human Rights Advisory Panel membership based on nomination by the President of the very Court – the European Court of Human Rights – that declined to order interim emergency measures that likely would have been abided by and resulted in the relocation of the IDP RAE camp victims to safe non-lead contaminated locales. One can speculate that, given the aforementioned, the RAE U.N. Kosovo IDP camp victims may feel that to describe the Human Rights Advisory Panel to UNMIK as *"semi-independent"*, as does Human Rights Watch,[138] is overly generous at a minimum. (Note also that the legal system in Kosovo is not entirely independent of UNMIK.)

The Advisory Panel may or may not hold a public hearing in any particular case, and may or may not recommend reparations in any particular case against UNMIK that it rules admissible. The Panel has no enforcement powers and simply makes recommendations to the Special Representative of the U.N. Secretary General about the Panel's preferred disposition of admissible cases that it has ruled meritorious. Findings and recommendations are made public.[139] Applications to the Human Rights Advisory Panel to UNMIK if successful on the merits result in:

[138]Human Rights Human Rights Watch (2009c).

[139]Human Rights Advisory Panel (for UNMIK) information leaflet for organizations. http://www.unmikonline.org/human_rights/documents/Leaflet_organisations.pdf. Accessed 13 August 2009.

(i) public acknowledgement of the fundamental human rights violations victims have suffered due to the acts of commission and omission of UNMIK, and (ii) sometimes what the Panel holds are just reparations for the violations perpetrated.

B.2 ***Alternate Flexible Compensation Systems***

The RAE U.N. IDP former and current camp inhabitants in Kosovo are victims of a humanitarian crisis who have arguably been *doubly victimized*; the second time by those working under the auspices of an international body (UNMIK) that was supposed to protect and assist them. When these victims come forward with a human rights complaint against the international body (i.e. UNMIK and its various constituent elements, etc.), the system hearing the complaint one would hope and expect would be responsive and flexible as to rules of procedure and evidence. In this regard, recall the alternative compensation system in Norway previously discussed, for instance, where the rules of evidence, etc., are not as stringent as in the Norwegian courts. That system was set up to address, in particular, the compensation claims of a specific population of victims of human rights violations; namely Norwegian war children or so-called 'Lebensborn' who had been discriminated against by the Norwegian government in post WW II Norway. The Norwegian alternate compensation system recognizes that the victim applicants, due to circumstances beyond their control, may not always have access to all the necessary documents or resources they require to present their human rights complaint in as strong a fashion as might otherwise be the case though certain incontrovertible facts are known. Similarly, in the lead contaminated U.N. IDP camps case, RAE victims may not have access to sufficient blood lead level data for every year they were in the IDP camp given that UNMIK did very little testing and then on a sporadic basis. Due to lack of funds, they may not have access to medical experts who could testify on their behalf before the Human Rights Advisory Panel to UNMIK or to counsel versed in international law and immunity issues who could effectively act on their behalf. Family members (indirect victims) may be unable to prove definitively that a family member who lived in the IDP camps died due to lead poisoning given the fact that UNMIK did not arrange for an autopsy. These RAE IDP camp victims nonetheless are greatly deserving of a more flexible approach to determination of their human rights claims than currently is embodied in the Advisory Human Rights Panel to UNMIK system (this is not to say that these victims should not be heard by the European Court of Human Rights if they choose that route instead; quite the contrary, as previously discussed, but as will be recalled their attempts to be heard by the Court to date have failed).

The direct victims of the U.N. lead contaminated IDP camps who have appealed to the Human Rights Advisory Panel to UNMIK are physically ill and traumatized, and exhausted due to years of mistreatment and very little regard, *in practice*, of their plight by the U.N. What is uncontested, given the World Health Organization's multiple reports and repeat sporadic sampling of blood lead levels for the RAE IDP camp occupants; as well as other independent medical testing; and KFOR testing of soil lead contamination; is that the IDP camps were and are uninhabitable. Yet, UNMIK and the participating States stranded the RAE in the life threatening IDP environment; not for weeks or months; but for years and for some; even to this date.

There is a *public interest* in demonstrating respect for these historically persecuted RAE minorities by rendering justice in the form of just reparations, *offered automatically at the U.N.'s own initiative*, not only to 'direct victims' harmed in the U.N. Kosovo lead contaminated IDP camps, but also to their close relatives as 'indirect victims'. One would have hoped that the U.N, given its charge of protecting human dignity, would have voluntarily offered such reparation as a matter of course to: (i) all current and former RAE IDP camp residents given, as is now uncontested, their suffering inhuman and degrading conditions in the U.N. IDP camps; not to mention the actual significant and chronic physical harms done to many, if not most of the camp occupants due to the lead toxic camp conditions and other aspects of the substandard conditions in the camps; and to: (ii) the close relatives of the living IDP camp victims who suffered significant mental or physical harm due to the camp conditions as well as to the close relatives of deceased camp victims who died of suspected lead poisoning due to living in the highly lead contaminated U.N. IDP camps.

The public interest would have been better served, it is suggested, by a flexible settlement scheme voluntarily entered into by UNMIK as opposed to the current UNMIK process involving the Human Rights Advisory Panel rigid formalistic process. This in that voluntary payments by the U.N. without a complex stringent quasi-judicial process before the Advisory Human Rights Panel would much better attest to: (i) an acknowledgment by the UN (UNMIK to be precise) that the RAE peoples have suffered over very many years in a *life threatening situation* in the U.N. IDP Kosovo camps due to the extremely high lead contamination in these camps which situation was dire enough to cause death due to lead poisoning already in some instances; and to (ii) an acknowledgement by the U.N. that the U.N. over many years did not remedy the situation despite knowledge of the consequences to human life of living in the lead contaminated camps, and, for several years, actively concealed from the camps' occupants information about the health hazards. A more accessible and flexible adjudication process is warranted for *all* former and current RAE IDP camp victims in that it is uncontested that the U.N. lead contaminated IDP camps (which were originally intended to provide but very temporary housing for the RAE displaced from their settlements due to an ethnic cleansing campaign perpetrated by the extremist element in the Albanian Kosovo community) became a death trap for some, and a path to serious and chronic ill health for others including children. Such a system, for instance, would *not* include a six month time limitation on any applications, but would rather provide a very generous allowable time period for filing of the human rights complaints and request for reparations. This is especially important given the very disadvantageous living circumstances and barriers with which these IDP camp victims still generally contend.

In this author's estimation, the Kosovo Human Rights Advisory Panel appears to be far from flexible or responsive to the plight of the RAE victims of the U.N. lead contaminated IDP camps. To illustrate, let us examine a few aspects of the case of *N.M. and Others v. UNMIK* heard 5 June 2009 as to admissibility.[140]

B.3 *The Human Rights Advisory Panel to UNMIK: The Case of N.M. and Others v. UNMIK*

The case of *N.M. and Others v. UNMIK*, was registered on 4 July 2008 with the Human Rights Advisory Panel to UNMIK and not heard until June 2009 despite the fact that the complainants provided medical evidence of serious physical ill health. Indeed, two of the listed complainants died of suspected lead poisoning complications before the complaint was even filed with the Panel. Though the complaint was filed by 143 named Roma victims' complainants and 3 non-Roma NGO workers who assisted them in the camps but were not residents of the camps, the complaint also referred to the situation of the RAE in all five lead contaminated IDP camps (that is, both the camps that are now closed and those still operational). A large number of the complainants had lived in the Zitkovac/Zhikoc, Casmin Lug/Cesminluke and Kablare camps for varying periods both before and after 23 April 2005; the date the Advisory Panel is held to have assumed temporal jurisdiction. Some of these residents were relocated to Osterode and Leposavic/Lepsaviq camps at some point while others were relocated to other locations in Kosovo (including their former living area of Roma Mahalla) while yet others migrated to Germany. The complaints alleged violations of *European Convention on Human Rights* Article 2 (right to life); Article 3 (prohibition against inhuman or degrading treatment); Article 6(1) (right to a fair hearing); Article 8 (right to respect for private and family life); Article 13 (right to an effective remedy); and Article 14 (prohibition against discrimination).[141] Here follows a commentary on the Advisory Panel's admissibility decision in *N.M. and Others v. UNMIK*.

B.4 *Commentary on the Human Rights Advisory Panel's Admissibility Decision in N.M. and Others v. UNMIK*

- ***Indirect victims of violations by UNMIK of the right to life (a right guaranteed under European Convention Article 2)***: The panel ruled on the admissibility of complaints filed by the respective close family members of three persons who had died of suspected lead poisoning due to high lead exposure as residents in one or other of the U.N. camps operated under the auspices of UNMIK. One complaint was brought by the parents of a deceased camp victim, the other two

[140] Decision of the Human Rights Advisory Panel of 5 June 2009, Case 26/08, NM and Others v. UNMIK heard by Mr. Marek Nowicki, Mr. Paul Lemmens, and Ms. Snezhana Botusharova under UNMIK regulation 2006/12 of 23 March 2006 on the establishment of the Human Rights Advisory Panel, para 5. http://www.toxicwastekills.com/downloads/Decision_eng_060609.pdf. Accessed 11 August 2009.

[141] Decision of the Human Rights Advisory Panel of 5 June 2009, Case 26/08, NM and Others v. UNMIK heard by Mr. Marek Nowicki, Mr. Paul Lemmens, and Ms. Snezhana Botusharova under UNMIK regulation 2006/12 of 23 March 2006 on the establishment of the Human Rights Advisory Panel, para 16. http://www.toxicwastekills.com/downloads/Decision_eng_060609.pdf. Accessed 11 August 2009.

complaints respectively by a husband and a wife. According to European Court of Human Rights case law:

> The victim's death does not automatically mean that the case is struck out of the Court's list. It is for persons with claims through the deceased – close relatives or heirs... to decide whether to pursue the case or not and up to the Court to assess whether it is appropriate to continue its examination for the purpose of protecting human rights.[142]

The Panel ruled these claims brought by close relatives as "indirect victims" *inadmissible as to the substantive requirements of Article 2* (right to life) of the European Convention on the basis that one of the deceased had died prior to 23 April 2005, and, in respect of the other two deceased, the complaints were filed more than six months after the deaths. Yet, these close relatives must continue to live with the mental anguish concerning the knowledge of their child or spouses' suffering in the IDP camps and the knowledge that their relative's death due to high lead exposure was preventable. On the view of the current author, there are 'continuing violations' for the indirect victims as well relating to the substantive element of Article 2. It therefore appears highly inappropriate to decline these claims on the *substantive requirements* of Article 2 on the alleged basis of *ratione temporis* as did the Advisory Panel. The complaints were ruled *admissible* as 'continuing violations' on the *procedural aspect* of Article 2. This in that UNMIK knew the camp conditions were highly hazardous to human health, but launched no investigations into the deaths of these complainants' loved ones who had resided in the lead contaminated camps;

- ***The human rights complaints of Non-Roma NGO workers suffering lead contamination after working in the RAE IDP camps***: The Human Rights Advisory Panel to UNMIK ruled inadmissible the human rights complaints of three NGO workers who had been lead poisoned working in the Kosovo RAE IDP camps providing humanitarian assistance to the RAE minority population there as best they could under harrowing conditions. The Advisory Panel held that:

> In order to qualify as victims, individuals must be directly affected by the act or omission in question... Victim status implies a degree of involuntary suffering or involuntary exposure to the human rights violation in issue... It is reasonable to expect persons to take preventative measures to avoid being subjected to human rights violations *where possible* and where they are aware of likely risks. If they choose to place themselves in a situation of some quantifiable risk, they must be considered responsible for their own actions, even if they are well-intentioned and act for humanitarian purposes, as appears to be the situation in this case... The information... indicates that the NGO workers were aware of the potential risks of lead contamination in the camps... *The Panel considers that the three NGO workers voluntarily assumed the risks of working in the camps.* ***It was open to them not to work in the camps and thus avoid any perceived harm to themselves.*** *Consequently, they cannot be said to be the involuntary victims of harm or suffering through acts or omissions by the respondent.*

[142]European Court of Human Rights (2007) Key case law issues: The concept of victim. http://www.echr.coe.int/NR/rdonlyres/0F2B45AE-4F54-41AB-AA8B-1E12D285110C/0/COURT_n1976742_v4_Key_caselaw_issues_Article_34_The_concept_of_the_victim_trad_eng.pdf. Accessed 14 August 2009.

> The Panel finds the complaints made by the three NGO workers inadmissible *rationae personae*... (emphasis added).[143]

With respect, on the above cited *illogic* of the Human Rights Advisory Panel to UNMIK, one would be able to argue, following the Panel's line of *fallacious* reasoning to its ultimate end, that the Kosovar RAE (so-called 'gypsy') occupants, past and present, of the U.N. lead contaminated IDP camps also voluntarily subjected themselves to the lead poisoning. This, the Advisory Panel might argue, was the case since the RAE were not being detained by UNMIK in the camps and the situation in the camps was life threatening. Note that in later years, (once the Albanian ethnic cleansing campaign against the RAE had wound down considerably given the UNMIK and KFOR prolonged presence in Kosovo), the lead contaminated IDP camps generally posed much more of a risk to the life and well being of the RAE IDPs than would have a return to the Roma Mahalla. Obviously, to suggest that the RAE IDPs voluntarily exposed themselves to harm in the U.N. lead contaminated camps would be a ludicrous claim and reveals that *the Advisory Panel's conception of victim and what constitutes involuntary suffering is erroneous*. The RAE were reliant on UNMIK and hence were involuntary victims, while the humanitarian workers, as true humanitarians, had no choice but to come to the IDP camp victims' assistance and work in the camps where others (including KFOR and UNMIK contingents) feared to tread once aware of the high lead contamination. *The voluntariness was rather in the hands of UNMIK and the States' delegates cooperating with UNMIK which, over many years, did virtually nothing to adequately ensure the safety and preservation of the human dignity of the RAE internally displaced peoples. It is, on the view here, unwarranted for the Human Rights Advisory Panel to UNMIK to attempt to shift the burden from UNMIK to these humanitarian NGO workers for the harms the NGO workers suffered in lead contaminated camps allowed to remain operational despite UNMIK being fully aware as early as 2000 of the risk to human life of the high lead levels in the camps.*

In any case, the European Court of Human Rights has well-established case law setting out government's *positive obligation* to protect all persons within its jurisdiction or control against European Convention human rights violations. Recall in this regard that: (i) the Human Rights Advisory Panel to UNMIK relies on the European Court of Human Rights' case law for guidance in applying the European Convention to the facts of the cases it considers; and that (ii) from 1999 to 2008 UNMIK (an international body) was the *de facto* government of Kosovo, and that currently it is still heavily involved in government in Kosovo performing a monitoring and advisory function. Hence, whether or not persons

---

[143]Decision of the Human Rights Advisory Panel of 5 June 2009, Case 26/08, NM and Others v. UNMIK heard by Mr. Marek Nowicki, Mr. Paul Lemmens, and Ms. Snezhana Botusharova under UNMIK regulation 2006/12 of 23 March 2006 on the establishment of the Human Rights Advisory Panel, paras 27–28. http://www.toxicwastekills.com/downloads/Decision_eng_060609.pdf. Accessed 11 August 2009.

wish to be the victims of human rights abuses, (a rather unique and dubious concept that the Advisory Panel promulgates in the above quote), is *irrelevant* to the positive obligation of the States delegates participating in UNMIK and UNMIK itself to protect the European Convention rights of the complainants. UNMIK's positive obligation to protect fundamental human rights is derived; furthermore, from the U.N. Charter as the protection of human rights is the sine qua non of the United Nations according to its stated mandate;

- ***Violation of the right to life and the imposition of a six month time limitation for filing of complaints to the Advisory Human Rights Panel regarding this non-derogable right and other rights***: Recall that the application to the Human Rights Advisory Panel in *N.M. and Others v. UNMIK* was filed 4 July 2008. The Advisory Panel held, based on a six month time limitation rule, that the complaints of those who had left their IDP camp *prior* to *4 January 2008* were *inadmissible as pertained to the life threatening camp conditions*. That is, their complaints with respect to violation of Article 2, the right to life, *relating to camp conditions* were ruled inadmissible on the contention that the violation had ceased once they left the camp and they were no longer exposed to those hazardous conditions. However, their complaints were ruled *admissible* as a 'continued violation' regarding UNMIK's breach of its positive obligation to protect their lives.

  The Advisory Panel ruled *admissible* as 'continuing violations' the complaints regarding violation of the right to life due to the camp conditions for those complainants who resided in an IDP lead contaminated camp on 4 July 2008, or who resided in a camp at least until 4 January 2008 (6 months before the application was filed).

  The six month time limitation rule appears to be inspired by Article 35(1) of the *European Convention on Human Rights*:

> **Article 35 Admissibility criteria**
> 1. The Court may only deal with the matter after all domestic remedies have been exhausted, according to the generally recognised rules of international law, *and within a period of six months from the date on which the final decision was taken.*[144]

However, it appears to be highly inappropriate to apply the 6 month rule if it is meant to reflect the logic of that rule as it is incorporated in the *European Convention on Human Rights.* This in that neither the domestic courts, nor the European Court of Human Rights, nor any other body has accepted jurisdiction and rendered a decision on the RAE human rights complaints from which the 6 month time could conceivably toll. Further, in ruling inadmissible complaints regarding violation of the right to life from applicants who had left the lead

[144] *European Convention on Human Rights and Fundamental Freedoms* (as amended by Protocol Number 11 and with protocols 1, 4, 6, 7, 12 and 13), entry into force 1 November 1998 (original Convention adopted by the Council of Europe 1950 and entered into force 3 September 1953), Article 35(1). http://www.echr.coe.int/NR/rdonlyres/D5CC24A7-DC13-4318-B457-5C9014916D7A/0/EnglishAnglais.pdf. Accessed 17 July 2009.

contaminated IDP camps prior to 4 January 2008, the Advisory Panel based its approach on the contention that:

> Those complainants no longer resident in the IDP camps at the relevant date of 4 January 2008 ceased to be exposed to the allegedly life threatening conditions at the time they left the camps. For those residents, their complaint in relation to [life-threatening] camp conditions must be found inadmissible as not lodged within six months of the alleged violation.[145]

In fact, however, there are continuing violations due to the high lead contamination of the camps and the overall deplorable inhuman camp conditions *even after the victims leave the camps* their having lived in those conditions in most, if not all instances, for many years. Those 'continuing violations' related to the camp conditions are comprised of continuing mental harms, and chronic serious physical problems due to lead poisoning; and for some, shortening considerably of the victim's life span due to the high lead exposure. *That is, the victim's body and mind is still responding to the camp conditions experienced even after the victim has departed from the camp*;

- ***Violation of the right to be protected against inhuman or degrading treatment (European Convention Article 3)***: The Human Rights Advisory Panel to UNMIK ruled the complaints *admissible ratione temporis* – even for victims who filed their complaints more than six months after leaving a lead contaminated IDP camp – as related to alleged *continuing violations due to UNMIK's failure to meet its positive obligation to prevent inhuman or degrading camp conditions*. However, the Advisory Panel, at the same time, ruled the complaints *inadmissible ratione temporis* in regards to *exposure to the indecent and inhuman camp conditions* in respect of former residents who filed their complaints more than 6 months after leaving the camps on the contention that the harmful living situation, and the rights violation in this regard, had ended for them once they left the camp. Yet, it can be argued that the mental harms caused by inhuman and degrading camp conditions, which often are correlated also with physical consequences due to chronic high stress, are often expressed in the form of a continued traumatic *reliving of the camp conditions*. Hence, there is a 'continuing violation' regarding exposure to inhuman camp conditions even if there was departure from the IDP camp prior to 4 January 2008;
- ***Violation of the right to respect for private and family life (European Convention Article 8)***: The Advisory Panel ruled complaints regarding violations of the right to respect for private and family life *due to the camp conditions inadmissible* for those who had left the camps prior to 4 January 2008 even if the latter complainants had spent many years living in the life threatening and squalid

[145]Decision of the Human Rights Advisory Panel of 5 June 2009, Case 26/08, NM and Others v. UNMIK heard by Mr. Marek Nowicki, Mr. Paul Lemmens, and Ms. Snezhana Botusharova under UNMIK regulation 2006/12 of 23 March 2006 on the establishment of the Human Rights Advisory Panel, para 51. http://www.toxicwastekills.com/downloads/Decision_eng_060609.pdf. Accessed 11 August 2009.

conditions of the U.N. lead contaminated IDP camps. In fact, however, it can be argued that there are 'continuing violations' of the right to respect for private and family life relating to the camp conditions also for complainants who departed the camps prior to 4 January 2008. This in that *even after leaving the camps*, family relationships amongst those family members who lived together in the camps in a constant state of fear, (once learning of the high lead contamination in the camps), and who had to contend with the degrading camp living conditions, and with the ill health of family members are inexorably altered and adversely affected by persistent and pervasive feelings of insecurity and other psychological ramifications.

All the complainants, even those who left the camps prior to 4 January 2008, had their complaints ruled *admissible* as continuing violations of the right to private and family life *as related to UNMIK's failure, at least from 2000 to 2005, to provide information on the health hazards in the camps* despite repeated requests from the camp inhabitants for such information;

- ***Violation of the right to a fair hearing of rights claims by an independent tribunal (European Convention Article 6(1))***: The Human Rights Advisory Panel to UNMIK ruled *admissible* all RAE IDP camp victim complaints regarding the complainants' alleged inability to receive a fair hearing by an unbiased independent tribunal which matter constitutes a 'continuing violation' regarding European Convention Article 6(1). Also ruled admissible then in this regard were complaints filed more than 6 months after the complainant's departure from the IDP camp in question as these victims too had received no hearing of their rights claims to date;
- ***Violation of the right to an effective remedy (European Convention Article 13)***: All complaints regarding violation of the right to an effective remedy, including those filed after the six month time limitation period, were ruled *admissible* as 'continuing violations'. The Advisory Panel, in regard to this category of alleged continuing violations noted the following:

> *The question of the availability of any remedies, in light of the respondent's immunity from legal proceedings, is a central issue in this complaint.* The Panel considers that this aspect of the complaint raises complex issues of law and fact, the determination of which should depend on an examination of the merits.[146]

Note that the treatment accorded the Kosovo RAE IDP camp victims by UNMIK personnel and States delegates participating with UNMIK (i.e. in regards to the placement of RAE in life threatening highly lead contaminated IDP camps with inhuman and degrading living conditions, relocation to equally highly lead contaminated camps, inadequate monitoring of blood lead levels for camp occupants, inadequate provision of medical treatment, etc.) may rise to the

[146]Decision of the Human Rights Advisory Panel of 5 June 2009, Case 26/08, NM and Others v. UNMIK heard by Mr. Marek Nowicki, Mr. Paul Lemmens, and Ms. Snezhana Botusharova under UNMIK regulation 2006/12 of 23 March 2006 on the establishment of the Human Rights Advisory Panel, para 79. http://www.toxicwastekills.com/downloads/Decision_eng_060609.pdf. Accessed 11 August 2009.

level of international crimes which possibility warrants thorough criminal investigation. If international crimes were involved, immunity would *not* attach to individual perpetrators if prosecuted by the International Criminal Court (for those who are nationals of States Parties to the Rome Statute, or perhaps even in regards to nationals of non-States Parties to the Rome Statute, as previously discussed, depending on how Kosovo is regarded in terms of whether it should be considered a State Party to the Rome Statute given its previous status as part of Serbia). The Advisory Human Rights Panel to UNMIK, however, makes no mention of the possibility of international crimes having been committed in relation to the U.N. lead contaminated IDP camps, nor of the potential implications, if any, for the question of *civil* immunity as it relates to UNMIK as a legal entity;

- ***Violation of the right to adequate housing, and health care and an adequate standard of living***: The RAE IDP camp victims alleged a breach of Article 25(1) of the Universal Declaration of Human Rights:

> (1) Everyone has the right to a standard of living adequate for the health and well-being of himself and of his family, including food, clothing, housing and medical care and necessary social services, and the right to security in the event of unemployment, sickness, disability, widowhood, old age or other lack of livelihood in circumstances beyond his control.
> (2) Motherhood and childhood are entitled to special care and assistance.. . .[147]

The complainants also alleged violations *due to the IDP camp conditions* of various international human rights treaties relating to breach of the right to a decent standard of living including adequate standards for shelter, clothing, health care, sanitation, food and water, nutrition, and adequate care during pregnancy.[148] The Advisory Panel ruled these complaints admissible regarding the *IDP camp conditions except* with respect to complaints by persons who had left the camps prior to 4 January 2008 and hence who had filed their complaints more than six months after leaving the IDP camps. However, it is here argued that *the victim's body and mind is still responding to the camp conditions experienced even after the victim has departed from the camp and hence there is a continuing violation relating to issues such as lack of food and water experienced in the camp*. For instance, very young children who were in the IDP camps at a critical period in their brain development, and who received grossly inadequate nutrition while in the camp, may have suffered irreversible brain damage especially when combined with the high lead exposure in the camps. There were many reported instances of miscarriages as well; and these

[147]Universal Declaration of Human Rights (1948). Adopted 10 December 1948 by the U.N. General Assembly (see Article 25). http://www.ohchr.org/EN/UDHR/Pages/Language.aspx?LangID=eng. Accessed 15 August 2009.

[148]Decision of the Human Rights Advisory Panel of 5 June 2009, Case 26/08, NM and Others v. UNMIK heard by Mr. Marek Nowicki, Mr. Paul Lemmens, and Ms. Snezhana Botusharova under UNMIK regulation 2006/12 of 23 March 2006 on the establishment of the Human Rights Advisory Panel, para 80. http://www.toxicwastekills.com/downloads/Decision_eng_060609.pdf. Accessed 11 August 2009.

were most likely attributable to the poor living conditions in the IDP camps and inadequate medical care afforded the women during their pregnancy while they were resident in the camps. At the same time, the Advisory Panel accepted the complaints of all IDP camp residents, present and former, relating to violation of UNMIK's positive obligation and, in certain cases ongoing positive obligation to provide the RAE internally displaced peoples with adequate housing, health care and an adequate standard of living;

- ***Violation of the right to be protected against discrimination (European Convention Article 14):*** The applicants alleged:

> *a policy or pattern of direct or indirect discrimination against the complainants as Roma.* This pattern of discrimination is said to have manifested itself through the respondent's acts or omissions in failing to relocate them to a safe environment, to provide them with adequate information about the health risks faced by them [in the U. N. IDP camps] and to take steps to improve their living standards (emphasis added).[149]

The Advisory Panel accepted these discrimination complaints as they related to the camp conditions and failure to relocate to safe areas as admissible *except* for those who had filed their applications outside the six month window since their departure from the IDP camps. The Panel held that any discriminatory acts related to failure to improve conditions in the camps or to relocate the camp occupants ceased when the person departed from the camp. This author would, however, in contrast, maintain that the discrimination relating to the camp conditions and the respondent's failure to relocate these camp victims constitutes a "continuing violation" even after RAE persons left the IDP camps. This being the case since the RAE IDP camp victims still suffered the severe physical and psychological consequences of their being on the receiving end of alleged grossly discriminatory treatment in the IDP camps which seriously adversely affected their long-term health and well-being.

At the same time, the Advisory Panel accepted as admissible all complaints from current and former residents of the IDP camps (even those who departed the camps prior to 4 January 2008) as to the respondent's positive obligation to protect this vulnerable minority from discrimination and to provide heath information about the risks that they had been exposed to in the IDP camps due to high lead exposure. The Advisory Panel ruled in the same way as to discrimination against, in particular, women and children due to the camp conditions and the failure to relocate (inadmissibility if the complaint was filed more than six months after leaving the IDP camp).[150] Note that with regard to children, one

---

[149]Decision of the Human Rights Advisory Panel of 5 June 2009, Case 26/08, NM and Others v. UNMIK heard by Mr. Marek Nowicki, Mr. Paul Lemmens, and Ms. Snezhana Botusharova under UNMIK regulation 2006/12 of 23 March 2006 on the establishment of the Human Rights Advisory Panel, para 86. http://www.toxicwastekills.com/downloads/Decision_eng_060609.pdf. Accessed 11 August 2009.

[150]Decision of the Human Rights Advisory Panel of 5 June 2009, Case 26/08, NM and Others v. UNMIK heard by Mr. Marek Nowicki, Mr. Paul Lemmens, and Ms. Snezhana Botusharova under UNMIK regulation 2006/12 of 23 March 2006 on the establishment of the Human Rights

could reasonably argue that to exclude as inadmissible complaints filed on behalf of children outside the six month window since departure from the IDP (i.e. complaints relating to the camp conditions and failure to relocate as a manifestation of discrimination) is especially legally insupportable. This as children have no say in where they live and are at the mercy of adults to obtain the good care in all respects they require for good health and development.

Note that as late as 5 February 2009, the European Parliament was continuing to express grave concerns for the health and safety of the RAE still living in the highly lead contaminated IDP camps of Osterode and Cesmin Lug, and the lack of funding for their return being allocated by the Kosovo government:

> The European Parliament... expresses grave concern at the *acute ill-health of Roma families in the Osterode and CesminLug refugee camps*; believes that this is directly linked to the improper siting of those camps, which are located on the highly toxic tailing stands of the Trepca lead mines... and urges the Commission to continue to work to secure the relocation, *as a matter of urgency*, of the families concerned.[151]

However, to date, (i) nothing has been done by the various States (i.e. those involved in Kosovo and their delegates working with, and in support of UNMIK, and the Kosovo government's reconstruction efforts), or by UNMIK or the Kosovo government itself to actually relocate the RAE Osterode and Cesmin Lug camp victims to safe areas and to alleviate their suffering due to high lead exposure in the camps, and the generally inhuman IDP camp living conditions, or (ii) to settle the stateless status of the Kosovo RAE who fled to Western States and having been living there for some time. Note that most were accepted on an ad hoc basis and never really had their asylum applications processed in the normal fashion and hence are vulnerable to expulsion. In fact, the European Parliament does not eschew 'forced returns', but attempts rather to assuage humanitarian concerns in this regard by reference to a so-called measured, sensitive approach to the issue of "forced repatriation" of members of [Kosovo] ethnic minorities such as the Roma who continue to face widespread discrimination and other human rights violations in Kosovo.[152,153] Indeed, Roma human rights and advocacy NGOs such as Chachipe, in accord with international

Advisory Panel, paras 88–95. http://www.toxicwastekills.com/downloads/Decision_eng_060609.pdf. Accessed 11 August 2009.

[151]European Parliament Resolution of 5 February 2009 on Kosovo and the Role of the EU (European Union) at para 27. http://www.eusrinkosovo.eu/pdf/European%20Parliament%20resolutionKosovo.pdf. Accessed 17 August 2009.

[152]European Parliament Resolution of 5 February 2009 on Kosovo and the Role of the EU (European Union) at para 28. http://www.eusrinkosovo.eu/pdf/European%20Parliament%20resolutionKosovo.pdf. Accessed 17 August 2009.

[153]EU must find a sustainable solution for the Kosovo Roma refugees, (letter of 9 June 2009 from Chachipe Roma rights and advocacy NGO to the President of the European Council regarding the situation of Roma refugees in Kosovo and in other European States). http://romarights.files.wordpress.com/2009/06/lettre-ec-10th-anniversary-kosovo-conflict-090609-eng.pdf. Accessed 17 August 2009.

humanitarian law, urge in 2009 **genuinely** *voluntary* returns to Kosovo, and the abandonment of 'forced returns' given that the protection of the fundamental human rights of the Roma and other minorities cannot be, in actuality, assured as of yet.[154] Note also that concerns have been expressed by the head of the OSCE mission in Kosovo in June 2009 concerning human rights issues related to the return of internally displaced RAE peoples in Kosovo and RAE from other European States.[155]

C. *Comments on the So-Called 'U.N. Supremacy Clause'*

In the above discussion, the argument was made that States are not obligated to abide by U.N. Security Resolutions when the organs of the U.N. with whom the States are cooperating in a peace-building operation (i.e. as with UNMIK) are *not* functioning in accord with the fundamental principles of the U.N. (i.e. as embodied in the U.N. Charter preamble and various Article provisions of the U.N. Charter). Recall that the preamble of the U.N. Charter makes reference to the following fundamental human rights principles amongst others:

- To reaffirm faith in fundamental human rights, [and] in the dignity and worth of the human person,. . . and
- To establish conditions under which justice and respect for the obligations arising from treaties and other sources of international law can be maintained. . .
- To promote social progress and better standards of life in larger freedom. . .[156]

Let us consider then the so-called supremacy clause of the U.N. Charter (Article 103) and whether it mandates blind obedience to the dictates of the United Nations, (i.e. expressed in the form of U.N. Security Council Resolutions), in all contexts, and regardless of specific extenuating circumstances. Note also in regards to this issue that Article 25 of the U.N. Charter states that member States "agree to accept and carry out the decisions of the Security Council *in accordance with the present Charter* (emphasis added)."[157]

The Supremacy Clause of the U.N. Charter (Article 103) reads as follows:

[154]European Council of Refugees and Exiles Position on returns to Kosovo (June 2000). http://www.unhcr.org/refworld/pdfid/3ae6a665c.pdf. Accessed 17 August 2009.

[155]Sustainable return to Kosovo remains a challenge, says OSCE Head of Mission (19 June 2009). http://www.osce.org/kosovo/item_1_38265.html.

[156]Charter of the United Nations (excerpts from the Preamble), entered into force 24 October 1945. http://www.un.org/en/documents/charter/preamble.shtml. Accessed 2 September 2009.

[157]Charter of the United Nations (Article 25), entered into force 24 October 1945. http://www.un.org/en/documents/charter/preamble.shtml. Accessed 2 September 2009.

> In the event of a conflict between the obligations of the Members of the United Nations under the present Charter and their obligations under any other *international agreement*, their obligations under the present Charter shall prevail (emphasis added).[158]

The question is then: 'where the Security Council decision or resolution is interpreted by a subsidiary organ of the U.N. body to allow the knowing placement or maintenance of persons of a particular ethnic or cultural heritage in a life threatening situation (i.e. highly lead contaminated refugee camps), is the State obligated under Articles 25 and 103 of the U.N. Charter to participate in effecting this strategy in contravention of its international human rights treaty obligations (i.e. under the *European Convention on Human Rights*) to protect persons under its jurisdiction from inhuman or degrading treatment and from injury or death resulting from human rights violations?'.

Liivoja points out that Article 103 of the U.N. Charter has been open to varying interpretations as to just what obligations it entails, and whether those obligations supersede only any conflicting obligations under various treaties that the State may have entered into.[159] The issue is of relevance in the context of the discussion in Chap. 2 of this monograph as regards to the question of whether the European States Parties to the *European Convention on Human Rights* violated their European Convention obligations while participating with UNMIK in Kosovo in accord with a U.N. Security Council resolution concerning peace-building in post-conflict Kosovo. Those State violations then would have involved placing Roma refugees in highly lead contaminated U.N. refugee camps in Northern Kosovo. The question is whether these States ought to have been held accountable in this regard by the European Court of Human Rights.

It will be recalled that the European Court of Human Rights considered *inadmissible* a complaint brought on behalf of the Kosovo Roma IDP camp lead poisoning victims on the grounds that the States were actually reporting to UNMIK, (a subsidiary organ of the U.N.), and as UNMIK was allegedly in control, the case was out of the jurisdiction of the Court given that UNMIK is not a party to the European Convention. In essence, the European Court of Human Rights, (in making the inadmissibility decision regarding the U.N. Roma lead contaminated refugee camps), disregarded the fact that where the U.N. (i.e. UNMIK) exceeds its jurisdiction, (by acting ultra vires of its basic human rights principles as articulated in the Charter of the United Nations), responsibility for the actions of States participating in U.N. initiatives under Security Council resolutions reverts to the participating States. Put differently, the supremacy clause of the Charter of the United Nations is only operative in regards to State participation in peace-building operations where the subsidiary organs of the U.N. (i.e. UNMIK) act in accord with the Charter of the United Nations:

---

[158] Charter of the United Nations (Article 103), entered into force 24 October 1945. http://www.un.org/en/documents/charter/preamble.shtml. Accessed 2 September 2009.

[159] Liivoja (2008, p. 584).

> While the Security Council's discretion is extremely wide, its powers [and that of its subsidiary organs] are limited by the rules of the Charter and, more generally, the object and purpose of the organization... ultra vires resolutions [or decisions taken by subsidiary bodies of the U.N. such as UNMIK] do not give rise to any obligations that could come within the scope of Article 103 (portions in square brackets added).[160]

Recall that Article 25 of the Charter of the U.N. requires that member States carry out their obligations to the U.N. *in accordance with the U.N. Charter*. Clearly, that was not possible in regards to the highly lead contaminated U.N. IDP camps in Kosovo where placement of persons in those camps violates the fundamental human rights tenets of the Charter of the United Nations. Note also that Article 103 of the Charter of the United Nations as a preemptory rule of international law is ***not*** intended to overrule customary international *jus cogens* principles as evidenced by the preamble to the U.N. Charter setting out the foundational human rights principles and objectives of the United Nations (in fact one would expect that Article 103 read in context with Article 25 requires adherence to *jus cogens* principles):

> The clear meaning of 'international agreements' [the term used in the text of Article 103; the Article referred to as the supremacy clause of the Charter of the United Nations]... does ***not*** by any stretch of the imagination encompass customary international law [dealing with *erga omnes* obligations; that is obligations States owe to the international community as a whole] (nor for that matter, [does Article 103 encompass] general principles of law).[161]
>
> ... the practice of the [U.N.] General Assembly and the [U.N.] Security Council seem to provide little support for the claim that obligations under the Charter prevail over obligations under customary law by virtue of Article 103.[162]

Hence, the supremacy clause of the U.N. Charter does *not* dictate that U.N. obligations are inconsistent with, or supersede customary international law such as *jus cogens* principles:

> The relief which Article 103 of the Charter may give the Security Council in case of a conflict between one of its decisions and an operative treaty obligation ***cannot*** – as a matter of simple hierarchy of norms – extend to a conflict between a Security Council resolution and *jus cogens*. (emphasis added).[163]

Thus, where U.N. subsidiary organs such as UNMIK violate *jus cogens* principles such as the right to life and the prohibition on inhuman or degrading treatment, they are operating *ultra vires* of the U.N. Charter and have no legitimate authority in the situation. No State obligation to that U.N. body ensues even under Article 103 *in that circumstance* as previously explained. Hence, U.N. Charter Article 103 in no way relieves States participating in U.N. initiatives (under the direction, to

160 Liivoja (2008, p. 586).

161 Liivoja (2008, p. 602).

162 Liivoja (2008, p. 607).

163 Liivoja (2008, p. 610) (citation of the Separate Opinion of Judge Lauterpacht in *Bosnia and Herzegovina v. Yugoslavia (Serbia and Montenegro) (Provisional Measures)* [1993] ICJ rep 325, para 100).

whatever extent, of a U.N. subsidiary body such as UNMIK) of accountability where they violate the *jus cogens* principles of customary international law (as in the Roma U.N. lead contaminated refugee camps case). It is here contended then, given the foregoing, that the U.N. lead contaminated refugee camp case was well within the jurisdiction of the European Court of Human Rights as UNMIK (with the participation of cooperating States) clearly acted ultra vires in violating the Charter of the United Nations from at least 2000 on, (if not before), when it intentionally and knowingly left hundreds of Kosovo Roma and other so-called gypsy persons in U.N. refugee camp situations that posed a grave risk to the lives and health of the camp occupants. As a result, *the participating European States bear responsibility* for *not* acting in accord with the *European Convention on Human Rights* in their dealings with the Roma internally displaced persons of post-conflict Kosovo and are *not* shielded by Article 103 or Article 25 of the U.N. Charter.

We turn now from our consideration in this part of the European Court of Human Rights as a pathway to impunity for fundamental human rights violations (by States and State agents, as well as by the U.N. personnel and organs) in post-conflict situations and times of relative peace to its contributions to impunity for human rights violations likely rising to the level of international crimes occurring in times of war or in the context of the tense "cold war" between East and West.

References

Arbour L (2008) Address by Louise Arbour, United Nations High Commissioner for Human Rights, Opening of the Judicial Year 2008 of the European Court of Human Rights, Strasbourg, 25 January 2008. http://echr.coe.int/.../Ouverture_Annee_Judiciaire_Louise_Arbour.pdf. Accessed 24 July 2009

Causevic J, Singula D (2006) A report for the society for threatened peoples: the Osterode refugee camp in Kosovo: unhealthy surroundings for the Roma refugees who have been contaminated by lead. http://www.icare.to/hdim2006/kosovo-questions2.pdf. Accessed 31 July 2009

European Rights Centre (2006) Ambulance not on the way: the disgrace of health care for Roma in Europe. Westimprim bt, Budapest

Giegerich T (2009) The is and the ought of international constitutionalism: how far have we come on Habermas's road to a "Well-considered constitutionalization of international law"? German Law Journal 10 (special edition). http://www.germanlawjournal.com/print.php?id=1076

Grover S (2008) The extraterritorial application of the Canadian charter to detainees in Canadian military custody: a re-examination of the Federal Court of Canada case Amnesty International Canada v. Canada (Canadian Forces) [2008] F.C.J. No. 356; FC 336. High Court Q Rev 4:40–53

Grover S (2009) Canada's refusal to repatriate a Canadian citizen from Guantanamo Bay as a violation of the humanitarian values underlying the principle of non-refoulement: a reanalysis of the reasoning in Omar Ahmed Khadr v. The Prime Minister of Canada et al FC 405. High Court Q Rev 5:42–48

Human Rights Watch (2009a) Kosovo: act now to close poisoned camps (crisis conditions for Roma stuck in lead-tainted site for a decade). News release dated 24 June 2009. http://www.hrw.org/en/news/2009/06/23/kosovo-act-now-close-poisoned-camps. Accessed 31 July 2009

Human Rights Watch (2009b). Poisoned by lead: a health and human rights crisis in Mitrovica's Roma camps. http://www.hrw.org/sites/default/files/reports/kosovo0609webwcover_0.pdf. Accessed 31 July 2009

Human Rights Watch (2009c) Poisoned by lead. http://www.hrw.org/en/node/83938/section/2. Accessed 13 August 2009

Larsen KM (2008) Attribution of conduct in peace operations: the 'ultimate authority and control' test. Eur J Int'l Law 19:509–531

Liivoja R (2008) The scope of the supremacy clause of the United Nations Charter. Int'l Comp Law Q 57:583–612

Milanovic M, Papic T (2009) As bad as it gets: the European Court of Human Rights's *Behrami* and *Saramati* decision and general international law. Int'l Comp Law Q 58:267–296

Roma Rights Centre (2006) Written comments of the European Roma Rights Centre concerning Kosovo for consideration by the United Nations Human Rights Committee on the occasion of review of the country report of task forces on UNMIK (20 February 2006). http://www.errc.org/cikk.php?cikk=2531. Accessed 31 July 2009

Roma Rights Centre (2007) European Court of Human Rights has no jurisdiction in Kosovo lead poisoning case. http://www.errc.org/cikk.php?cikk=2568

Romea Press Release (2009) Czech doctor not to be punished for sterilising Romany women, 2 March 2009. http://www.romea.cz/english/index.php?id=detail&detail=2007_1171

Slager EB (Counsel for International Law) (2006) European Court rules in critical Czech school desegregation case. Article for the U.S. Helsinki Commission 39(21), February 2006. http://csce.gov. Accessed 18 July 2009

UNMIK (2000) Policy paper on the repatriation of Kosovar Albanians, October 2000, No. 2. UN Interim Administration Mission in Kosovo. http://www.unhcr.org/refworld/docid/3ae6b33d7.html. Accessed 13 August 2009.

Yannis A (2004) The UN as government in Kosovo. Global Govern 10:67–81

Zampas C, Barot S, Bukovska B (in association with Zoon I) (2003) Body and soul: forced sterilization and other assaults on Roma reproductive freedom in Slovakia. Centre for Reproductive Rights, New York. http://reproductiverights.org/en/search/node/body%20and%20soul. Accessed 20 July 2009

PART III: The European Court of Human Rights' Reluctance to Classify European Convention Violations as International Crimes Even When Those Violations Likely Constitute 'War Crimes' or 'Crimes Against Humanity in Times of Armed Conflict'

Abstract In this part certain cases are analyzed in which there was a reluctance by the European Court of Human Rights to even consider whether various European Convention violations may potentially have constituted 'war crimes' or 'crimes against humanity in times of armed conflict'. Consideration is given to the implications of this reticence for fostering impunity. Also considered are certain troubling landmark *European Convention on Human Rights* Article 7 cases in which the European Court of Human Rights substituted its own characterization of the facts for that of the domestic courts and, *in effect*, exonerated applicants of international crimes as a by-product of its examination of whether there was State compliance with Convention Article 7.

I. Introduction

In this part, we will consider in what ways, if any, the European Court of Human Rights may have contributed to impunity, or, at a minimum, lack of full accountability for individual perpetrators of alleged international crimes (specifically 'war crimes' and/or 'crimes against humanity committed in times of armed conflict') due to: (i) the Court's reluctance to assess, in particular cases, whether the uncontested grave human rights violations committed by the applicant rose to the level of international crimes, or (ii) the Court's declaring in various Article 7 cases – after having substituted its own characterization of the facts for that of the domestic courts – that individual perpetrators of grave human rights violations did *not* commit the international crimes for which they were convicted domestically.

As evident from the discussion in the previous part; crimes against humanity can occur in peace time *or* in the context of impending or actual armed conflict,[1] but our focus in this section is on the latter. As Heintze explains, (i) the non-derogable right

[1]Heintze (2004, p. 789).

DOI 10.1007/978-3-642-10799-3_3,

to life (i.e. except in relation to lawful acts of war, or certain limited lawful acts taken in specified delimited peacetime circumstances where no other options were reasonably available) and to (ii) protection from torture among other non-derogable rights (as stipulated in the European Convention on Human Rights and in Article 3 common to the Geneva Conventions of 12 August 1949) means, in practice, that "The traditional impermeable border between international humanitarian law, which applies during armed conflicts, and the law of peace is thereby crossed."[2] Hence, where fundamental human rights are violated in times of armed conflict, the conduct may simultaneously violate international human rights treaties and constitute an international crime given the violation of international humanitarian norms which have been both codified (i.e. in Common Article 3 of the Geneva Conventions)[3] and become part of international customary humanitarian law.

It is essential to note that "there is no individual complaints procedure available to the victims of violations of international humanitarian law at the international level."[4] Hence, in respect of the States of the European Union, insofar as the European Court of Human Rights is reluctant to classify a European Convention violation as a potential international crime relating to a breach of international humanitarian law (where the facts prima facie support such a classification), there is no possibility for acknowledgement of this potential fact in the international human rights court context. This may do little to facilitate possible prosecution for international crimes at the International Criminal Court, or even prosecution and/or just sentencing at the domestic level for international crimes committed by a State national in times of war. This point will be discussed in our consideration of the European Court of Human Rights cases such as the case of *Streletz, Kessler and Krenz v. Germany*,[5] for instance, where the Court's classification of the conduct of individual perpetrators at the heart of the case stopped far short of the label of *potential* war crime.

Note that the judges of the European Court of Human Rights have often proclaimed that the *European Convention on Human Rights* not only sets up a system of collective rights and freedoms guarantees for persons within the jurisdiction of the States Parties as well as positive obligations for the States Parties in this regard, but that it must be interpreted also in the context of international law:

> *... the Convention must also be interpreted in the light of the Vienna Convention on the Law of Treaties of 23 May 1969 ... more particularly Article 31 § 3(c), which provides that there shall be taken into account, together with the context, "any relevant rules of international law applicable in the relations between the parties*". The Court is amenable

[2]Heintze (2004, p. 791).

[3]Geneva Convention IV relative to the Protection of Civilian Persons in Time of War, (common Article 3). http://www.icrc.org/ihl.nsf/385ec082b509e76c41256739003e636d/6756482d86146898c125641e004aa3c5. Accessed 1 September 2009.

[4]Heintze (2004, p. 800).

[5]European Court of Human Rights Grand Chamber judgment dated 22 March 2001 in the *Case of Streletz and Kessler v. Germany* (Applications 34044/96, 35532/97 and 44801/98). http://www.menschenrechte.ac.at/orig/01_2/Streletz.pdf. Accessed 15 August 2009.

> to this idea that the Convention cannot be interpreted in a vacuum and has often based its reasoning on other sources of international law ... (emphasis added)[6]

We will examine the aforementioned claim by the European Court of Human Rights in respect of the extent to which the Court is, *in practice*, amenable to referencing international codified and customary humanitarian law in assessing the facts of the case giving rise to the complaints. Such is critical if the European Convention is to be considered anything more than simply an international quasi-constitutional legal instrument applicable to the European States Parties in assessing their domestic law for conformity with Convention human rights standards (as important as that function is undoubtedly). Judge Francoise Tulkens raises the following questions with respect to the European Convention on Human Rights:

> ... does the fact that the rights guaranteed by the European Convention are enshrined in an international treaty mean that they must be interpreted differently from equivalent rights and liberties that are protected by national constitutions? ... *In the final analysis, should the European Convention on Human Rights be perceived more as an expression of international law or rather as resembling constitutional law as applied by the constitutional courts*? (emphasis added)[7]

The current author in this part argues that the European Convention should be regarded as in part an expression of international law rather than an expression of law resembling exclusively a super-ordinate Constitution covering the European States Parties to the European Convention. It will be argued here that to the extent that the European Court of Human Rights, *in practice*, treats the *European Convention on Human Rights* as only akin to constitutional law; its judgments in those cases are likely to hinder advancement of, and advocacy for consistent international human rights and humanitarian standards applied to all persons and collectivities regardless of status or background characteristics (ethnicity, place of origin, sexual orientation, disability, etc.) in times of war as well as in peacetime. That is, the suggestion is made that unlike the rights guarantees and State obligations specified under national constitutions; the *European Convention on Rights and Freedoms* must be interpreted expansively consistent with international human rights and international humanitarian law standards or norms which reach beyond the European States Parties. (Contrast this with, for instance, the example of the national constitution of Bosnia–Herzegovina which (at the time of writing) denies Roma and Jewish populations, as well as certain other minorities in the jurisdiction, certain democratic rights by restricting the types of elected office for which they are eligible to run; their being barred from running for the Presidency or standing for election to the House of Peoples of the Parliamentary Assembly.)[8] The problem is,

---

[6]Council of Europe (2007, p. 11), Presentation by Francoise Tulkens (then Judge of the European Court of Human Rights).

[7]Council of Europe (2007, p. 12 and p. 14), Presentation by Francoise Tulkens (then Judge of the European Court of Human Rights).

[8]Sejdic and Finci v. Bosnia and Herzegovina (applications 27996/06 and 4836/06). European Court of Human Rights case relinquished to the Grand Chamber. The Grand Chamber Judgement

however, that many times the European Court of Human Rights appears to take a rather insular view:

> *Like any court, the European Court of Human Rights has a natural tendency to want exclusively or primarily to apply "its" law – the European Convention on Human Rights … and its Protocols* – to such an extent that it might have been thought to lose sight occasionally of the fact that *the Convention* itself is governed by international law and, in particular, the Law of Treaties (emphasis added).[9]

Note, at the same time, that the European Court considers the European Convention on Human Rights as a 'living instrument':

> It would probably not have survived if it had not been regarded as a living instrument that has to be interpreted in line with developments in the society in which we live.[10]

One new development in the society in which we live is the establishment of the International Criminal Court which began hearing its first case in January 2008. We will consider as well then to what extent the European Convention is currently being interpreted by the European Court of Human Rights in manner consistent with that new reality (as indicated, for instance, by the extent of the European Court of Human Rights' willingness to declare whether the case before it *potentially* involves international crimes that may be ripe for, at a minimum, investigation and possible prosecution by the domestic courts as 'war crimes', or 'crimes against humanity in war time,' or should there be unwillingness or inability of the State to do so, and the case appears to be potentially admissible to the ICC, investigation and possible prosecution by the latter). Let us turn then to cases in which the European Court of Human Rights, it is contended here, declined to interpret the case facts and the European Convention, in part or in whole, with adequate consideration of codified international humanitarian law and customary international humanitarian law norms.

II. *Case 1 Streletz, Kessler and Krenz v. Germany* (Applications 34044/96, 35532/97 and 44801/98) European Grand Chamber Judgment

A. *Background Facts and Procedural History*

Background Facts: The applicants are German nationals who were convicted of war crimes by the German courts of the new Germany after reunification and imprisoned in the FRG after reunification then released after serving two-thirds of

of 22 December, 2009 found the bar to certain elected office discriminatory. http://www.soros.org/initiatives/justice/litigation/bosnia-and-herzegovinia/grand-chamber-judgment-20091222.pdf

[9]Council of Europe (2007, p. 21), Presentation by Lucias Caflisch (then member of the International Law Commission and Former Judge of the European Court of Human Rights).

[10]Council of Europe (2007, p. 13), Presentation by Francoise Tulkens (Judge of the European Court of Human Rights).

their sentences. Streletz and Kessler, at the time of the Grand Chamber hearing and judgment, were living in Germany (in Strausberg and Berlin respectively). The third applicant Krenz had been incarcerated since 2000 and was so at the time of the Grand Chamber hearing. In the instant case, the convicted men pleaded a violation of their European Convention rights under Article 1 which guarantees the rights and freedoms of the European Convention on Human Rights to all persons within the State Party's jurisdiction, and of Article 7(1) which prohibits retroactive application of the law (i.e. the applicants alleged that the conduct for which they had been convicted was not a criminal offence in the old GDR at the time the acts were committed).

The case concerned what happened at the Berlin Wall due to the actions of the applicants who were very senior leaders in the former German Democratic Republic prior to reunification of Germany. Recall that the Berlin Wall was built 13 August 1961 to prevent any further refugees fleeing from East Germany (i.e. from the German Democratic Republic or GDR) to West Germany (i.e. the Federal Republic of Germany or FRG). Between 1949 and 1961 two and one-half million Germans had fled from the GDR to the FRG.[11] That border wall dividing the GDR from the FRG was reinforced with antipersonnel mines, automatic fire systems and by East German border guards. Many who tried to escape to the West lost their lives at the Berlin Wall having inadvertently triggered the mines, or automatic weapons fire and/or after being shot by the German border guards. The official death toll resulting from such events, according to the government of the FRG, was 264; though according to other reputable sources this may be an underestimate. The GDR border policy as regards the wall was the creation of the Political Bureau of the Central Committee of GDR's Socialist Unity Party which was at the time the most powerful authority in East Germany. Both applicants were senior members of the GDR's State apparatus and of the Socialist Unity Party leadership. In autumn of 1989, the Berlin Wall fell after thousands had escaped from East Germany to the FRG's embassies in Prague and Warsaw, and to Hungary which in 1989 had opened its borders to GDR refugees. The GDR system crumbled and the reunification process began.[12] In the summer of 1990, the newly elected parliament of the FRG pushed the legislature for prosecution of the crimes committed by the Socialist Unity Party.

The Berlin Regional Court proceedings: The applicants were convicted 16 September 1993 by the Berlin Regional Court of '*incitement to commit intentional homicide*' due to their role in causing the deaths of a number of persons aged between 18 and 28 who had attempted to flee the GDR between 1971 and 1989 by crossing the border between the two German States. None of the victims of the

---

[11]European Court of Human Rights Grand Chamber judgment dated 22 March 2001 in the *Case of Streletz and Kessler v. Germany* (Applications 34044/96, 35532/97 and 44801/98), para 13. http://www.menschenrechte.ac.at/orig/01_2/Streletz.pdf. Accessed 15 August 2009.

[12]European Court of Human Rights Grand Chamber judgment dated 22 March 2001 in the *Case of Streletz and Kessler v. Germany* (Applications 34044/96, 35532/97 and 44801/98), para 17. http://www.menschenrechte.ac.at/orig/01_2/Streletz.pdf. Accessed 15 August 2009.

former GDR government's actions at the Berlin Wall had endangered anyone else and all had just attempted to flee to the West. Note that the conviction was based on GDR law in existence at the material time prior to reunification. The Regional Court found that the applicants were members of the National Defence Council which gave the directives to the Ministry of Defence regarding what security policy and correlated actions would be operative in guarding the Berlin Wall and in the effort to prevent crossings from East Germany to the West. In that regard, "Border guards had been ordered to *protect the border of the GDR at all costs*, even if that meant that 'border violators' ... thereby lost their lives."[13] The Regional Court found that the actual orders given to the border guards went far beyond what the GDR statute held permissible and that the border guards were instructed and trained to prevent border crossings at all costs and either arrest or "annihilate anyone who attempted to cross".[14] That is, it was made clear that border guards were expected to stop all crossings by whatever means necessary and that failure to do so would result in the border guard being investigated by a military prosecutor. The Regional Court ruled that the former GDR State practice regarding border security (i.e. at the Berlin Wall) "flagrantly and intolerably infringed elementary precepts of justice and human rights protected under international law."[15]

The Federal Court of Justice proceedings: The convictions were appealed to the Federal Court of Justice of the FRG. The sentences were reduced by that court in part based on the fact that the criminal law in the Federal Republic of Germany after reunification regarding sentencing provisions was more lenient than what would have been the sentencing under the German Democratic Republic penal code prior to reunification. The Federal Court of Justice also revised the nature of the offence for which the applicants had been convicted to "intentional homicide as indirect principals."[16] They were held guilty of this charge in that as members of the National Defence Council, they had been instrumental in formulating the border policy for the Berlin Wall that ultimately led to the deaths of certain young people at the Wall for which deaths the applicants were being held accountable. Both the lower Court and the Federal Court of Justice held that the defendants could *not* plead 'justification' based on the relevant statutes (the States Border Act) operative in the GDR at the time. This since that statute violated fundamental tenets of

[13]European Court of Human Rights Grand Chamber judgment dated 22 March 2001 in the *Case of Streletz and Kessler v. Germany* (Applications 34044/96, 35532/97 and 44801/98), para 19. http://www.menschenrechte.ac.at/orig/01_2/Streletz.pdf. Accessed 15 August 2009.

[14]European Court of Human Rights Grand Chamber judgment dated 22 March 2001 in the *Case of Streletz and Kessler v. Germany* (Applications 34044/96, 35532/97 and 44801/98), para 19. http://www.menschenrechte.ac.at/orig/01_2/Streletz.pdf. Accessed 15 August 2009.

[15]European Court of Human Rights Grand Chamber judgment dated 22 March 2001 in the *Case of Streletz and Kessler v. Germany* (Applications 34044/96, 35532/97 and 44801/98), para 19. http://www.menschenrechte.ac.at/orig/01_2/Streletz.pdf. Accessed 15 August 2009.

[16]European Court of Human Rights Grand Chamber judgment dated 22 March 2001 in the *Case of Streletz and Kessler v. Germany* (Applications 34044/96, 35532/97 and 44801/98), para 20. http://www.menschenrechte.ac.at/orig/01_2/Streletz.pdf. Accessed 15 August 2009.

international law concerning freedom of movement and right to life (i.e. as enshrined in the *International Covenant on Civil and Political Rights* ICCPR (Articles 12 and 6 of the ICCPR respectively) which had been ratified by the former GDR on 8 November 1974 (though the ICCPR had not been incorporated into the domestic law of the former GDR)) as well as the GDR Constitution.[17,18] The constitution of the former GDR was almost identical to that of the FRG after reunification and both provided guarantees regarding respect for human dignity and for the principles of international law.[19]

Federal Constitution Court proceedings: The applicants appealed next to the Federal Constitutional Court alleging that their impugned actions were lawful in the GDR at the relevant time. Specifically then the defendants held that the Federal Court of Justice had applied the law retroactively and this had resulted in a wrongful conviction being upheld. The Constitutional Court dismissed the appeals

Relevant Law: In this section, only selected points are highlighted regarding the relevant law in the former GDR at the time the offences were committed for which the applicants were convicted. The introduction to the special part of the 1979 criminal code of the former GDR was titled: "Crimes against the national sovereignty of the German Democratic Republic, peace, humanity, and human rights" and read in part as follows:

> The merciless punishment of crimes against the national sovereignty of the German Democratic Republic, peace, humanity and human rights, and of war crimes, is an indispensable prerequisite for stable peace in the world, for the restoration of faith in fundamental human rights . . . and the dignity and worth of human beings, and for the preservation of the rights of all.[20]
>
> *Any person whose conduct violates human or fundamental rights*, international obligations or the national sovereignty of the German Democratic Republic may *not* plead . . . statute law, an order or written instructions in justification; *he shall be held criminally responsible* (emphasis added).[21]

---

[17]European Court of Human Rights Grand Chamber judgment dated 22 March 2001 in the *Case of Streletz and Kessler v. Germany* (Applications 34044/96, 35532/97 and 44801/98), para 20. http://www.menschenrechte.ac.at/orig/01_2/Streletz.pdf. Accessed 15 August 2009.

[18]*International Covenant on Civil and Political Rights* adopted by the U.N. General Assembly 16 December 1966 and entry into force 23 March 1976. http://www2.ohchr.org/english/law/ccpr.htm. Accessed 15 August 2009.

[19]European Court of Human Rights Grand Chamber judgment dated 22 March 2001 in the *Case of Streletz and Kessler v. Germany* (Applications 34044/96, 35532/97 and 44801/98), para 28. http://www.menschenrechte.ac.at/orig/01_2/Streletz.pdf. Accessed 15 August 2009.

[20]European Court of Human Rights Grand Chamber judgment dated 22 March 2001 in the *Case of Streletz and Kessler v. Germany* (Applications 34044/96, 35532/97 and 44801/98), para 29 (citation from the introduction to a section of the criminal code of the former GDR dealing with "Crimes against the national sovereignty of the German Democratic Republic, peace, humanity, and human rights"). http://www.menschenrechte.ac.at/orig/01_2/Streletz.pdf. Accessed 15 August 2009.

[21]European Court of Human Rights Grand Chamber judgment dated 22 March 2001 in the *Case of Streletz and Kessler v. Germany* (Applications 34044/96, 35532/97 and 44801/98), para 30. http://www.menschenrechte.ac.at/orig/01_2/Streletz.pdf. Accessed 15 August 2009.

Crimes against peace, humanity or human rights, and ***war crimes*** shall *not* be subject to the rules on limitation set out in this law ... (emphasis added)[22]

Article 258 of the Penal Code of the former GDR set out that: (i) members of the armed forces that commit acts which violate international law cannot plead justification based on the fact that they were ordered to do so; (ii) both those committing the acts that violate international law and those who ordered them are criminally liable, and (iii) those who refuse to obey orders that manifestly violate public international law are *not* criminally liable for doing so:

(1) Members of the armed forces shall not be criminally responsible for acts committed in execution of an order issued by a superior *save where the execution of the order manifestly violates the recognised rules of public international law or a criminal statute.*
(2) *Where a subordinate's execution of an order manifestly violates the recognised rules of public international law or a criminal statute, the superior who issued that order shall also be criminally responsible.*
(3) Criminal responsibility shall *not* be incurred for refusal or failure to obey an order whose execution would violate the rules of public international law or a criminal statute.[23]

Further, the Constitution of the former GDR Article 30 sections 1 and 2 stipulated that:

"The person and liberty of every citizen of the German Democratic Republic are inviolable" and "citizens' rights may be restricted only in so far as the law provides and when such restriction appears to be unavoidable ..."[24]

Section 27 of the State Borders Act of the former GDR set out that: (i) there were very limited situations in which firearms could properly be used by State agents; (ii) that use of firearms was a last resort and that (iii) human life should be preserved wherever possible.[25] Until 1 January 1989, due to the legal provisions that had been passed in the former GDR (Passport Act of 1963 and the Passport Act and

[22]European Court of Human Rights Grand Chamber judgment dated 22 March 2001 in the *Case of Streletz and Kessler v. Germany* (Applications 34044/96, 35532/97 and 44801/98), para 31. http://www.menschenrechte.ac.at/orig/01_2/Streletz.pdf. Accessed 15 August 2009.

[23]European Court of Human Rights Grand Chamber judgment dated 22 March 2001 in the *Case of Streletz and Kessler v. Germany* (Applications 34044/96, 35532/97 and 44801/98), para 36. http://www.menschenrechte.ac.at/orig/01_2/Streletz.pdf. Accessed 15 August 2009.

[24]Constitution of the Former German Democratic Republic, Article 30(1) and (2) cited in European Court of Human Rights Grand Chamber judgment dated 22 March 2001 in the *Case of Streletz and Kessler v. Germany* (Applications 34044/96, 35532/97 and 44801/98), para 61. http://www.menschenrechte.ac.at/orig/01_2/Streletz.pdf. Accessed 15 August 2009.

[25]European Court of Human Rights Grand Chamber judgment dated 22 March 2001 in the *Case of Streletz and Kessler v. Germany* (Applications 34044/96, 35532/97 and 44801/98), para 38. http://www.menschenrechte.ac.at/orig/01_2/Streletz.pdf. Accessed 15 August 2009.

Order on Passports and Visas of 28 June 1979, as supplemented by the Order of 15 February 1982), only those who were at retirement age, had certain political privileges or who were exempted from normal passport or visa requirements on account of urgent family business could leave the GDR legally. Further, under the order of 28 June 1979 until 1 January 1989, no reasons had to be given by the government for refusals of permission to leave the former GDR and there was no appeal available. From 1981 to 1983, there were more than 50 complaints lodged to the U.N. Human Rights Commission by individuals who had been refused permission to leave the former GDR; the number required for the Commission to be able to refer to a systematic gross violation of human rights in the former GDR. The GDR, however, allowed some of these complainants to leave its territory thus bringing the numbers to below 50 and avoiding the censure of the Commission.

European Court of Human Rights Proceedings: The parties agreed to have jurisdiction relinquished to the Grand Chamber of the Court. The applicants argued before the Grand Chamber that their actions did not constitute offences at the time under the laws of the former GDR, or under international law, and that it was unforeseeable that they would be prosecuted after Germany's reunification. They suggested that this was why they had not been prosecuted in the courts of the former GDR and that there was no basis for prosecution in the criminal courts of the FRG after reunification. The applicants argued that there was no basis for the rejection by the criminal courts after reunification of the affirmative defense they had proffered; namely one of 'justification', and that this dismissal of their defence was not based on a gradual interpretation of the laws of the former GDR. The applicants suggested, further, that they had not violated the International Covenant of Civil and Political Rights since that international law did not apply to individuals but to States and in any case the former GDR had not been officially censored by any United Nations body for violations of international law. They also suggested that their border activities were essential to the preservation of the integrity of the territory of the former GDR and that other countries authorize the use of firearms at border crossings if individuals do not heed warnings from the border guards.

The government's counterargument was that it was in fact entirely foreseeable that the nondiscriminatory and ruthless use of firearms by the border guards combined with automatic weapons fire systems and mines at the Berlin Wall against civilians trying to flee who posed no threat to anyone would constitute a criminal offence once the government in the former GDR changed.

Analysis of the case by the Grand Chamber of the European Court of Human Rights: The Court held that under the European Convention on Human Rights, Article 19,[26] the Court is not charged with correcting any errors of fact or law made by the domestic courts *unless* these constitute a violation of the individual's

[26]*European Convention on Human Rights and Fundamental Freedoms* (as amended by Protocol Number 11 and with protocols 1, 4, 6, 7, 12 and 13), entry into force 1 November 1998 (original Convention adopted by the Council of Europe 1950 and entered into force 3 September 1953) (Article 19). http://www.echr.coe.int/NR/rdonlyres/D5CC24A7-DC13-4318-B457-5C9014916D7A/0/EnglishAnglais.pdf. Accessed 17 July 2009.

Convention rights or freedoms. The Court acknowledged, as a non-derogable right articulated in Article 7 of the European Convention, the right to be protected against prosecution for an act of commission or omission which was not defined as an offence in the criminal statutes at the relevant time and against retrospective application of the law. The Grand Chamber held that it must decide "whether the applicants' acts, at the time when they were committed, constituted offences defined with sufficient accessibility and foreseeability by the law of the GDR or international law."[27] The Court concluded that the applicants were responsible for the deaths of numerous persons trying to flee the GDR; mostly young people aged 18–20, and none of whom were armed or posed a threat to anyone. The Court concluded that none of those trying to flee were committing a 'serious offence' under German law as defined in the law of the former GDR which would justify the border guards using deadly force to prevent their escape. The Grand Chamber thus held that the conviction of the applicants by the German criminal courts (FRG courts) after reunification was *not* arbitrary or contrary to Article 7 of the *European Convention on Human Rights*.[28] The Grand Chamber held further that the practice of using deadly force as a matter of routine implemented at the Berlin Wall to stem the flow of the multitudes of persons attempting to flee the former GDR was contrary to the former GDR's Constitution, the Criminal Code in place at the time and even the State Borders Act of the former GDR.[29] The Grand Chamber also, based on general principles of criminal law, rejected the applicants' argument that the order to fire (for which they were largely responsible) formed a legitimate *State practice* and therefore constituted a justification for the applicants' acts. The Grand Chamber held that the applicants were *individually culpable* for the following reasons, among others: (i) the State practice regarding the border policy was unlawful according to the statutes of the former GDR, and international law, (ii) the Constitution of the former GDR held individuals culpable for violations of the international human rights obligations of the former GDR, (iii) the order to "annihilate" anyone attempting to flee the former GDR was a practice authored and implemented – as indirect principals – by the applicants. The Grand Chamber, in addition, held that it was entirely *foreseeable* that the applicants would face prosecution and probable conviction for their acts when the government of the GDR changed given that: (i) the former GDR's border policy had been severely criticized in the international community as a violation of fundamental human rights; and (ii) the Border policy and practice was not consistent with the statutes

---

[27]European Court of Human Rights Grand Chamber judgment dated 22 March 2001 in the *Case of Streletz and Kessler v. Germany* (Applications 34044/96, 35532/97 and 44801/98), para 51. http://www.menschenrechte.ac.at/orig/01_2/Streletz.pdf. Accessed 15 August 2009.

[28]European Court of Human Rights Grand Chamber judgment dated 22 March 2001 in the *Case of Streletz and Kessler v. Germany* (Applications 34044/96, 35532/97 and 44801/98), para 64. http://www.menschenrechte.ac.at/orig/01_2/Streletz.pdf. Accessed 15 August 2009.

[29]European Court of Human Rights Grand Chamber judgment dated 22 March 2001 in the *Case of Streletz and Kessler v. Germany* (Applications 34044/96, 35532/97 and 44801/98), para 73. http://www.menschenrechte.ac.at/orig/01_2/Streletz.pdf. Accessed 15 August 2009.

existing at the time in the former GDR, but was instead one superimposed on the latter by the applicants via secret orders and service instructions that emphasized protecting the border "at all costs" and "annihilating" anyone who tried to cross from the GDR to the West. The Grand Chamber noted also that the applicants' acts were offences under the law existing in the former GDR even though they had not been prosecuted prior to reunification of East and West Germany and that the failure to prosecute the applicants in the former GDR was related to their power in the former GDR. The Grand Chamber also found that the German courts' interpretation of the statutes of the former GDR in the instant case was consistent with, for instance, the Articles of the *International Covenant on Civil and Political Rights* with respect to right to life and freedom of movement.

Most importantly, the Grand Chamber held that the applicants had, by various means, attempted to create the "appearance of legality" in implementing the border policy and practice but, in fact, there was in actuality no domestic (under former GDR statute), or international legal basis for their acts:

The Court considers that a State practice such as the GDR's border-policing policy, which flagrantly infringes human rights and above all the right to life, the supreme value in the international hierarchy of human rights, cannot be covered by the protection of Article 7 § 1 of the Convention. That practice, which emptied of its substance the legislation on which it was supposed to be based, and which was imposed on all organs of the GDR, including its judicial bodies, cannot be described as "law" within the meaning of Article 7 of the Convention (emphasis added).[30]

The Grand Chamber thus concluded that the applicants had committed criminal offences at the time the acts were performed, and that this was the case was abundantly clear in the law of the former GDR at the time such that it was foreseeable that they could, and likely would be convicted if there was a democratic government elected in the GDR.

B. Commentary on Streletz, Kessler and Krenz v. Germany

1. ***The Grand Chamber's consideration of international human rights law in addition to the European Convention***: The Grand Chamber of the European Court of Human Rights (ECHR) in the instant case stated that "***The Court considers that it is its duty to examine the present case from the standpoint of the principles of international law also, particularly those relating to the international protection of human rights*** ... (emphasis added)"[31] In this regard, the ECHR noted the

[30]European Court of Human Rights Grand Chamber judgment dated 22 March 2001 in the *Case of Streletz and Kessler v. Germany* (Applications 34044/96, 35532/97 and 44801/98), para 87. http://www.menschenrechte.ac.at/orig/01_2/Streletz.pdf. Accessed 15 August 2009.

[31]European Court of Human Rights Grand Chamber judgment dated 22 March 2001 in the *Case of Streletz and Kessler v. Germany* (Applications 34044/96, 35532/97 and 44801/98), para 90. http://www.menschenrechte.ac.at/orig/01_2/Streletz.pdf. Accessed 15 August 2009.

preeminence given to the right to life in various international human rights treaties including the *International Covenant on Civil and Political Rights* which the former GDR had ratified on 8 November 1974.[32] The ECHR rejected the applicants arguments that their acts had been lawful under Article 2(2) of the *European Convention on Human Rights* in that the Court held that the use of deadly force at the Berlin Wall was in no way absolutely necessary to prevent a serious crime. The fugitives, in fact, the Court held, were not committing a 'serious crime' under the former GDR's Criminal Code in existence at the time and posed no security risk to anyone.[33] In addition, constitutional law and statutory law in the former GDR, the Court pointed out, enshrined the right to life and the necessity of preserving life wherever possible. The ECHR in the instant case also referred to international law regarding when restrictions on citizen movement are lawful and found that: (i) none of these circumstances were present in the instant case (i.e. restrictions in movement provided by law to protect national security, public order, public health or morals or the rights and freedoms of others), and that (ii) the FRG was justified in punishing the offence of violating the right to life as articulated in the *International Covenant on Civil and Political Rights* since international law obligations were incorporated into the penal code of the former GDR at the relevant time.[34] The Court held further that the applicants, as State leaders of the former GDR, could *not* have been ignorant of the actual law of the country which offered protection for the right to life and of the State's international law obligations in this regard. The Grand Chamber concluded that the applicants did bear individual criminal responsibility for the deaths at the Berlin Wall for which they had been convicted given that, for instance: (i) they were amongst the leading architects of the policy and orders that gave rise to those deaths, and (ii) Article 95 of the former GDR Criminal Code stipulated that individual criminal responsibility would attach for anyone who violated the GDR's international obligations of fundamental human rights and freedoms. *Hence, the Grand Chamber found that: (i) the State (i.e. the criminal courts of the FRG after reunification and the installment of a new elected Parliament) had not violated Article 7(1) of the European Convention by convicting the applicants (i.e. there was no retroactive application of the law), and (ii) it was not necessary in the view of the Court to consider article 7(2) of the Convention.*

---

[32]*International Covenant on Civil and Political Rights* adopted by the U.N. General Assembly 16 December 1966 and entry into force 23 March 1976, Article 6 (Rights to life). http://www2.ohchr.org/english/law/ccpr.htm. Accessed 15 August 2009.

[33]European Court of Human Rights Grand Chamber judgment dated 22 March 2001 in the *Case of Streletz and Kessler v. Germany* (Applications 34044/96, 35532/97 and 44801/98), para 96. http://www.menschenrechte.ac.at/orig/01_2/Streletz.pdf. Accessed 15 August 2009.

[34]European Court of Human Rights Grand Chamber judgment dated 22 March 2001 in the Case of Streletz and Kessler v. Germany (Applications 34044/96, 35532/97 and 44801/98), para 98 and100. http://www.menschenrechte.ac.at/orig/01_2/Streletz.pdf. Accessed 15 August 2009.

The Grand Chamber also held that there was *no violation* of the applicants' Article 1 rights. The applicants' had argued that their Article 1 rights had been violated due to the alleged discriminatory application – in criminal cases concerning former leaders of the old GDR – of a principle which permitted retroactive application of the law (the latter on the presumption that the failure to do so would allow for an intolerable conflict between statute law and justice). The Grand Chamber held, in contrast, that: (i) Article 1 is a European Convention on Human Rights framework provision and cannot be violated on its own, and (ii) the general principles of law applied by the Federal Constitutional Court in the instant case were relevant and broad in scope, and not applied in a discriminatory manner against citizens of the former GDR.

2. **The Grand Chamber's refusal to consider whether the applicants had committed crimes against humanity and the implications for justice and respect for the victims of the applicants' conduct of 'intentional homicide as indirect principals'**:

(a) ***The gravity of the crime issue***: What is of interest for the purposes of the discussion here is that, despite the references to international human rights law and the multitude of references by the European Court of Human Rights in *Streletz, Kessler and Krenz v. Germany* to the non-derogable right to life, ***the Grand Chamber declined to comment on whether the applicants' offences constituted 'crimes against humanity' holding it was "unnecessary" to so***:

> In addition, the applicants' conduct could be considered, likewise under Article 7 § 1 of the Convention, from the standpoint of other rules of international law, notably those concerning *crimes against humanity. However, the conclusion reached by the Court (see paragraph 105 above) makes consideration of that point unnecessary* (emphasis added)[35]

The Grand Chamber took an identical approach in the case of *K.H.W. v. Germany* where it also declined to make a finding with respect to whether the applicant when he was aged 20 had committed a crime against humanity. The applicant had killed a single unarmed civilian as a border guard at the Berlin Wall and the issue arises whether he was, as a result, thereby complicit in a State practice of killing unarmed civilians (who were trying to flee over the Berlin Wall and at other border points in the former GDR) where such a practice constitutes crimes against humanity. The Grand Chamber of the European Court of Human Rights (ECHR) held it was "unnecessary" to make a finding on whether the applicant K.H.W. had committed a crime against humanity since he was held by the Grand Chamber to be guilty of violating international human rights law and the statutory law of the former GDR. At the same time, the Grand Chamber had gone so far as to hold that when the applicant (K.H.W.) had enlisted for three years with the military, he was demonstrating allegiance to the socialist regime of the former GDR, and, at

[35]European Court of Human Rights Grand Chamber judgment dated 22 March 2001 in the *Case of Streletz and Kessler v. Germany* (Applications 34044/96, 35532/97 and 44801/98), para 106. http://www.menschenrechte.ac.at/orig/01_2/Streletz.pdf. Accessed 15 August 2009.

the relevant time, knew full well he could be posted at the border where he would be required by his superiors to use deadly force against unarmed civilians trying to flee the former GDR and that this was the State's systemic practice. The Court held that K.H.W. should have known that blind obedience to such orders would constitute a violation of international human rights law. In *K.H.W.* the accused had been convicted by the domestic court and sentenced to a term *as a juvenile*.[36]

Thus, the European Court of Human Rights held that it was unnecessary to consider whether the applicants in *K.H.W v. Germany* and *Streletz, Kessler and Krenz v. Germany* had committed crimes against humanity as they were found to have violated international law and the statutes of the GDR. However, it is here contended, with respect, that this is in fact *no answer* to the question of why the Grand Chamber in *Streletz, Kessler and Krenz v. Germany* declined to consider whether the applicants had committed 'crimes against humanity' by ordering the "annihilation" of anyone who tried to flee the former GDR which order resulted in the unlawful deaths of numerous persons, including young persons trying to exercise their basic human right to freedom of movement. After all, crimes against humanity are of a different order than are non-systemic crimes involving human rights violations. Crimes against humanity, as will be recalled, are a category of crime which are potentially prosecutable by the International Criminal Court. They are amongst the most grave of all crimes and held to offend humanity itself. *It is thus a key issue just what order of crimes the applicants are held to have committed as this has several implications; including what is considered just sentencing and for public acknowledgment of the gravity of the crimes committed. Both are essential for delivering justice to the victims.*

Consider then the comparatively very lenient sentences imposed on the applicants by the criminal courts of the FRG after reunification (five years six months for Streletz, seven years and six months for Kessler and six years and six months for Krenz; *all of whom were required to serve only two-thirds of their sentences*). This was the punishment for the murder of numerous persons; including several young victims who were unarmed and simply trying to exercise their fundamental human right to free movement. The applicants were convicted of perpetrating an unlawful *widespread and systematic campaign* (implemented prior to reunification) to stop flight from the former GDR *at any cost*, and orchestrated, in large part, by the applicants as senior leaders of the former GDR. It may appear to many to be unreasonable to suggest that such comparatively light sentences for deaths which constitute violations of fundamental human rights comports with justice. In addition, recall that all three applicants had served *semi-custodial* sentences; a fact also inconsistent, many would agree, with the notion of just punishment given the brutality and systematic nature of the crimes committed.

---

[36]*K.H.W. v. Germany* (Application no. 37201/97), European Court of Human Rights Grand Chamber Judgment of 22 March 2001. http://cmiskp.echr.coe.int/tkp197/view.asp?item=3&portal=hbkm&action=html&highlight=humanity&sessionid=28180616&skin=hudoc-en. Accessed 17 August 2009.

That the domestic court sentences were *inordinately light* is a view which would have been more consistent with the European Court of Human Rights' holdings in the case had the Grand Chamber found the applicants individually culpable for *crimes against humanity* under the findings of fact of the domestic criminal courts regarding the specifics of the crimes. However the Grand Chamber, it will be recalled, declined to make a finding in that regard on the contention that to do so was unnecessary. Yet, in regards to the *Streletz, Kessler and Krenz* case, (involving over 250 deaths due to the conduct of the applicants as architects of the border policy and practices in the former GDR), many in Germany may have expected the European Court of Human Rights to make a finding as to whether the applicants should be regarded as having committed crimes against humanity. Note that, in fact, the case was regarded by many as "... the Cold War's Nuremberg Trials"[37]

Note that a European Court of Human Rights' finding that the applicants did in fact commit international crimes may have had an impact on any future civil litigation in the domestic State (brought by the close family relatives of the victims who lost their lives due to the conduct of *Streletz, Kessler and Krenz and of K.H.W.*) in terms of the amount of civil damages awarded should the suits have succeeded.

3. **Exceptions to double jeopardy in the case of the international crimes of genocide, war crimes and crimes against humanity where the initial trial was a sham**: In the cases *of Streletz, Kessler and Krenz v. Germany* and *K.H.W. v. Germany*, the criminal courts of the FRG found the defendants guilty of: (i) intentional homicide of unarmed civilians (as indirect principals or as the person directly responsible respectively), and (ii) of violations of the right to life guaranteed under *international human rights law*. However, it was still imperative, on the view here, to determine whether the defendants had committed 'crimes against humanity', and whether the trials in the domestic courts fell under the legal exceptions (discussed below) which would eliminate 'double jeopardy' in respect of possible criminal prosecution by, for instance, another domestic court exercising universal jurisdiction in regards to 'crimes against humanity.' (This author takes no position on whether double jeopardy was defeated in the aforementioned cases concerning the Berlin Wall and the border policy of the former GDR). Given the temporal jurisdiction of the International Criminal Court, and the fact that the events in the instant case took place *before* the Rome Statute of the international Criminal Court entered into force, prosecution by the ICC would *not* have been possible even if double jeopardy did not apply. Nevertheless, let us consider the relevant Article in the Rome Statute concerning double jeopardy as not all such cases fall outside the temporal jurisdiction of the ICC.

Under Article 20(3) of the International Criminal Court statute (the Rome Statute), where a domestic trial is determined to have been held for the purpose of shielding a person from ICC prosecution, or the trial was not conducted impartially and independently with the intent to bring the person to justice, double jeopardy does ***not*** attach for alleged crimes falling within the jurisdiction of the

[37] German Law Journal (2001, para 4).

ICC even though the person has been previously tried by another court for the same conduct. (Note that the same principles apply in other court systems. For instance, in the U.S. courts, double jeopardy has been held *not* to apply where judicial bias or corruption had resulted in the defendant's acquittal).[38,39] Thus, on the legal principles discussed, sham trials will *not* trigger double jeopardy to shield the individual from potential accountability before the ICC for genocide, crimes against humanity or war crimes:

> **Article 20**
> Ne bis in idem
> No person who has been tried by another court for conduct also proscribed under article 6, 7 or 8 shall be tried by the Court with respect to the same conduct ***unless*** the proceedings in the other court:
> (a) Were for the purpose of shielding the person concerned from criminal responsibility for crimes within the jurisdiction of the Court; or
> (b) Otherwise were not conducted independently or impartially in accordance with the norms of due process recognized by international law and were conducted in a manner which, in the circumstances, was inconsistent with an intent to bring the person concerned to justice.[40]

The European Court of Human Rights in *declining* to rule on whether, in its opinion, the defendants in any particular case have committed crimes against humanity is *not* in fact taking a neutral stance. Rather, the European Court of Human Rights' refusal to make a finding as to whether the applicants have committed crimes against humanity contributes (rightly or wrongly) to protecting the applicants under the principle of double jeopardy from potential further criminal prosecution. This since the European Court of Human Rights then does *not* take the opportunity to assess whether: (i) the domestic trial, in all aspects, was intended to deliver justice to the direct and indirect victims of the applicants' conduct, *or* (ii) whether, in contrast, the trial, in any way, was intended to keep the matter in-house (i.e. *avoid* potentially airing the State's dirty laundry before the International Criminal Court where the Court has jurisdiction, or before the criminal courts of a foreign State exercising universal jurisdiction over 'crimes against humanity', or even to avoid another trial within the original State itself; this time where the process is intended to deliver justice). If the trial was intended to subvert justice in this way; then double jeopardy would *not* apply. Hence, this author takes the view that it is the duty of the European Court of Human Rights in considering complaints

---

[38]See *People v. Aleman*, Nos. CR 28786, 93 CR 28787, 1994 WL 684499 (Ill. Cir.1994) cited in Scheffer and Cox (2008, p. 1053).

[39]See *Commonwealth v. Gonzalez* 771 N.E. 2.d 134 (Mass. 2002) cited in Scheffer and Cox (2008, p. 1053).

[40]Rome Statute (2002). Text of the Rome Statute circulated as document A/CONF.183/9 of 17 July 1998 and corrected by process-verbaux of 10 November 1998, 12 July 1999, 30 November 1999, 8 May 2000, 17 January 2001 and 16 January 2002. The Statute entered into force on 1 July 2002 (Article 20(3)). http://www.icc-cpi.int/NR/rdonlyres/EA9AEFF7-5752-4F84-BE94-0A655EB30E16/0/Rome_Statute_English.pdf. Accessed 18 August 2009.

under Article 7(1) of the European Convention, (concerning alleged retroactive application of the law by the domestic State), to address not only whether the applicants violated international human rights law, but also whether they breached international humanitarian and/or international criminal law norms especially jus cogens norms which: (i) were and are widely accepted, *codified and/or unwritten*, (ii) existed at the time the acts of commission or omission were committed and (ii) were international norms of which the applicants were or should have been aware. This is required in order to give proper consideration as to whether Article 7(2) of the European Convention is a factor in the case (i.e. the Convention provision which stipulates that the European Convention prohibition in Article 7(1) against retroactive application of the law does *not* prejudice the prosecution of applicants who have violated the norms of civilised States).

This author, as mentioned previously, is *not* making a pronouncement one way or the other on the question of whether or not double jeopardy was *inoperative* in *Streletz, Kessler and Krenz v. Germany* and *K.H. W. v. Germany* (i.e. the question of whether or not the domestic trials as conducted triggered an *exception* that would *defeat* double jeopardy). Rather, what is being suggested is that the question should have been addressed by the European Court of Human Rights in the aforementioned cases, and that it was instead deftly sidestepped when the European Court declined *at the outset* to address whether the applicants had in fact committed 'crimes against humanity'. Note that foreign States exercising universal jurisdiction, and the domestic courts are even more likely to consider double jeopardy defeated (where there are serious flaws in the first proceedings) if the crimes alleged are crimes against humanity, war crimes or genocide rather than crimes not classed as international crimes (the ICC as will be recalled only has jurisdiction over crimes against humanity, war crimes or genocide in any event).

It is of course correct to say that the European Court of Human Rights, as an international human rights court, does *not* have a punitive focus relating to individual accountability *per se*, but rather the objectives of the Court are to: (i) ensure compliance by the States Parties with the European Convention on Human Rights, and to (ii) make the victims of European Convention on Human Rights violations whole, to the extent possible, via financial reparations and/or other remedies awarded due to (a) the State's failure to adequately protect the victims against European Convention on Human Rights violations, or (b) the State itself having sponsored such violations in some way. Notwithstanding the foregoing, however, the European Court of Human Rights' decisions, nevertheless, have implications for whether those who commit grievous human rights violations – even those which rise to the level of international crimes under the Rome Statute – do so with complete impunity, or suffer only the consequences of a sham form of extraordinarily lenient 'justice' delivered by domestic courts. The latter may be more likely where the European Court reinforces the perception that double jeopardy applies in all cases, and, *in practice*, disregards the possibility of exceptions to the double jeopardy rule, i.e. where domestic courts seek to protect defendants from prosecution for international crimes before the ICC or by other courts rather than to deliver justice.

4. **Further implications of the European Court of Human Rights' refusal to rule on whether the applicants in *Streletz, Kessler and Krenz v. Germany* had committed crimes against humanity**: The failure of the European Court on Human Rights to acknowledge whether international crimes such as 'crimes against humanity' have been committed in a particular case, (such as in *Streletz, Kessler and Krenz v. Germany* where the issue arises due to the systemic and/or widespread violations of international human rights law, and the nature of the human rights violations involved, i.e. violations of the right to life, etc.), creates the ***illusion*** of ambiguity in respect of knowing when grave international crimes such as crimes against humanity and war crimes have been committed. This problem *allegedly* arises in that some would argue that a non-democratic regime would interpret the law differently than does a democratic regime. Hence, under the non-democratic regime in the former GDR, where, for instance, the Criminal Code made reference to the need to respect and preserve human dignity and human life, (and the need to punish crimes which violate human rights and the individual's responsibility not to engage in conduct that violated the former GDR's international obligations and was contrary to peace), these provisions could *supposedly* be interpreted as still being consistent with the brutal border practice of the former GDR of killing unarmed civilians trying to flee (while the same text would be interpreted by the criminal courts in the new unified Germany as wholly inconsistent with that border practice which resulted in the death of so many unarmed civilians):

> The Court [European Court of Human Rights] comes to the conclusion that the conduct of the applicants at the material time was contrary to both international law [i.e. the *International Covenant on Civil and Political Rights*] and the national law [i.e. the Constitution, the People's Police Act and other laws] of the GDR. The applicants ... contested that approach ... saying in fact that in the GDR international law and national law were interpreted and applied differently and that in light of that interpretation and application of the law their conduct had been lawful. ... that objection raises one of the most serious issues of the present judgement – a point which is very important in situations where a previous non-democratic ... regime has been abolished and a new democratic regime has been established. It shows clearly that interpretation and application of the law depend on the general political order, in which the law functions as a sub-system. In fact, the courts of the GDR, by applying the same provisions of the GDR Constitution ... and other laws, and also the International Covenant on Civil and Political Rights (Article 12) would never have come to the same result as the German courts did after the reunification and this Court has done in the present judgment because of their completely different approach to interpretation and application of the law.[41]

If the above citation from Judge Levits is correct – if international human rights law, even jus cogens provisions, can be interpreted differently in different political contexts under various State regimes – then applicants to the European Court of Human Rights can argue lack of accessibility and lack of forseeability with respect

[41]Concurring opinion of Judge Levits in the European Court of Human Rights Grand Chamber judgment dated 22 March 2001 in the *Case of Streletz and Kessler v. Germany* (Applications 34044/96, 35532/97 and 44801/98), para 2–5 of the concurring opinion. http://www.menschenrechte.ac.at/orig/01_2/Streletz.pdf. Accessed 15 August 2009.

to not knowing that their conduct was unlawful. The argument made by the current author is, however, that: (i) the meanings of international human rights and international humanitarian law are abundantly clear when it comes to violations rising to the level of crimes against humanity and that (ii) violations constituting crimes against humanity as defined under the Rome Statute and under customary international law are manifestly unlawful. "The requirement of 'unlawfulness' found in the [Rome] Statute or in other parts of international law, in particular international humanitarian law, is generally not specified in the elements of crimes."[42] Furthermore, unlawfulness is considered to be intrinsic to the crime itself (the crime is manifestly unlawful) when it is a crime against humanity, or genocide regardless the national law. Hence, it is imperative that the European Court of Human Rights not evade a determination as to whether the applicant's offences in cases such as the Berlin Wall border guard cases involve crimes against humanity. Where crimes against humanity have been committed then the crimes are, and always have been, manifestly unlawful regardless the political context and alleged justifications for the offences proffered, for instance, in terms of interpretations under 'old law' or 'old interpretations' under the same law (i.e. the applicants erroneously argued in *Streletz, Kessler and Krenz v. Germany* and *K.H.W. v. Germany* that interpretations under GDR law would not have criminalized their acts; which arguments are not, on the analysis here, legally supportable).

This notion of the *manifest unlawfulness* of genocide, and crimes against humanity is incorporated into the elements of the crime as previously discussed and also into the Rome Statute at Article 33:

> **Article 33**
> **Superior orders and prescription of law**
> 1. The fact that a crime within the jurisdiction of the Court has been committed by a person pursuant to an order of a Government or of a superior, whether military or civilian, *shall not relieve that person of criminal responsibility* ***unless***:
>   (a) The person was under a legal obligation to obey orders of the Government or the superior in question;
>   (b) The person did not know that the order was unlawful; ***and***
>   (c) The order was *not* manifestly unlawful
> 2. ***For the purposes of this article, orders to commit genocide or crimes against humanity are manifestly unlawful*** **(emphasis added)**.[43]

Hence, one is misled to consider the question in cases such as the instant cases (of the German border guards during the time of the Berlin Wall) as one of old law

---

[42]Introduction to the Elements of the Crime Rome Statute, Elements of the Crime, General Introduction at point 6. http://www.icc-cpi.int/NR/rdonlyres/.../Element_of_Crimes_English.pdf. Accessed 18 August 2009.

[43]Rome Statute (2002). Text of the Rome Statute circulated as document A/CONF.183/9 of 17 July 1998 and corrected by process-verbaux of 10 November 1998, 12 July 1999, 30 November 1999, 8 May 2000, 17 January 2001 and 16 January 2002. The Statute entered into force on 1 July 2002 (Article 33). http://www.icc-cpi.int/NR/rdonlyres/EA9AEFF7-5752-4F84-BE94-0A655EB30E16/0/Rome_Statute_English.pdf. Accessed 18 August 2009.

vs. new law (where old law may be textually different or the same but allegedly interpreted differently by the courts and other bodies of the former regime). *The conduct was ipso facto manifestly unlawful if it constituted crimes against humanity* (*under international customary law and as now codified in the Rome Statute*). The European Court of Human Rights, in the aforementioned Berlin Wall border guard cases, however, declined to rule on whether or not the conduct for which the applicants had been convicted fit the criteria for crimes against humanity. The Court instead held that: (i) the applicants followed a State practice that was *superimposed* on the national law of the former GDR in violation of that law (i.e. the ECHR held that, in actuality, there was no room for variation in the interpretation of the national law between the old and new political regime insofar as the interpretation of the illegality of the killing of unarmed persons trying to flee the former GDR was concerned *as the relevant constitutional and statutory text in that regard was unchanged*) and (ii) the applicants' conduct was unlawful under international human rights law which the GDR had ratified (i.e. *the International Covenant on Civil and Political Rights*). However, by relying on alleged consistency in the meaning and interpretation of the national law *given the same relevant textual elements* in the law of the former v. the new reunified Germany, the Court still leaves room for argument on this point as reflected in the concurring judgment of Judge Levits who accepts the applicants' notion that the old regime would interpret the national law and international human rights law differently than the new regime in the reunified Germany.

Judge Levits holds that the human rights language in the legal statutes of the GDR, while similar to that in the national law of the new Germany, was, under the non-democratic regime of the GDR, used purely as a propaganda tool. Hence, Judge Levits concluded that: "... the ability of the courts in the newly established democracies to deal with the 'legacy' of former non-democratic regimes should *not* depend solely on the wording of the legal norms of the non-democratic regimes, formulated in the first place not for legal but for propaganda purposes (emphasis added)."[44] Hence, Judge Levits points out that to say that the wording in the old regime's legal statutes was similar or the same as under that in the new democratic regime is *not* sufficient to avoid the charge of retroactive application of the law given the differing interpretations and applications of the "same" statutory text in the two regimes.

Reliance on classification of the conduct, (where the facts warrant), as an international crime, (i.e. crime against humanity, etc.), which, as discussed, may properly be considered *manifestly unlawful in all circumstances*, would eliminate

[44]Concurring opinion of Judge Levits in the European Court of Human Rights Grand Chamber judgment dated 22 March 2001 in the *Case of Streletz and Kessler v. Germany* (Applications 34044/96, 35532/97 and 44801/98), para 15 of the concurring opinion. http://www.menschenrechte.ac.at/orig/01_2/Streletz.pdf. Accessed 15 August 2009.

the viability of any justification under Article 7(1) of the European Convention on Human Rights concerning alleged retroactive application of the law when grievous human rights violations constituting such international crimes are involved. It would also eliminate the need for the contentious legal "solution", such as that advanced by Judge Levits in *Streletz, Kessler and Krenz v. Germany*, to the issue of whether, when there is a change from a non-democratic to a democratic regime, it is legitimate or illegitimate to apply the 'old law' according to the interpretation and application of the law as endorsed by the new regime. Judge Levits, in regard to this question, held that such is permissible: "Democratic States can allow their institutions to apply the law-even previous law, originating in a pre-democratic regime-only in a manner which is inherent in the *democratic* political order ... Using any other method of applying the law (which implies reaching different results from the same legal texts) would damage the very core of the *ordre public* of a democratic State (emphasis added)."[45] Further, Judge Levits held that *non-democratic interpretations* of national law as reflected in the existing legal practice of current non-democratic regimes, or in the ex post facto assessment of the practice of past regimes should be considered to be "wrong" and a "misuse of the law".[46] The latter perspective Judge Levits bases on the "inherent universality of human rights and democratic values."[47]

5. **On the application of customary international criminal law norms**: Interestingly, Judge Levits, in *Streletz, Kessler and Krenz v. Germany*, alluded to the potential for application of international criminal law norms regarding, for instance, 'crimes against humanity' in the instant case concerning alleged retroactive application of the law (as opposed to reliance only on the national law of the former GDR and on international human rights law which the GDR had formally endorsed) (such a reliance on international criminal law norms is, it will be recalled, discussed by this author above). Yet, Judge Levis endorsed the majority view that it was *not* necessary to rule on whether the crimes of which the applicants had been convicted (violations of international human rights obligations and intentional homicide as indirect principals) were crimes against humanity. Judge Levits did not elaborate on how such a reliance on international criminal law norms, had it

---

[45]Concurring opinion of Judge Levits in the European Court of Human Rights Grand Chamber judgment dated 22 March 2001 in the *Case of Streletz and Kessler v. Germany* (Applications 34044/96, 35532/97 and 44801/98), para 8 of the concurring opinion of Judge Levits. http://www.menschenrechte.ac.at/orig/01_2/Streletz.pdf. Accessed 15 August 2009.

[46]Concurring opinion of Judge Levits in the European Court of Human Rights Grand Chamber judgment dated 22 March 2001 in the *Case of Streletz and Kessler v. Germany* (Applications 34044/96, 35532/97 and 44801/98), para 10 of the concurring opinion of Judge Levits. http://www.menschenrechte.ac.at/orig/01_2/Streletz.pdf. Accessed 15 August 2009.

[47]Concurring opinion of Judge Levits in the European Court of Human Rights Grand Chamber judgment dated 22 March 2001 in the *Case of Streletz and Kessler v. Germany* (Applications 34044/96, 35532/97 and 44801/98), para 11 of the concurring opinion of Judge Levits. http://www.menschenrechte.ac.at/orig/01_2/Streletz.pdf. Accessed 15 August 2009.

occurred, might have affected the European Court of Human Rights existing analysis in *Streletz, Kessler and Krenz v. Germany*, but rather he simply made the following provocative statement:

> *The judgment* [*in Streletz, Kessler and Krenz v. Germany*] ***left the door open*** *also for examination* [by the European Court of Human Rights] *of such conduct as the applicants' under the heading of criminal offence under international law* ... In that connection, I would like to stress recent developments in international law in respect of strengthening of the protection of human rights, including norms on crimes against humanity. Despite the fact that many legal problems in this field are not yet entirely resolved, the direction of these developments is obvious. *I therefore endorse the view of Judge Loucaides in his concurring opinion, that at the material time the applicants' conduct was not only a criminal offence under domestic law but could also be considered an offence under international* [*criminal*] *law (emphasis added).*[48]

It has been argued here, in contrast, that it is essential that the European Court of Human Rights consider international customary and codified law norms regarding 'crimes against humanity' and other international crimes where the applicants' alleged crimes, which are the focus of the case, may meet the legal definition for international crimes (i.e. under customary humanitarian law or the Rome Statute). This is necessary both for the logical consistency and perceived legitimacy of the Courts' judgments in the international community and in terms of ensuring that the Court not contribute in any way, great or small, to fostering impunity for such crimes.

Note also the concurring opinion by Judge Zupancic in *Streletz, Kessler and Krenz v. Germany*:

> The applicants did not simply "rely" on the "GDR's State practice". They helped create that very real State practice of impunity. This practice of impunity, however, was not formalised through legislative means, no doubt because to the outside world the GDR wanted to maintain the image of a *Rechtsstaat* [a State under the rule of law].[49] *If the practice of impunity had been legitimated through positive legislation this would have been a different case since it probably would have fallen under Article 7(2) of the Convention* (emphasis added).[50]

The suggestion has been here, however, that regardless of whether State practices of impunity are codified in State positive law or not, the basic principle or value articulated in Article 7(2) of the European Convention on Human Rights is

---

[48]Concurring opinion of Judge Levits in the European Court of Human Rights Grand Chamber judgment dated 22 March 2001 in the *Case of Streletz and Kessler v. Germany* (Applications 34044/96, 35532/97 and 44801/98), para 16–18 of the concurring opinion of Judge Levits. http://www.menschenrechte.ac.at/orig/01_2/Streletz.pdf. Accessed 15 August 2009.

[49]Online English Collins dictionary, definition of the German word *Rechtsstaat*. http://dictionary.reverso.net/german-english/Rechtsstaat. Accessed 21 August 2009.

[50]Concurring opinion of Judge Zupancic in the European Court of Human Rights Grand Chamber judgment dated 22 March 2001 in the *Case of Streletz and Kessler v. Germany* (Applications 34044/96, 35532/97 and 44801/98), para 12 of the concurring judgment. http://www.menschenrechte.ac.at/orig/01_2/Streletz.pdf. Accessed 15 August 2009.

triggered where international crimes have been committed. This is the case since nothing may prejudice the prosecution of the perpetrators for such grave fundamental human rights abuses. (In *Streletz, Kessler and Krenz v. Germany,* the majority of the European Court of Human Rights held that there had been no retroactive application of the law and, hence, no violation of Article 7(1) of the European Convention prohibiting the same. Therefore, there was no need for the Court's reliance on Article 7(2) of the European Convention to reach the result which the European Court of Human Rights did in fact reach in the case – no violation of Article 7(1)).

6. **The European Court on Human Rights and a misplaced deference to domestic courts in cases involving potential international crimes**: When it comes to the issue of potential international crimes having occurred, (in an Article 7 case), the European Court of Human Rights cannot, on the view expressed here, rely on its standard approach of only determining if the domestic proceedings were fair and if the result of those proceedings comports with Convention requirements. The European Court is obligated, it is here argued, instead in such cases as, for example, the instant cases: (i) to make a determination as to whether a crime against humanity or other international crimes involving grave human rights violations have, or have not occurred where this was *not* decided by the domestic courts, or where there is some question about the legitimacy of the domestic court process; and (ii) where the domestic court has decided that such an international crime has or has not occurred; to determine if that ruling is correct. The latter determinations are essential in deciding Article 7(1) European Convention on Human Rights cases concerning possible retroactive application of the law given the potential implications of the Court's ruling for: (i) real or imagined concerns about double jeopardy in any potential criminal proceedings; (ii) consideration of varying alleged interpretations of "old law" in the old versus the new political contexts associated with changing regimes if such applies and (iii) determinations about whether Article 7(2) of the European Convention is triggered by the facts. However, to date, the European Court of Human Rights' majority in the relevant cases has avoided determining whether international crimes have been committed where the domestic courts have declined to rule on that issue, and instead the Court has relied exclusively for its conclusions on national law and, in some instances, international human rights law obligations. For instance, in *Streletz, Kessler and Krenz v. Germany, the* European Court of Human Rights relied *exclusively* on: (i) its interpretation of national and constitutional law in the GDR, and on (ii) international human rights treaties such as the ICCPR (ratified by the GDR and alluded to in the former GDR's constitution and Criminal Code), so that the European Court of Human Rights did *not* rely on international criminal law norms in reaching its conclusions. That is, the European Court of Human Rights assessed whether the criminal courts of the new reunified Germany had complied with European Convention on Human Rights guarantees in convicting the applicants of violations of Article 95 of the GDR Criminal Code that provided for *individual criminal culpability* for violating the GDR's international human rights obligations.

For a discussion of international customary law *in existence at the relevant time* which, in the view of Judge Loucaides, rendered the conduct of German border guards' use of deadly force practices at the Berlin Wall (and other border points) *a crime against humanity*; see his concurring opinion in *Streletz, Kessler and Krenz v. Germany*.[51] Let us consider next a case in which the European Court of Human Rights *did* address the issue of crimes against humanity, but only it would appear because the domestic court had convicted the applicants of that particular international crime.

III. Case 2 Kolk and Kislyiy v. Estonia (Application 23052/04), European Court of Human Rights Chamber Judgment of 17 January 2006 on Admissibility

A. *The European Court of Human Rights' Reasoning in Kolk and Kislyiy v. Estonia*

In *Kolk and Kislyiy v. Estonia*,[52] in contrast to the aforementioned cases regarding the German border guards, the European Court of Human Rights did address the issue of crimes against humanity but only, it appears, because the applicants had been convicted of that specific crime by the domestic criminal courts. In *Kolk and Kislyiy v. Estonia*, the European Court of Human Rights affirmed the conviction of the applicants by the domestic courts for crimes against humanity. The applicants in *Kolk and Kislyiy v. Estonia* submitted that the acts of which they had been convicted in 2003 had taken place in Estonia in 1949 and that the criminal law in the territory of Estonia at the time did *not* include the offence of 'crimes against humanity' (the applicable law was the 1946 Criminal Code of the Russian Soviet Socialist Republic (Russian SSR) operative in the territory of the Estonian SSR). The applicants were sentenced to eight years *suspended* imprisonment with a *probation period of three years*. Their crimes committed in 1949 involved participating in the forced deportation of Estonian civilians from occupied Estonia to remote areas in the Soviet Union. The applicants also contended that the

---

[51]Concurring opinion of Judge Loucaides in the European Court of Human Rights Grand Chamber judgment dated 22 March 2001 in the *Case of Streletz and Kessler v. Germany* (Applications 34044/96, 35532/97 and 44801/98), 6–12. http://www.menschenrechte.ac.at/orig/01_2/Streletz.pdf. Accessed 15 August 2009.

[52]*Kolk and Kislyiy v. Estonia* (Application 23052/04), European Court of Human Rights Chamber Judgment of 17 January 2006 on Admissibility. http://www.derechosorg/nizkor/impu/kolk.html. Accessed 21 August 2009.

deportations did not take place before or during World War II and that they were therefore allegedly not acts within the jurisdiction of the Nuremberg Tribunal. The applicants also maintained that the forced deportations had not been committed in execution of, or in connection with, a crime against peace or any war crime. The applicants contended further that their acts were legal under the Soviet law applicable at the time in the Estonian SSR, and that it was, therefore, not at all foreseeable that so many decades after the fact the same acts would be considered to be crimes against humanity.

The European Court of Human Rights held in *Kolk and Kislyiy v. Estonia* that the *universal* validity of the principles concerning the prohibition on crimes against humanity had been confirmed via U.N. resolution in 1946. Hence, the Court held, responsibility for crimes against humanity *cannot* be considered to be confined to acts meeting the criteria for crimes against humanity that occurred in World War II, or to those acts only if committed by particular State nationals. Further, the Court stressed that the statute of limitations did *not* apply in relation to crimes against humanity and that when Estonia acceded to the *Convention on the Non-Applicability of Statutory Limitations to War Crimes and Crimes Against Humanity*[53] on 21 October 1991 (the point at which Estonia gained its independence once more after occupation first by the Germans 1941–1944 and then by the Soviets); it was duty bound to implement the Convention's principles. The Court further held that Article 7(2) of the *European Convention on Human Rights* requires that the prohibition of retroactive application of the law not prejudice the trial and punishment of persons for acts or omissions that, at the time of their occurrence, violated international customary law as recognized by civilized nations. Hence, the Court held that: (i) Article 7(2) of the *European Convention on Human Rights* applied to crimes against humanity, and (ii) Article 7(2) underscored the viability of the absence of any time bar to the prosecution and punishment of persons who have committed crimes against humanity.

The European Court of Human Rights deferred to the State of Estonia in regards to the interpretation and application of its domestic law which also referenced international law. This approach was in accord with that established in the previous case law of the European Court of Human Rights. The Court held that:

> . . . even if the acts committed by the applicants could have been regarded as lawful under the Soviet law at the material time, they were nevertheless found by the Estonian courts to constitute crimes against humanity under international law at the time of their commission. The Court [European Court of Human Rights] sees no reason to come to a different conclusion. It is noteworthy in this context that the Soviet Union was a party to the London Agreement of 8 August 1945 by which the Nuremberg Charter was enacted. Moreover, on 11 December 1946 the United Nations General Assembly affirmed the principles of

[53] *Convention on the Non-Applicability of Statutory Limitations to War Crimes and Crimes Against Humanity*, ratification and accession by U.N. General Assembly Resolution 2391 XXIII of 26 November 1968 and entry into force 11 November 1970. http://www2.ohchr.org/english/law/warcrimes.htm. Accessed 21 August 2009.

> international law recognized by the Charter ... The Court finds no reason to call into question the Estonian court's interpretation and application of domestic law made in the light of relevant international law. *It is satisfied that the applicants' conviction and sentence had a legal basis [in the Estonian Criminal Code*]. Accordingly, the matters complained of disclose no appearance of a failure to respect Article 7 of the Convention [i.e. Article 7(1) of the *European Convention on Human Rights* prohibiting retroactive application of the law] (emphasis added).[54]

B. Commentary on Kolk and Kislyiy v. Estonia

1. **The Article 7(2) *European Convention on Human Rights'* (ECHR) stipulation that neither the trial *nor punishment* of an individual perpetrator shall be prejudiced by rules regarding "no law no punishment" (as in Article 7(1) of the ECHR) where there has been a criminal act that violates "the general principles of law recognized by civilised nations"**: The European Court on Human Rights (ECHR) in *Kolk and Kislyiy v. Estonia* held that the Estonian domestic court's conviction ***and sentence*** of the applicants was legally supportable, and, therefore, in compliance with Article 7 of the *European Convention on Human Rights*. However, the *inadmissibility* decision of the European Court of Human Rights in the instant case refers rather holistically to the conviction and does not explore the reasons for the light sentence; if in fact any were given by the domestic courts. The ECHR also referenced the large 'margin of appreciation' that it affords States in the interpretation and application of domestic law. Recall in this regard that the sentences imposed on the applicants were *suspended* eight year prison sentences and only three years probation. Considering the gravity of the offence – crimes against humanity involving the forced deportation of Estonians to remote areas of the Soviet Union – the sentences imposed on the applicants by the Estonian criminal courts were arguably inconsistent with: (i) the gravity of the crime, and also inconsistent with: (ii) the principles or values underlying Article 7(2) of the *European Convention on Human Rights* in that the sentences are so light as to be, many victims and international law experts would likely hold, virtually no sentence at all in the circumstances (i.e. especially when one considers the devastating implications of the forced deportations for the direct and indirect victims of the applicants' conduct). If the foregoing is correct, then the question arises as to whether the European Court of Human Rights' holding the *suspended prison sentences* and brief probationary period to be legally sound: (i) *inappropriately reinforces the perception of double jeopardy* where the domestic trial result – *in regards to sentencing* – may not be legally sound, and should bring the domestic

[54] *Kolk and Kislyiy v. Estonia* (Application 23052/04), European Court of Human Rights Chamber Judgment of 17 January 2006 on Admissibility, para 9 under "The Law." http://www.derechosorg/nizkor/impu/kolk.html. Accessed 21 August 2009.

procedure potentially under one of the exceptions that *defeat* double jeopardy in any potential criminal proceeding; and (ii) *inappropriately discourages the potential exercise of universal jurisdiction by another State over the applicants for crimes against humanity.* Consider that a suspended sentence and three years probation may appear to approximate complete impunity for such a grave international crime as forced deportations carried out in the context of State sponsored attacks on civilians in Russian occupied Estonia. While sentencing is generally considered something to be determined according to: (i) the sentencing guidelines of the domestic statutes, and (ii) the discretionary leeway allowed domestic courts under the domestic criminal code, suspended sentences of imprisonment and a brief probationary period for 'crimes against humanity' may be so far removed from genuine accountability in the view of the international community so as to trigger the rightful exercise of universal criminal jurisdiction by another State.

The Estonian courts may have rationalized this light sentencing on the basis of the advanced age of the convicted, but it is entirely unclear whether advanced age, on its own, provides a sufficient justification for less than full accountability for such grievous crimes as crimes against humanity. It is also unclear to what degree, if any, socio-political factors were weighed by the Estonian courts in determining that a suspended prison sentence was warranted in *Kolk and Kislyiy v. Estonia.* More specifically, the domestic court in imposing such a light sentence may have considered: (i) the alleged desire for reconciliation in Estonia and also (ii) the fact that many Estonian nationals, as members of the Soviet communist party, or otherwise, participated in implementing the forced deportations. Indeed, in the instant case, one of the convicted was an Estonian national. It is an open question then whether suspended prison sentences (combined with probationary periods as in the instant case) amount to impunity and render the entire trial as a mere token exercise. This is not simply an academic question; however, since if this is the case then double jeopardy may *not* apply.

2. **The importance of considering article 7(1) of the European Convention in the context of article 7(2) of the *European Convention on Human Rights*:** Note that the European Court of Human Rights ruled the instant case *inadmissible* holding that Article 7 of the European Convention had *not* been violated by the State. The *European Court of Human Rights held that even if the applicants' acts had been lawful under Soviet law at the material time, this would not have altered the lawfulness of their conviction by the domestic courts. This in that the Estonian courts found the applicants' acts violated (customary) international law in that the acts constituted crimes against humanity at the time they were committed.* Hence, the prohibition against retroactive application of the statutory law was not a bar to prosecution and conviction in the instant case. The European Court did not challenge that interpretation of domestic law which domestic law had incorporated international law in respect of crimes against humanity, war crimes and genocide in 1994 after the end of the Soviet occupation (i.e. Article 6 of the Estonian Criminal Code – which provided for punishment of crimes against humanity, genocide and war crimes without any statute of limitations being operative – entered into force in 1994 after the Estonian Criminal Code was amended by Article 61-1 which was

decades after the commission of the offences by the applicants. Such provisions are also in the 2002 amended version of the Estonian Criminal Code, but were *not* part of the Soviet criminal code operative in Estonia at the time of the applicants' crimes involving orchestrating forced deportations). *Note then that the Court's consideration of Article 7(2) of the European Convention on Human Rights was essential to the inadmissibility ruling in the case.*

We will shortly consider two cases involving applicants convicted domestically of war crimes or crimes against humanity where the European Court did *not* get to an analysis of the case under Article 7(2) and we will consider the problems that such an approach creates for the search for justice. The outcome in those cases was quite different than in the instant case, and from that in the German border guard cases previously discussed. In the two cases to be discussed, the convicted were essentially exonerated of international crimes by the European Court of Human Rights and there was a finding by the Court of a State violation of Article 7.

3. **The more general implications of Article 7(2) of the European Convention on Human Rights**: The European Court of Human Rights in *Kolk and Kislyiy v. Estonia* may have done as much harm as good for the cause of advancing human rights when it held erroneously, (on the view expressed here), that the sentencing in *Kolk and Kislyiy v. Estonia* was consistent with the principles of Article 7 of the *European Convention on Human Rights* (this by implication given that the conviction, in all aspects, was held to be in compliance with Article 7 of the European Convention). In this regard, recall that Article 7(2) of the European Convention requires that there be no prejudice to the trial *or punishment* of any person for any act or omission which, at the time when it was committed, was criminal according to the general principles of law recognized by civilized nations. More specifically, Article 7(2) stipulates that "no prejudice" should result from the prohibition against retroactive application of statutory or codified law as articulated in Article 7(1) of the European Convention on Human Rights in regards to the trial and punishment of those who commit crimes that offend humanity and were violations of international customary law at the time the crimes were committed. However, it can be argued that Article 7(2) of the European Convention implicitly embodies also the more general principle or value that not just prohibitions against retroactive application of law should **not** interfere with the "trial" or "punishment" of perpetrators of crimes against humanity, war crimes or genocide; but neither should sham trials (to establish a false double jeopardy), wrongful acquittals, amnesties or immunities, nor any other factor create any wrongful barrier to the rightful prosecution and punishment of those who commit crimes that are an outrage to humanity.

In the instant case, however, there was arguably a sentence imposed that was *inconsistent* with justice for the victims of the forced deportations perpetrated by the applicants. An argument could be made that in *Kolk and Kislyiy v. Estonia*, the *suspended* prison sentences and brief probationary periods for defendants convicted under domestic law of crimes against humanity amount to a State violation of the *legal spirit* of Article 7(2) of the *European Convention on Human Rights*. This in that Article 7(2) requires that perpetrators of *crimes that offend humanity* (i.e. crimes that violate the international legal norms of "civilized nations") be *both* duly tried *and* duly punished in order that they be held to full account for their crimes. Recall in this regard that the crimes of the convicted in *Kolk and Kislyiy v. Estonia* constituted crimes against humanity in that they were part of a widespread systematic attack on the civilian population of Estonia. In fact, the forced deportations carried out by the applicants occurred in 25 March 1949 subsequent to the decision of the USSR Council of Ministers of 29 January 1949. The deportees who met that fate due to the actions of the applicants were amongst the nearly 100,000 Baltic nationals who were arrested and shipped in cattle cars to Siberia on the orders that followed from the January 1949 USSR Council of Ministers directives. Among the deportees were 40,500 Latvians, 33,500 Lithuanians and 20,500 Estonians.[55] Malksoo, referencing authorities on the topic, reports that: "Of the people deported in 1949, approximately 10% died in Siberia." She also points out that, in fact, the deportations were targeted at particular ethnic groups regarded as likely to engage in, or already engaged in rebel activities as well as against nationalists and others.[56]

Note that Article 6 of the 1994 modified ex-Soviet Estonian Criminal Code incorporated a section entitled "Crimes against Humanity" which included also reference to genocide, and combined the elements of both 'crimes against humanity' and of 'genocide'. Article 6 of the 1994 modified ex-Soviet Estonian Criminal Code elaborated on the concept of genocide and included also reference to acts intended to destroy in whole or in part "a group offering resistance to the occupation regime or other social group"; (thus extending the definition of genocide compared to that found in the 1948 Genocide Convention, which extension, as Malksoo notes, was particularly relevant to the Estonian situation given the forced deportations and executions under Soviet occupation).[57] Arguably, the forced deportations to Siberia may be considered as a form of genocide reflecting: (i) the intentional infliction of serious mental and physical harm intended to destroy the targeted groups in whole or in part, and (ii) the imposition of conditions of life calculated to bring about the physical destruction of the group in whole or in part. If, in fact, the forced deportations of Estonians of which the applicants in *Kolk and Kislyiy v. Estonia* were convicted formed part of a genocidal campaign against targeted identifiable groups in Estonian society, (i.e. the kulaks among others who offered resistance to the Soviet occupiers), then this highlights all the more that the virtual non-sentence imposed on the applicants violates article 7(2) of the *European Convention on Human Rights* which calls for full accountability of perpetrators in such cases. Malksoo notes that, according to some legal scholars, the Estonian Courts have convicted persons of genocide under Estonian law – in respect of defendants' involved in the mass forced deportations of Estonians during the Soviet occupation era – even though the judgment may not specifically use the word 'genocide'.[58] Particularly relevant in considering the issue of whether forced deportations can

[55]Malksoo (2001, p. 765).

[56]Malksoo (2001, p. 765).

[57]Malksoo (2001, p. 772).

[58]Malksoo (2001, p. 779).

amount to a form of genocide is the International Criminal Tribunal of the Former Yugoslavia (ICTY) case of *Prosecutor v. Jelisic*. In the latter case, the ICTY held that genocidal intent can be manifest in selectively removing a certain segment of the population, ('the disappeared'), given the devastating effect this would have on the survival of the rest of the group for various reasons. It may be argued that the mass deportations of nationalists and others may have served that function during the Soviet occupation of Estonia.[59]

We next examine the issue of impunity for international crimes further in the context of cases in which: (i) the European Court of Human Rights ruled that domestic convictions for crimes against humanity (*Korbely v. Hungary*) or war crimes (*Kononov v. Latvia*) allegedly violated the European Convention prohibition against retroactive application of the law and (ii) cases in which persons who committed widespread crimes against humanity were *not* convicted by the domestic courts and where the European Court of Human Rights once more declined to consider whether the individual perpetrator's European Convention violations rose to the level of international crimes.

IV. The European Court of Human Rights De Facto Exoneration of Persons Convicted Domestically of 'War Crimes' or 'Crimes Against Humanity' and the Implications for Impunity

A. Case 3 Korbely v. Hungary *(*Application 9174/02*)* European Court of Human Rights Grand Chamber Judgement of 19 September 2008

Key Background Facts and Procedural History

Actions for Which the Applicant Was Convicted of a Crime Against Humanity
Korbely alleged that he had been convicted for an action that did not constitute a crime at the time that he committed it and that this constituted a violation of Article 7 of the *European Convention on Human Rights*. Further, he also alleged that the proceedings were unfair and unduly delayed in his criminal trial in violation of Article 6 of the Convention. He had been charged as a military captain – ordered to regain control of a police department building taken over by insurgents – of having, during that assignment, shot at civilians and of having ordered his men to shoot at civilians causing injury to several persons and the death of several persons. After an

[59]*Prosecutor v. Jelisic*, Case IT-95-10 at para 82, cited in Malksoo (2001, p. 784).

investigation, Korbely was charged 27 December 1994 by the Budapest Military Public Prosecutor's Office with 'crimes against humanity' in violation of common Article 3 of the *Geneva Conventions relating to the Protection of Civilian Persons in Times of War* (Convention IV) (proclaimed in Hungary by law decree number 32 in 1954 and punishable pursuant to Act 90 of 1993 which made certain crimes committed during the 1956 revolution prosecutable; namely war crimes and crimes against humanity).[60] That is, common Article 3 of the Geneva Conventions prohibited attacks on civilians or those otherwise 'hors de combat' (that is, those outside of, or no longer engaged in combat such as members of an armed force who had surrendered or were in the process of surrendering, the wounded members of the armed forces no longer fighting, etc.) and this formed the basis then for the charge against the applicant of having committed a crime against humanity.

The applicant was a military captain in charge of training junior officers at the time of the Hungarian Revolution in Budapest 23 October 1956. *On 24 October 1956 martial law was imposed and the order was given by the State authorities that anyone who was bearing arms without authorization could be punished by death.* The applicant had successfully persuaded insurgents to leave a prison and the Prosecutor's office they had occupied in an incident on 26 October 1956. The applicant was ordered 26 October 1956 to regain control of a local police building that the insurgents had taken over. Tamas Kaszas was amongst those insurgents who had taken control of the police building on that date and he had armed himself. The applicant and 15 of his officers were deployed to the besieged police building each armed with a submachine gun and pistol with the group also having at its disposal 25 hand grenades and two machine guns. On arrival, the applicant's military contingent found five civilians belonging to the insurgent group outside the building along with several disarmed police. The members of the applicant's military platoon pointed their submachine guns at the insurgents standing in the outside yard. One of the insurgents, Istvan Balazs, stated that they were unarmed, but one of the police officers yelled that Tamas Kaszas had a pistol. Istvan Balazs told Tamas Kaszas to hand over his weapon to the applicant's group. Immediately after Istvan Balazs called out the instruction, Tamas Kaszas and the applicant exchanged some heated words of alleged unknown content. Tamas Kaszas reached for his pocket and drew his handgun whereupon the applicant *simultaneously* ordered his officers *who had their weapons trained on the insurgents the whole time* to fire while he also fired at Tamas Kaszas. Tamas Kaszas was shot in the chest and abdomen and died instantly. *One of the shots fired on the applicant's orders hit another insurgent and three hit yet another. An additional insurgent was also shot and killed. Two of the remaining insurgents ran into the street where the platoon of*

[60]Common Article 3 of the 1949 Geneva Conventions, *Geneva Convention relating to the Protection of Civilian Persons in Times of War* (Fourth Geneva Convention), Diplomatic Conference of Geneva of 12 August 1949, entry into force 21 October 1950. http://www.unhcr.org/refworld/docid/3ae6b36d2.html. Accessed 24 August 2009.

the applicant's men fired on them; one suffered non-lethal injuries while the other died at the scene. The applicant was shot at as he left the scene and fell off his motorcycle and then suffered some injuries.

Relevant Law and Domestic Court Proceedings

(a) *Constitutional Court Proceedings*

On 16 February 1993, the Hungarian Parliament passed an Act removing the statute of limitations in regards to certain acts that were committed during the 1956 uprising (pursuant to the U.N. *Convention on the Non-Applicability of Statutory Limitations to War Crimes and Crimes Against Humanity*[61] proclaimed as law in Hungary by a 1971 decree). The Constitutional Court held on 13 October 1993 that it was constitutional to remove the statute of limitations if the acts were classified as a war crimes or crimes against humanity under international law and if Hungary was duty bound, pursuant to its international obligations, to remove the statutory time limitations on such offences. The Constitutional Court reasoned that "the significance of these offences is too great to allow their punishment to be made dependent upon their acceptance by, or the general penal-law policy of, individual States."[62] The Constitutional Court further held that international law applies the *nullum crimen sine lege* ('no crime no punishment') principle to itself and *not* to domestic law:

> 'Customary international law', 'the legal principles recognized by civilised nations' and 'the legal principles recognized by the community of nations' constitute a *lex* which classifies certain types of behaviour as prosecutable and punishable according to the norms of the community of nations ... irrespective of whether the domestic law contains a comparable criminal offence or whether the relevant treaties have been incorporated into domestic law. The gravity of war crimes and crimes against humanity – namely the fact that they endanger international peace and security and mankind as such – is irreconcilable with leaving their punishability within the ambit of domestic laws ... For those States which incorporate into domestic law the international legal norms concerning war crimes and crimes against humanity *subsequent* to the commission of these crimes, the second paragraph of the aforementioned Articles [i.e. of Article 7 of the *European Convention on Human Rights*] amount to authorizing retroactive criminal legislation in the State's domestic legal system. *It is the international, rather than the domestic, law which must have declared, at the time of their commission, these acts to be punishable* (emphasis added).[63]

[61]U.N. *Convention on the Non-Applicability of Statutory Limitations to War Crimes and Crimes Against Humanity*, ratification and accession by U.N. General Assembly Resolution 2391 XXIII of 26 November 1968 and entry into force 11 November 1970. http://www2.ohchr.org/english/law/warcrimes.htm. Accessed 21 August 2009.

[62]*Korbely v. Hungary* (Application 9174/02) European Court of Human Rights Grand Chamber Judgement of 19 September 2008, p. 4, para 18IV(1). http://cmiskp.echr.coe.int/tkp197/view.asp?item=1&portal=hbkm&action=html&highlight=korbely%20%7C%20v%20%7C%20hungary&sessionid=28582191&skin=hudoc-en.

[63]*Korbely v. Hungary* (Application 9174/02) European Court of Human Rights Grand Chamber Judgement of 19 September 2008, p. 5, para 18 IV(4)(a). http://cmiskp.echr.coe.int/tkp197/view.asp?item=1&portal=hbkm&action=html&highlight=korbely%20%7C%20v%20%7C%20hungary&sessionid=28582191&skin=hudoc-en.

The Constitutional Court also noted that crimes against humanity in international law were no longer inextricably linked to the context of war in all cases (i.e. so that the concept of crimes against humanity is of such a scope as to include instances in which these crimes occurred in peacetime or in immediate post-conflict situations). *The Constitutional Court held further that "Acts defined in Article 3 common to the Geneva Conventions constitute crimes against humanity;* [this Article] contains those 'minimum' requirements which all conflicting Parties must observe, 'at any time and in any place whatsoever.'... the prohibitions contained in common Article 3 of the 1949 Geneva Conventions are based on 'elementary considerations of humanity' and cannot be breached in an armed conflict, regardless of whether it is international or internal ... (emphasis added)."[64] The Court held it was irrelevant whether the Geneva Conventions were properly promulgated or whether the Hungarian State had implemented them prior to the 23 October 1956 uprising in Hungary since: (i) war crimes and crimes against humanity are punishable regardless of the domestic law; and (ii) the responsibility of the perpetrators for these crimes existed under international law.

(b) *First-instance Proceedings Before the Military Bench of the Budapest Regional Court*

On 29 May 1995 the Military Bench of the Budapest Regional Court held that: (i) the accused Korbely had in fact been charged with committing actions that constituted the offences 'homicide' and 'incitement to homicide' *not* crimes against humanity, and that (ii) the statute of limitations had run on the homicide and incitement to homicide offences in this case hence barring prosecution.

Consequently, the Military Bench discontinued the criminal proceedings against the accused. The Military Bench of the Budapest Regional Court based this decision on its view that the insurgents were *not* an organized group under central command with different combatant units and, hence, the Geneva Conventions relating to protection of civilians during non-international conflicts was allegedly not engaged and the domestic law regarding crimes against humanity not applicable.

(c) *Suspension of the Appeal Proceedings Pending the Outcome of a Case Before the Constitutional Court*

The relevant bench of the Supreme Court suspended the appeal proceedings in November 1995 pending the outcome of a case before the Constitutional Court challenging the constitutionality of the Act that provided for prosecutions of certain actions committed during the 1956 Hungarian Revolution (thus dropping the statute of limitations for certain of those offences, i.e. for crimes against humanity). On 4 September 1996 the Constitutional Court held the Act to be unconstitutional *due to certain errors in the Act* that created an unconstitutional barrier to the prosecution of crimes against humanity under the Act.

[64] *Korbely v. Hungary* (Application 9174/02) European Court of Human Rights Grand Chamber Judgement of 19 September 2008, p. 6, para 18 V(4)(b). http://cmiskp.echr.coe.int/tkp197/view.asp?item=1&portal=hbkm&action=html&highlight=korbely%20%7C%20v%20%7C%20hungary&sessionid=28582191&skin=hudoc-en.

(d) ***Remittal and Repetition of the Proceedings De Novo Before the Military Bench of the Budapest Regional Court***

On 6 December 1996, the Supreme Court's appeal bench quashed the 29 May 1995 decision of the Military Bench of the Budapest Regional Court and remitted the case back to that court with instructions that the case be restarted from the investigation stage onward. The Budapest Regional Court was instructed to determine, on the facts, whether the accused had committed a "crime against life" that was statute barred, or alternatively, "a crime against humanity" that is *not* statute barred and to which the Geneva Conventions apply. The Supreme Court held that the Military Bench of the Budapest Regional Court had failed to elaborate on the facts sufficiently to distinguish which of these two categories of offence was applicable in the instant case. On 16 February 1998 an expert military historian presented evidence on whether the insurgents were an organized armed group under central command exercising control over part of the territory and carrying out sustained and concerted operations. On 7 May 1998, the Military Bench held a hearing and the Prosecutor argued that Korbely had committed crimes against humanity prohibited under Article 3 common to the Geneva Conventions and punishable under the Criminal Code of Hungary. The Defence argued that the Fourth Geneva Convention was not applicable to the facts, and that its application would amount to retroactive application of the law.

The Military Bench of the Budapest Regional Court held, pursuant to the Constitutional Court's holding of 13 October 1993, that the Geneva Conventions were part of Hungarian domestic law without any further transformation; that the legal system of the State of Hungary recognized these rules of international law and that the application of common Article 3 of the Geneva Convention would *not* amount to retroactive application of the law. The Military Bench then turned to the conduct of the accused to determine whether it met the elements of the crime against humanity under common Article 3(1) of the *Geneva Conventions relative to the Protection of Civilian Persons in Time of War. (Protocol II).*[65]

The Military Bench of the Budapest Regional Court then again discontinued the criminal proceedings against Korbely. The Military Bench held that the insurgents were *not* an organized armed group under central command exercising sustained operations in a part of the State's territory. On that basis, the Military Bench concluded that there was allegedly no armed non-international conflict between 23 October 1956 and 4 November 1956 in Hungary which would trigger the application of Common Article 3 of the 1949 Geneva Convention with respect to protected persons (i.e. civilians and members of the armed group who were 'hors de combat', etc.). The Military Bench's reasoning was based on the presumption that

[65]Common Article 3 of the 1949 Geneva Conventions, *Geneva Convention relating to the Protection of Civilian Persons in Times of War* (Fourth Geneva Convention), Diplomatic Conference of Geneva of 12 August 1949, entry into force 21 October 1950 (Article 3(1)). http://www.unhcr.org/refworld/docid/3ae6b36d2.html. Accessed 24 August 2009.

Protocol II additional to the Geneva Conventions altered the interpretation of common Article 3 of the Geneva Conventions and required that the belligerent parties *both* be formal (institutionalized) *organized armed forces* under central command engaged in a non-international conflict.

The Military Bench of the Budapest Regional Court held thus that the applicant's acts did not fall under the category of 'crimes against humanity', but rather that of 'multiple homicides'; partly as a perpetrator and partly as an inciter. The Regional Court held the latter crimes to be statute barred under the domestic Criminal Code operative at the material time as the statute of limitation period of 15 years specified under that Criminal Code had elapsed since the commission of the crime of multiple homicides (*not* constituting a crime against humanity). *The Military Bench of the Budapest Regional Court also held that the exception to the application of the 15 year statutory limitation period specified in the domestic Criminal Code regarding aggravated murder was also* ***not*** *applicable.*

The Military Bench of the Budapest Regional Court was careful to say that it had "not established condemnatory findings of fact in regard to the defendant [Korbely] relating to the crime of multiple homicides as perpetrator and inciter".[66] At the same time, the Military Bench of the Budapest Regional Court stated in its conclusion that it had *not* rendered an acquittal [regarding the crime of multiple homicides as perpetrator and inciter] simply because "... in its view, in the case of statute-barred conduct, the ground which eliminates punishability – that is, statutory limitation – has precedence over the fact that the impugned act has not been proven in any event."[67]

(e) ***The Appeal Proceedings Before the Supreme Court***

The Supreme Court on 5 November 1998 upheld the decision of the Military Bench of the Budapest Regional Court (rendered on remittal of the case to the Military Bench). Its ruling was based on the reasoning that the Geneva Convention protections in common Article 3 of the Geneva Conventions of 12 August 1949 – relating to the protection of victims of non-international armed conflicts – *allegedly* did not apply to the victims of the defendant as the defendant's impugned acts allegedly did *not* occur in the context of a non-international war involving the armed forces of the State versus an *organized* opposing armed force (i.e. organized armed freedom fighters).

---

[66] *Korbely v. Hungary* (Application 9174/02) European Court of Human Rights Grand Chamber Judgement of 19 September 2008, under "remittal to, and repition of the proceedings before, the Regional Court", para 31, p. 13. http://cmiskp.echr.coe.int/tkp197/view.asp?item=1&portal=hbkm&action=html&highlight=korbely%20%7C%20v%20%7C%20hungary&sessionid=28582191&skin=hudoc-en.

[67] *Korbely v. Hungary* (Application 9174/02) European Court of Human Rights Grand Chamber Judgement of 19 September 2008, under "remittal to, and repition of the proceedings before, the Regional Court", para 31, p. 13. http://cmiskp.echr.coe.int/tkp197/view.asp?item=1&portal=hbkm&action=html&highlight=korbely%20%7C%20v%20%7C%20hungary&sessionid=28582191&skin=hudoc-en.

(f) *The Supreme Court Review Panel Decision*

On 28 June 1999, a review panel of the Supreme Court quashed the 5 November 1998 Supreme Court decision. The Review Panel held that Protocol II of the Geneva Conventions did *not* restrict the application of common Article 3 of the 1949 Geneva Conventions, i.e. there was no requirement, in order that the common Article 3 protections be triggered in an internal conflict, that the group opposing the State armed forces be an armed organized group and under central command:

> Through Article 3 common to the Geneva Conventions, the community of nations intended to secure safeguards for protected persons in civil-war situations where the population of a given State and the armed forces of that State confronted each other. The wording of this provision does *not* contain any further condition in addition to this. *To require further criteria would impair the humanitarian character of the Conventions. If the Convention and the Protocol [Protocol II additional to the Geneva Conventions] were to be interpreted in conjunction with each other, it would mean that, should the resistance of the population under attack by the armed forces of the State not attain the minimum level of organization required by the Additional Protocol, Article 3 common to the Geneva Conventions would not be applicable even if the armed forces of the State were to exterminate a certain group of the population or the entire population* ... (emphasis added).[68]

The Review Panel of the Supreme Court held that from 23 October 1956 onwards the State "waged war against the overwhelming majority of the population of Hungary" and that a non-international conflict was occurring during that period until the Soviet occupation on 4 November when the conflict became international.[69] Hence, the Supreme Court Review Panel held that the appropriate charge against Korbely was in fact crimes against humanity and the Supreme Court should not have discontinued proceedings against him. Based on the ruling by the Review Panel, the Supreme Court: (i) held additional hearings, and (ii) quashed the 7 May 1998 decision of the Military Bench of the Budapest Regional Court on the basis of inadequate findings of fact underlying the decision and remitted the case back to that court for yet another rehearing.

(g) *Repetition of Proceedings De Novo Before the Regional Court*

New hearings were held in January 2001 by the Military Bench of the Budapest Regional Court and on 18 January 2001 Korbely was convicted of crimes against humanity consisting of multiple homicides as perpetrator regarding the murders committed inside the police building and as inciter regarding the murders outside

---

[68] *Korbely v. Hungary* (Application 9174/02) European Court of Human Rights Grand Chamber Judgement of 19 September 2008, under "remittal to, and repition of the proceedings before, the Regional Court", p. 16. http://cmiskp.echr.coe.int/tkp197/view.asp?item=1&portal=hbkm&action=html&highlight=korbely%20%7C%20v%20%7C%20hungary&sessionid=28582191&skin=hudoc-en.

[69] *Korbely v. Hungary* (Application 9174/02) European Court of Human Rights Grand Chamber Judgement of 19 September 2008, under "remittal to, and repition of the proceedings before, the Regional Court", para 34, p. 17. http://cmiskp.echr.coe.int/tkp197/view.asp?item=1&portal=hbkm&action=html&highlight=korbely%20%7C%20v%20%7C%20hungary&sessionid=28582191&skin=hudoc-en.

the police building in violation of common Article 3(1) of the Geneva Conventions. The Court relied on: (i) testimony from the accused; (ii) testimony from the victims; (iii) testimony from numerous witnesses; (iv) extensive documentation including, for instance, the Army Service Regulations in force in 1956; the defendant's personal service file; death certificates of the victims; minutes of the investigation; hospital records, photographs; sketches of the scene, etc., and (v) the testimony of a forensic medical and firearms expert.

The applicant was sentenced to three years imprisonment and five years deprivation of certain rights. On appeal, the Supreme Court amended the judgment to a five year prison sentence which was then reduced by one-eighth under an amnesty provision. Several requests for a retrial were rejected as were a request for a review by the Supreme Court and a pardon. The applicant began serving his prison sentence 24 March 2003 and he was conditionally released on 31 May 2005.

Reasoning of the Grand Chamber of the European Court of Human Rights in Korbely v. Hungary

The European Court of Human Rights began its analysis by noting the importance of Article 7 of the European Convention and the fact that it is non-derogable even in times of war or public emergency. The goal of Article 7, the Court noted, was to "provide effective safeguards against arbitrary prosecution, conviction and punishment."[70]

The Grand Chamber analysis of the case further included the following key points:

1. An acknowledgment of the fact that the Review Panel of the Supreme Court in *Korberly* had noted that the dictatorship in 1956 in Hungary had essentially "waged war" against the majority of the unarmed civilians and used the armed forces to attack peaceful demonstrators. (*However, the Grand Chamber, nevertheless, alleged that the Supreme Court had* ***not*** *addressed whether the applicant's acts were part of that systematic attack*).
2. Acceptance of the domestic court's view that the level of organization of the freedom fighters was irrelevant in determining whether common Article 3 of the Geneva Conventions was applicable. (*The Grand Chamber held that common Article 3 of the Geneva Conventions was applicable in the instant case*).
3. Rejection of the domestic court findings of fact as to the incident in relation to Tamas Kaszas. (*In direct contrast to the findings of fact of the domestic courts*, the Grand Chamber held that: (i) Tamas Kaszas was *not* in the process of

[70]*Korbely v. Hungary* (Application 9174/02) European Court of Human Rights Grand Chamber Judgement of 19 September 2008, under "remittal to, and repition of the proceedings before, the Regional Court", para 69, p. 37. http://cmiskp.echr.coe.int/tkp197/view.asp?item=1&portal=hbkm &action=html&highlight=korbely%20%7C%20v%20%7C%20hungary&sessionid=28582191& skin=hudoc-en.

surrendering when he was fatally shot by the applicant or, at the very least, that (ii) Kaszas was not clearly expressing an intention to surrender and that his intentions were unknown. *The Grand Chamber – based on its reinterpretation of the facts in this regard – held that Tamsa Kaszas could not be viewed as "hors de combat" according to the meaning ascribed to that term under common Article 3 of the Geneva Conventions*).

4. Rejection of the government's assertion that the applicant's conviction was *not* based solely on his having shot and killed Tamas Kaszas but also on his firing and shooting others who were unarmed and ordering his officers to shoot on these civilians as well resulting in deaths and also some non-lethal injuries. (The Grand Chamber held that the domestic court's conviction was focused on the Kaszas killing with the other deaths and injuries being considered as aggravating factors. *The Grand Chamber held that Kaszas could not be considered a "non-combatant" protected by common Article 3 of the Geneva Conventions and therefore it was not foreseeable that the applicant's acts in relation to Kaszas would be considered a crime against humanity.* The Grand Chamber held it was unnecessary to consider the applicant's complaint under Article 6 of the European Convention in relation to the fairness and length of the domestic proceedings against him; finding additionally that with respect to the length of the proceedings; the complaint was manifestly ill-founded).

The Grand Chamber awarded no damages as the applicant had not submitted a claim for damages and his legal costs had been covered by legal aid from the Council of Europe.

The applicant's complaint was ruled unanimously admissible under Article 7 and 6(1) of the European Convention.

The Grand Chamber judgment held by 11 votes to 6 that there had been a violation of Article 7 of the European Convention, and by 12 to 5 that it was not necessary to examine the unfairness of the proceedings under Article 6(1).

B. Commentary on Korbely v. Hungary

1. *The European Court of Human Rights as a De Facto Appeal Court in Korbely v. Hungary*: In *Korbely v. Hungary,* it would appear that the Grand Chamber took it upon itself to reinterpret facts in such a way that its interpretation contradicted the findings of fact of the domestic courts which actually heard from witnesses and experts on the stand and via written submissions. In this way, the European Court departs from its usual tact and, it may be argued, infringes its own self-described jurisdictional boundaries which require that: (i) it not function as an appeal court and substitute its opinion for that of the domestic courts, and (ii) restrain itself from reinterpreting facts, as well as from re-interpreting domestic law and its proper application, but rather confine itself to determining if the results of the domestic courts' interpretation and application of domestic law (which may or may not incorporate reference to international law) is compatible with the European Convention. According to the joint dissenting opinion of Judges Lorenzen, Tulkens, Zagrebelsky, Fura-Sandstrom and Popvic, however:

> *... the majority, without any explanation, head off in a different direction and, on a flimsy, uncertain basis, quite simply substitute their own findings of fact for those of the Hungarian judicial authorities* ... we see no reason to place more reliance on the conclusions reached by the Court [Grand Chamber of the European Court of Human Rights] than on those of the domestic courts. On the contrary, we consider that the national courts were in a better position to assess all the available facts and evidence.[71]

On the basis of its reinterpretation of the facts, the European Court of Human Rights' Grand Chamber, it would appear, essentially exonerated Korberly of crimes against humanity though it claimed simply to be ascertaining whether Article 7 of the European Convention had been complied with by the State. The simple disclaimer by the Court in Korbely that "it [the European Court of Human Rights] is not called upon to rule on the applicant's individual criminal responsibility, that being primarily a matter for assessment by the domestic courts"[72] is largely negated by its substituting its own findings of fact for those of the domestic courts in the instant case and contesting the domestic courts' conviction based on a reinterpretation of those facts. Exoneration regarding alleged 'crimes against humanity' in itself appears to have been victory enough for the applicant in the instant case as no damages were requested for the alleged violation of Article 7(1) of the European Convention affirmed by the ECHR.

If the European Court of Human Rights *improperly* finds in a *particular* Article 7 case that an individual was wrongly convicted of an international crime such as a crime against humanity or a war crime, that individual has, for all practical purposes, essentially been vindicated at the international level. Furthermore, the State in response to the European Court of Human Rights' judgment, may pay reparations to the accused; and/or release the defendant from prison if he or she is still in prison; and/or issue a pardon; or provide some other non-pecuniary as well as pecuniary reparation for an alleged violation of Article 7(1) of the European Convention thus adding to the suffering of victims and/or their relatives.

2. *The Erroneous Notion of a Required Nexus Between Armed Conflict and Crimes Against Humanity*: It has been recognized that crimes against humanity, *according to the Charter of the Nuremberg Tribunal* were linked to a war context *for the purpose of* ***demarcating the jurisdiction of the Tribunal*** *and* **not** *as a matter*

---

[71]Joint dissenting opinion of Judges Lorenzen, Tulkens, Zagrebelsky, Fura-Sandstrom and Popvic in *Korbely v. Hungary* (Application 9174/02) European Court of Human Rights Grand Chamber Judgement of 19 September 2008, para 2 of the dissenting opinion at pp. 49–50. http://cmiskp.echr.coe.int/tkp197/view.asp?item=1&portal=hbkm&action=html&highlight=korbely%20%7C%20v%20%7C%20hungary&sessionid=28582191&skin=hudoc-en.

[72]*Korbely v. Hungary* (Application 9174/02) European Court of Human Rights Grand Chamber Judgement of 19 September 2008, para 73, p. 38. http://cmiskp.echr.coe.int/tkp197/view.asp?item=1&portal=hbkm&action=html&highlight=korbely%20%7C%20v%20%7C%20hungary&sessionid=28582191&skin=hudoc-en.

of a substantive requirement of international law.[73] That crimes against humanity do *not* need to be linked to the conduct of a war and that they are prohibited as part of international customary law was affirmed through Resolution 95(1) of the United Nations General Assembly of 11 December 1946.[74] Notwithstanding the aforementioned, the Military Bench of the Budapest Regional Court twice, (the last time on remittal to repeat the proceedings anew), ruled in *Korberly* (later reversed) that the applicant had not committed crimes against humanity but rather multiple homicides partly as a perpetrator and partly as an inciter. The domestic Regional Court had erroneously focused on whether there were two organized opposing armed forces, each under their own respective central command, engaged in non-international conflict as an alleged prerequisite for crimes against humanity being the appropriate charge in the Korbely case. The Regional Court ruled incorrectly, (misinterpreting the implications of Protocol II additional to the Geneva Conventions), that a non-international conflict did *not* exist at the material time in the instant case (as the insurgents were not an organized armed group under central command carrying out sustained armed activities in that part of the territory under their control).

The Regional Court, furthermore, relied *incorrectly* on a presumed required nexus between 'crimes against humanity' and a war context in the first instance. However, as mentioned, such a nexus with a non-international war was *not* a requirement for a conviction for crimes against humanity. Neither was it required for the triggering of the protections under common Article 3 of the Geneva Conventions that the State be opposed in the internal conflict by an organized armed opposition under a central command with control over part of the territory and carrying out systematic and persistent attacks. The degree of organization of the insurgents was irrelevant to the case analysis in Korbely then on the issue of whether the applicant had committed crimes against humanity: (i) involving violations of the protections guaranteed under common Article 3 of the Geneva Conventions to persons who were not engaged in hostilities, or no longer engaged and (ii) as part of, or in furtherance of a systemic attack on the civilian population by the State.

3. *The Military Bench of the Budapest Regional Court's Initial Rulings Discontinuing Proceedings against the Applicant: Having It Both Ways in the Korbely v. Hungary case*: The Military Bench of the Budapest Regional Court *declined* to classify the applicant's alleged crimes as '*aggravated*' multiple murders as perpetrator and inciter. Furthermore, the Regional Court construed the crimes as

---

[73]Dissenting opinion of Judge Loucaides in *Korbely v. Hungary* (Application 9174/02) European Court of Human Rights Grand Chamber Judgement of 19 September 2008, p. 51 (citing Lord Millet in the Pinochet (3) case (House of Lords (1999) 2 Weekly Law reports 909). http://cmiskp.echr.coe.int/tkp197/view.asp?item=1&portal=hbkm&action=html&highlight=korbely%20%7C%20v%20%7C%20hungary&sessionid=28582191&skin=hudoc-en.

[74]Dissenting opinion of Judge Loucaides in *Korbely v. Hungary* (Application 9174/02) European Court of Human Rights Grand Chamber Judgement of 19 September 2008, p. 51 of the dissenting opinion. http://cmiskp.echr.coe.int/tkp197/view.asp?item=1&portal=hbkm&action=html&highlight=korbely%20%7C%20v%20%7C%20hungary&sessionid=28582191&skin=hudoc-en.

multiple homicides but *not* 'multiple homicides' constituting 'crimes against humanity'. This was the initial decision of the Regional Court despite the fact that it was uncontested that the multiple homicides were perpetrated in part against unarmed persons (while Tamas Kaszas was murdered arguably while trying to surrender his gun). The refusal to declare the alleged murders 'aggravated' meant that the statute of limitations still applied under the domestic Criminal Code.

In any case, the Regional Court, on the view here, in its initial decisions discontinuing proceedings against the applicant, declined its jurisdiction in that it rendered neither a conviction nor an acquittal, but relied rather on ruling the crime of multiple homicide statute barred. However, unless the Regional Court established whether or not multiple homicides had in fact occurred; it could not then consider if these homicides were aggravated thus falling under the *exception* to the domestic statue of limitations for such crimes. In this regard, note that the Military Bench of the Regional Court contended that it had declined to render an acquittal and instead held that it had simply ruled that the crimes committed by Korberly, (allegedly multiple homicides, but *not* crimes against humanity) were, even if proved, statute barred.

The Regional Court thus had, *in effect*, acquitted Korberly of the crimes charged, namely, *multiple murders constituting crimes against humanity* by: (i) defining the crimes away based on erroneous notions as to the contexts in which the Geneva Convention protections for civilians and others hors de combat under common Article 3 apply and a false presumption that crimes against humanity only occur in a war context and by (ii) substituting in its analysis and final decision the crime of 'multiple homicides as perpetrator and inciter' for the actual crime charged of crimes against humanity relating to multiple homicides of persons 'hors de combat' as part of a systemic State sponsored attack on civilians.

4. *The Grand Chamber's Blurring of the Boundaries Between 'Civilian' or "Non-Combatant" versus "Combatant" During Armed Conflict Undermines the Concept of 'Crimes against Humanity'*: *Reclassifying the victim, Tamas Kaszas, of Korbely's intentional killing, as a 'combatant' rather than a 'non-combatant' given the facts in the case, on the view expressed here, undermines the whole notion of crimes against humanity by blurring the distinction between 'non-combatant' and 'combatant' where in fact there is a bright line demarcation.* According to one of the dissenting judges in the case, Judge Loucaides, Korbely's crime of murder was on civilians as part of a widespread attack on civilians sponsored by the State of which he had knowledge, and the crime, therefore, meets the definition of a 'crime against humanity' under Article 7 of the Rome Statute.[75] Judge Loucaides concluded, on the facts, in addition, that Korbely's actions also meet the definition of a 'crime against humanity' under the minimum

[75]Rome Statute (2002). Text of the Rome Statute circulated as document A/CONF.183/9 of 17 July 1998 and corrected by process-verbaux of 10 November 1998, 12 July 1999, 30 November 1999, 8 May 2000, 17 January 2001 and 16 January 2002. The Statute entered into force on 1 July 2002 (Article 7(1)(2)). http://www.icc-cpi.int/NR/rdonlyres/EA9AEFF7-5752-4F84-BE94-0A655EB30E16/0/Rome_Statute_English.pdf. Accessed 18 August 2009.

requirements of the Charter of the International Military Tribunal of Nuremberg in that Korbely's actions, according to Judge Loucaides, comprised the following elements of the offence of 'crimes against humanity' under the Nuremberg Charter:

- Murder
- Committed against a civilian population
- Systematic or organized conduct in furtherance of a certain [State] policy[76]

Judge Loucaides held that the last element above is inferred from the combination of the other two. Judge Loucaides points out that the fact that there were systematic and widespread armed attacks against the civilian population by a dictatorship which led up to the October 1956 Hungarian uprising was well known internationally. He also contested the Grand Chamber's holding that the domestic courts in the instant case had not addressed the question of whether the applicant's actions were part of that systematic State policy of attacking the civilian population.

Judge Loucaides also disagreed with the Grand Chamber majority's reclassification of the murder victim Tamas Kaszas as a 'combatant'. The *domestic courts* had held that Tamas Kaszas was intending [or in the process of] surrendering his weapon when he reached into his pocket for his weapon. The domestic courts had tried to painstakingly establish the facts in this regard. *They noted that Korbely's officers had their submachine guns continuously pointed at the civilians including Tamas Kaszas at all times.* The Military Bench of the Budapest Regional Court, (in the last of several rounds of proceedings and the one resulting in a conviction), held that Korbely should have known that his military platoon had the superior force and that there was no need to resort to violence against the people. The Supreme Court held that: (i) Korbely was close enough to hear Istvan Balazs call (Kaszas' compatriot's call) for Kaszas to hand over his weapon to Korbely and that (ii) given that it was immediately after the call from Balazs to Kaszas to hand over the gun that a quarrel broke out between Korbely and Tamas Kaszas, that *Korbely knew that Tamas Kaszas intended to hand over his weapon rather than attack with it.* Judge Loucaides' position was as follows *based on the factual findings of the domestic courts*:

> I believe that the findings of the domestic courts to the effect that Tamas Kazas's behaviour in respect of his gun amounted to the gesture of a man attempting to hand over his gun, rather than to attack with it, were not unreasonable, bearing in mind in this respect that Mr. Kaszas, along with his companions, was facing officers who were continuously pointing their submachine guns at them and that the officers' force was superior to that of the civilians. *In the circumstances any attempt on the part of Mr. Kaszas to use his gun against*

[76]Dissenting opinion of Judge Loucaides in *Korbely v. Hungary* (Application 9174/02) European Court of Human Rights Grand Chamber Judgement of 19 September 2008, p. 52 of the dissenting opinion. http://cmiskp.echr.coe.int/tkp197/view.asp?item=1&portal=hbkm&action=html&highlight=korbely%20%7C%20v%20%7C%20hungary&sessionid=28582191&skin=hudoc-en.

> *the applicant would have amounted to suicide.* I do not therefore see any reason to overrule the relevant findings of the domestic courts (emphasis added).[77]

Judge Loucaides' interpretation of Tamas Kaszas as being a 'protected person' under common Article 3 of the Geneva Conventions in that he was 'hors de combat' after trying to surrender, seems consistent with the overall context in which the Tamas Kazas's killing took place. That is, the view of Kaszas as 'hors de combat' (a non-combatant when he was shot and killed) is consistent with the following facts ***uncontested*** by the Grand Chamber of the European Court of Human Rights which suggest that the incident was marked by the indiscriminate use of force: (i) the officers in the applicant's military platoon, on orders of the applicant, shot *randomly* with submachine guns at the others in Kaszas' group who were *unarmed* and standing around in the outside yard *near Tamas Kaszas*; (ii) the officers also shot with submachine guns on unarmed members of Tamas Kaszas group *who were attempting to flee* into the street; (iii) the officers, at the relevant time, were led to believe that Tamas Kaszas was the only one in the freedom fighters' group who was armed; yet they did not use their weapons against Kaszas alone; (iv) the applicant had killed persons inside the police building and incited killings outside the building as well as shooting Tamas Kaszas himself, and (v) the applicant did *not* order Kaszas to lie face on the ground or to take some other posture in which he could be safely disarmed. Note that the government of Hungry argued before the Grand Chamber that the applicant was convicted primarily for shooting and causing shootings of civilians and that the focus was not entirely on what happened in relation to Tamas Kaszas' killing (a point accepted by Judge Loucaides – based on the record – but contested by the Grand Chamber who held the conviction was focused on the Tamas Kaszas' killing).

5 (a) **The issue of reprisals as a violation of international humanitarian law and its relevance to the material events relating to the conviction in the domestic courts in the instant case**: *It would appear that the killing of Tamas Kazas, in the circumstances, and the firing on the others who were unarmed resulting in multiple deaths and injuries, may have amounted to: (i) a '**reprisal**' for the freedom fighters' activities, or the insurgent group's very existence as well as (ii) intimidation and terrorism intended to instil fear in all civilians, especially those contemplating offering resistance to the dictatorship or those already associating with resisters.* This becomes all the more plausible when one recalls, as Judge Loucaides points out, that it does not appear possible to disassociate the applicant's acts (for which he was convicted) from *the state policy of repression and systemic attack against the civilian population:*

> ... the applicant, in confronting and shooting Mr, Kaszas and the group near him, was acting as an agent of the dictatorial regime which was attempting to suppress by force those

[77]Dissenting opinion of Judge Loucaides in *Korbely v. Hungary* (Application 9174/02) European Court of Human Rights Grand Chamber Judgement of 19 September 2008, p. 53. http://cmiskp.echr.coe.int/tkp197/view.asp?item=1&portal=hbkm&action=html&highlight=korbely%20%7C%20v%20%7C%20hungary&sessionid=28582191&skin=hudoc-en.

> civilians, such as the victims of the applicant's attack, who were opposing that regime. *In short, the use of force by the applicant was on behalf of and for the purposes of that regime.* I do not see how we can dissociate the incident for which the applicant was found guilty from the general systematic attack by the military and the relevant state policy against the civilian population (emphasis added).[78]

Hence, on Judge Loucaides' analysis, the applicant's actions constituted a 'crime against humanity' as not only were the multiple victims 'hors de combat' as per common Article 3 of the Geneva Conventions (which alone is insufficient to establish a crime against humanity), but the other constituent elements of a crime against humanity were also present (the crime was part of a State sponsored systemic attack on the civilian population).

(b) **Reprisals and collective punishments**: Note that *reprisals* and *collective punishments* are intricately related and both directed at civilians or others 'hors de combat' (who are not at the relevant time participants in combat). Both are violations of international humanitarian law and customary law. Protocol II additional to the 1949 Geneva Conventions refers to violence against civilians intended to spread terror in the population and may be interpreted to encompass the notion of a prohibition against 'reprisals' and 'collective punishments' which are amongst the primary vehicles for spreading terror in the civilian population:

Protocol Additional to the Geneva Conventions of 12 August 1949, and relating to the Protection of Victims of Non-International Armed Conflicts (Protocol II), 8 June 1977.

> **Art 13.** Protection of the civilian population
>
> 2. The civilian population as such, as well as individual civilians, shall not be the object of attack. *Acts or threats of violence the primary purpose of which is to spread terror among the civilian population are prohibited* (emphasis added).[79]

(c) **The prohibition against reprisals applies also to unarmed resistance fighters; and to those who have, or are in the process of surrendering their weapons:** The fact that Tamas Kaszas and his group were a group of resistance fighters does *not* automatically mean that they should be considered as exempted from the Geneva Convention protections for civilians and those 'hors de combat.' Nor does it mean *ipso facto* that the applicant did not commit a 'crime against humanity' as defined, for instance, under Article 7 of the Rome Statute[80] as part of the State policy and practice (at the relevant time) of attacking civilians.

---

[78] Dissenting opinion of Judge Loucaides in *Korbely v. Hungary* (Application 9174/02) European Court of Human Rights Grand Chamber Judgement of 19 September 2008, p. 55. http://cmiskp.echr.coe.int/tkp197/view.asp?item=1&portal=hbkm&action=html&highlight=korbely%20%7C%20v%20%7C%20hungary&sessionid=28582191&skin=hudoc-en.

[79] Protocol Additional to the Geneva Conventions of 12 August 1949, and relating to the Protection of Victims of Non-International Armed Conflicts (Protocol II), 8 June 1977 (Article 13). http://www.icrc.org/ihl.nsf/7c4d08d9b287a42141256739003e636b/d67c3971bcff1c10c125641e0052b545. Accessed 25 August 2009.

[80] Rome Statute (2002). Text of the Rome Statute circulated as document A/CONF.183/9 of 17 July 1998 and corrected by process-verbaux of 10 November 1998, 12 July 1999, 30 November 1999,

The distinction between: (i) intentional multiple homicide which amounts to 'crimes against humanity' *versus* (ii) the same acts that do not meet the criteria for such an international crime, is usefully elucidated in the Estonian case (the Paulov case) involving the killing of 'forest brethren' resistance fighters by agents of the occupying Soviet State. The domestic courts, (Estonian Supreme Court), in the Paulov case held that: "... the murders qualified as crimes against humanity, since the intention to kill was not directed against the concrete victims, but anybody, whose killing would have come within the scope of the operations planned by the NKVD, could have become a victim of this crime."[81] This notion hearkens back to the fact that crimes against humanity occur in the context of systemic and/or widespread attacks on the civilian population. In the Korbely case, the murders and injuring of the unarmed freedom fighters and the murder of Tamas Kaszas, who arguably appeared to be in the process of trying to surrender his weapon, did occur in such a broader context of systemic attacks on the civilian population. The 1956 Hungarian uprising and resistance movement, in fact, may be considered, in large part, to have been in response to such brutal repression against the civilian population. By focusing only on the murder of Kazas, the Grand Chamber in the instant case disregarded the critical larger contextual elements of the particular incident during which Kaszas was murdered; as well as how the incident aligned at the time with State sponsored violence against civilians in Hungarian society at large. Judge Loucaides, rightfully, on the view expressed here, concluded that the incident involving Hungarian resistance fighters 'hors de combat', for which Korberly was convicted of crimes against humanity, was not an isolated incident, but rather one of "several separate incidents ... [that] would inevitably take place as part of the armed forces' organized activities against the population."[82] Viewing the matter from the forgoing perspective, and given *all* the facts, makes it arguably appear reasonable to reach the conclusion of the dissenting judges that a crime against humanity was committed by the applicant.

Notwithstanding the forgoing, however, the 19 September 2008 ruling of the Grand Chamber in the instant case, *in effect*, implies that there were no Geneva Convention protections applicable to any of those shot and injured during the 26 October 1956 incident at the police building in which the applicant led a group of military officers against a group of freedom fighters. (The Grand Chamber declared Kaszas a combatant and not eligible for the protections under common Article 3 of the 1949 Geneva Conventions and did not address the status of the others in his

---

8 May 2000, 17 January 2001 and 16 January 2002. The Statute entered into force on 1 July 2002 (Article 7(1)(2)). http://www.icc-cpi.int/NR/rdonlyres/EA9AEFF7-5752-4F84-BE94-0A655EB30E16/0/Rome_Statute_English.pdf. Accessed 18 August 2009.

[81]Malksoo (2001, p. 778).

[82]Dissenting opinion of Judge Loucaides in *Korbely v. Hungary* (Application 9174/02) European Court of Human Rights Grand Chamber Judgement of 19 September 2008, para 16 of the dissenting opinion. http://cmiskp.echr.coe.int/tkp197/view.asp?item=1&portal=hbkm&action=html&highlight=korbely%20%7C%20v%20%7C%20hungary&sessionid=28582191&skin=hudoc-en.

group who were murdered or suffered non-lethal injuries from the submachine gun fire at the hands of the applicant or his subordinate military officers on order of the applicant). With respect, the view is advanced here, in contrast to the Grand Chamber majority opinion, that Kaszas and his group were eligible for protection as civilians or persons otherwise 'hors de combat' under common Article 3 of the 1949 Geneva Conventions. The latter view is grounded on the fact that: (i) Kaszas' compatriots were *unarmed* and not engaging in hostilities at the time they were shot, and (ii) Kaszas, on a reasonable interpretation of the evidence adopted by the domestic courts, and based on *all* the relevant facts, appears to have been in the process of surrendering.

That the Geneva Convention protections apply also to resistance fighters who are unarmed and/or in the process of surrendering is evidenced, for instance, by common Article 3 of the Geneva Conventions and Article 4 of Protocol II to the 1949 Geneva Conventions which requires humane treatment of *all persons* without distinction who did not take part in hostilities, or who have ceased taking part in hostilities.[83] The important point is that in killing and injuring multiple *unarmed* members of Tamas Kaszas group, and in murdering Kaszas himself (even though he appeared to be trying to surrender), the applicant had ordered his platoon to deprive the victims of any due process before the imposition of penalties even though there was *no* threat to the life of any officer of the heavily armed military platoon who had their submachine guns continuously fixed on the freedom fighter group. The applicant's actions in ordering submachine gun fire on the entire group (unarmed civilians and Kaszas apparently trying to surrender) may have been a form of collective punishment and reprisal for resistance (perhaps triggered in the moment by Kaszas being *verbally* combative). Note that: *"the principle of the prohibition of reprisals against persons has now become part of international law* ***in respect of all persons*** *whether they are members of armed forces or civilians protected by the Geneva Conventions."*[84] *Hence, on the view expressed here, the Grand Chamber's judgment in Korbely v. Hungary inappropriately and inadvertently may reinforce the notion of justified reprisals. Such reprisals, as discussed, are directed ultimately at the civilian population in general, while the specific victims targeted are simply the symbolic vehicle for conveying a message of intimidation and repressive power.*

In the next case to be discussed, *Kononov v. Latvia*, the European Court of Human Rights appears, with respect, to have, *in effect*, once more rationalized a justification for what amounts to a reprisal involving multiple murders and

[83]Protocol Additional to the Geneva Conventions of 12 August 1949, and relating to the Protection of Victims of Non-International Armed Conflicts (Protocol II), (Article 4). http://www.icrc.org/.../d67c3971bcff1c10c125641e0052b545!OpenDocument. Accessed 1 September 2009.

[84]Commentary of the International Committee of the Red Cross on Convention IV Relative to the Protection of Civilians in Times of War, Geneva, 12 August 1949 and on "Reprisals". http://www.icrc.org/IHL.NSF/COM/380-600038?OpenDocument.

inappropriately, on the view here, reclassified civilians as combatants (contrary to the extensive factual findings of the domestic courts and their holdings as to the status of the victims).

V. Case 4 Kononov v. Latvia (Application 36376/04) European Court of Human Rights Chamber Judgment of 24 July 2008 (Referred to the Grand Chamber 26 January 2009)

A. *Background and Domestic Proceedings*

The applicant Kononov in the case *Kononov v. Latvia*[85] held Latvian nationality until 12 April 2000 at which time he was granted Russian nationality by special decree granted by the President of the Russian Federation, Mr V. Putin. The applicant had moved to Russia in 1941 after the Nazis occupied the whole of Latvia and other Baltic regions. In 1942, Kononov was drafted into the Soviet army where he received training in sabotage operations (i.e. learning how to lead commando raids behind enemy lines) and he quickly rose to the rank of sergeant. On 23 June 1943, Kononov and 20 fellow soldiers were parachuted into Belarus near the Latvian border which territory was under German occupation. After landing, Kononov joined a group of Soviet commandos known as the "Red Partisans" and in March 1944, he was put in charge of his own platoon by his superior commanders. On 27 May 1944, Kononov and his commandos allegedly attacked a village named Mazie Bati. It was uncontested that earlier in February 1944, in the village of Mazie Bati, the German army had discovered and killed a group of Red Partisans under the command of Major Chugunov (the Red Partisan group had consisted of nine men, two women and a small child). The men of the village after the killings of Major Chugunov and his group had allegedly feared reprisals and approached the Germans for weaponry purportedly for self-protection and were each given a rifle and two grenades.[86] Kononov and his fellow commandos suspected that the villagers of Mazie Bati had provided the information to the Germans that led to the deaths of the Red Partisan group under the command of Major Chugunov and they allegedly decided to take reprisals which resulted in the murders of nine of the

[85]*Kononov v. Latvia* (Application no. 36376/04) European Court of Human Rights Chamber judgment 24 July 2008. http://cmiskp.echr.coe.int/tkp197/view.asp?item=1&portal=hbkm&action=html&highlight=Kononov%20%7C%20v%20%7C%20Latvia&sessionid=29021422&skin=hudoc-en. Accessed 1 September 2009.

[86]*Kononov v. Latvia* (Application no. 36376/04) European Court of Human Rights Chamber judgment 24 July 2008, para 15. http://cmiskp.echr.coe.int/tkp197/view.asp?item=1&portal=hbkm&action=html&highlight=Kononov%20%7C%20v%20%7C%20Latvia&sessionid=29021422&skin=hudoc-en. Accessed 1 September 2009.

Mazie Bati villagers.[87] After the war, the applicant lived in Latvia and held various posts in the Soviet police apparatus until his retirement in 1988. For his military actions, Kononov had been decorated with the Order of Lenin which was the highest distinction offered by the USSR.

Latvia regained its independence after Soviet occupation on 21 August 1991. On 6 April 1993 a new law was passed in Latvia which became part of the Latvian Criminal Code and which allowed for prosecution of genocide, crimes against humanity or peace, war crimes and racial discrimination. Furthermore, new articles incorporated into the former Latvian Criminal Code allowed for retrospective application of the law to 'crimes against humanity' and to 'war crimes' and without any statutory limitation period being applicable in respect of these latter crimes.

The Latvian Courts Made the Following Findings of Fact

- The applicant and his commandos on 27 May 1944 entered the village of Mazie Bati near the area in which the applicant had grown up and where his parents still lived.
- The applicant and his fellow combatants were wearing German uniforms and entered and searched six houses in the village where they found the German-supplied rifles and grenades.
- Upon finding the weaponry, the applicant and his group shot and killed the male heads of the households and wounded two women. They then set fire to two of the homes with people in them burning those people alive. There were nine villagers killed in all by the applicant and his group and amongst the dead were six men and three women; one of whom was in the late stages of pregnancy.
- The murdered villagers *may* have been collaborators but, even if this were the case, this did not deprive them of their civilian status since they had not taken part in killing Major Chugunov and his group and these villagers had not organized any resistance to the applicant and his group though they had time to do so. Rather, their weaponry was for "self-protection" only.
- There was no firm evidence that the applicant and his group had been ordered by an *ad hoc* military tribunal organized by the Red Partisans to apprehend the villagers in question so that they could stand trial as collaborators of the Germans. The government held that: (i) the evidence on this point at trial had been contradictory at best and that (ii) even if such a body had existed and had issued the orders claimed, the orders would have been unlawful given that the villagers were tried in fact in their absence and without any possibility of advancing a defence to the charge of collaboration with the enemy.

[87] *Kononov v. Latvia* (Application no. 36376/04) European Court of Human Rights Chamber judgment 24 July 2008, para 14. http://cmiskp.echr.coe.int/tkp197/view.asp?item=1&portal=hbkm&action=html&highlight=Kononov%20%7C%20v%20%7C%20Latvia&sessionid=29021422&skin=hudoc-en. Accessed 1 September 2009.

The applicant contested the domestic courts' findings of fact and held that:

- The villagers in question were collaborators and traitors who were responsible for the deaths of 12 Red Partisans (Major Chugunov and his group).
- The villagers in question had been rewarded with various supplies and a sum of money for delivering the Chugunov Red Partisan group to the Germans.
- As commander he (Kononov) had been under order by an ad hoc military tribunal to bring the six male villagers in question to stand trial for collaboration and treason.
- He, Kononov, had *not* entered the village but was successful in having the order transferred to another commanding officer who actually entered the village and gave the orders resulting in the deaths of the nine villagers (he, Kononov, had not wanted to enter the area as everyone knew him there and he feared reprisal against his parents who lived in the area should he take action against the villagers and be recognized).
- He had hid in the bushes while his comrades carried out the raid and saw his comrades return with seized weaponry but denied his compatriots had pillaged the village.

In January 1998, a criminal investigation by the Centre for the Documentation of the Consequences of Totalitarianism was launched into the aforementioned 27 May 1944 Mazie Bati incident. The Centre maintained that the applicant might be guilty of war crimes under the amended Latvian Criminal Code which provided for penalties of 3–15 years *or* life imprisonment depending on the specific fact pattern in the case. The Criminal Code permitted retrospective application of the law in regards to war crimes that were not subject to statutory limitation. The applicant was charged 2 August 1998 with war crimes in respect of the aforementioned 27 May 1944 incident that had occurred in the village of Mazie Bati to which charge the applicant pleaded not guilty. He was placed in pre-trial detention and subsequently tried before the Riga Regional Court and convicted.

The Regional Court relied on eye witness testimony, and the applicant's admission that he had killed one person and burned six people alive; an autobiographical work found at the applicant's house that generally confirmed the prosecution's description of the facts relating to the incident in question as well as other documentary and testimonial evidence. The Regional Court ruled that the applicant had committed actions constituting war crimes and prohibited by the Charter of the International Military Tribunal for Nuremberg of 8 August 1945, the Hague Convention of 18 October 1907 concerning the laws and customs of war on land, and the Geneva Convention of 12 August 1949 relative to the Protection of Civilian Persons in Time of War.[88] Both the Prosecution and the Defense appealed to the Supreme Court.

---

[88]*Kononov v. Latvia* (Application no. 36376/04) European Court of Human Rights Chamber judgment 24 July 2008, para 37. http://cmiskp.echr.coe.int/tkp197/view.asp?item=1&portal=hbkm&action=html&highlight=Kononov%20%7C%20v%20%7C%20Latvia&sessionid=29021422&skin= hudoc-en. Accessed 1 September 2009.

The conviction was quashed on 25 April 2000 by the Criminal Affairs Division of the Supreme Court on the grounds that it was allegedly unclear from the findings of fact of the Regional Court whether the victims had been 'noncombatants' (i.e. civilians); whether the village of Mazie Bati was occupied territory, and whether the victims could have been considered 'prisoners of war' given that they had been armed by the Germans. The Supreme Court ordered that further inquiries/ investigations be made by the Principal Prosecutor's Office into these issues (i.e. by consulting expert historians and international law experts) and also ordered the applicant's immediate release in the interim. The Prosecution appealed this decision to the Supreme Court Senate, but that appeal was dismissed. However, the Supreme Court Senate amended the previous Criminal Affairs Division Supreme Court ruling regarding the need for specialist advice as to the facts and held instead that: "... the Criminal Affairs Division's direction that specialist advice should have been taken on international law was unfounded as expert evidence could not be sought on questions of pure law, which were solely for the courts to decide."[89]

On 17 May 2001, following a new investigation, the applicant was again charged with 'war crimes' under the amended Latvian Criminal Code which included Article 68-3 and the Supreme Court Senate held that the Latgale Regional Court would serve as the court of first instance.

On 3 October 2003, the applicant was acquitted by the Latgale Regional Court of the charge of 'war crimes' but convicted of 'banditry'. The charge of banditry under the former Latvian Criminal Code carried a penalty of 3- to 15-years imprisonment. The conviction was based on the grounds that the killings of the male villagers had purportedly been justified militarily (as the Court accepted the applicant's contention that he was under order of an ad hoc military tribunal and that the villagers were collaborators responsible for the deaths of the Chugunov Red Partisan group). The Court maintained that the applicant could not have foreseen that he would ultimately be regarded as an agent of the Soviet occupying State since Latvia had been incorporated into the U.S.S.R. and he had been fighting against the Nazis to free Latvia from German occupation.[90] The Court, however, held that the killings of the three women and the burning of the said villagers' homes was not justified. The Latgale Regional Court held the applicant responsible as the commanding officer for the crime of banditry in relation to the killing of the women and burning of the houses, but imposed no sentence as banditry was a crime subject to a statutory limitation period and that period had expired making any

[89] *Kononov v. Latvia* (Application no. 36376/04) European Court of Human Rights Chamber judgment 24 July 2008, para 39. http://cmiskp.echr.coe.int/tkp197/view.asp?item=1&portal=hbkm&action=html&highlight=Kononov%20%7C%20v%20%7C%20Latvia&sessionid=29021422&skin=hudoc-en. Accessed 1 September 2009.

[90] *Kononov v. Latvia* (Application no. 36376/04) European Court of Human Rights Chamber judgment 24 July 2008, para 42. http://cmiskp.echr.coe.int/tkp197/view.asp?item=1&portal=hbkm&action=html&highlight=Kononov%20%7C%20v%20%7C%20Latvia&sessionid=29021422&skin=hudoc-en. Accessed 1 September 2009.

punishment statute barred. Both parties appealed to the Criminal Affairs Division of the Supreme Court.

The judgment of the Latgale Regional Court was subsequently quashed on 30 April 2004 on appeal to the Criminal Affairs Division of the Supreme Court and a conviction for 'war crimes' under Article 68-3 of the Latvian Criminal Code substituted instead. The Regional Court ruled that the applicant had committed: (i) war crimes within the meaning of the second paragraph, point (b), of Article 6 of the Charter of the International Military Tribunal for Nuremberg and (ii) 'grave breaches' within the meaning of Article 147 of the . . . Geneva Convention . . . given its findings that:

> . . . Thus, V. Kononov and the Partisans from the special group he commanded stole the weapons that had been delivered to enable the villagers to defend themselves and killed nine civilians from the village, burning six of them – including three women, one in the final stages of pregnancy – alive in the process. They also burnt down two farms.
>
> By attacking those nine civilians from the village of Mazie Bati, who had not taken part in the fighting, by stealing their weapons and killing them, V. Kononov and the Partisans under his command . . . committed an appalling violation of the laws and customs of war as set out in . . . the Hague Convention of . . . October 1907 . . . the Geneva Convention of 12 August 1949 relative to the Protection of Civilian Persons in Time of War . . . the Protocol Additional to the . . .Convention [Geneva Convention relative to the Protection of Civilian Persons in Time of War] and relating to the Protection of Victims of International Armed Conflicts adopted on 8 June 1977 . . . .[91]

In consideration of the applicant's advanced age, the Court imposed a sentence of one year eight months imprisonment against which the applicant's appeal was unsuccessful. Note that in the final judgment, the applicant was not convicted of the crime of pillage.

Proceedings of the European Court of Human Rights Chamber in Kononov v. Latvia

The Chamber began its analysis by reaffirming that in accord with the subsidiarity principle of the European Convention human rights system, it was *not* the Court's task to reinterpret the domestic courts' findings of fact or their interpretation and application of domestic law (regardless of whether or not that domestic law referenced also international law). Rather, the Chamber's task, it held, was to monitor whether the effects of the domestic courts' handling of the case complied with State obligations under the European Convention on Human Rights. However, the Chamber noted that under Article 7 of the European Convention, it had the power to assess whether domestic law was complied with and if not this in itself

[91] *Kononov v. Latvia* (Application no. 36376/04) European Court of Human Rights Chamber judgment 24 July 2008, para 44. http://cmiskp.echr.coe.int/tkp197/view.asp?item=1&portal=hbkm&action=html&highlight=Kononov%20%7C%20v%20%7C%20Latvia&sessionid=29021422&skin=hudoc-en. Accessed 1 September 2009.

would constitute a violation of the European Convention. The Chamber further contended that: "... a careful distinction needs to be drawn in the present case between the existence of the facts and their characterisation in law."[92] Hence, the Chamber held that while it accepted the final findings of fact of the Latvian Supreme Court decision of 30 April 2004 (which was upheld by the Latvian Supreme Court Senate) and which it considered to have resulted from a fair legal process, it was *not* bound to accept the legal characterization and legal import of those facts by those same courts:

> the Court can and must consider the characterisation of these events under domestic and international law in order to determine whether the guarantees contained in Article 7 of the Convention were applied in the applicant's case. *In performing that task, it is free to attribute to the facts of the case, as found to have been established on the evidence before it, a characterisation in law different from that given by the applicant or, if need be, to view the facts in a different manner* (emphasis added).[93]

The Chamber noted that Article 7 of the European Convention: (i) stipulates that only the law can define a crime, and prescribe a penalty (*nullum crimen, nulla poena sine lege*), (ii) prohibits retrospective application of the law to conduct that was not a crime under the relevant law at the time the conduct took place; and (iii) prohibits broad interpretation of the law, i.e. by analogy, that is to the detriment of the accused. The Court further noted that section 7(2) of the European Convention is an exceptional derogation of the principles set out in Article 7(1) so as to allow for the trial and punishment of perpetrators of war crimes and crimes against humanity.

The Chamber framed its task as one of deciding whether the applicant's conduct on 27 May 1944 constituted offences under domestic or international law which were formulated *at the material time* in such a way that they should have been understood to be offences by the applicant such that, furthermore, it would have been entirely foreseeable for the applicant that he would be charged with such offences at some point (the offences hence meeting the accessibility and foreseeability criteria for offences required under Article 7(1) of the European Convention on Human Rights). (Hence, the analysis did *not* proceed from the perspective of Article 7(2) of the European Convention). The Court noted that the applicant had been convicted under a new 6 April 1993 law that listed offences classified as 'war crimes' that were defined by the Supreme Court with reference to international conventions; namely (i) the Hague Convention of 1907, (ii) the Geneva Convention of 1949 relative to the Protection of Civilian

[92] *Kononov v. Latvia* (Application no. 36376/04) European Court of Human Rights Chamber judgment 24 July 2008, para 111. http://cmiskp.echr.coe.int/tkp197/view.asp?item=1&portal=hbkm&action=html&highlight=Kononov%20%7C%20v%20%7C%20Latvia&sessionid=29021422&skin=hudoc-en. Accessed 1 September 2009.

[93] *Kononov v. Latvia* (Application no. 36376/04) European Court of Human Rights Chamber judgment 24 July 2008, para 111. http://cmiskp.echr.coe.int/tkp197/view.asp?item=1&portal=hbkm&action=html&highlight=Kononov%20%7C%20v%20%7C%20Latvia&sessionid=29021422&skin=hudoc-en. Accessed 1 September 2009.

Persons in Time of War and (iii) the Protocol Additional to that Convention adopted in 1977.

The Chamber challenged the (Latvian) Criminal Affairs Division of the Supreme Court's reliance in the final judgment in *Kononov* on the two international conventions that were *not* in effect at the time the alleged war crime offences were committed (namely, the Geneva Convention of 1949 relative to the Protection of Civilian Persons in Time of War and the Protocol Additional to that Convention adopted in 1977). The reliance on international conventions for the definitions of the 'war crimes' listed as offences in the amended 1993 Latvian Criminal Code, according to the Chamber, meant that international and domestic law had come to form a single body of law in respect of the war crimes offences listed in the domestic criminal law:

> Indeed, the Court considers that in cases such as the applicant's, in which domestic criminal law refers to international law for the definition of the offence *the domestic and international provisions form, in practice, a single criminal norm that is attended by the guarantees of Article 7 § 1 of the Convention* [European Convention on Human Rights]. Accordingly, that provision operates to preclude the retrospective application of an international treaty to characterise an act or an omission as criminal (emphasis added).[94]

The Chamber noted that at the time of the offences, neither the U.S.S.R nor Latvia had signed the 1907 Hague Convention. However, the Court held that since the Hague Convention merely codified well established customary law and practice (regarding the rules of war for "civilized nations"), and reiterated the 1899 Hague Convention, its application to the armed conflict in *Kononov* was not a violation of Article 7(1) of the *European Convention on Human Rights* (which Article covers both written and unwritten law). The Chamber held then that the applicant and those under his command were combatants and the applicant was responsible to know the universal rules of war regarding acceptable conduct (*jus in bello*) and comply with them. The Chamber held that the applicant was, in the final analysis, convicted of war crimes as the head of a unit that committed certain acts but that it was unclear from the domestic court final ruling whether he himself had committed some or all of those acts. The Chamber relied on the following further points:

- The villagers had *not* been engaged in combat at the material time when the alleged offences by the applicant were committed.
- The murdered male villagers were *not* members of the Latvian auxiliary police.
- The male villages had received rifles and grenades from the Germans (though the Chamber held that it was irrelevant that they were not carrying the weapons when they were killed).

---

[94] *Kononov v. Latvia* (Application no. 36376/04) European Court of Human Rights Chamber judgment 24 July 2008, para 119. http://cmiskp.echr.coe.int/tkp197/view.asp?item=1&portal=hbkm&action=html&highlight=Kononov%20%7C%20v%20%7C%20Latvia&sessionid=29021422&skin=hudoc-en. Accessed 1 September 2009.

- The Latvian domestic courts and the government had not contested that the murdered villagers were collaborators of the Germans and likely responsible for the deaths of the Red Partisans (Major Chugunov and his group) and that they had been rewarded for the same.

The Chamber held that:

> For present purposes, it suffices for the Court to say that, in view of the conduct of these men and the conditions obtaining at the time in the region in question, *the applicant and the other Red Partisans had legitimate grounds for considering these farmers* ***not*** *as "peaceable inhabitants" – the term employed in the present case by the Supreme Court Senate – but as collaborators of the German Army* (emphasis added).[95]

The Chamber rejected the contention of the Criminal Affairs Division of the Latvian Supreme Court that the villagers had collaborated with the Nazis in an effort to protect themselves from the Red Partisans *while, at the same time*, suggesting that: "the villagers must have known that by siding with one of the belligerent parties [the Germans] they would be exposing themselves to a risk of reprisals by the other [the Red Partisans]".[96] The Chamber rejected the notion that the six male villagers killed by the applicant's unit were civilians and noted that the regulations appended to the 1907 Hague Convention did not define the term 'civilian' or 'civil population'. The Chamber held in regards to the issue of whether the villagers killed by the applicant's unit had civilian status that: (i) the domestic court in Kononov had defined the term 'civilian' relying on *retrospective* application of the definition contained in the *Geneva Convention of 1949 relative to the Protection of Civilian Persons in Time of War and the Protocol Additional to that Convention adopted in 1977* and that (ii) the presumption (contained in the aforementioned Convention) that any person who was not a combatant, or in respect of whom there was doubt on that point, must be considered a "civilian" was *not* in existence in 1944 at the time of the offences in the instant case (i.e. the aforesaid presumption was *not* part of customary law in 1944 according to the Chamber). The Chamber made reference to Article 5 of the *Geneva Convention of 12 August 1949 relative to the Protection of Civilian Persons in Time of War* which allowed certain exceptions to affording various rights and privileges to persons under the Convention who threatened the security of the State (*but which Article still guaranteed these persons humane treatment, a fair trial and restoration of their full rights under the Geneva Convention IV at the earliest point at which they were no longer*

[95] *Kononov v. Latvia* (Application no. 36376/04) European Court of Human Rights Chamber judgment 24 July 2008, para 129. http://cmiskp.echr.coe.int/tkp197/view.asp?item=1&portal=hbkm&action=html&highlight=Kononov%20%7C%20v%20%7C%20Latvia&sessionid=29021422&skin=hudoc-en. Accessed 1 September 2009.

[96] *Kononov v. Latvia* (Application no. 36376/04) European Court of Human Rights Chamber judgment 24 July 2008, para 130. http://cmiskp.echr.coe.int/tkp197/view.asp?item=1&portal=hbkm&action=html&highlight=Kononov%20%7C%20v%20%7C%20Latvia&sessionid=29021422&skin=hudoc-en. Accessed 1 September 2009.

a threat to State security).[97] The Chamber held it was *not* necessary in order to make a ruling in the case for it to resolve the dispute between the parties as to whether the applicant had been under order of an *ad hoc* military tribunal organised from among the detachment of Partisans.

The Chamber suggested that the applicant's unit was selective and surgical in its imposition of suffering on the villagers:

> After arriving at the homes of each of the six heads of family and searching their homes, the Partisans executed them only after rifles and grenades supplied by the Germans – tangible evidence of their collaboration – were found. Conversely, with the exception of the three women . . . all the villagers were spared. In particular, no young children in the village at the time of the attack – including the children of those who were executed – suffered . . . Lastly, only two houses, those belonging to Meikuls Krupniks and Bernards Šķirmants, were burnt down [in which four persons were burned alive].[98]
>
> The instant case concerned a targeted military operation consisting in the selective execution of armed collaborators of the Nazi enemy who were suspected on legitimate grounds of constituting a threat to the Red Partisans and whose acts had already caused the deaths of their comrades.[99]

The Chamber concluded that:

> . . . it has *not* been adequately demonstrated that the attack on 27 May 1944 was *per se* contrary to the laws and customs of war as codified by the Regulations appended to the Hague Convention of 1907. Accordingly . . . it concludes that there was *no* plausible legal basis in international law on which to convict the applicant for leading the unit responsible for the operation.[100]

As regards the three women who were murdered, one of whom was nine months pregnant, the Chamber held that if the women were equally as guilty as the male villagers for collaborating with the Germans (thus leading to the deaths of Major Chugunov and his group of Red Partisans), then the Court's analysis applies also in the case of the women (i.e. they were not civilians) and their murders did *not* amount to a violation of the rules of war. The Court also held that if, under the

---

[97]*Kononov v. Latvia* (Application no. 36376/04) European Court of Human Rights Chamber judgment 24 July 2008, para 131. http://cmiskp.echr.coe.int/tkp197/view.asp?item=1&portal=hbkm&action=html&highlight=Kononov%20%7C%20v%20%7C%20Latvia&sessionid=29021422&skin=hudoc-en. Accessed 1 September 2009.

[98]*Kononov v. Latvia* (Application no. 36376/04) European Court of Human Rights Chamber judgment 24 July 2008, para 132. http://cmiskp.echr.coe.int/tkp197/view.asp?item=1&portal=hbkm&action=html&highlight=Kononov%20%7C%20v%20%7C%20Latvia&sessionid=29021422&skin=hudoc-en. Accessed 1 September 2009.

[99]*Kononov v. Latvia* (Application no. 36376/04) European Court of Human Rights Chamber judgment 24 July 2008, para 134. http://cmiskp.echr.coe.int/tkp197/view.asp?item=1&portal=hbkm&action=html&highlight=Kononov%20%7C%20v%20%7C%20Latvia&sessionid=29021422&skin=hudoc-en. Accessed 1 September 2009.

[100]*Kononov v. Latvia* (Application no. 36376/04) European Court of Human Rights Chamber judgment 24 July 2008, para 137. http://cmiskp.echr.coe.int/tkp197/view.asp?item=1&portal=hbkm&action=html&highlight=Kononov%20%7C%20v%20%7C%20Latvia&sessionid=29021422&skin=hudoc-en. Accessed 1 September 2009.

domestic criminal code at the material time, the murders of the women constituted an ordinary offence (not a war crime), the prosecution and penalties were statute barred due to a time limitation period in regards those offences. The Court rejected as allegedly irrelevant to the issue of the limitation period (for reasons which will not be detailed here) the fact that criminal proceedings could be brought only in 1991 after Latvia regained its independence.

Most significantly, the Chamber *rejected* the Latvian government's position that it was necessary to consider the instant case from the perspective offered by Article 7(2) of the *European Convention on Human Rights* which it held established that the offences of the applicant were criminal according to the 'law of civilized nations' (i.e. in this instance the customary international rules of war):

> *Since it has examined the case under the first paragraph of Article 7, it does not consider it necessary also to examine it under the second paragraph.* In any event, even supposing that that paragraph was applicable in the instant case, the operation of 27 May 1944 cannot be regarded as "criminal according to the general principles of law recognised by civilised nations" (emphasis added).[101]

In summary then the Chamber held that: (i) the applicant could *not* have foreseen that his acts of 27 May 1944 constituted war crimes at the material time and there is therefore no basis in international law to convict him of such an offences and (ii) even if his conduct amounted to offences (i.e. intentional homicide, etc.) under the domestic criminal law at the material time their prosecution was statute barred. The applicant was awarded EUR 30,000 in respect of non-pecuniary damage as well as an award for certain costs and expenses.

B. Commentary on Kononov v. Latvia

1. **The issue of reprisals**: As in the Korbely case, the European Court of Human Rights, (in this instance the Chamber), erroneously appears to implicitly suggest that there is such a phenomenon acceptable under the customary rules of war as justified reprisals against persons who, at the relevant time – that is when the reprisal is executed – are *not* actively engaged in hostilities against the attackers and especially; when it is not even clear that those attacked are official organs or agents of the enemy State (recall that even the applicant characterized the victims as his compatriots). In fact, as has been discussed in the commentary under the Korbely case, reprisals as a form of revenge; especially when against persons who are not engaged in combat at the material time, is a violation of customary humanitarian law and the rules of war. Reprisals, furthermore, were prohibited also

---

[101]*Kononov v. Latvia* (Application no. 36376/04) European Court of Human Rights Chamber judgment 24 July 2008, para 147. http://cmiskp.echr.coe.int/tkp197/view.asp?item=1&portal=hbkm&action=html&highlight=Kononov%20%7C%20v%20%7C%20Latvia&sessionid=29021422&skin=hudoc-en. Accessed 1 September 2009.

in 1944 at the time of the offences in *Kononov*, at a minimum, under the unwritten rules of acceptable conduct in war.

Note that the Chamber, as mentioned, rejected the contention of the Criminal Affairs Division of the Latvian Supreme Court that the villagers had collaborated with the Nazis in an effort to protect themselves from the Red Partisans *while, at the same time*, suggesting that the villagers must have known that by (allegedly) siding with the Germans they would be exposing themselves to a risk of reprisals by the Red Partisans. Hence, the Chamber essentially tacitly characterizes the attack (which attack occurred on order of the applicant) against the villagers to be a revenge reprisal. If in fact the attack was a revenge reprisal then, for the reasons previously explained, such an attack would constitute a war crime under international customary law concerning what falls outside of acceptable conduct in war. Note also that it had *not* been proven, in any case, that the villagers were collaborators with the Nazis and responsible for the deaths of Major Chugunov and his group, (this was only a suspicion), and even if they were collaborators, reprisal against them without military necessity would be unlawful under international humanitarian law as is discussed below. In fact, the domestic courts had established that the Red Partisans had used violence against the villagers and held that: (i) under international law the villagers were entitled to protect themselves against attack even in war and that (ii) the fact that the villagers held night watches did *not* prove they were engaged in military actions (i.e. against the Red Partisans) as opposed to trying to protect their families.[102]

2. **On the issue of whether the villagers had the legal status of 'prisoners of war'**: In *Kononov*, if the applicant had considered the villagers in question, (rightly or wrongly), to have been 'combatants' who, though not engaged in the hostilities at the time, nevertheless, posed a *potential* continuing threat to the Red Partisans, there was ample opportunity to simply take them into custody as *prisoners of war*. As prisoners of war, the villagers would have been entitled to humane treatment as required under international customary humanitarian law pertaining to war situations which *customary law* was codified in the 1907 Hague Convention (Annex to the Convention Regulations Respecting the Laws and Customs of War on Land):

> Prisoners of war
> **Article 4**: Prisoners of war are in the power of the hostile Government, but not of the individuals or corps who capture them.
> *They must be humanely treated* (emphasis added).[103]

---

[102]*Kononov v. Latvia* (Application no. 36376/04) European Court of Human Rights Chamber judgment 24 July 2008, para 44. http://cmiskp.echr.coe.int/tkp197/view.asp?item=1&portal=hbkm &action=html&highlight=Kononov%20%7C%20v%20%7C%20Latvia&sessionid=29021422&skin =hudoc-en. Accessed 1 September 2009.

[103]Convention (IV) respecting the Laws and Customs of War on Land and its annex: Regulations concerning the Laws and Customs of War on Land. The Hague, 18 October 1907 (Article 4 of the annexed regulations). http://www.icrc.org/IHL.NSF/FULL/195?OpenDocument. Accessed 1 September 2009.

The villagers, however, though coming into the custody and control of the applicant's unit were *not* treated as prisoners of war. Note that *even if the villagers had been combatants or enemy civilians, they as captives of the Red Partisans would still have had the legal status of prisoners of war under Article 3 of the Annex to the 1907 Hague Convention and as such were entitled to, at a minimum, the basic protections of prisoners of war under the Convention (i.e. right to life; right to be protected from torture, etc.)* (Recall that the Chamber of the European Court of Human Rights held that the 1907 Hague Convention – given that it was a codification of international customary law – was applicable at the material time). Instead, the six male and three female villagers in question, (one of the women being nine months pregnant), were summarily murdered, several in the most horrendous of ways having been burned alive. This conduct by the applicant's commando unit was, in any case, inconsistent with the provisions of Article 22 of the annexed regulations to the 1907 Hague Convention that stipulates that there are limits to the means chosen regarding how the enemy is injured. Such an approach as was taken by the applicant's unit under his order was inconsistent, furthermore, with the applicant's claim (unproven) that he was under order from an ad hoc military tribunal to capture the villagers suspected of collaborating with the Germans so that they could be tried.

Note that the Chamber does *not* address the key issue of whether the villagers should have been regarded as 'prisoners of war'; while, at the same time, the Court acknowledged that this would be a vital determination in deciding the outcome of the case.[104] In contrast, the Chamber was only too ready to definitively classify the victims as collaborators with the Nazis though there was no definitive proof on the matter. The *legal status* of the victims – whether they were 'prisoners of war' *which legal status can apply to captured collaborators and combatants as well* – is an essential element of the characterization of the facts in the case. Recall that the Chamber stated it would be engaged in making characterizations of the facts in the case which it held was well within the ambit of its mandate in assessing State compliance with the European Convention.

3. **On the issue of killing the enemy by means unacceptable (those that inflict maximum suffering) and killing or wounding the enemy when he has no means of defense**: Even putting aside the issue of whether the villagers in question had the legal status of 'prisoners of war' with all of the entitlement to Hague Convention protections, issues yet arise regarding the treatment meted out to the captured villagers by the Red Partisan commandos under the applicant's command and order. Several of the villagers were intentionally burned alive thus inflicting maximum suffering. Article 22 of the annex to the 1907 Hague Convention stipulates that there are limits to the means by which injury may be inflicted on the enemy. Clearly, Article 23(e) of the annex articulates that unnecessary suffering

[104] *Kononov v. Latvia* (Application no. 36376/04) European Court of Human Rights Chamber judgment 24 July 2008, para 38. http://cmiskp.echr.coe.int/tkp197/view.asp?item=1&portal=hbkm&action=html&highlight=Kononov%20%7C%20v%20%7C%20Latvia&sessionid=29021422&skin=hudoc-en. Accessed 1 September 2009.

is not to be imposed on the enemy. While burning the enemy alive is not explicitly listed as a means prohibited, this can be inferred from the legal intent of the following Articles of the 1907 Hague Convention (annexed regulations) taken together: Article 22 (stipulating that the lawful means of injuring the enemy are *not* unlimited); Article 23(d) (stipulating that declaring that no mercy will be given is prohibited); and Article 23(e) (stipulating that intentionally using means to inflict maximum suffering is prohibited). Recall that the Chamber seems to find particularly laudatory the fact that the suffering imposed by the applicant's unit was selective and that the children of the victims were not themselves attacked. Indeed, the Court makes the claim that essentially the children were spared suffering: "In particular, no young children in the village at the time of the attack – including the children of those who were executed – suffered."[105] Yet, the facts are uncontested that three of the children were eye witnesses to their parents' murders and others heard tell of the events from eyewitnesses; no doubt inflicting unfathomable suffering on these vulnerable indirect victims.

Note also that Article 23(c) of the 1907 Hague Convention (annexed regulations) stipulates that wounding or killing the enemy when that enemy no longer has a means of defence is prohibited. Recall in this regard that nine villagers in all were murdered by the applicant's unit though the victims posed no threat to the security of the Red Partisan unit once they were in custody and the weaponry in their homes had been confiscated. At the point that the villagers became captives, they were equivalent to those who surrender in respect of the fact that they, too, had no means of defense against their captors.

The aforementioned principles then are incorporated in the spirit of the law expressed in the provisions of the annex to the 1907 Hague Convention listed below. Note that the extreme gravity of the *particular* crimes contemplated is reflected in the wording that such conduct is "especially forbidden":

> CHAPTER I
> Means of injuring the enemy . . .
> **Art. 22**. The right of belligerents to adopt means of injuring the enemy is *not unlimited.*
> **Art. 23**. In addition to the prohibitions provided by special Conventions, it is *especially forbidden;*
> . . .
> (c) To kill or wound an enemy who . . . *having no longer means of defence . . .*
> (d) *To declare that no quarter will be given*;
> (e) To employ arms, projectiles, or material *calculated to cause unnecessary suffering; . . . .*[106]

[105]*Kononov v. Latvia* (Application no. 36376/04) European Court of Human Rights Chamber judgment 24 July 2008, para 132. http://cmiskp.echr.coe.int/tkp197/view.asp?item=1&portal=hbkm&action=html&highlight=Kononov%20%7C%20v%20%7C%20Latvia&sessionid=29021422&skin=hudoc-en. Accessed 1 September 2009.

[106]Convention (IV) respecting the Laws and Customs of War on Land and its annex: Regulations concerning the Laws and Customs of War on Land. The Hague, 18 October 1907 (Article 22, and Article 23(c)(d)(e) of the annexed regulations). http://www.icrc.org/IHL.NSF/FULL/195?OpenDocument. Accessed 1 September 2009.

4. **The prohibition on killing or wounding treacherously individuals belonging to the enemy group**: Article 23(b) of the annexed regulations to the 1907 Hague Convention prohibits killing or wounding treacherously individuals belonging to the enemy group. In the instant case, the applicant's commando unit dressed as German soldiers as a ploy in carrying out their attack on the villagers of Mazie Bati. However, the Chamber of the European Court of Human Rights held that this did *not* amount to 'treachery', but rather was permissible under Article 24 of the annexed regulations to the 1907 Hague Convention which regards as lawful "ruses of war and the employment of measures necessary for obtaining information about the enemy and the country . . . ."[107] The Chamber stated that: ". . . the domestic courts failed to explain in what respect the operation was considered to have been performed 'treacherously' within the meaning of Article 23 of the Hague Regulations and not as a legitimate 'ruse of war', as authorised by Article 24."[108] It would seem, however, with respect, more than obvious that the use of a ruse in the instant case to effect the massacre of nine persons may constitute treachery given that: (i) the victims were *not* actively engaged in combat at the time of their capture and murder, but were preparing for a religious event (Pentecost); (ii) were captured while *not* in possession of weapons on their person, and (iii) were murdered after confiscation of the weaponry in their homes. *The **alleged** legitimate ruse in the instant case then was used as a vehicle to inflict unnecessary suffering and death on persons who were taken into custody without armed resistance and who could justifiably have been regarded as prisoners of war and treated humanely if they were not to be considered simply as civilians.* The foregoing is the key point relating to the matter of possible treachery or the illegitimate use of a ruse of war. (Contrast the context for the use of deception in the instant case with a ruse used in the service of *protecting* human life where most in the international community would be loathe to classify the deception as treachery).[109]

There was, furthermore, no definitive evidence according to the domestic courts on the issue of whether in fact there was *organized* resistance from the village and whether or not the village could be considered a 'defended village' in that sense. The domestic courts rejected the notion that night watches constituted evidence of

[107]Convention (IV) respecting the Laws and Customs of War on Land and its annex: Regulations concerning the Laws and Customs of War on Land. The Hague, 18 October 1907 (Article 24). http://www.icrc.org/IHL.NSF/FULL/195?OpenDocument. Accessed 1 September 2009. See also *Kononov v. Latvia* (Application no. 36376/04) European Court of Human Rights Chamber judgment 24 July 2008, para 134–137. http://cmiskp.echr.coe.int/tkp197/view.asp?item=1&portal=hbkm
&action=html&highlight=Kononov%20%7C%20v%20%7C%20Latvia&sessionid=29021422&skin=hudoc-en. Accessed 1 September 2009.

[108]*Kononov v. Latvia* (Application no. 36376/04) European Court of Human Rights Chamber judgment 24 July 2008, para 134. http://cmiskp.echr.coe.int/tkp197/view.asp?item=1&portal=hbkm&action=html&highlight=Kononov%20%7C%20v%20%7C%20Latvia&sessionid=29021422&skin=hudoc-en. Accessed 1 September 2009.

[109]Dehn (2008, pp. 627–653).

organized military resistance. Since the nine villagers captured offered no resistance, the issue of 'defended' versus 'undefended village' is irrelevant to the question of: (i) whether there was any justification for the conduct of the applicant's unit under his order and (ii) whether or not that conduct was treacherous under the circumstances insofar as the fact that the unit summarily extinguished the lives of nine captive villagers. Clearly, the unit's conduct in murdering the nine villagers and burning two of their houses with numerous persons inside is inconsistent with the requirement of Article 46 of the Hague Convention annexed regulations requiring that: "Family honors and rights, individual lives and private property . . . must be respected"[110] Further, in the instant case, it does not appear that the ruse was used strictly to "obtain information about the enemy and the country . . ."[111] as required under Article 24 of the regulations annexed to the 1907 Hague Convention.

5. **The issue of whether or not the murdered villagers were civilians**: The Chamber challenged the domestic court's findings of fact that the murdered villagers were civilians and held that the definition of 'civilian' under Geneva Convention IV could not be applied retrospectively. Recall that the Chamber of the European Court of Human Rights maintained that the notion, as articulated in Geneva Convention IV, that: (i) anyone who was not a 'combatant' was a 'civilian', and that (ii) where there was doubt, the person should be considered a civilian, was *not* part of customary law in 1944 when the applicant's alleged offences took place. The Chamber, furthermore, made reference to Article 5 of the *Geneva Convention of 12 August 1949 relative to the Protection of Civilian Persons in Time of War (Geneva Convention IV)* which allowed certain exceptions to affording various rights and privileges to persons under the Convention who threatened the security of the State. *However, Article 5 of Geneva Convention IV still guaranteed these persons humane treatment, a fair trial and restoration of their full rights under the Geneva Convention IV at the earliest point at which they were no longer a threat to State security.* The Chamber appeared to suggest that the murdered villagers fell under the exemption provided by Article 5 of Geneva Convention IV (so that they were *not* clearly civilians that belonged to the 'peaceful population' entitled to the full protections guaranteed under the Convention), but failed to mention that Article 5 still required that persons who had the legal status contemplated under Article 5 of Geneva Convention IV be treated humanely and be afforded due process.

Pinzauti discusses numerous examples indicating that *as of 1944* there was in customary law and codified law already a prevalent notion of 'civilian' defined *a contrario* to the category of 'combatant' (that is, the notion that persons belonged to

---

[110]Convention (IV) respecting the Laws and Customs of War on Land and its annex: Regulations concerning the Laws and Customs of War on Land. The Hague, 18 October 1907 (Article 46 of the annexed regulations). http://www.icrc.org/IHL.NSF/FULL/195?OpenDocument. Accessed 1 September 2009.

[111]Convention (IV) respecting the Laws and Customs of War on Land and its annex: Regulations concerning the Laws and Customs of War on Land. The Hague, 18 October 1907 (Article 24). http://www.icrc.org/IHL.NSF/FULL/195?OpenDocument. Accessed 1 September 2009.

one group (i.e. combatant) or, by default, to the other (i.e. civilian)).[112] Certainly, core international humanitarian law principles such as Article 46 of the Hague Convention annexed regulations did *not* permit the gratuitous murder of civilians in 1944 *even if the civilians were collaborators* if they posed no security risk at the time of the murders and other viable options in the military circumstances were available at the relevant time (i.e. taking them as prisoners of war for instance).

It is noteworthy that the domestic courts made the following finding of fact on the issue of whether or not the villagers killed by the applicant's unit on orders of the applicant were in reality civilians. (*The Chamber did not comment on this finding in relation to the crucial issue of the actual legal status of the murdered villagers at the time of their murders*):

> Following the restoration of Latvian independence, all those killed were rehabilitated. It was stated in their rehabilitation certificates *that they [had] not committed 'crimes against peace [or] humanity, criminal offences ... or taken part ... in political repression ... by the Nazi regime'*.... (emphasis added).[113]

A great deal of emphasis was placed by the majority of the Chamber in *Kononov* on the fact that the victims were, in its estimation of the facts, likely collaborators of the Nazis though: (i) this was *not* established fact and, in any case, (ii) irrelevant to the analysis of the lawfulness of the applicant's conduct given the absence of military necessity for the murders or for the gratuitous infliction of extreme suffering on the victims. The impression created, based on the Chamber majority approach which focused on the victims as probable collaborators, inadvertent as it may be, is that 'lady justice' need not be blindfolded to ensure equity under the law (i.e. the right to due process for all without exception even in respect of suspected or actual collaborators).

Note in regard to the issue of possible collaboration, that dissenting Judge Bjorgvinsson makes an important point on the issue. He highlights the difficult situation in which the villagers found themselves; caught as they were between two international States each vying for control of Latvian territory as occupying powers with both States having had inflicted violence on the villagers:

> The aim of the Soviet Union was not to "liberate" Latvia from Nazi Germany and re-establish the country as an independent sovereign State, but to regain control over Latvia as one of the Soviet Socialist Republics. *History teaches us that such a situation facilitates conditions of war where both powers are inclined to be on the look out for likely collaborators with the enemy among the people of the occupied territory and use their own criteria – military, political or otherwise – to determine who should or should not be considered a collaborator, in accordance with their own aims and interests. However, from the Latvian standpoint both powers actions [Soviet and German] were based on an equally illegitimate claim for control over their territory*. It was under these conditions that the

[112]Pinzauti (2008, footnote 15).

[113]Kononov v. Latvia (Application no. 36376/04) European Court of Human Rights Chamber judgment 24 July 2008, para 44. http://cmiskp.echr.coe.int/tkp197/view.asp?item=1&portal=hbkm&action=html&highlight=Kononov%20%7C%20v%20%7C%20Latvia&sessionid=29021422&skin=hudoc-en. Accessed 1 September 2009.

killings in Mazie Bati took place. *Put in this historical context these atrocities were inflicted upon Latvian civilians by men under the command of the military representative of the Soviet Union, which was a hostile occupying power, not a liberator, of Latvia* (emphasis added).[114]

6. **The pregnant mother and her unborn**: The Chamber assigned no special status to the pregnant woman and her unborn in terms of their entitlement to protection. The latter were burned alive in clear violation of the regulation annexed to the 1907 Hague Convention regarding the killing and torture of prisoners who posed no threat at the time of their capture. The conduct of the applicant's unit under order of the applicant in regards to the woman who was nine months pregnant, furthermore, violates Article 16 of Geneva Convention IV which stipulates that "... expectant mothers, shall be the object of particular protection and respect."[115] It has been suggested that such principles of humanitarian law were already customary law in 1944 at the time of the impugned conduct of the applicant.[116]

7. **The Chamber majority deviated from past European Court of Human Rights analytic practice in cases involving alleged State violations of Article 7 of the European Convention**: The dissenting judges in *Kononov* (Fura-Sandstrom, David Thor Bjorgvinsson and Ziemele) noted that the majority had deviated from the Court's normal course in such cases ***by declining to examine under Article 7(2)*** whether the applicant had been properly convicted of war crimes in that the applicant should have been aware that his conduct constituted such an offence at the time it was committed (i.e. the offence met the required foreseeability criterion since it violated the laws of civilized nations). The dissenting judges noted also that: (i) in the previous case law of the European Court of Human Rights, the prosecution and punishment of crimes that had occurred many years previous was lawful where the offences were covered under Article 7(2) of the European Convention and (ii) the offences covered under Article 7(2) were not confined to those committed by the Nazis during World War II.

There appears to have been no explanation offered by the Chamber for its declining to examine *under Article 7(2)* the lawfulness of a conviction for war crimes, i.e. its compatibility or incompatibility with Article 7(2) of the European Convention *which was precisely intended by the drafters of the European Convention to address such specific alleged offences in particular and the special*

[114]Joint dissenting opinion of Fura_Sandstrom, David Thor Bjorgvinsson and Ziemele in Kononov v. Latvia (Application no. 36376/04) European Court of Human Rights Chamber judgment 24 July 2008, para 2 of the dissenting opinion at pp. 10–11. http://cmiskp.echr.coe.int/tkp197/view.asp?item=1&portal=hbkm&action=html&highlight=Kononov%20%7C%20v%20%7C%20Latvia&sessionid=29021422&skin=hudoc-en. Accessed 1 September 2009.

[115]Geneva Convention IV relative to the Protection of Civilian Persons in Time of War, Geneva, 12 August 1949 (common Article 3). http://www.icrc.org/ihl.nsf/385ec082b509e76c41256739003e636d/6756482d86146898c125641e004aa3c5. Accessed 1 September 2009.

[116]Pinzauti (2008, footnote 15).

considerations that must attend to an examination of such offences in determining whether their prosecution is lawful.

8. **Considering Article 7(2) of the European Convention on Human Rights and the core principle of humanitarian law**: In the instant case, the Chamber took the position that since it had considered the case under Article 7(1) of the European Convention it therefore did *not* need to analyze the case from the perspective of Article 7(2). However, Article 7(2) provides for retrospective application of the law in the domestic criminal code when it comes to war crimes, genocide and crimes against humanity (violations of the law of civilized nations) and, hence, it is a constraint on the prohibition against retrospective application of the law stipulated in Article 7(1) of the European Convention. Article 7(2) of the European Convention, as explained by the domestic courts in Korbely, requires only that the offences were crimes under *international* law – unwritten customary or codified – at the time they were committed in order for there to be a lawful prosecution (assuming a fair trial, etc.). Hence, an analysis *at the outset* under Article 7(2) appears a necessity where the applicant has been convicted of international crimes as in *Kononov* and an alleged State violation of Article 7(1) is claimed by the applicant.

Recall that the Chamber majority in analyzing the case made much of the fact that the domestic courts relied in part on the 1949 Geneva Conventions and additional Protocol I to the 1949 Geneva Conventions which postdated the offences for which the applicant was convicted. The aforementioned instruments clearly define the category of 'civilian' *versus* non-civilian or 'combatant', while the Hague Convention of 1907, upon which the domestic courts also relied, did not. It would appear that the Chamber majority attempts in *Kononov* to invoke the prohibition against retroactive application of the law under Article 7(1) of the European Convention, *not* by suggesting that war crimes were not already prohibited in customary law in 1944, but by suggesting that the distinction between 'civilian' and 'combatant' – as understood in the 1949 Geneva Conventions and Protocol I to the 1949 Geneva Conventions – was not in existence in 1944. *Such a suggestion would not have been possible had the analysis been carried out under Article 7(2) rather than Article 7(1) since Article 7(2) presumes that customary international humanitarian law and the rules of acceptable conduct in war are fundamentally based on practice and an intuitive knowledge of who is a combatant versus who is a civilian or otherwise 'protected person' (i.e. prisoner of war who may previously have been a combatant, collaborator, spy or previous combatant now 'hors de combat' due to injury, surrender, capture etc.) and what constitutes an atrocity.* In this regard, note that the preamble of the 1907 Hague Convention, (referred to by the dissenting judges in *Kononov*), appears to reference such an intuitive sense of humanitarian principles when it speaks of the "public conscience" and the need to behave in war in a manner dictated by "the laws of humanity" whether specifically written (codified) or not:

> the Preamble to the 1907 Hague Convention ... includes the so-called Martens clause, which provides: "The high contracting Parties clearly *do not intend that unforeseen cases should, in the absence of a written undertaking, be left to the arbitrary judgment of military commanders*". It goes on to explain: "In cases not included in the Regulations adopted by

> them, the *inhabitants and the belligerents remain under the protection and the rule of the principles of the law of nations, as they result from the usages established among civilized peoples, from the laws of humanity, and the dictates of the public conscience*" (emphasis added).[117]

It would seem safe to assume that a reasonable person would understand that summary execution of captives *without military necessity* and burning captives alive to inflict maximal suffering is likely incompatible with customary humanitarian law. Though one can readily understand the rage likely experienced by the applicant and his commando subordinates in their concluding (rightly or wrongly) that the villagers had collaborated with the maniacal Nazi regime; that outrage does *not* serve as a legitimate rationale; justification or affirmative defense for the violation of international customary law regarding acceptable conduct in war.

The Chamber essentially attempted to define away the war crimes offence at the heart of the Kononov case by: (i) substituting its own findings of fact (labeled as 're-characterizing' the facts) for that of the domestic courts in regards to the legal status of the victims and *retroactively reclassifying them as 'combatants' as opposed to 'civilians' without proof* that they had actually been engaged in military operations and *without applying the criteria in Article 1 of the 1907 Hague Convention* that distinguish 'combatants' from 'non-combatants' (the former being under command of a superior, having a fixed emblem that can be seen at a distance; carrying arms openly and carrying out operations in manner consistent with the laws and customs of war); (ii) holding, by implication, that the victims were *not* 'protected persons' as *prisoners of war* (whether they were formerly combatants or civilians) at the time of their capture by the applicant's unit of commandos, and (iii) *declining* to review the facts from the perspective of Article 7(2) of the European Convention which holds that the customary rules of war prohibit the murder and torture of persons who pose no threat at the time such conduct is perpetrated against them (i.e. as the foregoing conduct is a violation of the laws of civilized nations). *With respect, it may be argued that the majority Chamber decision in Kononov inadvertently undermines fundamental humanitarian law by suggesting that collaborators or even alleged collaborators are ipso facto not protected persons regardless of the circumstances in which they are apprehended.*

9. **On the European Court of Human Rights award of reparations for non-pecuniary damages in the Chamber judgment in *Kononov***: The applicant in the estimation of the Chamber majority had requested an exorbitant amount in non-pecuniary damage in the millions of Euros. In the end, however, non-pecuniary damages were awarded no doubt adding salt to the wounds of the surviving relatives of the villagers massacred.

---

[117] Joint dissenting opinion of Fura_Sandstrom, David Thor Bjorgvinsson and Ziemele in Kononov v. Latvia (Application no. 36376/04) European Court of Human Rights Chamber judgment 24 July 2008, at para 10 of the Joint Dissenting opinion referring to the preamble of the 1907 Hague Convention. http://cmiskp.echr.coe.int/tkp197/view.asp?item=1&portal=hbkm&action=html&highlight=Kononov%20%7C%20v%20%7C%20Latvia&sessionid=29021422&skin=hudoc-en. Accessed 1 September 2009.

Note that: "... traditionally, the Court [European Court of Human Rights] has recognised *that a judgment that establishes a violation of the ECHR [European Convention on Human Rights] has a 'declaratory' character ....*"[118] The award of damages in the instant case further serves to solidify the European Court of Human Rights Chamber majority's version of history based on the Chamber's 'characterizations of the fact' (or 'findings of fact'; depending on one's perspective), and its substitution of the same for the domestic courts' 'findings of fact', or 'characterizations of fact' in regards to: (i) whether the victims were civilians or otherwise 'protected persons'; (ii) whether the massacred villagers were collaborators with the Nazis, and (iii) whether the villagers murdered were the victims of 'war crimes' ordered by the applicant. The implications then go much beyond a ruling simply on whether Latvia had violated Article 7(1) of the European Convention in *Kononov* as important as undoubtedly is that outcome. The case represents, *to some extent*, a judicially constructed 'truth' as to the alleged historical facts (*as is the case with all court judgments regardless of the court*). However, that judicially constructed 'truth' is then open to question in terms of the extent to which it, in reality, coincides with the actual historical truth. It should be well appreciated that the Court's pronouncement on what it considers constitutes the truth in such cases is not just some necessary judicial and intellectual exercise, but rather a process the outcome of which profoundly impacts not just the lives of the parties concerned, but the international community itself. In this regard, it is relevant to note that some legal scholars, such as Naqvi, have discussed the notion of a possible *right to truth* in international law.[119] Indeed, the U.N. Commission on Human Right's resolution 2005/66 "recognizes the importance of respecting and ensuring the right to truth so as to contribute to ending impunity and to promote and protect human rights."[120] The European Court of Human Rights hence carries an awesome burden in this regard.

References

Coleandrea V (2007) On the power of the European Court of Human Rights to order specific non-monetary measures: some remarks in light of the *Assanidze, Broniowski* and *Sejdovic* cases. Hum Rights Law Rev 7:396–411

Council of Europe (2007) European Court of Human Rights: dialogue between judges. Council of Europe, Strasbourg, pp. 1–94. http://www.echr.coe.int/NR/rdonlyres/430DA534-F265-4407-9717-C43F3ADCA183/0/Dialogue_between_judges_2007.pdf. Accessed 6 August 2009

Dehn JC (2008) Permissible perfidy? Analysing the Columbian hostage rescue, the capture of rebel leaders and the world's reaction. J Int'l Crim Just 6:627–653

German Law Journal (2001) Victor's justice: Court of Human Rights and the conviction of East German leaders. German Law J 2(6). http://www.germanlawjournal.com/article.php?id=62. Accessed 20 August 2009

[118]Coleandrea (2007, p. 397).

[119]Naqvi (2006, pp. 245–273).

[120]Naqvi (2006, p. 248).

Heintze H (2004) On the relationship between human rights law protection and international humanitarian law. Int'l Rev Red Cross 86:789–814

Malksoo L (2001) Soviet genocide? Communist mass deportations in the Baltic States and international law. Leiden J Int'l Law 14:757–787

Naqvi Y (2006) The right to truth in international law: fact or fiction? Int'l Rev Red Cross 88:245–273

Pinzauti G (2008) The European Court of Human Rights' incidental application of international criminal law and humanitarian law: a critical discussion of *Kononov v. Latvia*. J Int'l Crim Just 6:1043–1060

Scheffer D, Cox A (2008) The constitutionality of the Rome Statute of the International Criminal Court. J Crim Law Criminol 98:983–1068

PART IV: The Importance of Moral Legitimacy in International Human Rights Court Rulings

Abstract In this part, we consider the importance of the 'moral legitimacy' of the rulings of the European Court of Human Rights, and international human rights courts generally. 'Moral legitimacy', in this context, is held to derive from the court protecting or advancing fundamental international human rights guarantees and fostering accountability at the State level for violations of those guarantees; while indirectly, where feasible, (i.e. where the identity of the perpetrators is known or discoverable), also contributing to ending impunity for the individual perpetrators of atrocity and other human rights abuses. The Inter-American Court of Human Rights' case of *Moiwana Village v. Suriname* is discussed as an example of an international human rights court demonstrating moral integrity where it could just as easily have denied access to a judicial remedy through the Inter-American human rights court system to the victims of crimes against humanity on an unjustly under-inclusive interpretation of its jurisdiction. The impact of such cases on the internationalization of the rule of law is discussed. Also addressed is the need for all levels of the international community to demand moral legitimacy in the rulings of the international human rights courts rather than to presume that characteristic as ubiquitous and essentially inherent in such rulings.

I. A Few Preliminary Points

In these concluding remarks this author confronts the fundamental question which it is difficult to sidestep in the context of the highly troubling and contentious cases discussed in this book. *That question is whether moral legitimacy should be considered a necessary requirement for rulings of the international human rights courts where moral legitimacy is understood to derive from the advancement or safeguarding of universal human rights guarantees and fostering an end to impunity wherever feasible.* The argument to be presented proposes that the answer to the foregoing question should be in the affirmative. Whether the European Court of Human Rights' controversial rulings discussed in this book have moral legitimacy

S.C. Grover, *The European Court of Human Rights as a Pathway to Impunity for International Crimes*,
DOI 10.1007/978-3-642-10799-3_4, © Springer-Verlag Berlin Heidelberg 2010

as here defined is ultimately for the reader to decide for him or herself, but hopefully the reader, based on the discussion in the forgoing pages, will have been encouraged to ponder the question rather than assuming such alleged moral legitimacy of the rulings to be an axiomatic given.

At a minimum, we can agree that there are universal human rights guarantees or norms against genocide, crimes against humanity and war crimes and these concluding remarks, as the discussion of the cases covered in this book, will focus on the latter. Those universal norms were already largely understood and accepted in customary international law before they were codified in part or in whole (i.e. in the 1949 Geneva Conventions such as Geneva Convention IV,[1] the Protocols Additional to the 1949 Geneva Conventions,[2] the Rome Statute,[3] the U.N. Convention Against Torture and other Cruel, Inhuman or Degrading Treatment or Punishment[4] and in other international legal instruments). The implicit presumptions underlying the provocative notion that moral legitimacy is a necessary requirement for international human rights court rulings include the following: (a) moral legitimacy is *not* intrinsic to all decisions and judgments of the international human rights courts simply by virtue of the fact that the rulings emanate from such prestigious and respected international bodies; and (b) neither philosophical appeals to moral or cultural relativism, nor rationales couched in terms of overly restrictive interpretations of the alleged dictates of court enabling statutes or conventions or rules of the court, nor reliance on the alleged impenetrable over-extended boundaries of State sovereignty can negate the necessity for moral legitimacy in the rulings of international human rights courts. All of humanity has a stake in the rulings of the international human rights courts in that fundamental human rights are universal and must not be eroded in any context. Furthermore, the rulings of the international human rights courts have an impact on international law more generally. This is no more the case than when the decisions and judgments of those courts are pronounced in respect of cases in which genocide, crimes against humanity and/or war crimes are clearly or potentially implicated. The international community, it is

[1]Geneva Convention IV relative to the Protection of Civilian Persons in Time of War (see common Article 3). http://www.icrc.org/ihl.nsf/385ec082b509e76c41256739003e636d/6756482d8614689 8c125641e004aa3c5. Accessed 26 September 2009.

[2]Protocol Additional to the Geneva Conventions of 12 August 1949, and relating to the Protection of Victims of International Armed Conflicts (Protocol I) and Additional Protocol II to the Geneva Conventions of 12 August 1949 and relating to the Protection of Victims on Non-International Armed Conflicts, (Protocols I and II entered into force 7 December 1978). http://www.icrc.org/ Web/Eng/siteeng0.nsf/html/genevaconventions. Accessed 26 September 2009.

[3]Rome Statute of the International Criminal Court (Text of the Rome Statute circulated as document A/CONF.183/9 of 17 July 1998 and corrected by procès-verbaux of 10 November 1998, 12 July 1999, 30 November 1999, 8 May 2000, 17 January 2001 and 16 January 2002). The Statute entered into force on 1 July 2002. http://www.icc-cpi.int/NR/rdonlyres/EA9AEFF7-5752-4F84-BE94-0A655EB30E16/0/Rome_Statute_English.pdf. Accessed 26 September 2009.

[4]United Nations Convention Against Torture and Other Cruel, Inhuman or Degrading Treatment or Punishment. U.N. General Assembly Resolution 39/46, 10 December 1984, entering into force 26 June 1987. http://www.unhchr.ch/html/menu3/b/h_cat39.htm. Accessed 17 June 2009.

contended, hence, has not only the right, but also the duty to demand nothing less than moral legitimacy in the rulings of the international human rights courts.

Let us begin this discussion then by considering a case in which an international human rights court was confronted with a legal dilemma which could have been resolved either with an *overly restrictive* interpretation of its jurisdiction or one which ensured moral legitimacy as previously defined. Thankfully, in that instance, the Court (on the view expressed here) chose the path which delivered genuine justice to the victims of atrocity. The case which is alluded to in the foregoing is *Moiwana Village v. Suriname*; an Inter-American Court of Human Rights' case. We will examine the latter case and the lessons it holds on the issue of moral legitimacy in the rulings of international human rights courts generally. We will consider also aspects of the international reaction to the decision in *Moiwana Village v. Suriname* including claims by some legal academics that the Inter-American Court overstepped its bounds in the context of that case.

II. Moiwana Village v. Suriname (IACHR): An Exemplary Case Regarding Moral Legitimacy in International Human Rights Court Rulings

A. *Case 1: Moiwana Village v. Suriname Inter-American Court of Human Rights Judgement of 15 June 2005*

Background and Commission Proceedings

The Inter-American Commission on Human Rights (which had received the Moiwana Village case in July 1997) submitted the case against Suriname (hereafter referred to as 'the State') to the Inter-American Court of Human Rights on 20 December 2002.[5] The Commission alleged that the State had violated Articles 25 (Right to Judicial Protection), 8 (Right to a Fair Trial) and 1(1) (Obligation to Respect Rights) of the *American Convention on Human Rights* ('the *American Convention*') thus adversely affecting certain former residents of Moiwana Village who had survived a massacre perpetrated by agents of the State. The complainants had survived a massacre of over 40 Moiwana villagers (who belonged to the Maroon ethnic group) by the National Army of Suriname (the Army taking retaliation for previous rebel attacks allegedly linked in some way to the Maroon peoples). The massacre occurred 29 November 1986 *prior to Suriname becoming a State Party to the American Convention* (Suriname became a party to the *American Convention*, thus also accepting the jurisdiction of the Inter-American Court,

[5]*Moiwana Village v. Suriname* Inter-American Human Rights Court Judgement of 15 June 2005. http://www.forestpeoples.org/documents/law_hr/suriname_iachr_moiwana_judg_jun05_eng.pdf. Accessed 26 September 2009.

on 12 November 1987 *approximately one year after the massacre at Moiwana Village*). The Army also razed the village and the survivors fled into the forest with some becoming internally displaced persons and others making their way to French Guiana. The survivors had not returned to their home territory in part for fear that their security could not be ensured.

There had been no adequate investigation of the case, nor prosecution of the perpetrators despite the passing of an inordinate period of time (though there had been *at least* one aborted attempt by certain officials to investigate). This then led to the complaint first to the Inter-American Human Rights Commission (brought on behalf of the victims by the human rights NGO Moiwana 1986) and then to the Inter-American Court of Human Rights fully 16 years after the massacre.

In 1993, a mass grave had been discovered in Moiwana Village containing several of the disappeared victims of the massacre (five adults and four children). The bodies were exhumed by a pathologist and civil and military police. Nevertheless, an amnesty law adopted by Suriname in 1992 pertaining to the perpetrators of the massacre remained in effect and no prosecutions were forthcoming. The Inter-American Commission found the complaints to have merit and recommended that Suriname be ordered to properly investigate the massacre and to bring the perpetrators to justice in the domestic criminal courts in conformity with Suriname's laws and, in addition, pay reparations to the surviving victims of the massacre. The Commission also recommended that the Suriname 1992 amnesty law be repealed insofar as crimes involving human rights violations and 'crimes against humanity' were concerned. As Suriname declined to provide any evidence that it had complied with the Commission's recommendations, the Inter-American Commission submitted the case to the Inter-American Court of Human Rights.

Proceedings Before the Inter-American Court of Human Rights

The Commission submitted to the Court that:

> ... while the attack [29 November 1986] itself predated Suriname's ratification of the American Convention and its recognition of the Court's jurisdiction [12 November 1987], *the alleged denial of justice and displacement of the Moiwana community occurring subsequent to the attack* [ongoing violations] *comprise the subject matter of the application* (emphasis added).[6]

The State, in response, challenged the *ratione temporis* jurisdiction of the Inter-American Court of Human Rights over the Moiwana case. The State held that the Commission had wrongly considered Suriname to be a State Party to the *American Convention* as pertained to the whole case and had applied the *American Convention ex post facto* (that is, retroactively to a set of events that occurred before the

[6]*Moiwana Village v. Suriname* Inter-American Human Rights Court Judgement of 15 June 2005, para 3. http://www.forestpeoples.org/documents/law_hr/suriname_iachr_moiwana_judg_jun05_eng.pdf. Accessed 26 September 2009.

State had ratified the *American Convention on Human Rights* or had officially accepted the jurisdiction of the Inter-American Court of Human Rights). The State, therefore, took the position that the petitioner's evidence was allegedly *not* evidence of treaty (*American Convention*) violations and, on that basis, the petition should have been dismissed as per Article 47(b) of the *American Convention*. The State then suggested that as there *allegedly* were no treaty violations in the first instance arising from the massacre of 29 November 1986; there could be no 'continuing violations'. Further, the State maintained that since the Commission had not declared a violation of Article 18 of the *Declaration of the Rights and Duties of Man*[7] in its merit ruling (concerning the right of individuals to access the courts to protect their rights and to avail themselves of judicial protection from acts of the State that would violate their fundamental constitutional rights); there was no basis to claim a violation of Articles 8 (the right to a fair trial) and 25 (the right to judicial protection) of the *American Convention*.

The Commission held that the State had made its jurisdictional objections too late according to the rules of Inter-American human rights system procedure (the objections were lodged only after the Commission had adopted the merit report leaving no opportunity for the petitioners to respond to the objections) and, therefore, the admissibility objections should be dismissed. The Commission also responded that: (a) claims regarding human rights violations pertaining to the 1986 massacre at Moiwana Village and related violations were formulated by the Commission in terms only of the *Declaration of the Rights and Duties of Man*[8] (applicable to non-State Parties to the Convention which are yet members of the Organization of American States), and that (b) the claims regarding *American Convention on Human Rights*[9] violations pertained only to the alleged *'continuing violations'* relating to an *ongoing* denial of justice and inability of the complainants to return to their traditional lands. The Commission thus contended that it was *not* asking the Court to apply legal norms retroactively. The Commission held it was instead petitioning the Inter-American Court to exercise the Court's jurisdiction in respect of human rights violations that occurred *after* 12 November 1987 (the date of the State's ratification of the Convention and its acceptance of the competence of the Inter-American Court); matters over which the Court clearly properly had jurisdiction.

The victim's representatives argued, among other things, as follows:

> ... whereas the alleged violations that were completed on November 29, 1986 are not before the Court, *the massacre constitutes a grave and systematic violation of a series of fundamental norms of international law that are nonetheless highly relevant to determining the nature and extent of Suriname's responsibility for the denial of justice under the American*

---

[7]American Declaration of the Rights and Duties of Man. http://www1.umn.edu/humanrts/oasinstr/zoas2dec.htm. Accessed 26 September 2009.

[8]American Declaration of the Rights and Duties of Man. http://www1.umn.edu/humanrts/oasinstr/zoas2dec.htm. Accessed 26 September 2009.

[9]American Convention on Human Rights entered into force July 18 1978. http://www1.umn.edu/humanrts/oasinstr/zoas3con.htm. Accessed 26 September 2009.

> *Convention, as well as the nature and extent of the measures required to remedy those violations* (emphasis added).[10]

The Court's Assessment

The Inter-American Court pointed out that when Suriname accepted the competence of the Court on 12 November 1987 *without* expressly stipulating any limitations; the State had accepted as binding without qualification the Court's interpretation and application of the *American Convention.* The Inter-American Court of Human Rights then went on to hold, relying on its own case law and on Article 28 of the 1969 *Vienna Convention on the Law of Treaties* (cited below), that the Court did in fact have jurisdiction over *American Convention* violations that began before Suriname's ratification of the Convention and acceptance of the Court's jurisdiction, but which continued after that State ratified the Convention and accepted the Court's jurisdiction:

> ... unless a different intention appears from the treaty or is otherwise established, its provisions do not bind a party in relation to any act or fact which took place *or any situation which ceased to exist* before the date of the entry into force of the treaty with respect to that party. [thus if the violation persists on or after the date of entry into force of the treaty in that State, then the Court has jurisdiction] (emphasis added).[11]

As to the State's second preliminary objection regarding the alleged failure of the petitioners to exhaust alleged domestic remedies, the Inter-American Court held that the State had waived the right to raise such an objection as the objection was *not* raised in a timely fashion at the appropriate stage of the proceedings (i.e. prior to the Commission's admissibility report). The Court noted also that domestic, exclusively civil remedies, such as suggested by the State, were inadequate in the present case which involved extra-judicial killings which required a prompt adequate criminal investigation and genuine attempts to bring the perpetrators to justice.

The Commission filed its petition to the Court only after two time extensions to the State for compliance had expired and the Court thus held that the Commission had filed the petition at the appropriate time and hence rejected the State's third preliminary objection regarding the timing of the Commission petition.

The Court rejected the State's fourth preliminary objection regarding Commission holdings pertaining to alleged violations of the *Declaration of the Rights and Duties of Man*[12] holding, in part, that the Commission interpretations of the alleged specific Declaration violations were *not* a matter before the Court in the instant case.

---

[10]Arguments of the Representatives, *Moiwana Village v. Suriname* Inter-American Human Rights Court Judgement of 15 June 2005, para 36(f). http://www.forestpeoples.org/documents/law_hr/suriname_iachr_moiwana_judg_jun05_eng.pdf. Accessed 26 September 2009.

[11]Vienna Convention on the Law of Treaties entered into force 27 January 1980. http://www1.umn.edu/humanrts/instree/viennaconvention.html. Accessed 26 September 2009.

[12]American Declaration of the Rights and Duties of Man. http://www1.umn.edu/humanrts/oasinstr/zoas2dec.htm. Accessed 26 September 2009.

Finally, the Court rejected Suriname's fifth preliminary objection that the Commission had allegedly not transmitted to the State critical documents in the case. The Court held that Suriname had presented its brief during the Commission proceedings only well *after* the Commission admissibility and merit reports had been issued and hence: "Having chosen not to exercise its right to defense during the appropriate procedural opportunities before the Commission, Suriname may not raise said objection now, before this Court."[13]

The Court held that it considered the facts regarding the massacre at Moiwana Village, which event occurred prior to the State accepting the jurisdiction of the Court, "only to place into the proper context those alleged violations over which the Tribunal actually exercises jurisdiction."[14] The Court clarified that the alleged victims in the petition (who were individually identified) comprised the following two groups: (a) the survivors of the 26 November 1986 massacre at Moiwana and (b) the relatives of the persons who were killed in that massacre. The Court took note of the fact that on 16 November 2004, the then President of Suriname promulgated an amendment to the Suriname Penal Code which removed the time limitations for prosecution of 'war crimes' or 'crimes against humanity'. The Inter-American Court made the following findings of fact among others:

> The Moiwana community members have *suffered emotionally, psychologically, spiritually and economically, owing to the attack on their village, the subsequent forced separation from their traditional lands, as well as their inability both to honor properly their deceased loved ones and to obtain justice for the events of 1986* (emphasis added).[15]
>
> The *ongoing impunity for the 1986 raid on Moiwana Village* and the inability of the community to understand the motives for that attack have generated a deep fear in the members that they may be subject to future aggressions, which is a central factor preventing them from returning to live in their traditional lands. Their permanent return to Moiwana Village, then, is contingent upon the State conducting a complete investigation into the events of 1986; according to the community members, only when justice is accomplished in the case will they be able to appease the angry spirits of their deceased family members, purify their land, and return to permanent residence without apprehension of further hostilities (emphasis added).[16]

Clearly, as revealed by the above paragraphs excerpted from the 15 June 2005 judgment of the Inter-American Court of Human Rights judgment in *Moiwana*, the

---

[13]*Moiwana Village v. Suriname* Inter-American Human Rights Court Judgement of 15 June 2005, para 68. http://www.forestpeoples.org/documents/law_hr/suriname_iachr_moiwana_judg_jun05_eng.pdf. Accessed 26 September 2009.

[14]*Moiwana Village v. Suriname* Inter-American Human Rights Court Judgement of 15 June 2005, para 70. http://www.forestpeoples.org/documents/law_hr/suriname_iachr_moiwana_judg_jun05_eng.pdf. Accessed 26 September 2009.

[15]*Moiwana Village v. Suriname* Inter-American Human Rights Court Judgement of 15 June 2005, para 86(42). http://www.forestpeoples.org/documents/law_hr/suriname_iachr_moiwana_judg_jun05_eng.pdf. Accessed 26 September 2009.

[16]*Moiwana Village v. Suriname* Inter-American Human Rights Court Judgement of 15 June 2005, para 86(43). http://www.forestpeoples.org/documents/law_hr/suriname_iachr_moiwana_judg_jun05_eng.pdf. Accessed 26 September 2009.

Court was keenly mindful of the ongoing suffering of the victims and of their right to justice in the form, in part, of having the perpetrators brought to justice by Suriname in accordance with State law.

The Court allowed the victim petitioners to argue among other violations: (a) a violation of Article 5 of the *American Convention* regarding every person's right to have their physical, mental and moral integrity respected, and (b) a violation of Convention Article 22 (the right to freedom of movement and residence) even though the Commission had not made claims regarding these alleged violations before the Court. The Court held that this was permissible as the State had had the opportunity to respond to these new alleged violations and, furthermore, it was permissible since:

> The petitioners are the holders of all of the rights enshrined in the Convention; thus, preventing them from advancing their own legal arguments would be an undue restriction upon their right of access to justice, which derives from their condition as subjects of international human rights law.[17]

The Court found that the victim petitioners' right to humane treatment under the *American Convention* included the right to have possible violations of Article 5 (regarding the right to respect for one's physical, mental and moral integrity) properly investigated by the State.[18] The Inter-American Court found in this regard that the State had failed to meet its obligation in upholding the Article 5 *American Convention* rights guarantee by denying the victims a proper investigation of the massacre and the possibility of prosecution of the perpetrators. This then caused the forced separation of the victims from their traditional land and made it impossible for the victims to honour their dead according to their traditions surrounding burial and other rites hence creating inordinate ongoing suffering for the victims. The Court further held, in relation to Article 22 of the *American Convention* that:

> ... the State has failed to both establish conditions, as well as provide the means, that would allow the Moiwana community members to return voluntarily, in safety and with dignity, to their traditional lands, in relation to which they have a special dependency and attachment – as there is objectively no guarantee that their human rights, particularly their rights to life and to personal integrity, will be secure. *By not providing such elements – including, foremost, an effective criminal investigation to end the reigning impunity for the 1986 attack* – Suriname has failed to ensure the rights of the Moiwana survivors to move freely within the State and to choose their place of residence. Furthermore, the State has effectively deprived those community members still exiled in French Guiana of their rights to enter their country and to remain there (emphasis added).[19]

[17]*Moiwana Village v. Suriname* Inter-American Human Rights Court Judgement of 15 June 2005, para 91. http://www.forestpeoples.org/documents/law_hr/suriname_iachr_moiwana_judg_jun05_eng.pdf. Accessed 26 September 2009.

[18]*Moiwana Village v. Suriname* Inter-American Human Rights Court Judgement of 15 June 2005, para 92. http://www.forestpeoples.org/documents/law_hr/suriname_iachr_moiwana_judg_jun05_eng.pdf. Accessed 26 September 2009.

[19]*Moiwana Village v. Suriname* Inter-American Human Rights Court Judgement of 15 June 2005, para 120. http://www.forestpeoples.org/documents/law_hr/suriname_iachr_moiwana_judg_jun05_eng.pdf. Accessed 26 September 2009.

Thus, in effect, the Inter-American Court of Human Rights held that the State's complicity in ensuring impunity for the perpetrators of the 1986 massacre of the Moiwana Villagers had resulted in *ongoing violations* of particular *American Convention* rights guarantees (namely; Articles 5 (right to humane treatment), 22 (freedom of movement and residence), 21 (right to property), 8 (right to a fair trial) and 25 (right to judicial protection), all in relation to Article 1(1) (the State Party's obligation to respect *without discrimination* the rights guaranteed under the Convention to every person (human being) within its jurisdiction). The Court ordered that reparations for material and moral damages be paid by the State to the victim petitioners (the moral harms to the victims being said to have arisen due to their "suffering…, [the] detriment to very significant personal values, as well as [due to the] non-pecuniary alterations to [the] victim's living conditions").[20] In addition, there was an order to establish a development fund of US $1.2 million to be used for health, housing and education so that the surviving Moiwana community members could successfully re-establish themselves on their traditional territory. The Court also ordered various non-monetary forms of reparations based on "*the extreme gravity of the facts and the collective nature of the damages suffered* (emphasis added)"[21] and the desire to prevent a repetition of such atrocity as the 1986 massacre at Moiwana Village. These non-financial reparations included requirements that the State provide safety guarantees to the surviving victims to facilitate their return to their traditional lands; make a public apology and acknowledge international responsibility for the atrocity committed at Moiwana Village in 1986, acknowledge the memory of Herman Gooding, the civilian police official who was murdered due to his attempts to investigate the events of 29 November 1986 and build a monument to honour the victims of the massacre. Further, the order for non-pecuniary reparations required that the State:

> … investigate the facts in question, identify, prosecute and punish the responsible parties, as well as recover the remains of the Moiwana community members killed during the 1986 attack.[22] [the Court also held that the victim petitioners had a right to the truth about the circumstances of the *American Convention* violations in the instant case].[23]
>
> … adopt such legislative, administrative and other measures as are necessary to *ensure the property rights of the members of the Moiwana community in relation to the traditional*

[20]*Moiwana Village v. Suriname* Inter-American Human Rights Court Judgement of 15 June 2005, para 191. http://www.forestpeoples.org/documents/law_hr/suriname_iachr_moiwana_judg_jun05_eng.pdf. Accessed 26 September 2009.

[21]*Moiwana Village v. Suriname* Inter-American Human Rights Court Judgement of 15 June 2005, para 201. http://www.forestpeoples.org/documents/law_hr/suriname_iachr_moiwana_judg_jun05_eng.pdf. Accessed 26 September 2009.

[22]*Moiwana Village v. Suriname* Inter-American Human Rights Court Judgement of 15 June 2005, para 201(a). http://www.forestpeoples.org/documents/law_hr/suriname_iachr_moiwana_judg_jun05_eng.pdf. Accessed 26 September 2009.

[23]*Moiwana Village v. Suriname* Inter-American Human Rights Court Judgement of 15 June 2005, para 204. http://www.forestpeoples.org/documents/law_hr/suriname_iachr_moiwana_judg_jun05_eng.pdf. Accessed 26 September 2009.

territories from which they were expelled, and provide for their use and enjoyment of those territories (emphasis added).[24]

Additional Proceedings

There was a subsequent request 4 October 2005 by Suriname for the Court to clarify and interpret the meaning and scope of aspects of its 15 June 2005 decision. The Court, however, viewed the substance of the State's October 2005 submission in that regard to be simply an expression of its disagreement with the Court's previous 2005 judgment in the case and a re-submission by the State of various issues of fact and law already decided and hence the request for interpretation was dismissed. However, the Court did emphasize again that, as regards to the return of traditional territories to the victims (property over which they held no formal legal title), the Court "left the designation of the territorial boundaries in question to 'an effective mechanism' of the State's design."[25]

III. On the Issue of Alleged Ex Post Facto Application of International Human Rights Conventions

The Inter-American Court of Human Rights in the case of *Moiwana Village v. Suriname* was guided by the Court's principled obligation to deliver justice to the victims and to prevent impunity of the perpetrators. The Court found a legal solution, *consistent with international law*, to the State's challenge of the Court's temporal jurisdiction and to the State's contention regarding the Commission's alleged *ex post facto* application of the *American Convention*. As a result, the Court was able to provide to the petitioners a judicial remedy for the fundamental and *ongoing* human rights violations which they continued to suffer; a remedy so long denied the surviving victims of the 1986 Moiwana Village massacre. This can be contrasted, it is here contended, for instance, with the thrust of the European Court of Human Rights' rulings in *Korbely v. Hungary*[26] and *Kononov v.*

---

[24] *Moiwana Village v. Suriname* Inter-American Human Rights Court Judgement of 15 June 2005, para 201(b). http://www.forestpeoples.org/documents/law_hr/suriname_iachr_moiwana_judg_jun05_eng.pdf. Accessed 26 September 2009.

[25] *Moiwana Village v. Suriname* Inter-American Court of Human Rights Judgement of 8 February 2006, para 19. http://www.wfrt.org/humanrts/iachr/C/145-ing.html. Accessed 28 September 2009.

[26] *Korbely v. Hungary* (Application 9174/02) European Court of Human Rights Grand Chamber Judgement of 19 September 2008. http://cmiskp.echr.coe.int/tkp197/view.asp?item=1&portal=hbkm&action=html&highlight=korbely%20%7C%20v%20%7C%20hungary&sessionid=28582191&skin=hudoc-en. Accessed 26 September 2009.

Latvia[27] (previously discussed). In the latter cases, the European Court of Human Rights appears, *in effect*, to have exonerated perpetrators of systemic acts of violence against civilians who were (on the arguments here) 'hors de combat' by finding, on what are here considered to be suspect grounds, that their conviction in the domestic courts for acts that arguably constituted 'war crimes' or 'crimes against humanity' *allegedly* violated Article 7(1) of the *European Convention on Human Rights* concerning purported retroactive application of the national and/or international law.[28] This is *not* to suggest that the European Court of Human Rights has not in other cases held that violations of the European Convention arose due to an ongoing denial of justice to the victims (i.e. the case of *Mahmut Kaya v. Turkey*[29] in which the European Court of Human Rights: (a) affirmed a positive duty of the State to protect life and prevent injury to its citizens, and (b) found Convention violations, in part, related to an infringement of the right to an effective remedy due to the ongoing failure *post State ratification of the European Convention* to properly investigate the torture and murder of an individual allegedly for his political connections and, by implication, the failure to bring the perpetrators to justice. See also the Grand Chamber case of *Varnava and Others v. Turkey*[30] where the European Court rejected a challenge to its temporal jurisdiction and found *'continuing violations'* in a case involving a group of 'disappeared' men who were last seen in the custody of agents of the respondent State. This ruling was based, in part, on the fact that the State had not, at any point, properly investigated the suspicious disappearances).

In regards to the *Moiwana Village v. Suriname* case, there is no consensus in the legal academic community as to whether the Inter-American Court overstepped its jurisdictional bounds and it is to that issue that we next turn our attention.

---

[27]Kononov v. Latvia (Application no. 36376/04) European Court of Human Rights Chamber judgment 24 July 2008. http://cmiskp.echr.coe.int/tkp197/view.asp?item=1&portal=hbkm&action=html&highlight=Kononov%20%7C%20v%20%7C%20Latvia&sessionid=29021422&skin=hudoc-en. Accessed 26 September 2009.

[28]European Convention on Human Rights and Fundamental Freedoms (as amended by Protocol Number 11 and with protocols 1, 4, 6, 7, 12 and 13), entry into force 1 November 1998 (original Convention adopted by the Council of Europe 1950 and entered into force 3 September 1953). http://www.echr.coe.int/NR/rdonlyres/D5CC24A7-DC13-4318-B457-5C9014916D7A/0/English Anglais.pdf. Accessed 28 September 2009.

[29]*Mahmut Kaya v. Turkey* European Court of Human Rights Chamber Judgement of 28 March 2000. http://www.coe.int/t/e/legal_affairs/legal_co-operation/family_law_and_children's_rights/Documents/Mahmut%20Kaya%20v%20Turkey_ENG.pdf. Accessed 26 September 2009.

[30]*Varnava and Others v. Turkey* Grand Chamber judgment of the European Court of Human Rights of 18 September 2009. http://cmiskp.echr.coe.int/tkp197/view.asp?item=2&portal=hbkm&action=html&highlight=Varnava%20%7C%20Others%20%7C%20v%20%7C%20Turkey&sessionid=30855967&skin=hudoc-en. Accessed 28 September 2009.

IV. Moiwana Village v. Suriname and the Issue of a Denial of Justice as an 'Ongoing (Convention) Violation'

Some legal academics have contended that the implication of the Inter-American Human Rights Court decision in *Moiwana Village v Suriname* is that the 'continuing violation' doctrine allows the Court to "remedy almost any violation [of the *American Convention*] that occurs in a given Latin American country" since under that doctrine "a State is obligated to investigate and prosecute all violations of human rights, even if that violation occurred before ratification of the Convention."[31] [According to the 'continuing violation' doctrine], "a failure to investigate [human rights violations] constitutes a failure to 'ensure' ... a citizen's rights to judicial protection and to a fair trial as long as that failure continues."[32] Some have contended that the Inter-American Court in the Moiwana Village v. Suriname case did in fact apply the *American Convention ex post facto* and that this (assuming this was the case) may (a) cause States to withdraw their recognition of the Court's jurisdiction as well as (b) discourage new potential States Parties to the *American Convention* from accepting the Court's jurisdiction.[33] Further, it has been held by some that ***allegedly*** "punishing a state for actions taken by previous regimes" fails to advance "... the main goal of the American Convention [of] ensuring that current sitting governments respect human rights" and "... could conceivably destabilize that government."[34]

This author would contend, however, that the foregoing critique of the 'continuing violation' doctrine fails in fact to consider the *ongoing* nature of the violations and the precise manner in which the Inter-American Court of Human Rights exercised its jurisdiction in the Moiwana Village v. Suriname case. The State in *Moiwana Village v. Suriname*, for instance, was held accountable ***not*** for what occurred prior to Convention ratification, and prior to State acceptance of the Court's jurisdiction, in terms of either the underlying events (i.e. the 1986 massacre at Moiwana Village), or the failure to investigate and prosecute perpetrators. Rather, the State, in regards to the Moiwana Village massacre, was held accountable by the Inter-American Court *only* for the failure to properly investigate and prosecute *post Convention ratification and acceptance of the Court's jurisdiction*:

> *The Commission has maintained throughout the present proceeding that the only violations which it attributes to Suriname before this Tribunal relate to "a series of acts and omissions," starting from the date of the State's acceptance of the Court's jurisdiction,*

[31]Ormachea (2008, p. 284).

[32]Ormachea (2008, p. 285).

[33]Ormachea (2008, p. 286).

[34]Ormachea (2008, p. 286).

which has allegedly caused an ongoing denial of justice in violation of the terms of Articles 8, 25 and 1(1) of the American Convention (emphasis added).[35]

These supposed State violations are based upon,. . .the following alleged facts cited by the Commission: the failure until 1989 to initiate an ex officio investigation into the 29 November 1986 occurrences at Moiwana Village; the army's forceful releasing of suspects in police custody in 1989; the 1990 murder of the police officer in charge of the Moiwana investigation and, as a consequence, a suspension of further official inquiries; and the additional "chilling effect" upon the investigation brought about by the 1992 enactment of an amnesty law. [all of which occurred *post* the State's 1987 ratification of the *American Convention* and its acceptance of the Inter-American Court of Human Rights' jurisdiction].[36]

For their part, the representatives argued that *"[t]he denial of justice alleged in this case is specifically linked to Suriname's acts and omissions occurring in 1989, 1992, 1993, 1995 and 1996–97* [after ratification of the American Convention and acceptance of the Inter-American Court's jurisdiction] and continues to the present day (emphasis added)."[37]

Hence, the 'continuing violation' doctrine eliminates the State's ability to elude accountability under international human rights conventions where (a) the underlying events (i.e. such as the massacre in Moiwana Village of 'protected civilians') took place prior to Convention ratification, and (b) the State's failure to investigate and prosecute *originated* with a previous government in a time period prior to Convention ratification *though that failure to investigate and prosecute remains un-remedied and ongoing under the new government which has ratified the Convention and accepted the Court's jurisdiction.* The doctrine of 'continuing violations' makes especially good judicial and moral sense in regards to cases involving international crimes, such as the 1986 Moiwana Village massacre. This is the case since international crimes have no statute of limitations respecting the possibility for prosecution of individual perpetrators. Hence, the State – whether or not a new government is installed – has an ongoing responsibility under international criminal and human rights law to make all feasible, reasonable efforts to bring the perpetrators of international crimes to justice. The 'continuing violation' doctrine – especially as applied in cases involving international crimes such as the 'crimes against humanity' in the Moiwana Village massacre committed by Suriname national army personnel – emphasizes the fact that even new State governments are accountable under the Convention for the failure to take reasonable steps *post-ratification* of the Convention to end impunity (i.e. for human rights violations, some rising to the level of international crimes, that occurred under the watch of

---

[35] *Moiwana Village v. Suriname* Inter-American Human Rights Court Judgement of 15 June 2005, para 40. http://www.forestpeoples.org/documents/law_hr/suriname_iachr_moiwana_judg_jun05_eng.pdf. Accessed 26 September 2009.

[36] *Moiwana Village v. Suriname* Inter-American Human Rights Court Judgement of 15 June 2005, para 41. http://www.forestpeoples.org/documents/law_hr/suriname_iachr_moiwana_judg_jun05_eng.pdf. Accessed 26 September 2009.

[37] *Moiwana Village v. Suriname* Inter-American Human Rights Court Judgement of 15 June 2005, para 42. http://www.forestpeoples.org/documents/law_hr/suriname_iachr_moiwana_judg_jun05_eng.pdf. Accessed 26 September 2009.

a previous government which did not investigate the circumstances surrounding the violations and/or make all reasonable and feasible efforts to lawfully prosecute the perpetrators of the human rights violations).

The notion of 'continuing violations' in regards to the denial of justice then *indirectly* reinforces the premise that all governments of a State, as well as the international community as a whole, have a responsibility to protect fundamental human rights and to end *ongoing* impunity for human rights violations and atrocity. There is a recognized international legal responsibility to end impunity for the international crimes of genocide, war crimes and crimes against immunity. Indeed, there are international treaties which provide for universal criminal prosecution of grievous violations of international jus cogens standards of civilized conduct in times of peace and war and these treaties have, in practice, become part of international customary law.[38] The 'continuing violations' legal principle under international human rights law enhances the ability of the international human rights courts: (a) to fulfil the international legal obligation of ending lack of moral and civil accountability for atrocity at the State level, and (b) to contribute to the likelihood also of bringing to criminal justice domestically (or perhaps through the international criminal court or foreign courts exercising universal criminal jurisdiction; depending on the specifics of the case) individual perpetrators as is evident in the inter-American Court of Human Rights case of *Moiwana Village v. Suriname*.

Respectfully, it is, furthermore, wholly inaccurate to characterize the Inter-American Court holding in *Moiwana Village v. Suriname* as standing for the proposition that the new government in place at the time of the Commission proceedings should be held responsible for the actions of the previous government. In fact, the new government in Suriname at the time of the Inter-American proceedings, under the 'continuing violation' doctrine, was held accountable by the Inter-American Court of Human Rights *only* for that *new government's own failings* in regards to the Moiwana Village massacre, i.e. the new government's failure to investigate and prosecute the perpetrators of the massacre, and institution of a 1992 Amnesty for the perpetrators of the Moiwana Village massacre. *All of the Convention violations attributed to the new government arose from State acts or omissions which*: (a) *occurred post Convention ratification*, specifically in 1989, 1992, 1993, 1995 and 1996–1997 (including a delay in initiating the investigation, the release of suspects, the murder of the chief investigator and the 1992 Amnesty law), or (b) *involved ongoing violations* (i.e. the denial of justice due to the failure to investigate or prosecute the perpetrators of the massacre and the forced separation of the massacre survivors from their traditional lands; both ongoing human rights violations at the time of the Inter-American Human Rights Commission and Court proceedings).

Note that the Inter-American Court of Human Rights did *not* consider potential *American Convention* Article 4 violations (right to life) in the Moiwana Village

[38]Cassese (2003, p. 591).

massacre case since the murders occurred before ratification of the *American Convention* by Suriname and the Court does *not* consider loss of life to constitute a "continuing violation". (However, 'forced disappearances' are considered to constitute continuing violations by the Court for as long as the status and whereabouts of the disappeared is unknown[39] even though the forced disappearance may have occurred prior to Convention ratification and also is effected via a single event such as abduction often followed by murder).

With respect, especially disheartening from this author's perspective is the notion that "Although enforcing the doctrine of 'continuing violation' would achieve the admirable goal of finally granting justice to the victims of human rights violations, it could do so at the expense of a still-fragile democracy."[40] It is here contended, in opposition, to the forgoing notion that respect for the right to justice and ending impunity for atrocity (especially where State sponsored) is a vital precondition for *sustaining* democracy; especially a fragile fledgling democracy. Be that as it may, however, such political considerations *cannot* properly drive how the Inter-American Court of Human Rights, or any other international human rights court for that matter, can or should function (for instance, whether or not it should apply the 'continuing violation' doctrine).

Some such as Gibson[41] have considered the 'continuing violation' doctrine to be an *alleged* 'legal fiction' since the Court did *not* explicitly make a finding that Suriname was responsible for the massacre in the first instance (an alleged legal fiction, Gibson speculates, perhaps premised on the Court's desire to hold Suriname accountable for its alleged involvement in the massacre or to prevent future State-sponsored atrocities). However, as discussed, Suriname was held accountable by the Court for: (a) the *ongoing impunity* it provided for the perpetrators of the massacre due to the *new* government's acts and omissions *post Convention ratification* as well as for: (b) *ongoing violations* relating to the de facto *forced expulsion* of the survivors from their traditional lands. Gibson suggests that "the Court [improperly] used an outcome determinative test, not a procedural test";[42] that is one focused on an outcome that would pressure Suriname to investigate the massacre and prosecute those responsible. Quite disconcerting is the following passage from Gibson (no doubt echoing the views of countless like-minded legal academics and reminiscent of Ormachea's[43] position previously discussed):

> There is nothing morally wrong with the Court's decision. In fact, it is morally justified, and as such, is a legitimate piece of international law *under the theories that find legitimacy in morality* [as opposed to theories that base legitimacy on State consensual agreement to

---

[39] Gibson (2007, pp. 153–166).

[40] Ormachea (2008, p. 286).

[41] Gibson (2007, p. 160).

[42] Gibson (2007, p. 163).

[43] Ormachea (2008, p. 284).

> respect certain human rights[44]]. However, the legal fiction cannot be denied. ... Courts should be concerned with how these fictions affect the advancement of human rights law.
>
> States may refrain from joining new human rights treaties for fear of retroactive application. This deterrent effect can retard the growth of new international norms. *The line between a morally legitimate judicial outcome and a decision that will pragmatically advance human rights is hazy* (emphasis added).[45]

As previously explained; the Inter-American Court of Human Rights in *Moiwana Village v. Suriname* did ***not*** in fact apply the *American Convention* retroactively, but rather held Suriname accountable for those State actions or inactions *post ratification* of *the Convention* that fostered *continued impunity* for the perpetrators of the massacre and *ongoing suffering* for the victims. The only 'legal fiction' to speak to is that created by those legal academics who maintain that international human rights courts holding States accountable for the *ongoing* denial of justice constitutes retroactive application of the law when it is (a) within the power of a *new* government to properly investigate fundamental human rights violations and to potentially bring the perpetrators of those often grave violations to justice; and (b) it is the duty of that new government also to do so; especially in regards to violations that constitute international crimes. It appears to have become intellectually fashionable (even perhaps 'politically correct' in academic circles) to *dissociate* 'justice' from any necessary connection to 'moral legitimacy' even when a case concerns an international crime as in *Moiwana Village v Suriname* which involved crimes against humanity ('moral legitimacy' here being a term used in a limited way to refer only to the requirement that international human rights court rulings advance and/or protect human rights rather than weaken them and/or contribute to impunity). While Gibson claims that: "The line between a morally legitimate judicial outcome and a decision that will pragmatically advance human rights is hazy";[46] surely, the Moiwana Village massacre case attests to the converse. This being the case since there is nothing unclear for the surviving victims about the Inter-American Court's ruling of 15 June 2005 finally delivering solace and justice and the means to rebuilding their lives in their traditional territory almost two decades after the massacre and after years of successive governments creating barriers to any judicial remedy for the ongoing gross violations of their fundamental human rights.

It appears that international human rights courts, when sufficiently inspired to do so, are generally quite competent to interpret their enabling texts as 'living instruments' and develop innovative legally and morally legitimate interpretations which combat State resistance to full accountability. Yet, there are instances, (one already being too many), in which the international human rights courts have declined jurisdiction in the face of *ongoing* grave systemic human rights violations arguably amounting to international crimes. In this regard, recall, for instance, the European Court of Human Rights declining jurisdiction, (improperly on the view

[44]Gibson (2007, pp. 153–154).

[45]Gibson (2007, p. 165).

[46]Gibson (2007, p. 165).

here as discussed in a previous section), over complaints to the Court regarding the role of States Parties to the *European Convention on Human Rights* in maintaining Roma and other so-called gypsy internally displaced persons in highly lead contaminated U.N. refugee camps in post-conflict Kosovo. These State acts or failures to act causing the victims to be exposed to highly lead contaminated environments occurred (a) even after the life-threatening character of the U.N. refugee camp environments was well known, and (b) even though it was apparent that the U.N. mission in Kosovo (as a legal entity) was clearly acting in a manner beyond its jurisdiction and contrary to the U.N. Charter in housing the internally displaced Roma and other minorities in deadly toxic U.N. refugee camp environments.

V. Moral Legitimacy of International Human Rights Court Rulings as Essential to the Promotion of an Internationalized Rule of Law

The notion of the 'rule of law' has been defined in abstract terms by former U.N. Secretary General Kofi Annan as follows:

> … a *principle of governance in which all persons, institutions, and entities, public and private, including the State itself, are accountable to laws* that are publicly promulgated, equally enforced and independently adjudicated, and which are *consistent with international human rights norms and standards.* It requires, as well, measures to ensue adherence to the principles of the supremacy of the law, equality before the law, *accountability to the law*, fairness in the application of the law, separation of powers, participation in decision-making, legal certainty, avoidance of arbitrariness and procedural and legal transparency (emphasis added).[47]

One need look no further, however, than to the lack of accountability of States and of the U.N. mission (UNMIK) in post-conflict Kosovo for their involvement in overseeing the maintenance of internally displaced Roma and other so-called 'gypsy' refugees in highly lead contaminated U.N. IDP camps to understand that the realization of the 'rule of law' is, for the vulnerable, often but an empty promise. As discussed, the European Court of Human Rights had the opportunity to deliver some modicum of justice to these refugee Roma and other Kosovo minorities who had been languishing for years suffering from serious chronic health problems (and dying) in the lead toxic IDP camps. However, the European Court of Human Rights (on the view expressed here) declined its jurisdiction in rejecting for consideration the case against the European States Parties to the European Convention involved in UNMIK. That refusal, it will be recalled, was communicated to the victims' representatives via a private faxed letter to the European Roma Rights Centre.

---

[47]Secretary-General Kofi Anan (2004) The rule of law and transitional justice in conflict and post-conflict societies. Report of the Secretary General, UN Doc. S/2004/616 (3 August 2004), para 6. http://documents.un.org. Accessed 28 September 2009.

This outcome (the denial of judicial protection in terms of *interim measures* and a judicial remedy in other respects such as reparations) and the manner in which it was communicated, would seem to mitigate against the perception that the international human rights system *consistently* contributes to the 'rule of law' when presented with that opportunity, and dare we say, responsibility (i.e. contributes to the rule of law in post-conflict societies to the benefit of all; including the most vulnerable of the population).

It is well recognized by international legal scholars that "international (human rights) law [frequently] strengthens and supports the domestic rule of law".[48] However, it is here contended, that international human rights law as sometimes applied by international human rights courts can also undermine the internationalization of the rule of law and weaken the domestic human rights context. The latter may occur when interpretations of international human rights law by the international human rights courts inadvertently undermine respect for justice by, *in practice*, giving rise to rulings that fail to affirm and protect the human rights of the most vulnerable and/or rulings which contribute to lack of accountability for gross human rights violations at both the State level and, indirectly also, in respect of the individual perpetrators. The contentious cases discussed in this book, it is suggested, appear to fall into that latter category with the consequence that the European Court of Human Rights, in those cases, did not afford the human rights victims involved substantive justice.

As has been highlighted by Stromseth, there is great value for promoting and maintaining the rule of law in "empowering civil society – individuals and groups- to insist upon justice and accountability."[49] This Stromseth terms "the *demand side* of justice on the ground."[50] She contends that "building the rule of law is as much about strengthening public demand and confidence in justice as it is about building better legal institutions."[51] Her point then is also relevant to the issue of whether, and to what degree, the international human rights courts inspire the demand for and confidence in justice as fashioned and delivered by these courts.

As has been discussed, international human rights court rulings often have a profound impact both on State accountability and the likelihood of impunity for individual perpetrators of grave human rights crimes – even international crimes (see for example *Moiwana Village v. Suriname*).[52] This book has, in that regard, explored how the European Court of Human Rights exercised, or failed to exercise, its jurisdiction and mandate in various highly important and contentious cases and examined the result in terms of State accountability and the potential for impunity

---

[48]Nolkaemper (2009, p. 75).

[49]Stromseth (2009, p. 96).

[50]Stromseth (2009, p. 96).

[51]Stromseth (2009, p. 96).

[52]*Moiwana Village v. Suriname*, 8 February 2006 Judgement of the Inter-American Court of Human Rights (Interpretation of the 15 June 2005 Judgement of the State's Preliminary Objections and Merit and Reparations). http://www.wfrt.org/humanrts/iachr/C/145-ing.html. Accessed 26 September 2009.

of individual human rights violators. This book has been then this author's attempt to make a modest contribution to the so-called 'demand side' of justice in the hopes of encouraging others also to insist on rulings from international human rights courts that have 'moral legitimacy' ('moral legitimacy' here defined, as discussed previously, as rulings that protect or advance human rights, rather than weaken them or contribute to impunity for those who have committed human rights violations or even grave human rights violations amounting to international crimes). That insistence on moral legitimacy in the rulings of the international human rights courts will undoubtedly bring us closer to achieving justice not only for the direct victims of human rights violations and atrocity and their immediate relatives and community, but ultimately for us all.

References

Cassese A (2003) Is the bell tolling for universality? A plea for a sensible notion of universal jurisdiction. J Int'l Crim Just 1:589–595

Gibson TR (2007) True fiction: competing theories of international legal legitimacy and a court's battle with *ratione temporis Loy*. LA Int'l Comp L Rev 29:153–166. http://ilr.lls.edu/documents/Article629.1Gibson.pdf. Accessed 27 September 2009

Nolkaemper A (2009) The internationalized rule of law. Hague J Rule Law 1:74–78

Ormachea PA (2008) Recent developments: Moiwana village: the Inter-American Court and the "continuing violation" doctrine. Harv Hum Rts J 19:283. http://www.law.harvard.edu/students/orgs/hrj/.../ormachea.shtml. Accessed 26 September 2009

Stromseth J (2009) Justice on the ground: can international criminal courts strengthen domestic rule of law in post-conflict societies? Hague J Rule Law 1:87–97

Index

MIX
Papier aus verantwortungsvollen Quellen
Paper from responsible sources
FSC® C105338

If you have any concerns about our products,
you can contact us on
ProductSafety@springernature.com

In case Publisher is established outside the EU,
the EU authorized representative is:
Springer Nature Customer Service Center GmbH
Europaplatz 3, 69115 Heidelberg, Germany

Printed by Libri Plureos GmbH
in Hamburg, Germany